D1544448

Ford:

THE DUST AND
THE GLORY

A RACING HISTORY
VOLUME 2 (1968–2000)

Other SAE books

Ford: The Dust and the Glory, A Racing History,
Volume 1 (1901–1967)
By Leo Levine
(Order No. R-292)

The Golden Age of the American Racing Car
By Griffith Borgeson
(Order No. R-196)

Henry Ford: A Hearthside Perspective
By Donn P. Werling
(Order No. R-266)

The Fords in My Past
By Harold L. Brock
(Order No. R-270)

Edsel Ford and E.T. Gregorie: The Remarkable Design Team
and Their Classic Fords of the 1930s and 1940s
By Henry Dominguez
(Order No. R-245)

Chevrolet—Racing? Fourteen Years of Raucous Silence, 1957–1970
By Paul Van Valkenburgh
(Order No. R-271)

For more information or to order this book, contact SAE at 400 Commonwealth
Drive, Warrendale, PA 15096-0001; (724)776-4970; fax (724)776-0790;
e-mail: publications@sae.org; web site: www.sae.org/BOOKSTORE.

THE DUST AND
THE GLORY

A RACING HISTORY
VOLUME 2 (1968–2000)

LEO LEVINE

Society of Automotive Engineers, Inc.
Warrendale, Pa.

Library of Congress Cataloging-in-Publication Data

Levine, Leo.
Ford: the dust and the glory, a racing history / Leo Levine.
   p. cm.
Vol. 1 was originally published: New York : Macmillan, 1968.
Includes bibliographical references and index.
Contents: v. 1. 1901-1967
ISBN 0-7680-0663-5
   1. Ford Motor Company. 2. Automobile racing--History.
3. Ford automobile--History.
I. Title.

GV1029.15.L49 2001
796.72--dc21   00-059522

ISBN 0-7680-0814-X (Volume 2)

Published by: Society of Automotive Engineers, Inc.
                     400 Commonwealth Drive
                     Warrendale, PA 15096-0001 U.S.A.
                     Phone: (724)776-4841
                     Fax: (724)776-5760
                     E-mail: publications@sae.org
                     http://www.sae.org

SAE Order No. R-293

DEDICATION

For Sam,
Who has never seen an automobile race,
and
For Mose,
Who has seen many and had an impact on thousands more,
and whose loyalty to Ford over nearly five decades
has been an example to dozens of others like him
who have worked in relative anonymity, but whose contribution
to the performance effort has been most important.
Without them, it wouldn't have happened.

Author's Note

Although literally hundreds of people have been helpful in the writing of this second volume, there are a few who have either devoted a considerable amount of time to the project, or who were instrumental in getting it done. They are:

Chris Economaki, the doyen of racing writers and broadcasters not only in the United States, but in the rest of the world as well, whose assistance and judgement were invaluable.

Graham Robson, whose assistance made the rally section possible and who also helped with many other British and European subjects, especially when Cosworth history was involved. He is the authority on the latter and the author of several books on the subject.

John Chuhran, whose research on the history of CART, IMSA, the SCCA and related subjects was most helpful.

Judy Levine, for the considerable amount of time and effort she devoted to cleaning up this manuscript.

E. Gabriel Perle, for his advice and counsel.

And David Scott and Tom Rhoades of Ford, who got this started.

Acknowledgements

Gary Anderson • Mario Andretti • Peter Ashcroft • Dave Ashley • Elizabeth Aves • Phillip Baker • Pauline Baldwin • Georgina Baskerville • Ernie Beckman • Kenny Bernstein • Ian Bisco • Adrian Bourne • Ray Brock • Bruce Cambern • Dean Case • John Clinard • John Cooper • Mike Costin • Tom Cotter • Eric Dahlquist • Donald Davidson • Russell Datz • David E. Davis, Jr. • Mac Demere • Hank Dertian • Burt Diamond • Gene Dicola • Jimmy Dilamarter • Keith Duckworth • Dee Duncan • Corinne Economaki • Roger Edmondson • Paul Eggert • Tom Elliman • Bill Elliott • Dan Erickson • Wayne Estes • John Ewert • Bernard Ferguson • Greg Fielden • Sal Fish • Herb Fishel • Casey Folks • Edsel Ford II • Jim Foster • W.C. France • Dave Friedman • Brad Frohn • Torrey Galida • Jerry Gappens • Mike Gearhart • Paul Gentilozzi • Bob Glidden • Tom Gloy • Leslie Gowan • Charlie Gray • Gavin Green • Jerry Green • John Griffin • Dan Gurney • Carl Haas • Lee Hamkins • Walter Hayes[1] • Don Hayward • Dave Hederich • Lincoln Hill • Phil Hill • David Hobbs • Martin Holmes • Wade Hoyt • Jim Hunter • Dale Jarrett • Ned Jarrett • Robert (Junior) Johnson • Dan Jones • Parnelli Jones • Tom Jones • Al Kammerer • Tom Kendall • Kevin Kennedy • Charles Kim • Juergen Klauke • Bill Kniegge • Michael Kranefuss • Dick Landfield • Bob Latford • Steve Lockwood • Klaus Ludwig • Karl Ludvigsen • Dan Luginbuhl • Glenn Lyall • Pete Lyons • Leon Mandel • Dutch Mandel • Mickey Matus • Phil McCray • Buzz McKim • Ak Miller • Don Miller • Preston Miller • Ralph Moody • Bud Moore • Peter Morris • Lee Morse • Sir Stirling Moss • Max Muhleman • Jochen Neerpasch • Jay Novak • Mose Nowland • Bill Oursler • Jim Owens • Wally Parks • Richard Parry-Jones • Ed Pearlman • David Pearson • Harold Poling • Len Pounds • Don Prudhomme • Bob Puffer • Bobby Rahal • Mel Record • Neil Ressler • Bob Rewey • Barry Reynolds • Dan Rivard • Marti Rompf • Jack Roush • Greg Rubenstein • Horst Sass • Dick Scammell • Sam Scott • Greg Shea • Carroll Shelby • A.B. Shuman • Dan Smith • Greg Specht • John Sproat • Simon Sproule • John Starkey • Jackie Stewart • Dan Stuczynski • Bob Tasca • Deb Taylor • Simon Taylor • Brian Tracy • Stuart Turner • John Valentine • Steve Van Houten • Jason Vines • Robert Vizcarra • R.R.C. Walker • Rusty Wallace • Barry Wally • Bonnie Walworth • Dick Wells • H.W. Wheeler, Jr. • Martin Whitaker • Lee White • Mark Wilford • Glen Wood • Bruce Wood • Cale Yarborough • Douglas Yates • Robert Yates • Dan Zacharias

[1] Deceased

CONTENTS

FOREWORD

This nation, and for that matter the world, has been concerned of late with the summing up of man's adventures through the 20th century and the second millennium. Adventures is perhaps a better word than achievements because the latter, according to Webster, implies something praiseworthy, and much that transpired during the past 100 years (or 1000, take your pick) is more fit for condemnation than applause.

Automobile racing is a sport that started out as a pastime for the rich and in recent years could make those involved in it rich if they were successful. Yet despite all the money, when the starter's flag drops it reverts to being a sport, and one in which the Ford Motor Company has been involved, in one way or another, for a century. This is one of two volumes with the same name, the first having been published in 1968 and considering the first 67 years (it was republished earlier this year, as part of the observation of Ford's racing centennial). This one treats the last 33, in which the exponential growth of the sport has moved it from being a regional attraction to a television staple.

The story of the first book, and therefore this one, began at the Sebring twelve-hour race in the late winter of 1966. We were standing behind the Ford pits when Don Frey and Leo Beebe, then Ford Division general manager and special vehicles manager, respectively, asked if I was interested in writing the racing history of the company.

The result was what is now Volume 1, which was originally published shortly before I exchanged a typewriter for a career with Mercedes-Benz of North America. After I retired the question of "When are you going to do the next one?" arose on an annual basis. Finally, after a decade's worth of off-and-on discussions the decision was made. This, plus some minor changes to the original, is the result.

The "why" of spending this much time—more than two years—on another "racing book," (the term somehow carries an air of denigration) is simple: Racing is part of America's culture—it always was, but people in the media centers didn't know it and the promoters didn't know how to explain it—and Ford is the quintessential American company. As such, as part of the social history of this country, it deserves some attention. Although the use of superlatives in any context is dangerous, no other company has seen its reputation laid on the line in so many forms of the sport for so long a period of time. (That being said, it should also be noted that the Ford Motor Company had no right of editorial approval of either volume.)

As we enter the third millennium, with scientific and industrial progress of an order that would be inconceivable to people of the year 1000 (or even to people of 1900), racing has changed greatly since Volume 1 of this work was first published, and so has society. Among other innovations we now have the Internet, a form of communication unknown four decades ago, which gives us instant contact to people and services previously undreamed of, and which will transform our world even more than the television camera, although it embodies elements of the latter.

The Iron Curtain and Vietnam are memories, except as tourist stops, as is our decades-long estrangement from China, and the U.S. has had eight presidents since that summer's day when Ford first won at Le Mans. If there is a cause for immediate concern it centers on the Middle East, which in 1968 was taken for granted as the place from which cheap oil flowed.

The Ford Motor Company has also changed. At the close of the first volume it was only a decade into its existence as a public company, and despite sales in many parts of the world it was still very much a Midwest-oriented organization, and running a poor second to General Motors with Chrysler not far behind. In the year 2000 the company was the industry's most aggressive, and was most profitable. Although a member of the Ford family is once again chairman, the chief executive is an Australian of Lebanese birth.

The more things change, the more they do not stay the same.

Leo Levine
Stamford, Connecticut
May, 2001

INTRODUCTION

There were 1301 automobile racing venues in the United States at the beginning of this year. These ranged from the Indianapolis Motor Speedway, the world's best-known, to the Geographical Center Speedway in Rugby, North Dakota, a quarter-mile clay oval that is the scene of events for stock cars and so-called "modifieds" that comply with IMCA rules, and also for a class known as "Bombers."

The total, which includes a number of multi-purpose facilities, has gone up in recent years (from 1253 in 1995, for example) probably due to the long-term bull market and despite rising real estate values and environmental considerations. It is far greater than that of any other country, due in part to the size of the U.S. but also because of Americans' predilection for oval tracks of a quarter- or half-mile in length, which fit conveniently into the landscape. This number includes ovals, both paved and dirt (and even some indoors), road courses (72) and drag strips (277).

IMCA is the abbreviation for International Motor Contest Association, a Midwest-oriented sanctioning body that is one of more than 270 such groups organizing automotive competitions as part of the happy anarchy that makes up the sport-cum-business in the U.S. The exact number can only be estimated, because no one knows from one day to the next how many are still with us, or how many new acronyms have joined the racing lexicon in the last months or even weeks.

The reasons for the proliferation of the sport in this country are several, but the basic one is that the automobile, almost from birth, and primarily due to Ford's Model T, has been a populist machine. It was affordable for almost everyone—and thus the Model T was the foundation of grassroots racing in the first three decades of the 20th century. It was available for many, and therefore available for modifying into a racing car of one sort or another. And the tracks were available, too, many being adapted from other sports—the first ovals were originally built for horse racing. Beginning in 1934, when the first midget race was held in California, quarter-mile and even shorter ovals were found, some on high-school running tracks, or plowed out of a farmer's field.

So the cars were available, and so were the tracks, and then came the most important technological advancement—the television camera, which has given us what can be termed the universal race track, seemingly available at any time of the day or night by pushing a button. Before the advent of cable television, racing, in social terms, can be said to have been a subculture. But that changed in the past decade. It has changed to the point where certain minor-league series are even owned by television networks.

About the only constant, since the beginning, is the fact that Ford has been there, in the hands of kids right off the farm or out of the body shop or filling station, or in the care of high-tech teams running with full Dearborn involvement. There have been more successes than failures, but this is not a review designed to emphasize the winning and hide the losses: It is, rather, an attempt to look at Ford's ongoing involvement in one of the world's great sporting pastimes, one that despite its obvious business overtones still carries with it the need to be fiercely competitive in order to win, and to be willing to lay one's reputation on the line on a daily basis. No other American manufacturer has done this so consistently, or has done this for a century. Before the Ford Motor Company existed it was racing that enabled Henry Ford to raise money for one of his early companies, the one that eventually became the Cadillac Division of General Motors. Ford was astute enough to see that his future lay in building cars, not driving them, but he also realized success in motorsports could be a valuable promotional device.

The company he left behind tended to forget this from time to time, and there were also earlier periods when it did not realize that the youth of America, equipped with Ford's flathead V8 of the 1930s and '40s, was keeping the performance flame alive for it. By the 1960s, however, the understanding that motorsports participation, on a worldwide basis, was a necessity had spread through most of the company. Since then, with the notable exception of the decade of the 1970s in the U.S., Ford has been consciously involved—and for the most part successful—at a time when worldwide motorsports competition has become more intense than ever.

The winning, however, has become only part of it: Being there, and being competitive, and being able to communicate this, has become the major task of motorsports marketing. This latter occupation, one sadly overemphasized in recent years, has seen various manufacturers perpetrate all sorts of nonsense in efforts to make silk purses out of sow's ears. Not being competitive, of course, is a synonym for losing badly. That is not permissible.

This volume treats the years 1968–2000 and deals with seven different disciplines:

- Stock-car racing on a major league basis—NASCAR

- American single-seater racing—USAC and later CART

- Drag racing—the NHRA and some others

- World championship (grand prix) racing—Formula One

- Road racing—a mixture of everything from European sports-car and GT championships to the SCCA's Trans Am series.

- Off-road racing—the Baja 1000 and its relatives

- International rallying—outside the U.S. as important to manufacturers as stock-car racing is here.

What it does not do is deal with the myriad of smaller organizations, or for that matter even with such relatively important circuits as NASCAR's Busch Grand

National or Craftsman Truck series. There is just too much of it. It would take a small library, rather than one book, to do it all justice. The exponential growth of the sport in the past four decades has made anything done before pallid by comparison, and these organizations, combined with television exposure and now with the Internet, have been the leading edge. It has become part of our culture; not necessarily good or bad, but part of it.

It is a sport that has always had a great visceral appeal for spectators, even though we live in a country populated, as author Ken W. Purdy once said, by mechanical illiterates. The vast majority of Americans have no clue about the four strokes of the reciprocating engine that powers both their personal car and a racing car, and it doesn't make any difference. The roar, the scream, the flash of color that comes with the racing car somehow provides a subconscious relationship with his or her more mundane version, and that is enough.

What makes the technical part of the sport even more difficult to understand is the fact that every one of the 270-odd organizations mentioned previously have their own regulations. Combine this with the fact that the media by and large makes no attempt to educate the public—television is particularly guilty—it is a wonder that the sport has reached its current level of popularity.

But it is morning, and it is time to go racing again. Roger Penske, Jack Roush and the other Ford team owners drive to their waiting jets, aircraft costing sums that not so long ago would have represented the annual expenditure for a sanctioning body's entire series, much less for one team.

It is also morning near Rugby, North Dakota, where a carpenter or plumber or garage mechanic is already at work, earning a living during the day before he can compete at Geographical Center Speedway in the evening. Prize money would make his week, or even his month.

Someday, maybe, he'll be noticed by Penske, or Roush, and he'll be on his way.

That is racing in the 21st century.

Chapter 1

---◆---

THE KINGDOM OF FRANCE

Stock-car racing, the most American form of the sport, was codified, promoted, defended and is run by one family. From time to time others have a say in the matter, but in the end the Frances decide what happens.

William Henry Getty France (1904–1992) is the most important person in the history of American motorsports, and his son, William Clifton France, is not far behind. The father took a bunch of ragtag southeastern drivers and dirt-track promoters, complete with cars that were never designed for competition by their Detroit creators, and transformed the lot into a cohesive group that became a regional institution and an interesting fringe player on the national scene. The name chosen was the National Association for Stock Car Automobile Racing—NASCAR. The acronym was a fortunate choice, as it was easily recognizable, and rolled off one's tongue.

The son took what his father built and by the close of the century had turned stock-car racing into the country's hottest new television sports attraction. It drew

The founder: William Henry Getty France.
—Daytona Archives

The successor: William C. France.
—Don Hunter

attention even from those who weren't fans, and it moved the Frances into the ranks of America's 400 richest families. They did it all from Daytona Beach, and as a consequence revived this North Florida town that in the first three decades of the 20th century was the scene of land speed record attempts. They made Daytona as synonymous with the sport as Indianapolis, Le Mans, Silverstone or the Nürburgring.

The Frances created the most competitive form of auto racing ever seen, and they were able to offer this week after week, year after year. Much of the growth of NASCAR, and of all auto racing, came with the growth of cable television. At the outset cable was merely a provider of better reception for the networks in areas of the country where the signal was weak, but this changed in the late '70s and early '80s, when cable channels began to provide their own programming, led by ESPN (1979) and CNN (1980).

ESPN had about 1.5 million households out of the roughly 7 million cable homes in 1980. In 2000 these figures had grown to 78 million out of the approximately 80 million homes with a cable connection. Speedvision, a cable channel with auto racing as its principal fare, was established in 1996, and by mid-2001 was in more than 40 million homes. NASCAR was a prime candidate for broadcast; NASCAR understood what television wanted, and understood how to be attractive to sponsors who made consumer products that were not auto related.

Had anyone in 1950 suggested that a half century later a stock-car race on national network television would include vehicles sponsored by everything from detergents to breakfast cereals to a drug that fought impotence, they would have been dismissed as deranged. When the networks finally got around to covering a complete season of an auto racing series, starting in early 2001, it was NASCAR that was chosen. Just as the cable channels had reached their maturity, stock-car racing was able to move onward and upward. The Frances were powerful enough to decree a split TV season, half with one network, half with another.

In the middle of all this were the automobile manufacturers, commonly referred to by racing people as "the factories," who found they were involved whether they liked it or not. When auto racing began, at the outset of the 20th century, the phrase "Win on Sunday, sell on Monday" had a direct application. Automobiles were an untested product, and if a manufacturer could demonstrate that his was better than others, sales could result. There were exceptions to this rule but it was by and large a workable method of promotion. However, as time went on this would change. "Win on Sunday" was the primary purpose, but insurance, in the form of maintaining a performance image regardless of Sunday's outcome, was also needed. The marketing task was figuring out how to do this. And there was a basic problem: NASCAR knew it was in the entertainment business; the automakers thought it was in the racing business.

By the end of the century technical development had practically eliminated "bad" cars from series production thanks to the computer, which was now a key factor in design and manufacturing and which controlled engine-management systems. Bell Laboratories' invention of the transistor in the late '40s, which led to Intel's microprocessor in 1971, among many other things, made compliance with emission-control laws possible and contributed greatly to the advancement of the production automobile. Despite emission-control standards, which were considered impossible to meet at the time of their promulgation, specific power outputs went up.

There was more horsepower per cubic inch in normal road-going cars than ever before, and the word "tuneup," for example, disappeared from car owners' vocabularies. At the same time, America's population went from 152 million in 1950, to 281 million in 2000. There were 49 million vehicles on our roads in 1950. This increased to roughly 214 million today. There are nearly 190 million licensed drivers in this country, the disparity coming because practically every truck and bus driver owns a passenger car.

This combination of more people and better technology reduced the everyday, go-to-market automobile to either a fashion statement or an expensive household appliance, depending on one's point of view. Concurrently, the very computer that improved the automobile was replacing it as the Freedom Machine in the minds of America's youth. The reality of running full bore down a moonlit country road was surpassed, in the minds of many who no longer had a country road in their neighborhoods, by the PC. They had learned that a few keystrokes could put them in any place at any time and behind the wheel of any car. In racing, by the turn of the century they could even be a part of the race itself. Virtual reality was in some ways an improvement on the real world.

Despite all this, the popularity of stock-car racing grew and the stock-car franchise in the racing firmament eclipsed those of its single-seat and sports-car cousins (and competitors in the race for the spectator and sponsor dollars). Veteran fans felt there was no substitute for being there, and the glow cast by the television screen, plus the daily barrage of stock-car related TV programs, only served to increase the audience.

But before all this happened, before the growth of cable television, before the birth of ESPN, TNN and Speedvision, before the demand for ready-made live programming, France the Elder, the ultimate pragmatist, was at work. He started with promotion of the beach races in the late 1930s, also tried promoting midgets, larger single-seat cars with production engines, and even drag races. None of these ventures produced anything like the success of what were known at first as "strictly stock" events. He founded NASCAR in the winter of 1947; the first stock race, later to be known as Grand National and even later as Winston Cup, was run in June of 1949. And having found that he had touched a nerve France stayed with these, which would eventually become stock in name only.

What France had developed, or invented if you will, was the closest, most colorful form of racing. He did it with a product to which the average onlooker could relate, because he or she also owned something that carried the same name despite a steadily increasing number of modifications that made the car on the track bear little resemblance to the car in the parking lot. If the name on the nose said Ford, or Chevrolet, or Dodge or whatever, that was good enough. France operated with certain simple principles:

- The first was that the promoters, not the car owners or the drivers, should control racing. He ruled with the classic iron hand, and in doing so avoided the internecine struggles that have contributed to the decline of single-seater, open-wheel racing in America.

- The second was that the rules should be written so the racing would be close—and when it wasn't, then change the rules, either between seasons, between races, or even during races if necessary.

- Third, and at least as important as the first two, was that everyone should get a fair share. France made money for himself but he made sure the others also did well, contrary to the practices of many promoters in the pre- and immediate postwar eras.

These were American cars with American drivers and the competition in NASCAR was close, always. Purists, many of them fans of road racing, where left and right turns and braking were needed, or of single-seaters purpose-built for the sport, tended to look down at stock-car racing. Eventually they realized it took just as much skill, if not more, to maneuver a large sedan around an oval track and do it better than anyone else, as it did to compete in a more sophisticated vehicle. Competition was the watchword.

In the rarified atmosphere of Winston Cup racing, less than half a second can separate the first 30 cars after qualifying. Wind tunnels and computers are standard equipment for any team desirous of even so much as making an appearance, and engines are modified from race to race so that power and torque curves match track configurations. It is a long way from the beach races of the '30s.

Zora Arkus-Duntov, for many years the Corvette chief engineer, summed up oval-track racing best when he said "driving an oval is like playing a violin on one string—very easy to make noise, very hard to make music." There was much music in a Grand National race and the players were the drivers, who soon became heroes in the Southeast, an area that in the '50s and '60s had no presence in major-league baseball, football or basketball.

In this climate, in a part of the nation in the process of converting from an agrarian to a manufacturing economy, a place where mill workers were looking for their "own" heroes, it was easy to put Glenn (Fireball) Roberts, Curtis Turner, Junior Johnson, Lee Petty and the rest on pedestals.

There were several milestones in the first two decades of NASCAR, and one of these involved an event that took place thousands of miles distant, in France. This was the Le Mans accident of 1955, in which at least 83 persons lost their lives during the 24-hour race. The Le Mans disaster took place less than two weeks after two-time Indianapolis winner Bill Vukovich was killed while going for his third straight win. The combination gave the American Automobile Association, for years the group that controlled so-called championship racing in this country, the excuse it needed (and had wanted for years) to abandon its role as the principal U.S. sanctioning body. There is little doubt that the Frances would have succeeded anyway, but

Among the early heroes: Junior Johnson (left) and Fireball Roberts.
—Don Hunter

there was no love lost between *arriviste* NASCAR and AAA. The departure of this Establishment organization, and the subsequent birth of Midwest-oriented successor USAC, made the task that much easier.

Another major impact on the fortunes of the Frances was the discovery of Daytona, while races were still run on the beach in the 1950s, by the auto industry. Hudson, Chrysler, Chevrolet and Pontiac, and finally Ford, became eager participants in Speed Week, which took place on the hard-packed sands. Even if you were a tourist, you could pay your entry fee and be timed for the flying mile, and receive a certificate attesting to this.

Factory-prepared cars were there as well, posting much better times, and factory cars were also in the races that were a climax to the activities. Detroit had finally realized what racing fans knew all along. It was the start of a long relationship with the manufacturers that saw NASCAR strive to put itself in a position where Detroit participation was welcome, but would be found not necessary for survival or even prosperity.

This was proven first in 1957, when the Automobile Manufacturers Association invoked a GM-sponsored ban on racing. The ban wasn't worth the paper it was printed on, but Ford played by the rules for several seasons, abandoning a leadership position, and this lowered the quality of the entries for what was then known as the Grand National series (this period is treated in some detail in Volume I). NASCAR's ability to survive was proven again in the early '70s, when first Ford and then Chrysler withdrew. There were times when the fields were thin, but the races went on and the fans showed up. Eventually the manufacturers came back. Even Dodge, after a three-decade hiatus, was back in 2001.

The building of the Daytona Speedway, with the word "International" between the other two, was another major step, with its first race in 1959. Despite the fact that Darlington's big oval was nine years older, a story datelined "Darlington" did not create the echo that Daytona did. This town had been the scene of world records dating back to the early 1900s, and so it had tradition. There was brief consideration given to building the Speedway in the Palm Beach area, but the fact that Daytona had such a longtime association with speed was the principal reason Daytona was chosen. The other—in the years before the interstate highway system—was that France knew Palm Beach was another day's drive from the Carolinas, and he knew his core audience would come from there. So France merely moved a few miles inland. It was also the start of the International Speedway Corporation, a public company that holds a 99-year lease on the land under the Daytona track. After a merger with a Roger Penske-led group in 1999, ISC would own eleven major tracks, ten of them ovals and the other a road course. In addition another major speedway was under construction in Kansas City, ISC was a partner in a Chicago project, and had various other racing-related subsidiaries, and the two new tracks were awarded Winston Cup dates for 2001. NASCAR remained privately held.

By the turn of the century this France-owned organization was the sanctioning body for 13 different series conducted at 135 tracks in 40 states. There were approximately 2200 races per year that paid a sanctioning fee to the family. All of these operated in the reflected glow of the Winston Cup series—the big leagues for every kid in the Carolinas, Nebraska, California or anywhere else, who took his home-built car to the local bullring on Saturday nights and hoped to make it to Daytona some day. In the '50s and '60s he just heard about Roberts, Turner and Freddy Lorenzen. In the year 2000 he could watch them on his television screen, not only in Winston Cup events, but also every evening as NASCAR-oriented racing shows were the staple fare of several cable channels. In addition the NASCAR web site was available 24 hours a day, and this year was averaging 4.6 million "unique" visits per month, meaning that many people were using their computers to join the NASCAR party every 30 days.

In 1984 the Daytona 500 was televised on the same day as the closing ceremonies of the Sarajevo Winter Olympics, and came up with a better Nielsen rating, thus gaining the attention of the advertising agencies. In July of that year, at Daytona's Firecracker 400, the race was started by President Reagan, via radio from Air Force One. Reagan then landed before it was over and later posed for pictures with Richard Petty, who won his 200th race that day. *The New York Times* ran the picture at the top of page one—and stock-car racing took another quantum leap as even the *Times* recognized its importance. In the mid-'90s the CART-IRL schism, brought about by Indianapolis Motor Speedway owner Tony George, sent American open-wheel racing into a tailspin from which it has not recovered—and NASCAR was there to reap the benefits.

These three events were also milestones for NASCAR. The people in Daytona had little to do with what happened, but they were smart enough to take advantage of them.

There was some television coverage in the 1960s, but at the time it played only a minor role in racing's growth. The general populace had never heard of cable and the networks had (they thought) more than enough sports programming with stick and ball games. When theater TV was tried in the mid-'60s—a few years after the Indianapolis Motor Speedway flirted with the same idea—it was approached with caution. It wasn't until the start-to-finish live network telecast of the 1979 Daytona 500 that both broadcasters and the Frances were convinced they had been missing something. There was a National Football League-type share-the-wealth agreement in the late '50s, but television revenue was minimal at best. Charlotte Motor Speedway broke away from this agreement in 1977, and it wasn't until late 1999 that NASCAR was able to put together the $2.4 billion package that took effect in 2001. For those who equated money with importance, that agreement established stock-car racing as major league.

Finally there was the arrival of R.J. Reynolds, in time for the 1972 season and the reason for changing the name to Winston Cup. Until then the Grand National series had run wherever and whenever a track was available, in one year as many as

62 races, an average of 51 on either dirt or pavement, once even holding an event on the two-tenths-mile oval at Islip, Long Island, in 1968. In that one the 25-car field occupied more than a quarter of the track surface when the green flag dropped. The last dirt-track event was held in 1970.

Reynolds changed all that. The number of events dropped to the low 30's starting in 1972, and remained there until the late '90s, when new tracks meant new races (the schedule grew to 36 events for 2001). Minimum length of Winston Cup events was set at 250 miles. In addition to cash payments to NASCAR, Reynolds put many times that amount into promotion of the series. With the assistance of Reynolds NASCAR was able to survive the withdrawal of manufacturer support, and become successful financially. This led not only to a healthy bank balance, but Reynolds' help and the attendant national merchandising campaigns helped spread the word to parts of the country where NASCAR was not popular—yet.

Superlatives are always dangerous, but Reynolds' early recognition of the television industry ban on tobacco advertising, which became effective at the end of 1971, gave the company three decades' worth of a promotional bonanza unmatched by any other marketer. Whatever it cost, it was worth it for someone selling a product known to cause cancer. It was simple: If you aren't allowed to pay for a commercial, pay for the sponsorship of a race that is televised—and also make sure that everything else connected with the race has your brand name on it. Reynolds even paid for the painting of many smaller tracks—as long as they were painted in the Winston color scheme.

(Reynolds was not the first cigarette manufacturer to use modern-era automobile racing as a means of promotion. That distinction went to the British Gold Leaf brand, which sponsored the Formula One Lotus team in 1968. By the '90s, with tobacco television advertising banned in various European countries, six of the eleven Formula One teams had cigarette companies as their principal sponsors.)

Ford's involvement, in the 1968–2000 period, saw teams running the company's products use, basically, only four different models, although the outer skins may have caused some of them to be called by different names. These were:

- The Galaxie of the '60s, which had a 119-inch wheelbase, and which was powered by a 427-cubic-inch engine and later by the 429-inch "Boss" engine. The former, used from 1964 through 1968, produced anywhere from 500 to 570 horsepower, depending on its stage of development. The latter was only slightly more powerful (up to 600 horsepower in its last year, 1974). Both ran at the (then) NASCAR limit of 12.5/1 compression ratio. At times these cars ran with Mercury sheet metal, especially after the company withdrew at the close of the 1970 season. The reason was that some of the Mercury shapes—especially the Cyclone—were more aerodynamic.

- The Fairlane, with a 427-inch engine, was used from time to time, most notably by Mario Andretti when he won the 1967 Daytona 500 with a Holman-Moody car, H-M being Ford's principal stock-car racing arm in the '60s.

- The Torino (there were Talladega and Cobra versions) and Mercury Cyclone and Montego of the 1970s.

- The Thunderbird (sometimes with Cougar sheet metal), which made its competition debut in 1978 and lasted through the 1997 season. The 427- and 429-inch engines disappeared after the 1974 season, when NASCAR reduced the maximum displacement to 358 cubic inches (5.9 liters) and Ford teams went over to a version of the company's "small-block" V8, which was introduced as a 260-inch production engine in the early 1960s, but which has seen many modifications over the past four decades. This engine started its NASCAR career producing approximately 600 horsepower, and by 2000 was turning out a reliable 760 hp (at 12.0/1 compression) with some qualifying engines at close to 800. The "Yates Head," developed by master engine builder and team owner Robert Yates, introduced in competition in 1998, was responsible for the last 20 or 25 horses.

- The Taurus, which appeared on the circuit in 1998 and in 2001 is still the Ford of choice. By the time the Thunderbird was finished the company no longer made a two-door sedan that was deemed suitable for NASCAR, so it created one. This was another step in NASCAR's recognition of what was needed to maintain a rivalry between major manufacturers and to maintain a level playing field. The sanctioning body had given Pontiac approval of important aerodynamic changes in the early '90s, and then gave the Chevrolet Monte Carlo permission to make radical alterations to its hindquarters in 1999. It was simple: NASCAR wanted Fords in its races. Ford wanted to race. Once again the rules were changed to suit the situation.

The model used for competition was dictated not only by marketing considerations but also by the rules, which basically specified minimum weight, measured with oil, water and a 22-gallon load of gasoline; wheelbase; and maximum allowable engine size. In the late '60s wheelbases were set at 119 inches, engines were limited to 430 cubic inches, and minimum weights were at 3900 pounds.

The 430-inch limit (later increased to 433 to allow for overbore) lasted until 1982, but by that date practically all competitors were using a 115-inch wheelbase "intermediate" car with a 358-inch engine. Wheelbases dropped to 110 inches the same year that Detroit was producing smaller cars, but minimum weight stayed at 3700 pounds, where it had been since 1975. It finally went to 3500 in 1987 and to 3400 in 1995. Beginning in 1992, the old 305- or 358-inch regulation was changed to read from 350 to 358 inches.

Chapter 2

———•———

JUST BEFORE MIDNIGHT

The multi-faceted campaign to prove that Ford was the dominant high-performance make in the United States, and by extension the world, was already losing steam at the beginning of 1968, when the company decided to withdraw from sports-car racing, leaving Sebring, Le Mans and the rest to private entries. As a consequence, the stock-car effort was more intense than ever. At the time, no one on the operational level suspected that this too would soon end.

1968

> *The Tet Offensive gives Americans a new look at North Vietnamese determination.... Robert Kennedy and Martin Luther King, Jr. are assassinated.... Frenchman Jean-Claude Killy wins three gold medals in the Winter Olympics at Grenoble.... Bob Beamon long-jumps 29 feet, 2½ inches at the Mexico City Summer Games, setting a record that will last for 24 years.*

———•———

At the start of the 1968 Grand National season—there were two "1968" events counting for points in November of 1967—the company was still basking in the glow of its second Le Mans victory the previous June. The Indianapolis 500 and the entire USAC single-seater circuit were dominated by Ford engines, even though the turbocharged Offenhauser would upset that picture in a few months. Leo Beebe, who had brought order and leadership to the racing effort, was promoted to an executive position at Ford of Canada, and Jacque Passino, Beebe's second in command and a man with very close ties to John Holman of Holman-Moody, was Ford's new head of the performance effort.

On a top management level, Henry Ford II brought stock-car fan Semon (Bunkie) Knudsen over from General Motors to be the president of the Ford Motor Company, and this would set off an inner-company war that hurt the performance program. Knudsen was president from February 1968 through mid-September 1969, and his sudden departure would play a role in the fortunes of NASCAR.

Knudsen initiated the development of the "Boss" 429, a more or less hemispherical combustion chamber engine that produced little more horsepower than did the 427-incher with its wedge-shaped chambers, was expensive and played hob with the racing department budget. Former NASCAR program manager Charlie Gray: "We even had to use a separate engine for qualifying and they cost us $4000 apiece, which was astronomical for those times." Lee Iacocca, who wanted Knudsen's job, made use of this impact on the racing budget as part of his campaign to oust the ex-GM executive, and when Knudsen departed in the fall of 1969 Ford was left with the Boss 429.

Holman-Moody, now complete with a marine engine business in Miami and a West Coast operation at Bill Stroppe's facility in Long Beach, California, had more than 450 employees, with most of them at the Charlotte airport headquarters. H-M was for all intents and purposes Ford Racing South—or Ford Racing for Anything Aside from Single Seaters. If it had to do with stock cars and Ford, it went through Charlotte—everything from basic race car construction, to the machining of rough castings shipped from "Up North," to the running of Ford's premier teams, to supplying the other Ford teams with parts. Carroll Shelby, despite his positive image for Ford fans, and despite his two Le Mans wins, was now history as sports-car activity was cut back, and the Indianapolis engine program had been farmed out.

The opposites: Ralph Moody (left) and John Holman.
—Don Hunter

At the beginning of 1968 there were five tracks considered "super speedways," at least one mile in length and banked sufficiently to allow high velocities: Daytona (2.5 miles), Atlanta and Charlotte (1.5 miles), Darlington (1.375 miles) and Rockingham (1 mile). The flat 1.5-mile oval at the New Jersey State Fairgrounds in Trenton was also used that year, as was the 2.7-mile road course in Riverside, east of

Los Angeles. Two more were under construction—the Frances' 2.66-mile Talladega track in Alabama, and Lawrence Lopatin's two-mile oval in Brooklyn, Michigan, approximately 75 miles west of Detroit—and they would eventually bring about a sea change in stock-car racing.

The problem for Ford, as the 1968 season unfolded, was Richard Petty. Ford's nemesis in a "Petty Blue" Plymouth had just come off the most successful season in NASCAR history, winning 27 of his 48 starts—more than 13 percent of the 200 victories he would collect in a 30-plus year career. Most of those wins were achieved not with a 1967 model, but with his 1966 car, reskinned with '67 sheet metal after the new one proved unsuccessful. Petty was NASCAR's first truly public relations-conscious driver, and became the prototype for all the fan-friendly drivers who would follow him. He had a great smile, and he would sign autographs as long as there were fans who wanted them, Plymouth's public relations apparatus was behind him, and 27 wins were unheard of.

Ralph Moody: "He won a load of races—he was a hell of a race driver, don't get me wrong—but he won a lot of races when there was nobody there to race against. It wasn't until later, when they had incentives to run all the races ... that we ran all the races and we won the championship...."

That is when Holman-Moody brought in David Pearson, who came from Cotton Owens' Dodge team and who would be managed by Dick Hutcherson, just retired as an H-M driver. Pearson, who normally avoided a full season, completed one this time, running 47 of the 50 events and winning 16, as did Petty. The difference was that Pearson won the Grand National title with Petty third behind Dodge driver Bobby Isaac, who won only three times. Pearson would wind up with 105 lifetime

Brief interlude: Richard Petty with his Ford, 1969.—Don Hunter

*Teammates and rivals: LeeRoy Yarbrough (top) and
Cale Yarborough (bottom).—Don Hunter*

victories, second only to Petty in a career that was considerably shorter and which, in his later years, concentrated on major events. This was Pearson's second championship, the first having come in 1966 when he was driving for Owens.

The lineups, for most of the season, looked like this:

For Ford, Pearson in the Holman-Moody car; Cale Yarborough with the Wood Brothers; LeeRoy Yarbrough with Junior Johnson, Bobby Allison in another H-M car, and cameo appearances by Mario Andretti, Parnelli Jones, Dan Gurney and A.J. Foyt in major races.

For Chrysler, in addition to Petty there was Bobby Isaac in Harry Hyde's Dodge, Darel Dieringer in Mario Rossi's Plymouth and Buddy Baker running Cotton Owens' Dodge. Paul Goldsmith, on his way into retirement, made some appearances in Ray Nichels' Dodge. Pearson, Isaac, Petty, Bobby Allison, Yarborough and Yarbrough won 46 of the 49 races, Pearson and Petty accounting for 32.

Chevrolet was still operating under a no-race policy, under the table help was minimal, and appearances of GM cars in general were limited to what one could consider as extras in large-scale movies. The one exception to this was Smokey Yunick, the man with the best pipeline to Chevrolet, who appeared at Daytona qualifying with a Chevelle that never stood a chance of making it through tech inspection. GM's policy would change, but not now.

Gurney, driving for the Wood Brothers, won the Riverside road race for the fifth time, an event in which Ford products ran first through fifth. Fords won 21 of the season's 49 events and Mercurys added another six, incurring the displeasure of the Ford Division, which as the more profitable had been the principal beneficiary of the NASCAR program. The reason for Mercury's renaissance was aerodynamics, which were becoming more important with the increase of high-speed tracks.

Cale Yarborough, who was as fast as Pearson and Petty, won both Daytona events and the Southern 500 at Darlington with the Wood Brothers Cyclone. The new

The road course king: Dan Gurney, who won the Riverside race five times, with crewman Leonard Wood, 1969.—Ford/Dave Friedman

Setting an example: Bill France and the car he drove at Talladega in an effort to foil the drivers' strike in 1969. The 59-year-old France reached approximately 175 mph during an August testing session.—Don Hunter

fastback models boosted speeds considerably, Daytona qualifying up about ten miles an hour, close to 190 mph. The Dodge and Plymouth Hemis were good for at least the same power, but the slippery shapes—and the drivers—made the difference.

France was still taking every opportunity to expand the NASCAR area of influence, including the northeastern swing that had become standard. This time it included four races in eight days in such places as Oxford, Maine; Fonda, New York; the aforementioned Islip; and Trenton. A better opportunity to make an impact in the north, albeit in the Midwest, was being born in Michigan, where Lopatin's two-mile oval held its inaugural event for USAC's single-seater cars and attracted 55,000 spectators to the Irish Hills area southeast of Jackson.

Lopatin, a Detroit businessman in his early 40s from outside the NASCAR and USAC communities, formed American Raceways, Inc., a public company; built the Michigan track, soon afterward bought into Riverside and Atlanta; and started construction of a two-mile oval near College Station, Texas. What he did, in essence, was predate the International Speedway Corporation's expansion activities. France attended Lopatin's inaugural race in October, and the day afterward signed a ten-year agreement to hold two NASCAR races per season at Michigan. In addition, he guaranteed Lopatin that the Texas track would be the venue for the 1969 Grand National final event.

While all of this was going on France broke ground for Talladega in May, with a considerable amount of support from segregationist Governor George Wallace, who made sure access roads from the interstate highway were adequate. France had originally considered the Greenville, South Carolina, area, but couldn't put the necessary real estate together, so the project was moved west and south.

And finally, a few days before Thanksgiving, Richard Petty, the Plymouth paradigm, announced he would be switching to Ford for 1969.

As incidental intelligence, when the first race of the 1968 season was held at Macon, Georgia, in November of 1967, Federal agents uncovered an illegal still located under the track. A trap door in the floor of one of the ticket booths led to a 35-foot ladder, at the end of which was a 125-foot tunnel ending at a still capable of turning out 200 gallons every five-day cycle. The track president was brought to trial but a local jury found him innocent after deliberating for two hours.

The point standings: David Pearson (Ford) 3499, Bobby Isaac (Dodge) 3373, Richard Petty (Plymouth) 3123.

Wins: Ford 21, Plymouth 16, Mercury 6, Dodge 5, Chevrolet 1.

Manufacturer's Trophy: Ford 304, Plymouth 237.

1969

> *The Boeing 747 makes its debut. ... Willie Mays hits his 600th home run. ... "Sesame Street" is introduced on public television. ... Neil Armstrong becomes the first man on the moon. ... Dwight D. Eisenhower and Ho Chi Minh die, Steffi Graf is born. ... The Woodstock festival in upstate New York draws 400,000 and later would be considered the defining moment for a generation.*

There were 17 races on tracks of one mile or more in 1969; factory-backed Ford Motor Company products took part in 16 of these—and won 15. Seven went to the credit of LeeRoy Yarbrough, driving Junior Johnson's Ford that twice early in the year was wearing a Mercury skin because of better aerodynamics. Although Petty's success on the smaller tracks was annoying and had been stopped to a degree the previous year, Ford knew national publicity came from winning the major races, and so emphasis was on these.

The front-line teams were Pearson with Holman-Moody, Cale Yarborough with the Wood brothers, LeeRoy Yarbrough with Johnson, plus Bobby Allison with Banjo Matthews, and finally newcomer Petty. Gurney, Jones, Andretti and Foyt drove one or two races each, Gurney as usual for the Wood brothers, Jones and Andretti for H-M. Foyt used a Jack Bowsher car, the latter being a top driver on the Midwest-oriented ARCA circuit and the recipient of Ford assistance in what was essentially a Holman-Moody vehicle. Thanks to Knudsen's move to Ford, even Smokey Yunick, the longtime GM stalwart and a friend of Knudsen's, showed up at the Daytona 500 with a Ford for Indianapolis star Bobby Unser. Unser started eighth, but crashed on the 57th lap.

Engines were still limited to 430 inches, but minimum weight went back up to 3900 pounds. Engines were limited to one four-barrel carburetor but were now allowed dry-sump lubrication systems. Ford showed up with a long-nose "Talladega" version of the Torino, Mercury had a Cyclone Spoiler II and Dodge added a Charger 500. Holman-Moody's 1968 creation of the four-sidebar roll cage became mandatory for all makes.

The one race the Ford factory teams missed was the opening event at Talladega in Alabama. The longest and steepest (32-degree banking), Talladega is now just another one of NASCAR's so-called "super speedways," but when it opened it was a lightning rod for controversy and obscured much of the season's competition.

The trouble with Talladega was it was too fast—too fast for the tires, and too fast for the drivers, due to its uneven surface. The Ford team went to Alabama for initial testing in early August, with Yarbrough and Allison doing the driving. Speeds were in the 195-mph range, and no one was comfortable. The word got out, and the drivers' reaction to what was unknown, and considered unsafe, was to form a union.

By mid-August, with Talladega as the catalyst, the Professional Drivers Association was born, with Richard Petty as president and New York attorney Lawrence Fleisher, the creator of the National Basketball Association players' union, as legal counsel (the difference between the NBA and NASCAR was that one group was composed of employees, and the other of independent contractors). Whatever the PDA's concerns were—pensions, insurance and the like—there was little question this had been brought to a head by the testing at Talladega, and the tire troubles that resulted from venturing into speed ranges unheard of for stock cars.

At Talladega the action off the track was as intense as on it, where tires were being destroyed on a regular basis and which resulted, finally, in Firestone packing up and going home, not willing to risk the adverse publicity that would result from a crash caused by tire failure. Goodyear stayed, but only after France had a talk with company officials. Petty and 31 others pulled out on Saturday afternoon after several garage-area confrontations with France. The race started with 13 Grand National cars and a group of 23 make-weights left over from the preliminary event run Saturday afternoon. Caution flags were displayed every 25 laps to allow tire changes, and Richard Brickhouse, who had filled an empty seat in a factory Dodge, won the only event of his five-year, 39-race NASCAR career, averaging 153 mph, more than 40 miles slower than qualifying speeds.

Early in the week, while things were coming to a head, France sought support in Dearborn and called Knudsen, an old friend. "As long as I'm president," Knudsen told France, "you'll have your cars." Two days later Henry Ford II fired Knudsen.

The upshot was that France won. No one was killed, no one was injured, there were 62,000 (announced) spectators. The PDA was dissolved in the following year, never to be heard from again. Another result was that Talladega speeds brought restrictor-plate racing to NASCAR, and today they are used at Daytona and Talladega. Restrictor plates are devices that limit the amount of air that can be taken into the engine. Over the years they have varied in size and the power penalty has varied accordingly. By the year 2000, horsepower in restrictor-plate engines was down 35 to 40 percent compared with that of engines built for the other races. In 2000 Ford's 358-inch NASCAR engines were producing about 760 horsepower for other tracks, the exact number depending on the individual builder. In restrictor-plate (and race) configuration they were down to approximately 435–450 hp, and still running over 190 mph at Daytona and Talladega. Restrictor plates make for a different kind of racing where passing is more difficult and occurs relatively infrequently. These races are decided by the pit stops, by who can avoid accidents, and by who can "draft," or slipstream, better than others. But the fans came anyway, and have continued to do so.

Fords won 26 of the 54 events on the 1969 calendar and Mercury added four. Dodge had 22 wins, 17 of them by Bobby Isaac in the car prepared by Harry Hyde. Plymouth had only two, both by Petty in late-1968 races counting for the '69 title before he got his new Fords in shape to compete. Pearson, whose mission for Ford and Holman-Moody was to take the Grand National title, did so, winning eleven times in 51 starts and placing in the top five no less than 42 times, a remarkable tribute to the car's reliability and his skill. Petty, who won ten times (eight in Fords) was second while Isaac, despite all of his wins, placed sixth. The NASCAR point system of 1969, like all the organization's various systems, placed emphasis on participation and finishing well as opposed to just winning—designed to delay the clinching of the championship until the very end of the season. Isaac was in the top five only 29 times in 50 starts. James Hylton, Neil (Soapy) Castles and Elmo Langley, none of whom managed to win a race, were third through fifth in the standings.

The aerodynamics race continued, with Dodge and Plymouth coming up with limited-production winged models—first the Dodge Daytona and later on the Plymouth Superbird—in order to gain an advantage on the high-speed tracks. Regulations called for a small minimum number of units to be built for these to be legal for competition and this was done, supposedly. The net effect, years later, was to provide something special for collectors of '60s–'70s muscle cars.

Despite the controversy NASCAR continued its climb toward recognition by the television industry. In December of the year ABC Sports signed a contract to televise nine races in 1970, and included options for 26 events in 1971 and 1972. The first agreement was for a total of $1,365,000, with payments spread among the tracks staging the events, some money to those not having TV coverage, and some to the drivers. Left out of all this were Lopatin's American Raceways properties—by now including Michigan, Atlanta, Riverside and Texas. Lopatin, now a relative footnote in racing history, was the first major multi-track owner—and he almost made it work.

Lopatin had been openly critical of France's position during the Talladega confrontations in August and for a promoter to disagree with the president of NASCAR displayed a remarkable lack of judgement. Lopatin, it is assumed, thought he could take over stock-car racing, but soon found otherwise. His 1969 races suffered from an unusual run of bad weather, with Riverside rained out twice, Atlanta delayed a week by rain, Michigan stopped after 330 miles by rain, and Texas hit by pre-race storms that left the infield too soggy to accommodate spectators. Lopatin was running out of money to service American Raceways debt and he also lost executive Les Richter, who sided with France in the Talladega affair and resigned soon afterward. Richter went on to a long and fruitful career as one of France's key people.

Lopatin would not survive the following year.

The 1969 point standings: David Pearson (Ford) 4170, Richard Petty (Ford, Plymouth) 3813, James Hylton (Dodge) 3750, Neil Castles (Dodge) 3530, Elmo Langley (Ford) 3383, Bobby Isaac (Dodge) 3301.

Wins: Ford 26, Dodge 22, Mercury 4, Plymouth 2.

Manufacturer's Trophy: Ford 375, Dodge 320.

1970

After five years of drilling, oil is discovered in the North Sea.... "Doonesbury" makes its national debut.... The Beatles dissolve their partnership.... Salvador Allende is elected president of Chile, the first avowed Marxist to win a free election in a western country.... Janis Joplin, Vince Lombardi, Charles de Gaulle die.... The Environmental Protection Agency is created.

———————◆———————

It was November and still pitch black when Mose Nowland got to Kar Kraft at six one morning. Nowland, a veteran Ford racing technician and program manager, was supervising a project at this Ford vendor's building on Haggerty Street in East Dearborn, and was the first to arrive. When he tried to unlock the door his key wouldn't fit.

"Never had heard a word about anything," Nowland said. "I came in, and no kidding, my key wouldn't fit the door. At first I thought the kids in the neighborhood have been screwing around—maybe shot some airplane glue in the lock ... so I pulled the car up the front walk so the lights were on it and I could see a brand new shiny brass tumbler. I jumped the fence, went to the back door—and the same thing.... Then a couple of my employees arrived and we were standing around and I didn't know what to tell them ... and then a Ford security man drove up and he asked for me by name. He said, 'You are instructed to send your employees home and you will be in touch with them later, and you are to go home and wait for a phone call, and [Ford engineer] Joe Macura will be calling you with some instructions and some explanations.' So I hung around until 9 or 9:30 because the others wouldn't leave, they were wondering, 'Well, what is it?'

"So our designers, our inspectors, our mechanics, the engineers, were saying, 'What's going on?' And I said, 'I don't know, it's a lockout'.... So we went home, and I did get a call later from Joe Macura, and he said, 'I don't know the full story yet, but you folks are welcome to stay home until I call you back,' and then he said, 'I hope to have a good explanation in a day or so and then I'll bring you in and tell you what we have to do.'

"The very next day, he (Macura) was sitting in a temporary office—he was locked out too—and he called me in and told me, 'Here's the deal. We're out of racing. I don't know the reasons why yet, but we're not going to be back in the building for some time because there are discussions as to who owns all the equipment. But eventually we'll go in and pack up our material, unbolt the machines that belong to Ford, take our inventory and move it out....' Eventually we did move it all to a storage area in the middle of the Triple E building and that's when I brought the guys back in to work.... then finally we got a token job.... we did a small engineering job, converting tractor engines to propane so they could be run on fork lift trucks."

Nowland went from that to working on Ford's experimental rotary engine program, to building Presidential limousines Ford was doing for the White House, and would eventually, when motorsports became a priority again, be called back.

That's how he learned the company was pulling out—at least in the United States, or at least in 49 of the states. For some reason the off-road program in Southern California was not touched, possibly because much of it was funded by the truck marketing money rather than through the racing department.

Others were informed in different ways, but the effect was the same.

Henry Ford II was still the chairman and chief executive officer and he was the one who made the decision. One reason was the money spent on the performance program in the past eight years. It had produced winners at Indianapolis, in Formula One, in long-distance sports-car racing (most notably Le Mans), in Trans-Am events, even some in drag racing, and obviously in stock-car racing. What it had not done was increase Ford's market penetration, which stayed, domestically, in the 29 percent range from 1962 to 1969. The root of this problem was that, while Ford was winning races, there was no transfer to what Ford was selling in dealer showrooms. The youth market, which Ford had lost to Chevrolet when that GM division's "small-block" V8 was introduced in 1955, was still in the enemy camp—and would remain there for years to come.

Also contributing to the decision was the discovery of certain abuses of company policy, perhaps inevitable any time a large corporation gets involved in something as fast-moving as racing, with field decisions needed practically every day and oversight being something that came much later, if at all. The hard look came in 1970. Harold (Red) Poling, then controller of the Product Development Group and two decades later to serve as chairman, was the man entrusted with the shutdown. He did it quickly. Certain persons were allowed to resign, among them Passino, while others were reassigned within the company once Poling was satisfied they had not been involved in anything questionable.

Nevertheless, in a company the size of Ford, there are certain exceptions to every rule and the performance program did not disappear completely even though the support for outside vendors did. A small group of engineers, including Gray, Lee Morse and Danny Jones, were placed in a small department where they continued to design high-performance equipment. This group would remain more or less intact for over a year before it was broken up, with most of the engineers going to the emission-control work that was top priority not only at Ford, but at every other automaker as well. A decade later some of these people would be called back to racing.

In Britain, deeply involved in practically every facet of the sport, including sponsorship of Cosworth's all-conquering Formula One engines, there wasn't a ripple. Stuart Turner, then Ford of Europe's motorsports manager: "Indifference. We kept on with what we were doing." Walter Hayes was there. Hayes had become personally friendly with HF2, and the subject of stopping motorsports in Europe was hardly discussed.

It was different down south.

Ralph Moody: "We knew before that something was going on; we'd get things in the mail, asking us how much it cost to build cars, what we got for them, and all kinds of stuff.... There was a lot going on, but I was too busy building cars to know about it.... Finally, when I found out, I had them vote me out of the company and then they couldn't put me in the middle of anything." Moody would stay with the company as an employee until the fall of 1971, when another disagreement with Holman—they were never personally close—caused him to leave.

One other factor contributing to Henry Ford's dissatisfaction could well have been the 1970 stock-car effort: There were 48 Grand National races, and despite all the money and the factory-sponsored teams the Chrysler Corporation wound up winning 38 of these. Plymouths took 21, including 18 by Petty, who had returned to his original make when the Superbird was introduced. Petty's teammate, New Englander Pete Hamilton, won three major races, the Daytona 500 and two 500-mile races at Talladega, which was now considerably slower thanks to the restrictor plates. Nevertheless, in one of them he was forced to make 14 pit stops and used seven sets of tires. Hamilton was another of those good drivers with an all-too-brief career in NASCAR. He had only 64 starts in a six-year span, with five of these in 1972 and two the next year before he was gone. Dodges added another 17, including eleven for Bobby Isaac, who also won the GN championship. Ford drivers won six, plus four more when the cars were reskinned as Mercurys for the high-speed tracks. It was a disastrous performance, and provided ammunition for every in-house critic of the program. Success had many fathers, failure had none.

It was the end of several eras: In the fall Chrysler announced it would reduce its stock-car effort to sponsorship of Petty in a Plymouth and Buddy Baker in a Dodge operating out of the Petty stable. Isaac and crew chief Harry Hyde were left out. NASCAR ran its last dirt-track event on September 30 at Raleigh, and five days later Curtis Turner, one of the heroes of stock-car racing's early days, was killed in the crash of his own plane near Dubois, in western Pennsylvania.

The final point standings: Isaac (Dodge) 3911, Bobby Allison (Dodge) 3860, James Hylton (Ford) 3788, Petty (Plymouth) 3447.

Wins: Plymouth 21, Dodge 17, Ford 6, Mercury 4.

Manufacturer's Trophy: Dodge 301, Plymouth 286.

And then it was quiet—or nearly so.

Chapter 3

THE ENGLISHMAN

He was one of the great name-droppers, fond of starting conversations with gambits like "… as Lord Beaverbrook was saying to me yesterday …" and he was on a first-name basis with Henry Ford II, which was a privilege extended to few in the company. He was of less than medium height, rather unimposing at first glance, usually fussing with his pipe or his necktie, and he could sell refrigerators to Eskimos.

He would have shipped them before he called at the igloo.

That was Walter Hayes (1924–2000), in his 30-year career at one time or another vice president of public relations of Ford of Britain, vice president of public affairs of the Ford Motor Company, and vice chairman of Ford of Europe. He was the outsider who became the insider, and he was, as Haymarket Publishing Chairman Simon Taylor wrote in his obituary, "The first industry executive to comprehend fully the huge marketing and corporate image-building power of motorsport."

Walter Hayes: He got things done.—Ford Motor Company

As such, he was the most important man in Ford's 100-year history of motorsports involvement.

He came to Ford of Britain in 1961 as director of public relations when the United Kingdom division of the company was building blue-collar cars that wouldn't have recognized charisma if it walked up and shook hands.

- He fostered the use of the 1000cc Anglia engine (known as the "Kent" engine in Britain) for Formula Junior in the late '50s and early '60s, and then helped create Formula Ford. He thus made the company a vital part of the cars that ruled—and still do—entry-level single-seater racing.

- He saw to it that Ford financed Keith Duckworth's Formula One engine of 1967 that dominated world championship racing for more than 15 years, and did this for less than $300,000.

- He brought in Stuart Turner, England's best rally team manager, and the two of them gave the plain-Jane Escort some sex appeal as it became a contender in a motorsports discipline important in Britain and on the European continent.

- He brought racing to Ford of Germany in the late 1960s when that company had no sporting image whatsoever.

- And he talked Henry Ford II into going back into racing in the U.S. in 1980 after the company had been out for a decade. And he did this while the company was undergoing the worst financial crisis in its history.

Iceboxes in the Arctic would have been easy....

Hayes was born into a family of printers, missed a university education when he spent five years in the RAF during World War II, then went to work as a newspaperman. He moved quickly, rising to the post of associate editor of the *Daily Mail*, one of Britain's leading publications, and was then editor of the *Sunday Despatch* before he came to Ford. Hayes: "Sir Patrick Hennessy, who was chairman of Ford [of Britain] at the time, asked me if I'd like to work for them, because they were told they had to have a director with a feel for the outside world...."

And Britain's world was different.

"Ordinary people didn't have cars in this country in any quantity until 1955, which was terribly late, when you think about it," Hayes says. "If you were rich you had a big car, if you were middle class you had a smaller car, if you were poor you didn't have anything. So it's from that time onward, particularly in the '60s, when the aspiration for car ownership, the excitement of the car, and a sort of general changing of things, that this whole boom began. When I asked when I got there what I was allowed to do they said, 'We're not laying down any rules for you,' so I was able to put motor racing forward from the beginning. I did it not just for motor racing, but it was perfectly clear, as I saw it, that excitement was the name of the game. Excitement could be motor racing."

Celebration: (left to right) Two-time world champion Emerson Fittipaldi, Keith Duckworth, Walter Hayes and Henry Ford II when the Cosworth DFV won its 40th grand prix race, 1971.—Ford Motor Company

"The reason we started here," he says, "was simply to add excitement and romance to the cars as such, particularly production cars, because in the early days I was never tempted into exotic motor racing, it was rallying that we started with…. In 1962 I got 85,000 pounds (approximately $240,000 at then-current rates of exchange) to build a rally center at an old airfield, Boreham, and that was the start…. But in addition to rallying, where we had great supremacy, we were into touring cars in the biggest way … and because there was less control I could feature Jimmy Clark driving Cortinas, winning the British touring car championship, going around Brands Hatch [racing circuit] on three wheels. There was a huge crossover in that period, and although people today can't believe this, you could go to a meeting, see a grand prix, a sports-car race and a touring car race, and the grand prix drivers would drive in all three."

When Ford shut down active sponsorship of motorsports in the U.S. in the fall of 1970 the decree did not extend to any of its international outposts, and what was going on in Britain and elsewhere kept right on going.

In the fall of 1979, when Henry Ford II made up his mind to retire as chief executive officer, he told Hayes he wanted him to take over the post of vice-president for public affairs. One of the reasons was Ford wanted someone on the executive floor with whom he had a more-than-business relationship, someone who would tell him what memos would not. The other was that Hayes was good at his job.

"I didn't want to go to the States," Hayes says. "I said to Henry, 'It's ludicrous to have an Englishman there—they won't even understand what I'm saying, apart from everything else, and what will I do?' And he said, 'Do what you want to do. [Philip] Caldwell is taking over, and you know Caldwell and you get on well with him.' I said, 'Well, I'm going to do motorsport,' and he said, 'OK.'"

There was some slight movement in this direction in the year before Hayes moved, but he was the one who got it done.

"I looked at the situation in late '79, just before I moved over," he said, "and I went to Las Vegas to talk to some dealers and I announced that we were going back into motor racing, and when I got back there was a blue letter [management letter] saying you can't go back into motor racing and I said you can tear it up, because I'll write you a new blue letter and you can send it out, because I can tell you we are."

"I think Americans never really got the demographic message. You have to simply stand up all the time in the marketplace and say, 'Look what my product can do.'"

There was a postscript to Hayes' career, and it occurred in 1987, when he was back in Britain, and Henry Ford was spending much of the year at a house he owned in Henley, outside of London. "I went down there one day," Hayes says, "and he said, 'What will we do today?' and because I'd just been to the Mille Miglia (the historic version) I said, laughing, 'Well, we could always buy Aston Martin.' And he said, 'That's funny, because I've been golfing with Victor Gauntlett, who said they really need to sell the company to a bigger manufacturer.' And so we bought Aston Martin. We started negotiations in May, we bought it in July.... Henry died in September so he never had the fun he was determined to have with this marque."

Chapter 4

—◆—

THE GERMANS

Jochen Neerpasch was one of Germany's better drivers in the late 1960s, when he was a member of the Porsche factory team. Before that, in 1965, he finished 7th in the 1000 Kilometers of the Nürburgring, sharing a Cobra with Bob Bondurant, and the following year he drove a few events in a Ford GT40. In 1968 he was in the winning Porsche in the Daytona 24 Hours, and consistently in the top three or four in most of the manufacturer's world championship races.

But for the greater part of that season he was also the director of the new motorsports department for Ford of Germany. Neerpasch, from Krefeld near Ford's German headquarters in Cologne, and whose father was a Ford dealer, had been contacted that spring. "I told Ford I had an arrangement with Porsche and I had to complete that," he says, "and since we weren't going to do any races until the next year they said OK."

All Neerpasch had was a contract and an assignment: Make a contender out of Ford's new Capri coupe, and give the new Escort a sporting image. Some wishful thinkers saw the Capri as possible competition for Porsche, which ruled the sports-car scene in its native land and in many others as well. The Escort, in the mother country of the Volkswagen … well, anything would be of help. The impetus for all this, as it did in Britain, came from Walter Hayes, who was pursuing his conviction that a sporting image could help with brand identification. Although it would be difficult to attribute Ford's German-market problems of the late '90s to the lack of a performance image, the fact remains that Ford was not seriously involved in performance there, at a time when Mercedes, BMW, Porsche and Audi were.

The Capri was produced for 15 years, nearly 2 million were built and more than 70 percent of them were exported, including 470,000 to the U.S., from 1970 through 1978. When this coupe was introduced in Germany in 1969 it came in several versions, ranging from a 1.3-liter four with 50 horsepower to a 2.3-liter V6 with 108 hp, neither of which convinced anyone they were performance cars. But before the Capri's run was finished, a racing version, complete with tube frame and 1.7-liter turbocharged four-cylinder, was turning out more than 600 horsepower. In addition to being the main weapon in Ford-Cologne's stable, this one also provided the basis for the company's return to racing in the U.S., being reskinned with Mustang sheet metal and making its American debut in 1981.

The leader and the band: Ford of Germany motorsports director Jochen Neerpasch (top left), Hans-Joachim Stuck (top right), Jochen Mass (bottom left), and Dieter Glemser (bottom right).—Ford Motor Company

The Escort, originally with an 1100cc, 40-horsepower, four-cylinder engine, worked its way up to the RS Cosworth of 1992, complete with 2.0-liter turbo producing 220 hp, the one beloved by rally enthusiasts throughout Britain and the Continent. In German racing form, complete with 2.0-liter Cosworth, it turned out 275 hp without a turbo, and weighed only 1850 pounds ready to race, without fuel or driver. Zero to 60 was achieved in less than five seconds and top speed, depending on axle ratio, was in excess of 150 mph.

Among the first people Neerpasch hired was a young enthusiast from Münster in Westphalia with some experience as a driver but whom he felt would do better as

The Capris: European touring car champions, 1971–72.
—Ford Motor Company

an administrator. This was Michael Kranefuss, whose career with Ford would last two decades, most of it in the U.S. Neerpasch laid the foundations for Ford of Germany's racing adventure, then moved to rival BMW in 1972 and Kranefuss took over. He did so in the middle of what can be considered the Capri's zenith as a competition car, both in terms of how well it did and in the talent level of those who were attracted to it.

The Capri and the Escort were stepping-stone cars for a number of young drivers in the early '70s, and they were also, from time to time, busman's holiday drives for many of Europe's biggest names. These included three-time world champion Jackie Stewart, who was, in effect, acknowledging Ford's support of his career by driving Capris when his Formula One schedule permitted. He was paired in long-distance races with 1979 champion Jody Scheckter once and with two-time (1972–74) champion Emerson Fittipaldi once, but despite the high hopes, nothing came of either entry. Even Niki Lauda, another triple world champion, did a brief stint in a Capri, as did 1982 titleholder Keke Rosberg.

The bulk of the work was done by young Germans on their way up, at the beginning most notably Dieter Glemser and Jochen Mass, the latter successful as a grand prix driver later. Glemser, driving an Escort TC, won the German racing championship in 1969, won the European touring car championship in 1971 in a Capri RS, and won the German racing championship in 1973 and '74 while driving an Escort. The last two titles were won while driving for Zakspeed, the team that at first had semi-official status and which starting in 1976 became Ford of Germany's *de facto* works team.

Mass was German closed-circuit (as opposed to hillclimb) champion in 1971, and then won the European touring car title in 1972, both times with a Capri RS, by now taken out to 3.0 liters and 300 horsepower. In the latter year the German racing championship went to Hans-Joachim Stuck, son of the great 1930s driver, also in a Capri RS. The major Capri news of 1972, however, was made by its successes at the Nürburgring 1000 Kilometers and at Le Mans.

Although the very thought of Capris—however modified—running against Ferraris, Porsches and Alfa Romeos of that era may seem preposterous, the results were otherwise. At the Ring, thanks to bravura performances by Glemser, Mass, Stuck and Spanish Formula One driver Alex Soler-Roig, the Capris finished seventh and eighth over-all, behind a group of racing sports cars and ahead of all the Porsche GT cars. Mass and Glemser were seventh, the other two eighth. At Le Mans, running in a special touring class, Scotsman Gerry Birrell and Frenchman Claude Bourgoignie finished tenth over-all, just ahead of Glemser and Soler-Roig in the second Capri. In addition, the Capris ran 1-2-3 in the 24-hour touring-car race at Spa, in Belgium. The next year the Capri RS did even better at the Ring, with Birrell and John Fitzpatrick finishing sixth over-all ahead of what seemed to be dozens of Porsches. The latter soon took Fitzpatrick on as one of its own drivers.

The program continued through a reduced 1974 season, the cutback coming because of the energy crisis that hit Europe as hard as the U.S. in the fall of 1973.

Hans Heyer won the European Touring Car championship driving both an Escort and a Capri RS, the 3.4-liter latter complete with four-valve Cosworth modifications that produced up to 450 hp. He won five of the six events counting for the title. But the economic downturn created by the oil shortage brought with it a Ford of Europe budget crisis for 1975. And so Hayes, in a memo to Ford of Europe President Bob Lutz, recommended shutting down the activities in either Cologne or Boreham, where British Ford based its rally team. Germany had a budget more than twice as large as Britain's, so that is where the axe fell. Kranefuss was retained. "I had to agree with the decision," he said, "because I knew of the difference in budgets, but I thought it was all over and I actually started looking for another job," he says. "In the meantime I looked for other company components who could support some of my people on their budgets, and looked for outside help to carry on the program, and we continued to work."

This was how the relationship with Zakspeed was cemented. In 1976, when funds were available, Zakspeed became the official Ford team, much in the manner that Holman-Moody ran the U.S. stock-car program in the 1960s.

Heyer won the German racing title in 1975 and 1976 in a Zakspeed Escort, this one with 275 horsepower in a car that weighed little more than 1700 pounds ready to race but without fuel. He won five events in 1975 and five more the next year, but had to contend with Klaus Ludwig, a newcomer to Ford who would eventually be well known in American road racing circles.

The affable, talkative Ludwig was raised in the Bonn suburb of Roisdorf, about an hour east of the Nürburgring, and was the son of a racing fan who happened to know the Ring's general manager, so tickets were always available. Ludwig knew the Ring from childhood, and knew he would become a racing driver.

The fastest drivers will seek out the fastest cars, and Ludwig was no exception. He moved to Formula Two for 1977 with little success, drove a Porsche 935 with mixed results the next year, then in 1979 won 12 of 17 starts with the 935, including the Watkins Glen 6 Hours and the first of his three Le Mans victories. Ludwig won the unlimited division of the German racing championship as well, and the under 2.0-liter honors went to Heyer in the new Capri, making a comeback after a two-year absence.

This one, a Zakspeed creation, had a tube frame with a skin that looked only vaguely like the production model, had a 1.4-liter four-cylinder with turbocharger and about 380 hp. And for the 1980 season, with the engine up to 1.7 liters and 580 horsepower, Kranefuss brought Ludwig back to Cologne. The Capri was approximately 200 horsepower down on the Porsche 935, but weighed considerably less— 2100 pounds with oil and water but without fuel. It had, at the beginning of the 1980, a giant wing at the rear, and the wing was protested by the competition. Ludwig lost his points from the first two events of the season, and although he won seven races with the car, he lost the championship as a result.

The next year was better: Ludwig took part in 13 German championship events, sat on the pole every time and won ten times in a car that was producing approximately

510 horsepower. By now, however, he had become a Trans-Atlantic commuter. Ford was back in the racing business in the U.S., the chosen stage for the comeback was the International Motor Sports Association, and IMSA would accept the turbo Capri with a Mustang skin. Kranefuss had moved to the U.S. in the fall of 1980 to revive the program, and Ludwig was his first choice as driver

The Sierra XR4Ti, complete with 2.3-liter turbocharged engine, became the principal competition model for Europe beginning in 1985 (the Sierra was marketed in the U.S. as the Merkur). This was the car with the odd-looking spoiler on the production versions, which was sold in Germany from 1983 through 1985, and in the U.S. from 1985 through 1989. It was intended as an additional model for Lincoln-Mercury dealers, but retail salesmen used to moving Lincolns to older people never quite knew how to treat this one. It was also used in IMSA and the SCCA's Trans-Am series in the U.S., and was successful, but that did little to convince buyers.

By 1986 the Swiss Eggenberger organization had replaced Zakspeed as the principal competition arm of Cologne, and by 1987 this paid off. The Sierras won what at the time was called the World Touring Car championship, with Ludwig and Klaus Niedzwiedz doing most of the winning. In addition, with Englishman Steve Soper as the third driver, Ludwig and Niedzwiedz and their Sierra won the 24 Hours of the Nürburgring, which had become the world's most prestigious event for small-displacement sedans.

In 1988 the Sierras won the European Touring car championship and the German Touring Car championship, the latter considerably enlivened by the presence of Mercedes-Benz. Eggenberger's team handled the European events, and three others—Grab, Ringhausen and Wolf Racing had factory support in the national events. Ford took the European team title with eight wins in the eleven races, including six for Soper. There were 22 races for the DTM crown and Fords won eleven, with the individual title going to Ludwig in his last year with the blue oval.

That was, unfortunately, the last year for Ford of Germany to compete on any sort of a major-league level. Budget and marketing considerations said otherwise.

Chapter 5

———◆———

THE REST OF THE WORLD

Ford of Europe's Escort, an ordinary kind of car but a willing candidate for conversion to a competition machine, carried the longest-running nameplate in the history of the company, being introduced in 1968 and produced until 2000—32 years. It thus outlived, in a sense, the Model T, which was built for 19 years, starting in 1908. For most of its life the Escort was the bell cow of Ford's worldwide rally program, an effort in British and other European markets best compared to Dearborn's NASCAR campaign when considering the image-building effectiveness.

It was the vehicle of choice during a period when Ford faced competition from makes that were more sophisticated (and expensive) in standard production form, and was finally replaced in 1999. That is when the new Focus, a remarkably good successor, took over the job of representing the blue oval in what had finally become a workable World Rally Championship.

Just as oval-track racing is a distinctively American version of motorsport, rallying is as popular in many other parts of the globe. It began in Europe before World War I, when the object was to see if production cars were reliable in long-distance, non-stop sporting events, and it progressed from there. Rallying has changed little in principle, but in actual fact it has evolved into something quite different, and something the International Automobile Federation (FIA) hopes will eventually be a successful television package. The original idea was to drive a predetermined route in a fixed time, with penalties for arriving early or late at the end of each stage. The first four decades saw major rallies run over thousands of miles and take two or three days and nights, with stops only for fuel and to clock in at checkpoints.

If there was a tie after all of this, a "special test"—a slalom or a hillclimb—was used as the tie-breaker. In the last three decades a number of what are euphemistically called "special stages" have become the decision makers and crowd pleasers. What these are, simply put, are races (except that cars start one at a time) over sections of road sometimes paved, sometimes unpaved, closed to other traffic. The fastest car, obviously, is the winner, after a vehicle's times from all the special stages are added up at the end.

Today events counting for the World Rally Championship (it has been called that since 1997) run over a distance of between 800 and 1000 miles, and the driving is done in three days. The routes are laid out in a rough cloverleaf pattern, which simplifies the logistics for both the teams and the organizers, and the driving is done almost exclusively in the daytime. Special stages usually number about 25, or eight or nine per day, and these will total somewhere near the maximum allowable 260 miles.

That is more than enough to come up with a decision as well as provide excitement for the spectators and television audience. There is also a provision that limits the average speed in the special stages to 132 kph (about 83 mph), but the roads used for the stages make this academic at best.

The factory-sponsored entries are something of a cross between undersized (and more sophisticated) NASCAR stock cars and off-road racing Trophy Trucks. When viewed at speed on winding, twisting roads that keep them at almost right angles to the line of flight, they offer a thrill to those spectators who have climbed through the forests, or snowbanks, or both. The current ones are right on the minimum weight limit of 1230 kg (about 2700 pounds), all have four-wheel drive and about 315 to 320 horsepower, and they can fly.

It is a form of motorsports that has attracted various manufacturers using it for sales promotion, the most successful of which, by far, was Lancia, one of Italy's great old nameplates which was taken over by Fiat in 1969. Lancia, to American audiences, meant little or nothing, since the make's sales in the U.S. were miniscule at best and nonexistent since 1984. Lancia has also been practically invisible in parts of Europe outside its native country.

But Lancia's management expended major sums. The company won the title ten times in the first 20 years of the world manufacturer's competition, and won one third of the events until its withdrawal after 1993. The net result was a decline in sales and a retreat from what had become a financial millstone. In other words, one more company learned that winning is nice, but it helps to have a product to which fans can relate. Between Lancia and parent company Fiat, which was also heavily involved in the late '70s and early '80s, the pair won 95 of the first 232 world championship events, counting through 1993.

Nevertheless the opportunities for promotion do exist, and rally participation has been a mainstay of various Japanese manufacturers attempting to penetrate the European market, most notably Toyota, Mitsubishi and Subaru. They have done a better job, translated to mean sales, than Lancia ever did. Although rally adherents are quick to point this out, they sometimes manage to forget that such factors as quality of product, price, and service network are the principal determinants of success.

Rally distances dropped under 2000 miles in the early '70s—with the notable exception of the East African Safari, which has almost always covered more than 3000—and by the mid-'80s the others were for the most part under 1500 miles. The decline in mileage, plus the fact that the "stages" are run over roads closed to normal traffic, happened for several reasons, one being that the increased traffic on European roads brought with it more stringent law enforcement. All-night events lost their popularity in the mid-'80s, with the Monte Carlo Rally being the last to give this up in 1995.

Rallying in the U.S., for the most part, has been a navigational rather than a driving test, sort of a stop watch-cum-calculator exercise ("go 5.63 miles, turn left on Route 43, average speed 32.4 mph...."). As a result rallies have never been interesting to the vast majority of American car enthusiasts. In Europe the absence of speed limits—or the ignoring of them by the authorities—enabled organizers to establish averages for the key rally sections that made them, in effect, races, with the fastest driver getting the fewest penalty points. If you stood by the side of a dirt road in the Alps and saw the cars come screaming by, tails out, drivers on opposite lock, well, it was really something, and you wanted to come back again—and maybe even buy that make the next time you needed a car.

Many European rallies were also used as promotional vehicles for certain areas of their organizing country, most notably the Monte Carlo Rally, which began life in 1911—the second oldest event, but the longest running—and was designed, among other things, to fill Riviera hotel rooms in the off-season.

There was some factory participation in the '50s, many of the British manufacturers and Mercedes-Benz from time to time, and by the '60s Porsche was also prominent. The French (Renault, Alpine, Citroen) and later the Italians also came aboard, and the Escort was in the middle of all this. It was a program limited to an extent by budgets, but most of the time, when the money was available, it worked.

Rallies, the cars that took part and the championship rules underwent changes in the three-plus decades treated here, with the principal over-all factor probably being the benign neglect exercised by the FIA. That organization, made up (for most of its life) of administrators and delegates with little commercial sense, realized far too late there was an advantage to inserting "world" into the rally championship.

A good portion of the responsibility for major-league rallying not being as popular as it could be can be laid at their door. That organization, especially in the years when blue blazers were more important than business sense, was delinquent in giving this form of motorsport the status it deserved, and in giving the manufacturers who supported it a full range of promotional possibilities.

The FIA, preoccupied with racing, finally got around to organizing a true world rally championship in 1973. And this was only for manufacturers. It took another six years before there was a driver's championship. And decades passed before the FIA revised the championship so that it could have an appeal for television—again, the "X Factor" in all forms of motorsports since the adaptation of satellites for commercial telecast. By 1999 the television rights for the World Rally Championship were used as a pawn in the FIA's struggle with the European Union over its alleged monopolistic practices, and as a result the rights were sold to an outside agency.

They went to an organization headed by David Richards, a veteran and important part of the international rally scene, and at the time of the rights sale the owner of the factory-sponsored Subaru team. The success of rally telecasts, based on attracting incremental audiences, is something watched closely by manufacturers.

To date, in the U.S. at least, the audience has been marginal, due—to a great extent—to the inability of the broadcasters to explain rallies in terms understood by the average channel surfer.

Ford of Europe's rally involvement can be divided, roughly, into five phases:

- The first can be called pre-Escort, when efforts were more amateur, or sporting, than designed as a marketing exercise.

- The second is the Hayes-Henry Taylor-Stuart Turner era, from 1968 through 1979, which ended when budget considerations caused the company to look to outside teams for assistance.

- The years in the wilderness, from 1980 through 1990, when the commitment to a major league program was lacking. Ironically, only the second world driver's championship ever won in a Ford vehicle (through 2000) came during this period.

- The return to being competitive in 1991, when the Sierra Cosworth was introduced, but an effort that went into decline in 1995.

- The current era, which began with the decision in 1996 to join the World Rally Championship the next year, to allocate sufficient budget, and to have Malcolm Wilson's M-Sport organization run the team. The chances for a championship, for both a Ford driver and for the manufacturer's title, then moved from wishful thinking to a real possibility with the introduction of the Focus in 1999. This happened despite more competition than ever from other manufacturers.

For Hayes and Ford of Europe in the late 1960s, long before television became a consideration, the rally program was part of a three-pronged effort: The Ford-sponsored Cosworth engine in almost everyone's Formula One car, German Ford racing in touring car events on the Continent, and British Ford in international rallying plus racing in its home country.

Ford had done well in rallies during the mid-'60s, but the Cortina sedan, in Lotus-Cortina form with the twin-cam head on its engine, was dated, and was on its way out. It would be succeeded by the Escort, originally a somewhat smaller car, and at the outset equipped with engines producing between 50 and 71 horsepower in civilian dress. The Escort was introduced in time for the 1968 model year, by late winter it was winning British rallies, and made its international debut in the Italian San Remo event in March, finishing third. Roger Clark, Britain's best rally driver of his era, gave the Escort its first European championship event in April when he won The Netherlands' Tulip Rally, and he added Greece's always-difficult Acropolis Rally in June.

Swedes Bengt Soderstrom and Gunnar Palm won the Austrian Alpine event, and Finland's Hannu Mikkola, a legend as a driver, won his home country's Rally of the 1000 Lakes. The company won four of the 14 events and took the manufacturer's championship. It was second to Lancia the next year, with Mikkola winning twice and Gilbert Staepelaere, a good Belgian driver, taking another two and also placing second twice. All of this was done with a version of the Escort called the TC, which indicated it had a 1.6-liter engine complete with twin-cam Lotus head that produced about 150 horsepower.

To shepherd the rally program, and the performance effort in general, Hayes brought in Turner, the talented former competitions manager of the British Motor Corporation who left a failing BMC to join an oil company for two years before coming to Ford in the summer of 1969. Taylor, the previous manager and a successful one, was moved over to run the advanced engine program, as Hayes expanded his motorsports initiative.

Turner had his eye on the real prize for a manufacturer, which was market penetration, and organized his schedule with this in mind. He was also the recipient of a great opportunity in his first full season, which had the 1970 World Cup Rally as a feature event. It would run from London to Mexico to tie in with that year's World Cup soccer championship; it would run from April 19 to May 27, and would cover 16,000 miles and 26 countries, including almost every South American nation. It was one of those events that for some reason have great appeal for Britons. They drive in them, they follow them in the media, and with a win and the right kind of publicity these automotive marathons can be an effective sales tool. With this event sponsored by the *Daily Mirror*, Britain's largest-circulation newspaper, the publicity was guaranteed.

There were 96 starters, 23 finishers. There were seven factory Escorts, equipped with pushrod four-cylinder engines bored out to 1800cc, and they placed 1-3-5-6-8. It couldn't have been better. Mikkola, with (later to be) Ford of Sweden public relations man Palm as his co-driver, were the winners.

Ford had won what was called the first rally World Championship of Makes in 1968, but in 1969 it was obvious other teams were getting stronger. In 1970 the Mexico triumph was to come in handy, because there was little else to celebrate. Porsche dominated the manufacturer's point standings, Renault's Alpines won six events and were second on points, and Ford was fifth, behind Lancia and Saab. Staepelaere finished tied for second in the driver's championship, but that was it.

The next year was worse, with Ford tenth as Alpine dominated once more, and part of the Renault team was Frenchman Jean Todt. He first came into view as a navigator for Ford France in the Monte Carlo Rally of 1969, in a Capri, and later on was the co-driver in successful Renault Alpines, but made his reputation as a manager. When he was with Peugeot in the 1980s his rally team showed other manufacturers new standards of preparation and organization. He did the same for Peugeot in winning four Paris-Dakar marathons, and also supervised its racing team to two world sports-car titles and a 1-2-3 finish at Le Mans in 1993. He moved to Ferrari in 1994, and that organization's success since then has been in no small part due to his abilities. Such is motorsports in Europe, where nameplates may be on the noses of the cars, but the names behind the wheel, or the desk, are often more important.

London-Mexico 1970: Winners Hannu Mikkola (with bottle) and Gunnar Palm on car. Escorts finished 1-3-5-6-8 in this 16,000-mile marathon.—Ford Motor Company

And the names behind the wheels of the Fords in the 1970s were the best. The hard-driving, hard-drinking Mikkola would go on to win the world championship (for Audi, unfortunately), Clark was the best Britain had produced. Then there was Staepelaere, plus Finn Ari Vatanen, a future world champion, Timo (not Tommi, who came later) Makinen, and Bjorn Waldegaard, the Swede who won the first driver's championship in an Escort. The Scandinavians, especially the Finns, have been the stars of rallying. They learned to drive on roads that were mostly unpaved, and also covered with snow for much of the year. So being sideways at speed was nothing special, and to be paid for doing this was even better.

Other countries would produce stars, but the standard was set by the Finns. They drove for all the major teams, and from 1979 through 2000 they won twelve of the 22 championships. In the years before the FIA finally got around to giving rally drivers the same recognition they had been according race drivers since 1950, the Finns were instrumental in helping the makes for which they drove win the manufacturer's title. Considering that this country has roughly 5 million inhabitants, this is all the more remarkable—and add to that two Formula One champions, Keke Rosberg and Mika Hakkinen.

If you want to win, find a Finn. They have won 118 of the 314 rallies counting for the world manufacturer's title through 2000, better than a third.

The "others" come from a variety of European countries, led by Carlos Sainz, the well-born Spaniard who had won 23 championship events—and won the title twice, in 1990 and 1992 (for Toyota), and who became a mainstay of the Ford team. Sainz's wins, counting through the 2000 season, put him even with four-time world title-holder Juha Kankkunen. They are at the top of the list. Markku Alen, who seemingly just missed out on the seasonal championships, won 20 rallies. Didier Auriol, the Frenchman who won 19 events during his career and was the 1994 titleholder, is one ahead of Colin McRae, the Scotsman who is the current leader of the Ford team and was 1995 champion while driving for Subaru. Tommi Makinen, the Finn who won for four straight years (1996–99) while driving for Mitsubishi, is another with 18, as is Hannu Mikkola. They are one ahead of Italy's Massimo (Miki) Biasion, who won the championship in 1988 and 1989.

Roger Clark

Timo Makinen

Ari Vatanen
—Ford Motor Company

Year by year, the international rally scene looked like this:

1971

The U.S. goes off the gold standard, the dollar is devalued by almost eight percent and would float, along with other currencies.... CAT scans are introduced.

———————●———————

Ove Andersson, the Swede who two decades later would be the man in charge of Toyota's international rally program and later on its new Formula One effort, led the French Renault-Alpine team to dominance in what was then called the European Rally Championship for Manufacturers. Andersson won four of the 19 events (only the best six results counted), including Monte Carlo and the Acropolis Rally in Greece. There was a driver's championship of sorts, but not given the distinction of "world." The peculiarities of the point system gave this title to Poland's Sobieslaw Zasada, a BMW driver who participated in a number of second-rank events that counted, for some odd reason. Ford was crippled by a lengthy strike, and did little.

Manufacturer's points: Alpine 36, Saab 18, Porsche 16.5.

1972

Mark Spitz wins seven gold medals at the Munich Olympics.... The Duke of Windsor and J. Edgar Hoover die.... The A300 Airbus, Europe's first wide-body aircraft, makes its debut.

———————●———————

Mikkola was still there in 1972, a year which saw nine events counting for the championship, and which saw only desultory efforts on the part of most manufacturers. Fiat and Lancia, the latter a division of the former, fought it out for the title with Lancia winning, to a great extent because the team competed in more events. The logic of having two branches of the same family competing for a single prize escaped most of the onlookers. Ford did not run a full schedule, but managed to salvage some promotional advantage when Mikkola and Palm won the East African Safari and Clark took the RAC Rally. The Mikkola-Palm triumph was the first for a European team in Kenya.

Manufacturer's points: Lancia 97, Fiat 55, Porsche 53, Ford 48.

1973

*The oil embargo results in mile-long lines at American gas stations. ...
The Supreme Court decides that restrictions on abortions in the first tri-
mester are unconstitutional—Roe v. Wade.*

———•———

Finally realizing it would help spectators and attract sponsors, the FIA called it
a world championship, but only for manufacturers, not for drivers. Alpine dominated, winning seven of the 13 events, including 1-2-3-5-6 in the Monte Carlo Rally.
Ford finished a bad third, but Timo Makinen won the Finnish Rally of the 1000 Lakes
and Ford, led again by Makinen and co-driver Henry Liddon, finished 1-2-3 in the
season-ending RAC Rally. Alpine's small factory, located on the French coast in
Dieppe, had 65 mechanics in the competition department, which also handled some
single-seater cars. The rear-engined rally cars had only 170–175 horsepower, but
their weight was down to 1500 pounds, unheard of for a normal road-going passenger vehicle.

Manufacturer's points: Alpine 160, Fiat 89, Ford 76.

1974

*The LSI chip reduces the cost of pocket calculators from $400 to where
they are given away as premiums. ... The Heimlich maneuver is invented. ...
Portugal's dictatorship is overthrown.*

———•———

The energy crisis of late 1973 caused some rallies to be canceled for the 1974
season, as organizers felt it would not be politically correct, and so only eight were
left on the schedule. Lancia dominated with the new Stratos, finishing well ahead of
Fiat and Ford, and the amount of money and manpower needed went up once more:
Fiat's effort was run by a 48-man crew, plus seven drivers, seven co-drivers. Approximately 100 rally and practice cars were built before and during the season, and there
were dozens of service vehicles. Makinen and Liddon were about the only bright
spots for Ford, repeating in Finland and in the RAC rally. The year 1974 also marked
the debut of a Toyota factory team in Europe, part and parcel of the Japanese
effort—successful, as it turned out—to penetrate the market. Nissan, Mitsubishi
and Subaru would not be far behind.

Manufacturer's points: Lancia 94, Fiat 69, Ford 54, Toyota 32.

1975

Jack Nicklaus wins the Masters golf tournament for the fifth time....
The Lebanese civil war begins in April.... The Helsinki Accords, new
human-rights standards, are endorsed by 35 nations.

———◆———

The Lancia-Fiat competition came to an end after the 1975 season, one that saw the Stratos dominate whenever it stayed in one piece. Smaller fields (only 96 entries for the Monte Carlo Rally) were the order of the year, thanks to the fallout from the energy crisis. Lancia won four of the ten events, and Fiat bowed out after a corporate decision to stop the internecine warfare. It had reached the ridiculous: the cars for both teams were being prepared and maintained in the same department.

Staepelaere did well in Belgian rallies and Clark did the same in Britain, but they were not to be found among the major winners. The Stratos, in rally form, had approximately 270 horsepower and weighed less than 2000 pounds.

Manufacturer's points: Lancia 96, Fiat 61, Alpine 60, Opel 56, Peugeot 40, Ford 35.

1976

College dropouts Steve Jobs and Steven Wozniak introduce their
first Apple computer.... Sylvester Stallone writes and stars in "Rocky."
... Dorothy Hamill wins the Olympic figure skating championship.

———◆———

The Stratos did it for the third straight year, and did it for four reasons. The first was the car, which was designed and built strictly for this type of event. The second was the drivers, led by Sandro Munari and Bjorn Waldegaard, the third was the massive organization behind the drivers, and the fourth was the fact that Lancia took part in nine of the ten events that counted—more than any other team.

The Escort, equipped with a 2-liter Cosworth BDA engine, was now up to 240 horsepower and weighed about 2160 pounds, as Ford mounted its first full-scale effort in several years, and had reliability problems through much of the season. It finally paid off in the season-ending RAC Rally, as Clark and Waldegaard—the latter having just moved over from Lancia—had a 1-3 finish. By that time, however, the championship was already long decided.

Manufacturer's points: Lancia 112, Opel 57, Ford 47.

1977

*Gordie Howe scores the 1000th goal of a 30-year hockey career....
The Pompidou Center opens in Paris.... "Star Wars" wins seven Academy
Awards.*

———•———

Ford was finally competitive again, finishing a close second to the Fiats modified by Italian tuner Abarth in the chase for the manufacturer's trophy, thanks to a 1-3-4-5 performance in the season-ending RAC Rally. Fiat had the title clinched by that time, but the RAC was good for sales promotion in the home market. The RS1800 was aging (the platform was many years old, the 16-valve engine eight years) but a better powerplant brought output up to 260 hp and a new suspension helped as well, at least on unpaved roads.

Had the suspension done as well on pavement, the result might have been different. Also helping was the fact that Lancia entered only five of the eleven championship rallies. Waldegaard won the Safari, the Acropolis and the RAC, Finland's Kyosti Hamalainen, in a partially Ford-supported car, won the 1000 Lakes. Clark, Vatanen and Russell Brookes were also on the team. The first FIA driver's cup—not a championship, according to that organization—went to Sandro Munari of Fiat.

Manufacturer's points: Fiat 136, Ford 132, Toyota 70, Opel 65.

1978

*It is the Ford Motor Company's 75th anniversary and Lee Iacocca is
fired in June.... Five-time Italian Prime Minister Aldo Moro is kidnapped
by terrorists and later murdered.*

———•———

Ford decided to emphasize British rally participation in 1978, the point system for the driver's championship became overly complicated, and the company was hit by a strike in the latter part of the year. The strike forced car preparation out of the team's Boreham headquarters and into the shops of several dealers who were also active in the sport. In the end, however, the result was the same: Fiat won again, and Ford finished second after a season-long battle with Opel for the runner-up spot.

The British rally championship was won easily, and Mikkola took four of the seven events counting for this, including the RAC Rally, which counted for both British and World—but by the time it was held, Fiat had its manufacturer's crown wrapped up. The driver's title went to Finland's Markku Alen, one of the leaders of the Fiat-Abarth team, in a season that was confused due to many rules changes (four-valve heads were banned as options, for example, but OK as standard equipment).

Manufacturer's points: Fiat 134, Ford 100, Opel 100.

1979

The nuclear power station at Three-Mile Island, Pennsylvania, brings the region to the brink of catastrophe when partial meltdown occurs. ... The U.S. and China resume formal diplomatic relations.

———•———

The FIA finally got around to calling the driver's championship just that, and this time it was Waldegaard who won, a point ahead of Mikkola as Ford's major effort got the company back on top in the competition for the manufacturer's championship. Boreham's Escorts finished well ahead of Nissan, which was mounting a massive campaign. Waldegaard won the Acropolis Rally, was second in Monte Carlo and Sweden, Mikkola won in Portugal, New Zealand and the RAC Rally, but his other finishes weren't good enough to get him past Waldegaard. Ford's team entered eight of the twelve events counting for the title, won five and placed second in the other three.

The RS1800 was now producing about 260 horsepower. The car in that form was, however, somewhat long in the tooth, it was called outmoded for competition purposes by many, and at the same time Ford was immersed in the corporate financial crisis that brought with it a reduction in European motorsports budgets. The effort would be given to independent David Sutton's team for the 1980 and 1981 seasons, with much support from cigarette manufacturer Rothmans.

Manufacturer's points: Ford 122, Nissan 102, Fiat 92, Lancia 68.

Driver's points: Waldegaard (Ford) 112, Mikkola (Ford) 111, Alen (Lancia) 68.

1980

The Cable News Network is inaugurated. ... The Chrysler Loan Guarantee bill is passed by Congress. ... John Lennon is murdered in New York.

———•———

Walter Roehrl, the lean and lanky German, led the Fiat-Abarth team to the 1980 championship and took the individual title for himself. This was the second year of the drivers being accorded the same recognition as the manufacturers. Fiats won four of the ten events counting and wound up with 120 points to 93 for Datsun and 90 for Ford, with a very expensive Mercedes-Benz effort finishing fourth with 79.

Roehrl collected 118 points, almost double the number amassed by Hannu Mikkola, who had 63 while splitting his time between Ford and Mercedes. The latter, running heavyweight 450SLC's in selected rallies, found the horsepower was fine but the weight was a decided disadvantage. Finland's Ari Vatanen won both the Acropolis Rally and the 1000 Lakes event for Ford, with the latter, for some reason, not counting for the manufacturer's title.

Ford's general over-all business situation—the corporation was losing money and cutting back wherever possible—led to the arrangement with Sutton. For 1980 Ford paid for Vatanen and Mikkola, but they drove for Sutton's Rothmans-sponsored team. The Ford team cars, vans, and other equipment were sold to Sutton at what were termed "favorable" prices. Toward the end of the year Kranefuss was transferred to Dearborn to rebuild the American effort, which had lain dormant, for the most part, since the fall of 1970.

Manufacturer's points: Fiat 120, Datsun 93, Ford 90, Mercedes-Benz 79.

Driver's points: Roehrl (Fiat) 118, Mikkola (Ford-Mercedes) 63, Waldegaard (Mercedes) 63.

1981

The TGV train, running from Paris to Lyon, is inaugurated.... Anwar Sadat is assassinated by Muslim fundamentalists.... A coup d'etat fails in Spain.... MTV makes its debut.

Ford was still losing money and the company was again represented by Sutton, with Rothmans tobacco empire once more providing the sponsorship. Even though the RS1800 was practically obsolete, this Escort wound up as the car that helped win the driver's championship, which went to Ari Vatanen. He took three of the twelve events (Acropolis, Finland and Brazil)—only 10 counted for the manufacturer's championship—and finished second in Sweden and in the season-ending RAC Rally. It was Ford's second driver's title in three years and would be the last through the year 2000.

The year marked the debut of the four-wheel drive Audi Quattro, clearly the fastest car, but dogged by mechanical problems throughout the season. The manufacturer's title went to Talbot, a division of Peugeot and a brand that has since disappeared, but was making one of its last sales-promotion attempts during 1981.

Manufacturer's points: Talbot 117, Datsun 106, Ford 90, Opel 69.

Driver's points: Vatanen (Ford) 96, Guy Frequelin (Talbot) 89, Mikkola (Audi) 62.

1982

AT&T agrees to divest itself of its 22 regional telephone companies, better known as the "Baby Bells"…. The Getty Trust turns the private art collection of late oilman J. Paul Getty into the world's richest museum, complete with $1.2 billion endowment.

Group B began this year, but no team had a real Group B car ready for the season, because Group B was a synonym for anything goes, and it would take a year before the rally equivalents of hot rods were ready. Group B meant a total of 200 cars had to be produced within a twelve-month period, and this opened the homologation process to all sorts of abuses. Group B, before the FIA belatedly stopped it after the 1986 season, would lead to 500-horsepower race cars thinly disguised as rally vehicles—cars that had little in common with what was sold to the public. Ford, not having a suitable four-wheel drive vehicle, was out of the picture, and would remain so as long as Group B was in effect. That was part of it.

Ford's new rear-wheel drive Escort RS1700T might have been a contender, but it wasn't ready in time, and that was one of the reasons Rothmans switched. The fact that Audi had four-wheel drive and was ready to compete was the other. The RS1700T would be canceled by Turner when he took over in 1983. Roehrl won his second championship, this time for Opel.

Rothmans' bet paid off, with the Audis edging the Opels for the manufacturer's title. But Roehrl managed to finish ahead of Audi's Michele Mouton, the Frenchwoman who was unquestionably the finest female rally driver ever. Roehrl did it on reliability, because there was no question the Audis were faster.

Manufacturer's points: Audi 116, Opel 104, Nissan 57, Ford 55.

Driver's points: Roehrl (Opel) 109, Mouton (Audi) 97, Hannu Mikkola (Audi) 70.

1983

Sally Ride becomes the first American woman in space. .... South Africa adopts a new constitution that grants limited representation to "Coloreds" and Indians, but not to blacks.

———————————•———————————

Ford would be absent until 1986, but Lancia came back, this time with the 037, the company's first Group B car—mid-engined, rear-wheel driven and supercharged.

Audi also had a hot car and the championship came down to a battle between the two, with Mikkola being Audi's number one driver and the leader of the team that took the manufacturer's crown in a twelve-event season. Roehrl, always looking for the best car, drove a Lancia.

Manufacturer's points: Lancia 118, Audi 116, Opel 87, Nissan 52.

Driver's points: Mikkola (Audi) 125, Roehrl (Lancia) 102, Markku Alen (Lancia) 100.

1984

*The worst industrial accident in history takes place at the Union Car-
bide plant in Bhopal, India, when more than 4000 persons die as the result
of a toxic gas leak.... The Los Angeles Raiders defeat the Washington
Redskins in the Super Bowl, 38-9.*

———•———

Audi got some revenge for the previous year, edging Lancia for the manufacturer's
title. Stig Blomqvist, thanks to some stage managing on the part of Audi, won the
driver's title with previous year's winner Mikkola—also a member of the team—
second.

Manufacturer's points: Audi 120, Lancia 108, 74, Toyota 62.

Driver's points: Blomqvist (Audi) 125, Mikkola (Audi) 104, Alen (Lancia) 90.

1985

*The wreck of the "Titanic" is discovered, some 13,000 feet down.... An
extra second is added to the calendar year.... The "new" Coca-Cola is
introduced and flops, prompting a quick return to "classic" Coke.*

———•———

Jean Todt, who made his debut as the Peugeot rally team manager in 1984,
brought his organization into the championship this year with a 205T16, a trans-
verse, mid-engined, four-wheel drive special that dominated the rally scene and
was a factor in causing Audi to find other motorsports opportunities. To offset
the Peugeot offensive Lancia came up with a Delta S4 model that had both supercharger *and* turbocharger, the former for low-end torque and the latter for high-
rev horsepower. It wasn't enough, but it was indicative of the lengths to which
an automaker would go.

Manufacturer's points: Peugeot 142, Audi 126, Lancia 70, Nissan 56.

Driver's points: Timo Salonen (Peugeot) 127, Stig Blomqvist (Audi) 75, Walter
Roehrl (Audi) 59.

1986

*The Statue of Liberty celebrates its 100th anniversary.... The U.S.
bombs Libya.... Former UN Secretary General Kurt Waldheim's Nazi past
is revealed.... The Mets beat the Red Sox in the World Series.*

———•———

This was the last year of Group B, FIA-speak for road-going race cars, and the
end came in the late spring of the year, when Lancia driver Henri Toivonen and his
navigator were burned to death in a flaming crash at the Corsican rally. This was the

second "incident" of the season, with three spectators killed in the Portugese rally earlier in the year, with a Ford of Portugal-entered RS200 (newly and finally homologated) being involved. Crowd control at the event was sorely lacking, and after the accident, which happened early in the rally—30 persons were injured, in addition to the fatalities—many of the leading drivers refused to continue.

The RS200, born a few years too late and now under a cloud, led the Acropolis Rally later in the season, but the demise of Group B spelled the same for the car. It remains a footnote, and not a happy one.

Group A, which required a minimum of 5000 identical cars to be built in a twelve-month period, was a quantum leap closer to standard production cars than was Group B, which only required 200, and that was a rule that was honored more in the breach.

The Todt-led Peugeot team once again outlasted Lancia, while Juha Kankkunen, his number one pilot, won the driver's title in a 13-event season. It was also the first year of the Olympus Rally, held in Washington State, and counting for the world title.

Manufacturer's points: Peugeot 137, Lancia 122, Volkswagen 65, Audi 29.

Driver's points: Kankkunen (Peugeot) 118, Markku Alen (Lancia) 104, Timo Salonen (Peugeot) 63.

1987

Henry Ford II dies at 70. ... The restoration of the Sistine Chapel of the Vatican is completed, to almost universal approval from art historians. ... Televangelist Jim Bakker resigns from his post as head of the $100 million Praise the Lord ministry after an affair with his secretary becomes public.

———•———

Ford, which had returned to rallying the year before for a brief (and unhappy) period, had to make its 1987 model decision between the Sierra RS Cosworth, with rear-wheel drive only (about 300 hp) and the Sierra XR4x4, which had four-wheel drive but was underpowered (about 220 hp). In the end the two-wheel drive car was the choice.

Peugeot was in litigation with the FIA, claiming an arbitrary decision to abandon Group B cost the company large development sums, and was therefore not about to enter any more rallies. Instead, the French devoted their attention to the Paris-Dakar marathon, and with Vatanen as the driver won in a first attempt. As a result Lancia had what was more or less a clear field, and won the manufacturer's title comfortably. Kankkunen, again with Lancia, edged Miki Biasion, his Italian teammate, for the driver's championship. Lancia, with the four-wheel drive Delta, won eight of the 13 events. The Olympus Rally was run as a championship event for the second and last time.

Manufacturer's points: Lancia 140, Audi 82, Renault 71, Volkswagen 64, Ford 62.

Driver's points: Kankkunen, (Lancia) 100, Biasion (Lancia) 94, Alen (Lancia) 88.

1988

The Iran-Iraq war ends after eight years and an estimated million deaths.... Chicago's Wrigley Field, the last major-league park without them, finally gets lights for night baseball.... The Human Genome Project, an effort to decode and map DNA, is begun.

Ford, handicapped by virtue of having only a two-wheel drive car (the Sierra RS Cosworth) while Lancia and the others had all four-wheel drive, finished second to Lancia for the manufacturer's title—but it was a distant second. Lancia won ten of the eleven events and finished second to Ford's Didier Auriol in the other event, Auriol giving the Sierra its only world championship win when he took the Tour de Corse.

Biasion won the driver's title, with teammates Alen and Alex Fiorio, the son of Lancia team manager Cesare Fiorio, third.

Manufacturer's points: Lancia 140, Ford 79, Audi 71.

Driver's points: Biasion (Lancia) 115, Alen (Lancia) 86, Fiorio (Lancia) 76.

1989

The U.S. topples Panamanian dictator Manuel Noriega.... Four years later he would be tried in Miami and sentenced to 40 years for drug smuggling ... but shipments from and through Panama continue unabated.

Lancia won the manufacturer's title again, thanks to the Delta Integrale, the same model that won the year before, and Lancia driver Biasion was again the world champion, finishing well ahead of Fiorio, his teammate.

Toyota, making a determined effort to gain market share in Europe as well as in the rest of the world, was second in the manufacturer's chase. But Lancia won the first six events of the year and seven out of the nine in which the company entered. Lancia didn't bother to go to the season-ending RAC Rally. Ford was conspicuous only by its absence.

Manufacturer's points: Lancia 140, Toyota 101, Mazda 67, Mitsubishi 58.

Driver's points: Biasion (Lancia) 106, Fiorio (Lancia) 65, Kankkunen (Toyota) 60.

1990

The Cold War ends.... John Major succeeds Margaret Thatcher as prime minister of Britain.... San Francisco defeats Denver in the Super Bowl, 55-10.

Carlos Sainz, the aristocratic Spaniard who was a newcomer to the international rally scene wound up as world champion, driving for Toyota. Sainz, who together with co-driver Luis Moya would become a valuable addition to the Ford team in future years, won four of the season's twelve events and placed second in three others in his much-modified Celica.

The manufacturer's championship, however, went to Lancia again, this time by the narrowest of margins over Toyota. The Japanese segment of the auto industry, by this time, was making an all-out effort: Toyota, Mitsubishi, Subaru and Mazda had teams in the series. The four-wheel drive Sierra was finally ready, but not until August, and the blue oval was absent for most of the year. Turner retired at the end of the year, a season in which the Escort RS Cosworth made its debut in a minor Spanish event, running as a prototype. It would not be homologated until the 1993 season.

Penti Airikkala and Malcolm Wilson, who would be heard from later, were signed for a Ford team that did little, entering only three events late in the season, and Alex Fiorio also drove for Ford in the last event. Turner's retirement gave the motorsports responsibility to Peter Ashcroft, a longtime and valued member of the Boreham team.

Manufacturer's points: Lancia 137, Toyota 131, Mitsubishi 56, Subaru 43.

Driver's points: Sainz (Toyota) 140, Didier Auriol (Lancia) 95, Kankkunen (Lancia) 85.

1991

The six Balkan republics that were combined to form Yugoslavia after World War I fall apart, and a bloodbath starts that would last for at least a decade.... In the Baltic region, Latvia, Estonia and Lithuania declare their independence from the Soviet Union.

It was Lancia again, this time winning six of the ten rallies on the schedule and placing second in the other four and finishing just ahead of Toyota in what was essentially a two-make battle. Kankkunen, with the Lancia Delta Integrale, won the title again, just ahead of Toyota's Sainz. The rest of the manufacturers, including Ford, were hardly visible.

Ashcroft, who had been competitions manager for almost 20 years, moved up to Turner's job for 1991, then retired at the end of the year. Colin Dobinson would run the program in 1992–93, and be succeeded by Australian Peter Gillitzer, who took over in 1994 and lasted until midway through 1996. The cost of competition was rising: Nissan was reported to have an $8 million budget for the Safari Rally alone, and Lancia had 14 service vans and 100 people on the ground for the 1200-mile Acropolis Rally.

Manufacturer's points: Lancia 137, Toyota 128, Mitsubishi 62, Ford 54.

Driver's points: Kankkunen (Lancia) 150, Sainz (Toyota) 143, Didier Auriol (Lancia) 101.

1992

New York Mafia boss John Gotti is sentenced to life in prison without parole.... Johnny Carson retires from "The Tonight Show" after 30 years.... Hurricane Andrew kills 14 persons in Florida and leaves 250,000 homeless in Florida and Lousiana.... Damages in South Florida run to more than $20 billion.

———•———

It was Lancia again, for the tenth time, and again ahead of Toyota, but Sainz took the individual title with Toyota's new Celica Turbo complete with four-wheel drive—the latter standard on any car hoping to be taken seriously.

Ford finally made it back to some sort of respectability with the Sierra Cosworth 4x4, in that model's last year. Former world champion Miki Biasion of Italy was number one driver, backed up by Frenchman Francois Delecour.

Manufacturer's points: Lancia 140, Toyota 116, Ford 94.

Driver's points: Sainz (Toyota) 144, Kankkunen (Lancia) 134, Didier Auriol (Lancia) 121, Biasion (Ford) 60.

1993

Israel and the Palestine Liberation Organization sign a peace accord, one that would be interrupted by armed strife many times in the future.... Janet Reno becomes the first woman named U.S. attorney general.... The World Trade Center explosion in New York kills five, injures many, traps thousands, but the buildings stand.... The attack is the work of Muslim fundamentalists.

———•———

Juha Kankkunen, with Nicky Grist as his co-driver, won the championship for the fourth time. Toyota, led by Kankkunen, displaced Lancia as the manufacturer's title-holder. Lancia, withdrawing from rallying thanks to a decision by parent company Fiat, turned its team over to the Jolly Club, an Italian organization, and they wound up fourth in the standings, although counting as a manufacturer. The Escort RS Cosworth, weighing the FIA minimum of 2700 pounds and producing 300 horsepower, was finally ready for competition, and made life on the rally circuit once again interesting for Ford fans, winning five events and placing second in three. This model was also, in series production form, probably the first standard passenger sedan designed to produce downforce that could be appreciated by "civilian" drivers.

Ford, making a strong effort once more, was second in the chase for the manufacturer's crown and Francois Delecour, Ford's lead driver this season, was runner-up to Kankkunen in the individual competition, winning rallies in Portugal, Corsica and Spain. Newcomers to the scene included Scotsman Colin McRae, driving for Subaru and winning the New Zealand Rally. McRae's father, Jimmy, was a five-time British rally champion, so it was obvious his son had been brought up with a rally career in mind. Toyotas won seven of the season's 13 events.

Manufacturer's points: Toyota 157, Ford 145, Subaru 110.

Driver's points: Kankkunen (Toyota) 135, Delecour (Ford) 112, Didier Auriol (Toyota) 92.

Miki Biasion and his Escort RS Cosworth winning
the 1993 Acropolis Rally.—Ford Motor Company

1994

The Whitewater investigation, which would eventually lead to the impeachment of President Clinton, gets under way.... O.J. Simpson's wife is murdered: He is accused, eventually found not guilty in a criminal proceeding, but found liable for damages in a civil trial.

———————●———————

Didier Auriol, for several years among the better drivers, finally ascended to the championship and led Toyota to the team title as well, at the wheel of a turbocharged Celica complete, as usual, with four-wheel drive. Carlos Sainz, now with Subaru, was second and Ford, despite a season-opening victory in Monte Carlo, finished a poor third to the two Japanese makes. By the end of the year Gillitzer announced he would be closing Boreham, where Ford's rally program had been located for more than three decades. Boreham remained, and is still in use as a Ford development facility, but this announcement brought morale at the old airfield to a new low.

This was the first year of the FIA-imposed "rotation" system, whereby only a certain number of the major rallies would count for the two world championships. The idea was to encourage a new "second-tier" championship for front-wheel drive cars, and make them the headliners in the rallies that were left out of the ones counting for the world titles. It didn't work, but it lasted three years.

Manufacturer's points: Toyota 151, Subaru 123, Ford 116.

Driver's points: Auriol (Toyota) 116, Sainz (Subaru) 99, Kankkunen (Toyota) 93.

1995

More than 100 die as a terrorist car bomb destroys the Oklahoma City Federal Building.... Army veteran Timothy McVeigh is arrested in a matter of hours and eventually convicted.... Republicans take control of Congress.

———————●———————

Colin McRae, in his third year of major-league rallying, wound up as the title-holder, again driving for Subaru in what was an eight-rally season. Actually it was a 14-rally season, but the FIA's new rotation system only counted eight of them, and this ridiculous arrangement had one more year to go.

Carlos Sainz, who would be McRae's teammate again with Ford in a few years, was his Subaru compatriot this time and finished second. The biggest news of the season, however, came in the fall, when a disgruntled former employee of the Toyota team told the FIA just how Toyota had been cheating—through an ingenious method of bypassing the 34-millimeter restrictor in the turbocharger.

The net result was that Toyota's points for 1995 were wiped off the books and the manufacturer was suspended for the 1996 season.

Because of this Juha Kankkunen's bid for a fifth world championship went down the tubes—or through the turbo, in this case—and Subaru, with the operation being run by Prodrive of Britain, walked away with the team championship. Gillitzer had been persuaded to make a deal with RAS Sport, a major Belgian rally team led by Bruno Thiry, so the Fords—still the Escort RS Cosworth—ran under different colors. In the end Ford was a poor third behind Mitsubishi, with the Escort showing its age.

Manufacturer's points: Subaru 350, Mitsubishi 307, Ford 223.

Driver's points: McRae (Subaru) 90, Sainz (Subaru) 85, Kenneth Eriksson (Mitsubishi) 48.

Chapter 6

---●---

DARK DAYS

Ford was out of stock-car racing in 1971, Chrysler was gone as well, and NASCAR was reminded that the manufacturers, from the standpoint of a sanctioning body, were unreliable. Daytona did not control the Detroit part of the equation, and as a consequence there came the realization that promotional efforts would have to be focused on the drivers rather than the cars.

And while the Frances were absorbing this change of status and continuing the struggle to build stock-car racing as a major sport, they became partners in the most successful ongoing promotion ever conceived by any manufacturer of non-automotive-related consumer goods. It was a piece of good fortune comparable only to being present during the television era, and being there when TV networks and cable operators were looking for new programming. And the reason for this good fortune was the report that cigarettes could cause cancer. As a consequence, among other restrictions, cigarette advertising would disappear from television screens, leaving tobacco companies searching for new ways to spend their promotional funds.

At the same time Junior Johnson was looking for a new sponsor, so he visited R.J. Reynolds headquarters in Winston-Salem, not far from his home in Wilkes County.

Johnson: "I went to Reynolds to try to secure a sponsorship because I knew they'd come off of TV, the government had banned them … but I'd been to Reynolds prior to that, talking to them, and then it happened.… I was sure I could talk them into sponsoring a race car.… I went with a guy who'd been with Hanes, who'd been involved with Hanes, and he knew the people at Reynolds, so he said he'd go with me and introduce me.… We got in a conversation about racing and sponsorship and so forth and one of the guys who was in the PR department or marketing department, or whatever, spoke up and said, 'We're looking for something a lot bigger than what you got,' and he had some kind of unbelievable number that they'd spent with TV, something like $500 or $600 million. So I said, 'Well, if you're looking for anything bigger than sponsoring a car you need to talk to Bill France and sponsor the whole thing, the circuit,' and they said, 'Well, how do we go about doing that?'

"They asked me to contact Bill France and I did, and told him what had happened… I had just met with Reynolds Tobacco Company about sponsoring my race car, and they said they were interested in doing a lot more than what I was planning on, and they were interested in sponsoring the whole thing.... Told him who to contact at Reynolds, and I called them back and told them he was going to call them and then I fell out of the picture, other than being good friends with both sides."

It turned out to be a marriage made in heaven. Superlatives are dangerous, but it is safe to say that few marketing and promotional agreements have been as valuable to both sides as the Reynolds-NASCAR partnership.

At first the arrangement was a simple one: Winston would sponsor a 500-miler at Talladega and would also come up with a $100,000 point fund, plus—and this would prove to be the most important part—provide promotional support for NASCAR. Newspaper ads, billboards and in-store displays gave the organization, reeling from Ford and Chrysler's withdrawal, a needed boost. There were still 48 races on the schedule, but this would be the last year for that many. Beginning in 1972 the Winston Cup calendar would include only 30 events, all 250 miles or more.

The shorter events at smaller tracks would be renamed Grand National East, which was comparable to what then was called Grand National West. Eventually (in 1982) Anheuser-Busch would take over the sponsorship of Grand National East and the name would change to Busch Grand National, with this series functioning as a sort of AAA minor league for Winston Cup, and as a provider of a second race series for track owners. The western segment was renamed Winston West when Reynolds assumed title sponsorship.

The Reynolds-NASCAR agreement was in certain respects like dropping a pebble in a pond: The waves emanating from the initial impact touched major package goods companies, and since Reynolds was acquainted with them their executives began attending races, and soon they were sponsors.

Howard A. (Humpy) Wheeler, Jr., the president of the Charlotte Motor Speedway (as well as of Speedway Motorsports, the publicly traded company that operates five other tracks as well), remembers how Reynolds became a role model for the others:

"They were the first non-automotive consumer company to come in, and RJR's tentacles among the consumer companies are huge, because they bump into the same people at the grocery chains and drug chains and so on, so what happened is RJR started inviting the big-chain brass, whether grocery store or drug chain [to the races].... These people are like modern-day feudal barons because they buy so much, and so other consumer companies decided, 'Hey, we can get next to these guys in a social setting—it's pretty tough to do that'.... It's just like Indianapolis was the gathering spot for Midwest industrialists.... The social scene that RJR brought in by the mid-'70s was introducing us to a lot of people...."

The second non-automotive-related company to get NASCAR religion was one with a low profile on the national scene, and also located in Winston-Salem—Goody's Headache Powders. Wheeler: "The company that really lit the fuse on this thing

*H.A. (Humpy) Wheeler: He helped
it grow.—Don Hunter*

was Goody's, and Goody's was sort of legendary among consumer companies because it's something that shouldn't work.... It's a headache powder, it's consumer unfriendly, and they never advertised, and they had no distributors. You bought it— if you were a store up in Dinwiddie, Virginia, you bought directly from Winston-Salem, or if you were K-Mart you bought directly from Winston-Salem. And they didn't have a hard growth pattern either. So they got in, and it was kind of like when Hershey's got in and M&M started advertising.... People started looking up and saying 'wow' ... And Goody's began to grow significantly as a company.... Whether it was racing that did it, it was at least part of it, and those were the two things that really started an inflow of other folks...."

(Reynolds' involvement in stock-car racing was followed by Phillip Morris, with its Marlboro brand, getting into American single-seater racing and eventually into Formula One—where it is now the biggest sponsor—world championship motorcycle racing, and even international rallying. Reynolds followed its stock-car involvement with sponsorship of the National Hot Rod Association in 1976, but government regulation was taking its toll: The agreement that restricted tobacco companies to sponsoring only one version of the sport caused Reynolds to announce its withdrawal from NHRA effective at the end of 2001. On a worldwide basis, cigarette advertising was expected to disappear from racing cars in 2006.)

Government regulation and the Reynolds marketing department were the architects of the Winston involvement in NASCAR, but the original workman on the scene, the missionary who made Winston "real" to the stock-car community, was

Ralph Seagraves. For a while in the 1960s he was Reynolds' man in Washington, and had even worked his way into the White House, where among other things he made sure that all the cigarette boxes were filled with their products. He was in the Oval Office on the November day in 1963 when John F. Kennedy was assassinated in Dallas, and was held in the White House for eight hours along with numerous others, since no one knew, at first, if Kennedy's murder was part of an organized attack. This dictated sealing the building.

Wheeler: "He was a wonderful character.... He never met a stranger, and you could have landed him in the middle of Moscow in the coldest time of the cold war and within days he'd have been in Khruschev's office having a drink.... He was from Wilkes County and was one of those guys who brought himself up by his own bootstraps, and when RJR decided to get into racing he was the perfect man for the job."

1971

> *Intel develops the microprocessor to where it is commercially viable and changes computing forever.... Hardly anyone knows what a microprocessor is.... East Pakistan becomes the sovereign nation of Bangladesh after a war in which approximately 1 million Bengalis are killed.... Lt. William Calley is court-martialed for his part in 1968 My Lai massacre....*

———•———

Holman-Moody, which had Ford's leftover parts inventory, went looking for sponsors and for appearance money, either for the entire season or for specific races. David Pearson opened the season as the H-M driver but quit in May and Bobby Allison took over for the longer races and drove a Dodge, of which he was the nominal owner, in the shorter events. Junior Johnson sold his Ford equipment and starting preparing a Chevrolet with backdoor help from GM. The Wood Brothers soldiered on, using A.J. Foyt for the big races at the start of the season—Foyt even won the 500-milers at Ontario and Atlanta—and Donnie Allison later.

The path the season would take was seemingly clear after the Daytona 500 in February: Petty and Baker ran 1-2, Foyt and Pearson were 3-4, and only Foyt managed to be on the same lap as the two Chrysler cars. Fred Lorenzen, still involved in his comeback, was fifth in a Plymouth. But something happened on the way to the winner's circle: Bobby Allison, in the H-M Ford, wound up the year as the king of the high-speed tracks. He won twice at Charlotte and Michigan, once at Talladega (and finished second behind brother Donnie in the other Alabama race), won the Southern 500 at Darlington and lost the other Darlington event when his engine let go shortly before the finish.

Bobby added the 400-miler at Riverside in his own Dodge. This was the year Riverside saw the upset victory of Ray Elder, a 28-year-old San Joaquin Valley farmer and Dodge pilot, in the season-opening 500-miler. Elder, who was one of the mainstays of West Coast NASCAR activity, was also the runner-up to Allison in the

Aerodynamics, '70s style: Donnie Allison with the Ford Torino
at Charlotte Motor Speedway.—Don Hunter

second Riverside event of 1971. The next year he was fourth in the 500 and won the 400, before disappearing into the record books.

Despite all the Allison heroics Petty was a runaway winner of the first Winston Cup, winning 21 of his 46 starts and finishing almost 400 points ahead of the steady James Hylton in his year-old Ford. Combined with his 27 wins in 1967, this meant Petty collected a quarter of his 200 victories in just two years. Bobby Allison also won at Bowman-Gray Stadium in Winston-Salem, driving a Mustang on the quarter-mile oval as NASCAR allowed cars from its Grand American series to fill out a depleted field. Petty may have won the championship, but there was little question who was fastest. The leader of what would turn out to be a star-crossed family was about all Ford had going for it. Bobby was fourth in the point standings, finishing behind third-place Cecil Gordon. The latter was in the top five only six times, but drove in 46 races—always a plus in NASCAR's point systems.

With the various Ford teams left to their own devices, they used Mercury Montego sheet metal for the super speedways since these were more aerodynamic than the Ford Torino. The upshot was that all the high-speed events the company won went to the credit of Mercury.

The final point standings: Richard Petty (Plymouth) 4435, James Hylton (Ford) 4071, Cecil Gordon (Mercury) 3677, Bobby Allison (Ford, Mercury, Dodge) 3636.

Wins: Plymouth 22, Mercury 11, Dodge 8, Ford 4, Chevrolet 3.

Manufacturer's Trophy: Plymouth 271, Dodge 187.

1972

In June a security guard at a Washington hotel and office complex discovers a burglary, and the Watergate scandal is under way, an event that shakes the nation to its roots and results in President Nixon's resigning the following year.... The Munich Olympics are the site of the Black September invasion of the Israeli team's dormitory, an attack which ends with the deaths of eleven team members, five terrorists and one German policeman.... The Olympics continue, to the dismay of many.

The biggest news came soon after New Year and before the 500-miler at Riverside. Bill France was stepping down as president of NASCAR and son Bill, still called Billy by many but not for long, would take over. His father was only 62 and in good health, but his interest now lay in assembling a group of tracks for the family-controlled International Speedway Corporation rather than the running of NASCAR. Whereas the father was outgoing, physically imposing, charismatic and with a great smile, the 37-year-old offspring was of average height, had little to say in public and most observers felt he existed only in the shadow of his father.

There was concern in some quarters as to whether he was up to the job. And it was his, without a doubt. Jim Foster, then executive assistant to France the Elder, said it best when he described the new father-son relationship as "a one-way door." The father was available for advice, but the son had to ask for it.

Years later John Cooper, a veteran member of the racing community and a former president of Ontario, Indianapolis and Daytona Speedways, would put it best: "Bill was a man for his time, and Bill Junior was a man for his time." He was faced with a practical void insofar as factory-supported teams were concerned and with small fields, but he had Reynolds, and he was used to hard times. He would turn them into good times before too many years passed.

Also faced with hard times were the teams affiliated with Ford. Their equipment was wearing out, and there were no replacement parts in sight. Holman-Moody, Ford's number one team and the dispenser of parts to all the others, passed into history over the winter of 1971–72. Holman and Moody were never personally close but formed a good team: John Holman was the promoter and deal maker, Ralph Moody took care of the cars. A taciturn New Englander who was a legend as a midget driver in the Northeast right after World War II, Moody was also successful on the USAC and NASCAR circuits in the mid-'50s before becoming the guru of the stock-car preparation industry. Moody, it was said, could set up a car on the telephone—and there were times when he did. Holman died of a sudden heart attack in the spring of the year.

This left Ford with the Wood Brothers as its number one team although NASCAR thought otherwise. For 1972, the Frances arranged for appearance money for four top teams, each with a different make of car: These teams would get $2000 for entering each race of more than 400 miles, and $1500 for races from 250 through 300 miles. Petty was the Plymouth recipient, and needed it now that Chrysler had pulled out. The Dodge money would go to Nord Krauskopf's team, with Harry Hyde as crew chief and Bobby Isaac as driver. The Chevrolet share went to Junior Johnson, now with Bobby Allison as driver. The Ford share was allotted to Bud Moore, who was planning on returning to NASCAR from the SCCA's Trans-Am series—and who in the end only had cars in ten races. The Wood Brothers, with first A.J. Foyt and later David Pearson as drivers, would not commit to running a full season and so got nothing up front.

Petty won the initial Winston Cup championship, finishing first eight times, and placing in the top five 25 times. It was his third NASCAR title, but much of the excitement was provided by Allison, driving Johnson's Chevrolet, with Robert Yates, of Holman-Moody, as the engine builder. Allison won ten events, with Yates working for H-M in the daytime and then driving the 80-odd miles to Johnson's garage in Wilkes County to work at night.

Mercurys, or Fords in different clothing, won nine events, with eight of these going to the Wood Brothers, two being early season races (Daytona and Ontario) when Foyt could spare the time from his single-seater efforts, with the other six being driven by Pearson. He won at Darlington (400 miles), Talladega (500), Michigan twice (400 each time), Daytona (400) and Dover (500). The other Mercury winner was independent James Hylton, a circuit fixture for a number of years who was noted more for his steady performance than for any flashes of brilliance, with a great deal of this due to his limited budget. Hylton won the second 500-miler at Talladega.

The final point standings: Richard Petty (Plymouth) 8701, Bobby Allison (Chevrolet) 8573, James Hylton (Ford) 8158, Cecil Gordon (Mercury) 7326.

Wins: Chevrolet 10, Mercury 9, Plymouth 7, Dodge 5.

Manufacturer's Trophy: Chevrolet 175, Dodge 152.

1973

Rather than face impeachment and a possible prison term for tax evasion, Vice President Spiro Agnew resigns.... Gerald Ford takes his place.... Paavo Nurmi, Lyndon Johnson die.... Juan Peron comes back and is reelected president of Argentina.... Israel wins the Yom Kippur War.

———◆———

The cars were wearing out and the parts were running out, but somehow the Wood Brothers kept their veteran Mercury together. With it, David Pearson put on a performance that would not be matched for more than a decade: The Woods entered only 18 of the 28 Winston Cup events and Pearson drove it to victory in eleven of these, including ten on the super speedways. But thanks to the NASCAR scoring system, Benny Parsons won the championship. Driving a Chevrolet at this stage of his career he won one race, but competed in all of them and that made the difference. Pearson, the hero of the year, was 13th in points. Not one Ford won a race.

Seldom has anyone been as dominant as Pearson in 1973. At Rockingham in the spring he led 499 of the 500 laps, and he won the spring Darlington 500-miler by 13 laps. He even won short-track races in a car set up for super speedways. Petty won six races in a Dodge and Cale Yarborough, back from two unsuccessful years in USAC single-seat racing, won four driving Johnson's Chevrolet. An interesting footnote was provided by Roger Penske, who entered a disc-braked American Motors Matador in the January 500-miler at the Riverside road circuit. Mark Donohue, the Indianapolis 500 winner for Penske a year earlier, a former Trans-Am champion (for Penske) and currently making a joke out of the Can-Am series with Penske's 1100-horsepower Porsche 917, won easily.

Disc brakes, at the time, were not used in stock-car racing, but Penske had read the rules. It was one of the first times Penske made an impact in NASCAR, but not the last. By midsummer he was the owner of Michigan International Speedway, having bought the track at the bankruptcy auction, and was thus a promoter of Winston Cup events. Penske would be heard from in the future.

The rules were once again the subject of discussion and evasion and controversy. Restrictor plates came back, replacing carburetor sleeves, and in mid-year

*A different role: Car owner (and later industrialist) Roger Penske
doing a stint with ABC television, interviewing Bobby Allison
at Daytona, 1973.—Don Hunter*

NASCAR changed specification of the plates used by Dodge and Plymouth hemi-head engines. In October, at the 500-mile race in Charlotte, Yarborough's Chevrolet win was not made official until the next day, after a questionable post-race inspection of his Chevrolet, Petty's Dodge and Allison's Chevrolet. Allison screamed the loudest after being stonewalled by Bill Gazaway, the chief inspector at the time, and it wasn't until after a private meeting with France the Younger a week later that matters were settled, with no details of the settlement announced. Yarborough kept his victory.

On Labor Day, in Darlington's Southern 500, Yarborough pulled away from Pearson with ease in the closing stages and both eyebrows and voices were raised. Charlotte a month later, it would seem, was the flash point of what started much earlier.

Petty resigned from the Professional Drivers Association in January, and in what was surely more than a coincidence, PDA founder Petty was named man of the year by the Daytona Beach newspaper soon afterward. The PDA disappeared before the end of the year.

The final point standings: Benny Parsons (Chevrolet) 7173, Cale Yarborough (Chevrolet) 7106, Cecil Gordon (Chevrolet) 7046.

Wins: Mercury 11, Dodge 8, Chevrolet 7, Plymouth 1, AMC Matador 1.

Manufacturer's Trophy: Chevrolet 163, Dodge 153.

1974

Richard Nixon resigns the Presidency on August 8 and is succeeded by Gerald Ford.... Patty Hearst is kidnapped by the Symbionese Liberation Army, later participates in a bank robbery and isn't apprehended for 20 months.... Lawyer F. Lee Bailey gets her off, claiming Patty had been brainwashed.... Hank Aaron hits his 715th home run, breaking Babe Ruth's record.

Richard Petty, still in a Dodge, won 10 of the season's 30 races and also won his fourth championship. Cale Yarborough, driving Junior Johnson's Chevrolet, won ten races and was second in the point standings. Both men drove in all of the season's 30 races. David Pearson, still with the Wood Brothers and about the only thing Ford had going for it—even though the car was called a Mercury—appeared in 19 events and won seven. Bobby Allison won two—one in Penske's Matador at Ontario—and Canadian rookie Earl Ross, in a Johnson car sponsored by Canadian brewer Carling, won the 500-lap event at Martinsville in September. The rules—and the manner in which they were enforced—were still in a state of flux. Bobby Allison drove Roger Penske's AMC Matador at Ontario and won, and afterward the engine was found to be illegal. Yet Allison kept the win and the points he earned, and only had to forfeit $9100 of the $15,125 paid for first place.

The oil embargo of the previous fall came at the close of the 1973 season, but it brought all spectator sports, and especially racing, under scrutiny. France the Elder was quick to form the National Motorsports Committee, a group that included representatives of his own organization, USAC, the SCCA, IMSA and the NHRA. Headed by former Ontario President John Cooper, the committee made a convincing argument to the Federal Energy Office, including canceling his 24-hour Daytona sports-car event and reducing the length of every Winston Cup race by 10 percent. The crisis passed, but France's leadership kept racing—not only NASCAR—intact.

Texas World Speedway closed its doors during 1974, the championship point system was overhauled for the fourth time in eight years—and was worse than ever. Smaller engines came into vogue, as they were also replacing 7-liter monsters in production cars. As a consequence NASCAR took the restrictor plates out of 427-inch engines, but saddled them with a special carburetor. This effectively ruled out big engines, and 366 cubic inches became the new standard. Petty even ran a 340-inch engine at first, as a new era in engine development, both cut-and-try and scientific (for those who still had Detroit connections) got started. NASCAR would eventually, in 1975, limit Winston Cup engine size to 358 cubic inches.

In 1974 the 366-inchers were producing in the neighborhood of 600 horsepower, with a compression limit of 12.5/1. In the fall and at locations far removed from the major leagues of NASCAR, there were two winners who would have an impact in the future: 18-year-old Bill Elliott won his first Sportsman class event at Woodstock, Georgia, and 15-year-old Mark Martin won the six-cylinder championship at the Benton, Arkansas, Speed Bowl, coming from tenth place to win the season finale.

The final point standings: Richard Petty (Dodge) 5037, Cale Yarborough (Chevrolet) 4470, David Pearson (Mercury) 2389, Bobby Allison (Chevrolet, AMC Matador) 2019.

Wins: Chevrolet 12, Dodge 10, Mercury 7, AMC Matador 1.

Manufacturer's Trophy: Chevrolet 195, Dodge 168.

1975

The U.S. pulls its last troops out of Vietnam in April. ... Spanish Dictator Francisco Franco dies and the country soon becomes a working constitutional monarchy under King Juan Carlos. ... Teamster leader Jimmy Hoffa disappears in August. ... The U.S. and the Soviet Union space ships link up as a symbol of their newfound spirit of cooperation.

It was all Petty again, winning 13 of the 30 races, this time in a Dodge, and the lack of factory support had crippled whatever Ford effort was left. Nevertheless, with David Pearson driving the Wood Brothers' two-year-old Mercury, and Buddy Baker in Bud Moore's Ford, they combined for seven victories—four for Baker in his most successful season—despite running a limited schedule. Petty took part in all 30 events, Pearson in 21, Baker in 23.

Moore and the Woods were running out of parts, especially engine blocks. Although production castings are more than sufficient for everyday use, even into the hundreds of thousands of miles, the stresses caused by hours of operating above 7000 rpm make longevity a problem—and longevity can mean five or six hours. As a consequence, in the '60s and '70s every major manufacturer involved in stock-car racing made sure there were special runs of castings with a different composition. These would be shipped to the racers, in Ford's case from the Cleveland foundry, which not only cast them but did the machining as well.

By this time the tooling for machining the blocks had been shipped from Cleveland to a Ford plant in Australia, and Cleveland was long out of the business of making limited-run castings.

The lack of Detroit involvement was creating financial problems for all concerned, and the Frances were doing what they could to present reasonable fields. The money situation being what it was, only twelve front-line teams towed to California for the early-season Riverside race, with the rest of the field being made up of West Coast drivers. Appearance money, called the "Awards and Achievement Plan," came into use, and has continued, in one form or another, to this day, when it carries the title "Winners' Circle."

In 1975 this meant Petty (himself), Junior Johnson (Cale Yarborough), Bud Moore (Buddy Baker) and K&K Insurance (Dave Marcis) would each get $3000 for super speedway appearances and $2000 for showing up at the shorter events. Lower-level teams would get $500 for the big events and $250 for the small ones, as long as they were in the top 20 in point standings. Johnson and Moore turned down the offers, figuring they could do better negotiating with individual promoters, and Moore wound up the season having eight different sponsors as a result. In addition, Goodyear would give a certain number of tires to the faster qualifiers.

The point system was changed—again—and about the only other thing that was new was the ascendancy of Darrell Waltrip, the talkative Tennessean who won his first Winston Cup race, the first of what would turn out to be 84 in a quarter-century career. Petty won his sixth championship, to no one's surprise. And despite the lean year, television exposure was on the increase, six races being televised live or on a delayed basis.

The final point standings: Richard Petty (Dodge) 4783, Dave Marcis (Dodge) 4061, James Hylton (Chevrolet) 3914, Benny Parsons (Chevrolet) 3820.

Wins: Dodge 14, Chevrolet 6, Ford 4, Mercury 3, AMC Matador 3.

Manufacturer's Trophy: Dodge 188, Chevrolet 160.

1976

The United States celebrates its 200th birthday.... Mao Zedong and Zhou Enlai both die, leaving China in a state of turmoil.... Jimmy Carter is elected president.... Seymour Cray introduces the first supercomputer.... The videocassette recorder is introduced to the consumer marketplace.

————◆————

He attracted little notice, but a tall blond 21-year-old from the north Georgia town of Dawsonville made his Winston Cup debut at Rockingham in late February, where the Ford sponsored by his father's dealership, with his brother as crew chief, had its engine let go after only 32 laps. Bill Elliott would be heard from again, and there would be a time when almost all of Ford's stock-car reputation would be riding in his Thunderbird, but that would come later. Another driver making his debut in 1976 would be Ford's nemesis in years to come. His full name was Ralph Dale Earnhardt, but in order to distinguish himself from his race-driver father of the same name, he dropped the Ralph in everyday use. He participated in one Winston Cup event, the World 600 at Charlotte, and finished 22nd.

The Elliotts, the Earnhardts and the rest were rookies in the literal sense of the word, since they were making their initial appearances at Winston Cup level, but they were hardly inexperienced as drivers. By the time someone got into a Winston Cup car, they normally had hundreds of lower-level events behind them, short-track, often dirt-track events that once again proved Darwin's theory about survival of the fittest.

The problem was that when they got to a Winston Cup race there was Pearson in the Wood Brothers' Mercury, Yarborough in Johnson's Chevrolet and Petty in his Dodge, plus Bobby Allison, Buddy Baker, and some others almost as quick and certainly as experienced. Darwin had to be proven right all over again.

Rookies also found graphic examples of what it meant to be tough: Bobby Allison, driving in an unsanctioned event in Minnesota on July 10, crashed when he skidded on an oil slick and was unconscious for half an hour while being freed from the wreck. He had a broken nose, fractured ribs, facial cuts, thoracic injuries, torn ligaments and other injuries to his feet. A week later he climbed into his Mercury at Nashville and drove one lap before handing the car over to Neil Bonnett in order to maintain his position in the point standings.

In 1976 it was all Pearson and Yarborough, with Pearson winning ten of the season's 30 events despite running in only 22, and Yarborough taking nine plus the title, thanks to another convoluted NASCAR point system that saw Pearson finish ninth. Petty, who won three events, was second and Benny Parsons, who took two in a Chevrolet, was third. But they drove in all the races.

The Wood Brothers' car, plus Moore's, finally got some good blocks, thanks to retired Ford vice-president of manufacturing planning Don Tope, whose son had been involved in Trans-Am racing. Tope saw to it that blocks with the right alloy mix were cast, shipped to Australia to be machined, shipped back to the U.S. and sold to the racing teams. It was all *sub rosa,* and even a quarter century later some of those involved were reluctant to discuss the matter.

Pearson won the season opener at Riverside, ahead of Yarborough, then won the Daytona 500 in a made-for-television thriller when he and Petty, running side by side, crashed at the entrance to the final straight. Pearson managed to find a gear and came across the line at about 20 mph while Petty remained on the infield grass. Pearson would win three in a row in mid-season, would win twice at Riverside, Michigan and Darlington, and also at Charlotte, Ontario and Atlanta. But Yarborough came on strong at the end of the year, winning four straight in September and early October. The Woods skipped two of those races: No money, no parts.

A move that would prove beneficial to NASCAR in general and Charlotte Motor Speedway in particular was made in 1976 when Bruton Smith, who had just bought out partner Richard Howard, named "Humpy" Wheeler general manager of the facility. Wheeler, a South Carolinian, had been working for Firestone's racing division, was known to all, and was a natural promoter. He made Charlotte's 600-miler in May his first big success, bringing in sports-car driver Janet Guthrie, who had just failed to qualify a single-seater for the Indianapolis 500, for his event. Smith was the money behind the car owner of record, Guthrie got some help from Ralph Moody in setting up the car, and she qualified 27th and finished 15th, 21 laps behind Pearson.

Guthrie's presence not only attracted the largest crowd in Speedway history, it brought in more women fans than ever before. This not only gave Wheeler a lesson in demographics, but it also pointed up the problems created by the lack of a sufficient number of ladies' restrooms and the amount of water needed for their use. Charlotte Motor Speedway increased its reservoir capacity dramatically after the World 600.

The final point standings: Cale Yarborough (Chevrolet) 4644, Richard Petty (Dodge) 4449, Benny Parsons (Chevrolet) 4304, Bobby Allison (Mercury) 4097.

Wins: Chevrolet 13, Mercury 10, Dodge 6, Ford 1.

Manufacturer's Trophy: Chevrolet 199, Mercury 149.

1977

Elvis Presley dies at 42.... The U.S. cedes control of the Panama Canal to the Republic of Panama, with changeover due Dec. 31, 1999.... *Egypt and Israel take the first steps toward reconciliation.*

———•———

A look at starting fields in any of the season's 30 events shows something on the order of 80 percent Chevrolets, with two or three Dodges—most notably Petty—the Matador of Bobby Allison, running independently—and a small collection of Fords. The old reliables were the Wood Brothers (Pearson), Bud Moore (Buddy Baker), the veteran Junie Donlavey (usually Dick Brooks) and newcomer Bill Elliott when

A.J. Foyt

Junie Donlavey   *Cale Yarborough*

—*Don Hunter*

he and his car-owner father could afford to enter. The other few Fords around could have gotten lost on their way to dealerships for all the good they did the company's image.

Yarborough won nine races and the Winston Cup championship for the second consecutive year. Petty won five races, Parsons four and Darrell Waltrip, now a threat to win on any Sunday, won six. Pearson and the Woods soldiered on, entering 22 events and winning two, at Riverside in January and Darlington in September. Moore had no luck, as Baker went winless even though he drove in all 30 races.

Guthrie, with Moody handling the crew, drove in 19 races and placed in the top ten four times. The point system had her finishing in front of Donnie Allison, who won two events but only appeared in 17. Bobby Allison left Penske's team before the start of the season after going winless for the first time since he became a front-line driver. Penske picked up Dave Marcis as a driver but was not successful and left NASCAR at the end of the year. He would be back, in more ways than one.

The final point standings: Cale Yarborough (Chevrolet) 5000, Richard Petty (Dodge) 4614, Benny Parsons (Chevrolet) 4570, Darrell Waltrip (Chevrolet) 4498.

Wins: Chevrolet 21, Dodge 7, Mercury 2.

Manufacturer's Trophy: Chevrolet 233, Dodge 125.

1978

The Jonestown Massacre in Guyana sees self-proclaimed Reverend Jim Jones and roughly 900 of his flock commit suicide.... There are three popes in office—Paul VI; John Paul I, who dies after 34 days; and Polish-born John Paul II, the first non-Italian pontiff in 456 years.... Ultrasound becomes an alternative to X-rays.... The Camp David Accords are reached.

———————•———————

Changes in what Mr. and Mrs. America would be driving on the highway, plus increased cost pressures, gave impetus to certain key rule changes. The small-block Chevrolet engine, which had already been granted "corporate" status by General Motors after a public relations black eye that involved some Oldsmobile owners suing after finding Chevrolet engines in their cars, was also granted the same dispensation for the Winston Cup series. This gave the starting fields, which more and more resembled a one-make event with the odd Ford added in, some variety. Oldsmobiles and Buicks started to appear and one of the Olds, prepared by Johnson and driven by Yarborough, won the championship. The fact that it was a new skin over an old Chevrolet bothered few. It was Yarborough's third straight title, something not accomplished before or since.

Petty, who used his 1974 Dodge Charger through 1977, tried it again in 1978 when the three-year-old limit was extended temporarily. He then went to a Dodge Magnum with little success before switching to a Chevrolet in late August, thus leaving the Chrysler Corporation for the first time in two decades.

All of this made little difference in the Ford camp.

The old teams were still there, with one notable difference: Moore had picked up Bobby Allison, winless for the past two years, and Allison proved to be the best thing that had happened to Ford since the pull-out of 1970. Pearson was still with the Wood Brothers, running a limited schedule. In addition there was Elliott, not yet a contender but at least getting some attention. Pearson and the Woods had a two-year-old Mercury Cougar, Elliott had a year-old Montego, while Moore had prepared a new Thunderbird for Allison. The "civilian" version of this made its debut in 1977, when the Thunderbird was reduced from its 120-inch wheelbase of the previous year to the 114-inch wheelbase of the two-door LTD replacement for the Torino. This move was dictated by the Government's corporate average fuel economy (CAFE) standards, which would take effect in 1978. The new T-Bird weighed 900 pounds less than the old one. And it could all be fitted into NASCAR's new 115-inch rule. It would be Ford teams' car of choice for the next two decades.

Allison won five races while running the full 30-event schedule, including the Daytona 500, Atlanta's spring event, plus Dover, Charlotte and Ontario in the fall. Pearson added four while running 22 times—Rockingham in the spring, Dover in May, the Firecracker 400 in Daytona on July 4, plus Michigan in August. He was also the pole-sitter seven times, one less than Yarborough.

The final point standings: Cale Yarborough (Oldsmobile) 4841, Bobby Allison (Ford) 4367, Darrell Waltrip (Chevrolet) 4362, Benny Parsons (Chevrolet) 4350.

Wins: Oldsmobile 11, Chevrolet 10, Ford 5, Mercury 4.

Manufacturer's Trophy: Chevrolet 176, Oldsmobile 162.

1979

Margaret Thatcher is named prime minister of Britain, the first European woman to hold her country's highest elected office.... The Soviet Union invades Afghanistan.... The Shah of Iran is overthrown by Islamic fundamentalists, who later imprison 52 Americans for 444 days.... Lord Mountbatten is assassinated by IRA terrorists, who blow up his sailboat.

———————◆———————

In Dearborn racing was about the farthest thing from anyone's mind. Imports had taken more than 22 percent of the market, the second energy crisis had panicked the public, and Ford's market share was on its way to a postwar low. Philip Caldwell, the finance man whom Henry Ford II promoted to president after Iacocca was fired, would shepherd the company through four dark years before the turnaround. If anyone had suggested that two decades later the import share would be at 33 percent but Ford would be setting sales and profitability records, well....

Bud Moore still had Bobby Allison, who won five times, but the Wood Brothers and Pearson split after the April race at Darlington. Neil Bonnett, another member of the Allison-led "Alabama Gang" from the steel-mill suburbs of Birmingham, took his place. Bonnett added three more but the championship went to Petty, the seventh and final one of his career. Petty's car was clothed as an Oldsmobile for the high-speed tracks and as a Chevrolet for the others. He won the title by the slimmest of margins when he finished the season-ending event at Ontario in fifth—but a lap in front of Waltrip. The difference, after a year's worth of racing, was eleven points.

Earnhardt won his first event and would be named rookie of the year. He had driven in Winston Cup before, but never more than five races in a season. This time he was in 27 of the 31, won at Bristol in the spring, and was the fastest qualifier four times. The biggest break for NASCAR—perhaps for racing in general—came in February, when CBS did the first live, start-to-finish telecast of the Daytona 500. The race wasn't decided until the last turn of the last lap and then the cameras also had the sight of the Allison brothers and Yarborough in a post-race fistfight. The race drew a better rating than the competing programs on NBC and ABC.

The final point standings: Richard Petty (Chevrolet, Oldsmobile) 4830, Darrell Waltrip (Chevrolet, Oldsmobile) 4819, Bobby Allison (Ford) 4633, Cale Yarborough (Oldsmobile) 4604.

Wins: Chevrolet 18, Ford 5, Oldsmobile 5, Mercury 3.

Manufacturer's Trophy: Chevrolet 212, Ford 108.

1980

The president of the Digital Equipment Corporation says, "There is no reason for any individual to have a computer in their home"…. Ronald Reagan is elected President…. Eric Heiden wins five gold medals at the Lake Placid Winter Olympics.

For the first time since becoming a public company in 1956, Ford lost money— the minus for the year was $1.545 billion, and there was little light at the end of the tunnel. Henry Ford II retired as chairman and chief executive officer on March 12, to be replaced by Philip Caldwell, with Don Petersen as president. For the first time since the company's founding, a Ford would not be sitting at its head.

Two other names cropped up in Dearborn for the first time, names that meant little to anyone involved with stock-car racing, but names belonging to men who would see to it that Ford returned. The first was Walter Hayes, Ford of Europe's vice-chairman, who would become head of public affairs for the entire corporation. Hayes understood what a performance image could do, and he was the man who financed the all-conquering Cosworth grand prix engine in the 1960s. That cost Ford roughly $280,000 and gave the company an image boost everywhere but the U.S., where Formula One was thought of by many as something from baby-food manufacturers. More importantly, Hayes had HF2's ear. The other was Michael Kranefuss, who would run the program.

Even though a performance image was needed, the state of the corporation in 1980 made providing budget money for this sort of venture something questionable at best. Harold (Red) Poling, who occupied the Chairman's seat in 1990–1993, was executive vice president in charge of corporate staffs at the time and remembered the situation well.

Poling: "You need to consider the environment. When I came back [in April 1979, after having been chairman of Ford of Europe] all you could sell were large cars with V8 engines, and then we had the energy crisis—and we just died. And so I was put in charge of North America [Poling was named head of North American

Automotive Operations in March, 1980] and the situation was quite dire. We were losing huge sums of money ... and so I had to take drastic cost reduction actions ... 15 percent personnel reductions immediately, across the line, I insisted, everybody, no one was excused, executive vice presidents right down.... Then in 1980 ... I was approached by Phil [Benton, head of the Ford Division] and Walter saying, 'We want to get back in racing,' and they persisted, and I concluded only if I could get the dealers' support and if we could control the amount of attention given to it, and I agreed to support it on that basis, I wanted to get the dealers involved, and that's how we got back."

But for the moment Fords at Daytona, Charlotte, North Wilkesboro and the rest of NASCAR territory would struggle along.

Earnhardt, in a Chevrolet, won the first of what would eventually be seven Winston Cup titles, just ahead of Yarborough. He won the rookie award the year before, so at the age of 27 he was sitting on top of the world, or at least the stock-car part of it. He won the 1980 title in the last event of the season, which coincidentally was the last race ever held at Ontario. The bondholders were bought out by the Chevron Land and Development Corporation, a division of Standard Oil of California, and the roughly 980-acre site became just another Southern California real estate project, with a Hilton hotel soon to rise on what was previously the fourth turn. Two decades later, just down the road in Fontana, Penske would build another speedway that turned out to be a financial success as well as an artistic one.

The final point standings: Dale Earnhardt (Chevrolet) 4661, Cale Yarborough (Chevrolet) 4642, Benny Parsons (Chevrolet) 4278, Richard Petty (Chevrolet) 4255.

Wins: Chevrolet 22, Ford 3, Mercury 3, Oldsmobile 3.

Manufacturer's Trophy: Chevrolet 226, Mercury 69.

The prospect of Ford being a threat to the General Motors dominance of NASCAR was still a dim one—but at least it was now a possibility. It would take a few years, however, while the company first returned to financial health, and for the upper floors of the headquarters building to realize that stock-car racing was the quintessential American form of the sport, and that factory support was a necessity.

Chapter 7

THE VETERANS

As in any other sport some people make brief appearances, some are around for a while, and others become an integral part of the culture, in part because of their success, in part because of their longevity. Stock-car racing has its own heroes, going back to the early days of Red Byron, Lloyd Seay, Roy Hall and the Flock brothers. There are seven from the last four decades. Some of their careers began before the '60s, but all have remained in NASCAR's collective memory.

David Pearson

He has aged gracefully, something not all former racing drivers do (those that are able to age at all, someone once said), and he has returned to his South Carolina roots although it would also be fair to say he never left them.

Ford's biggest winner:
David Pearson.—Don Hunter

Pearson, now in his mid-late 60s, came out of the mill town of Whitney, which is a section, more or less, of Spartanburg and now lives a few miles from there, comfortable, silver-haired, alone since his wife died a decade ago but with his children and grandchildren nearby, and he is at peace. Other drivers have stayed on long after their competitive time, but not Pearson.

A while back he was voted the stock-car driver of the 20th century by a jury of his peers. Not by a group of sportswriters and broadcasters, most of whom never saw him run, but by those who were on the track with him.

Not Richard Petty, but Pearson, who won three championships, who drove 574 NASCAR championship races to Petty's 1184, and who won 105 to Petty's 200. And who came out in front in their head-to-head meetings more often than not.

The election concerned him so little that it wasn't until months afterward that he was given to understand the vote was for the best stock-car driver, not the best of all. He had expressed some surprise that Mario Andretti or A.J. Foyt hadn't won, and that is when someone explained that there were votes for several categories. He just hadn't given it much thought.

David Pearson won more NASCAR championship races driving a Ford product than any other man, 29 with a Ford and 44 with a Mercury, or 73 in all, although the basic difference between the nameplates was the sheet metal skin on the tube frame of the Wood Brothers or Holman-Moody chassis.

Was he faster than Petty?

"Sometimes," he says. Pearson has few illusions. He knows who he is, and if a stranger doesn't that wouldn't bother him. He also knows he was good, and if there were days when someone else was better, that no longer bothers him either.

Pearson drove a full season in both 1968 and 1969, something he seldom did before or since, and won both championships. He did it because Ford wanted to shut down Petty, who won 27 races (of 48) in 1967 on his way to becoming a folk hero, and, as Ralph Moody said, "We got tired of watching Petty beat nobody out there on the small tracks, so we had to go after them."

Pearson left Holman-Moody after the spring race at Darlington in 1971 and found a home with the Wood Brothers: "... Like I said, we was good, I mean with the Woods especially.... They worked hard at pit stops and stuff like that ... and about every race I run, if I got behind they would usually catch me right back up when I made a pit stop.... I just had confidence in them... I don't reckon I went to a race that I didn't feel like I could have won. That's how comfortable I was."

Pearson is of the old school, men who gravitated to racing because it was a way out of the mills at a time when the South was beginning to convert from an agrarian economy, and there weren't that many jobs around. The money, by today's standards, was minimal, but if you never had any, a few hundred dollars from a dirt track feature was a lot. He and his parents worked at the Whitney yarn mill and from there he went to work at a gas station and was driving flathead Fords at night and on weekends, winning as many as 30 races one season.

The Spartanburg area was a stock-car hotbed, the home of such NASCAR worthies as Joe Littlejohn, Bud Moore, Joe Eubanks, Cotton Owens, Rex White and others, so there were role models, people Pearson could look up to, men he could emulate.

His friend Ralph Sawyer helped him raise money to buy a used Grand National car, going on the local radio station, soliciting contributions of a dollar or two. Then he borrowed the rest from his father, paid Jack Smith $3500 for the car and took it to Daytona for the 1960 500 and his first experience at high speed. He finished 18th, but it was a start, and he was on his way.

The next year Ray Fox was looking for a driver for his Pontiac for the World 600 at Charlotte, and came up with Pearson. He won by two laps, even after driving the final two laps with a blown tire. He was 26 years old. David collected $12,000, more than he had ever seen or dreamed of, and spent $5000 of it to purchase the small house that he and his wife were renting. It was his first equity position, but not his last.

He lives with his dog in the house he built in 1978, a nice but not ostentatious place, surrounded by about 100 acres of his own but in an area that is slowly being built up. When he moved in he said, "I was going to be a big farmer ... and I went to a cattle sale and of course I had some hogs and chickens and a little bit of everything ... but I ended up more or less giving them away because I killed one and couldn't eat the meat."

"You get attached to things like that, you know."

Ralph Moody

Healthy and hearty in his mid-80s, except for suffering from Old Racer's Disease, Ralph Moody likes to laugh about it.

"You know the favorite word of all old racers?," he asks. When told no, he yells, "WHAT?" and then laughs again.

Moody, the transplanted New Englander who came to Charlotte by way of Florida, was the racing half of Holman-Moody, the by-now legendary stock-car operation that Ford financed and which shut down a few years after the company withdrew from racing in the U.S. at the close of 1970.

Moody and partner John Holman were diametric opposites. They were never close, and in the final years they disliked each other and at times almost came to blows. But they were a good fit when it came to getting the job done, and that included not only winning races with their own team, but also supplying all the other Ford-supported teams as well.

If you ran a Ford stock car in NASCAR or USAC in the 1960s, you got your cars, engines, and whatever individual parts you needed from Holman-Moody. The operation grew into a 450-man empire with branches in Long Beach, California, and in Miami (for power boat racing) before everything imploded with the withdrawal of Ford support and some adventurous business moves on Holman's part.

Holman took care of the wheeling and the dealing—sometimes there was too much wheeling—and Moody took care of the race cars. He had a talent for it, one that was developed in his early years, when he was the scourge of the New England midget drivers in the late '40s. He was not only good behind the wheel, but was his own mechanic and learned that chassis setup could be as important as horsepower.

Moody even won five NASCAR races in 1956, and was a threat on the USAC stock-car circuit, before moving over to full time race team management for H-M. His influence, although kept confidential at the time, even extended to the 1966–67 Le Mans cars, when they were having problems. Moody was there when Marvin Panch ran three consecutive laps at 240 mph on Firestone's Fort Stockton, Texas, test track. Moody: "We left Fort Stockton ... 240 for three laps and then we quit. I said we ain't doin' this—no big argument there.... Running 240 in that place ... nothin' but rocks out there."

Moody was in charge of the J-Car testing at Riverside the day Ken Miles died: "They were going to let that thing run as hard as it would run and I'm telling 'em that sonofabitch is floating already, and they said they were going to do it, and Miles said 'It'll be all right,' and I said, 'Goddamn, you nuts? Can't you feel it? You can't run that wide open down that backstretch....' They decided they could, and I went to the phone to call Ford to get it stopped, and he did it in the meantime...."

Moody was the head man for Fireball Roberts, for Fred Lorenzen, for a young Cale Yarborough, for David Pearson, for Mario Andretti in his brief (and winning) Daytona 500 appearance, and for anyone else who had the big "Competition Proven" sign on their car. And many of his innovations, the building of subframes to carry the front suspensions, the first steps toward tube-frame chassis, were pace setters for the entire NASCAR community.

When Moody learned, too late in the relationship, that some of Holman's business practices were questionable, he sold his stock in the corporation but stayed as an employee. In 1971, after Ford's withdrawal, Moody took one of their 1969 Mercurys, put Bobby Allison in the seat and won eleven races, second only to Richard Petty in the number of wins, and then wanted Allison again for 1972, the first Winston Cup year.

"I wound up with money for next year," Moody says, "close to $3 million from Coca-Cola and other sponsors, and Holman said, 'I don't like that Bobby Allison.'" So Allison went to Junior Johnson (with H-M employee Robert Yates building the engines) and was the leading winner in 1972, finishing first ten times in 31 events with Johnson's Chevrolet.

Moody was gone by then and Holman died in 1972, the victim of a heart attack while at the wheel of one of his trucks. Ralph went on to another career as an engine builder, was called in to help with Janet Guthrie's stock car in the late '70s, set up sprint cars for a friend of his, still out on the road in his 70s, still enthusiastic ("You should see those things—you talk about flyin'!... that first year, the youngest boy,

I had him winnin' races and eatin' those guys up and they didn't know why.... you can't believe how those things would go ... 850 horsepower, 1800 pounds!").

He sits up in Mooresville now, a few miles north of Charlotte, having finally moved out of town a year or two ago, and his latest toy is a 34-foot motor home. There's a road out there, places to go and things to do, and being in your 80s is only a state of mind.

Cale Yarborough

There is a Mercury on the showroom floor of Cale Yarborough's Honda dealership in Florence, South Carolina, the car he drove for the Wood Brothers when he won the 1968 Daytona 500.

The car comes from the time before the 1970 shutdown, when the Ford and Lincoln-Mercury divisions were engaged in intramural warfare, much as the Dodge and Plymouth divisions of Chrysler had been doing. The bigger Ford Division had most of the money and the support and sympathies of Jacque Passino, who was then in charge of the racing effort, but a funny thing happened on the way to the race track: The Mercury body shapes were better aerodynamically than were the Fords, and so some of the teams reskinned their cars. At Daytona in 1968 Yarborough had a race-long duel with good friend LeeRoy Yarbrough in another Mercury, LeeRoy finishing second and giving the division a 1-2 punch.

That was almost four decades ago, before the shutdown caused Cale to move over to Junior Johnson's GM-sponsored team and win the Winston Cup championship three straight years, 1976-77-78. It was before Cale rose to fourth on NASCAR's list of most career wins with 83, and long before he retired from driving in 1988 after 30 years.

Florence is in the heart of the Pee Dee River country, where Yarborough grew up as a farm boy outside the hamlet of Sardis, population about 200, not far from where he lives now in Timmonsville, except that the farm boy has grown into a prosperous businessman, one who has aged gracefully.

Now in his early 60s Yarborough looks well, his stocky frame has added almost no extra poundage, he moves well, and he is busy. "I've worked seven days a week all my life," he says, and when he is in town, he can be found in his trophy-filled office over the dealership. He had three others, a Chrysler outlet, a Honda dealership in Savannah and a General Motors dealership, but they have been sold.

"I used to think the name of the game was accumulate, accumulate.... Well, now I think it's time to start getting rid of, and start doing things I want to do instead of things that I have to do." He sold his 18 Hardee's restaurants in 1999, the cleaning businesses and most of the rest are gone.

The 4000-acre farm in Sardis is home and someone works the land for him as he is, in many respects, the warrior in repose. When he was driving, his eye was already on the prize at the end, not just on the trophy that came with the checkered flag, but on the idea that there would be a life after racing.

He was second to Dale Earnhardt in 1980, in one of the closest points races in NASCAR history, and then cut back on his schedule, driving 18, then only 16 races a year until he stopped. "I wanted to spend more time with my family, that had a lot to do with it … and the business end had gotten so big that I needed to look after it."

Almost from the beginning, Cale knew how he wanted to end: "When I was a kid sports people were my heroes and I wanted to be like them, but when you look around, most of them did well, made a big name for themselves, but ended up broke … And I promised myself if I did well in the sports world I would not end up like my heroes did."

There is little danger of that.

Bud Moore

Walter Moore, better known as Bud, was just out of high school on May 25, 1943, when he turned 18, and a week later he was drafted. His Spartanburg, South Carolina, buddies, Joe Eubanks and Cotton Owens, went into the Navy, but that quota was filled and Bud's choices were Marines or Army, and he chose the latter.

He celebrated his 20th birthday in Pilsen, Czechoslovakia, after having made the D-Day landing at Utah Beach, been part of the force that relieved the 101st Airborne in Bastogne, and was the holder of two bronze stars and five purple hearts.

Moore spent most of World War II with the 90th Infantry Division, but on D-Day his 359th Infantry Regiment was attached to the 4th Division and he went in with the first wave. "I had a .30-caliber water-cooled machine gun and when I landed I had on my pack and I had the tripod—I was the first gunner—and the tripod weighed 51 pounds. The second gunner had the gun and we had seven ammunition bearers.… when we went off the front of that LCI, when the front of it went down and we went off, we was in water up to our shoulders, there I was, and I stepped in a hole and went under, and I had salt water in my eyes, and I finally managed to get goin' again and with all those shells comin' in it was something.…

"They always told us when you get off that boat get off that beach the fastest you can, but you can't do anything, you're in the water, it didn't make any difference if you had a rifle, you couldn't do anything to start with.… I had maybe 150 feet, 200 feet of water to get through and then about another 200 feet of beach and all I did was work as fast as I could, and I remember one time I looked behind me and I thought, 'Well, I got 5000 miles of water behind me, so I got to go this way, and I did.… I finally got out of the water and got across the beach and over behind a sand dune or something and I got out of the artillery fire.… they weren't shelling the beach, they were shelling the boats to stop them coming in, and they were hitting them, too.… It was just amazing to get out of the artillery.… The small arms fire was nothing, it didn't bother me or any of us."

In December of 1944 Moore's outfit had just crossed the Moselle River and been pulled back for a rest when General George Patton came into their small town. "He

Bud Moore—the recruit.
—Ford Motor Company

Bud Moore—the veteran.
—Don Hunter

was standing on the courthouse steps," Moore says, "standing there with his pearl-handled pistols and his little white dog and with a megaphone, and he was telling us about the 101st Airborne that was stuck in Bastogne, and he said, 'Let me tell you now, we're going to leave here in about 30 or 45 minutes, we can't wait.... I know you guys are needing hot meals.... Them poor guys up there are catching hell and we're going to go up there and get them out, and we're going to kill every son of a bitch on the road,' and he meant it."

Patton's speech to the troops "Was probably about 3 o'clock, 4 o'clock in the afternoon.... that night we were in snow about 12 inches deep and it was cold.... We hiked 28 miles that night and the next day we got a tank division, I don't know where they came from but they caught up with us and we started riding the tanks. When we got up there to Bastogne it was a mess ... and another thing happened [on the way to Bastogne].... There was a column of trucks, men, tanks, about a mile long, and every one of them was burned.... They put a couple of our TD's [tank destroyers] up there, they had bulldozer blades on them, and they just pushed tanks, everything, right off the road so we could get through."

When Bud got home he went into the used-car business with Eubanks in 1946 and eventually they wound up with a 1939 flathead Ford coupe that was set up for competition. "I told Joe, 'We got us a race car, why don't we start runnin' it?'"

Their debut was at a fairgrounds dirt track not far from home where "Joe said, 'Who's going to drive it?' and I went out and warmed it up, I run a few laps and the first thing I know I was through the fence, but it didn't really hurt it, so I went out and run a few more laps and I'm back through the fence again, so I come back in and I told Joe,

'You get in, I can't drive it'.... Joe run third or fourth in the consolation race.... we ran the feature and we finished seventh ... so that's sort of what got us into it."

For Moore, "into it" meant a four-decade career as one of NASCAR's leading car owners, a short stint as the leader of Lincoln-Mercury's dominance of Trans-Am racing, and a well-deserved reputation as the talent behind Ford's move from a 429-inch stock-car engine to the 351, effecting a sea change in the way not only Fords were raced, but also everyone else who competed in Grand National or Winston Cup events.

Advancing technology and the lack of adequate sponsorship finally caught up with Moore in 1999 and he sold his team midway through the season. When Moore retired his various drivers had started a total of 912 races, second only to the Petty team, and they had won 63, then seventh on the all-time list.

Four decades was enough. He didn't have anything left to prove.

Junior Johnson

Tom Wolfe's profile of Junior Johnson, published in a 1960s issue of *Esquire*, was a groundbreaking contribution to the New Journalism, and propelled Junior in particular and stock-car racing in general into the consciousness of new segments of the populace. The Northeast, complete with the advertising people of Madison Avenue, and even auto-oriented California, where other forms of racing were well established, knew little of this Southern pastime, except for vague rumors about whiskey runners and "revenooers" and some guy named Fireball.

*Junior Johnson: From Ford to GM
and back again.—Don Hunter*

Now here, in a national magazine that prized good writing was Junior, and he became the archetype of the NASCAR driver to a large part of the country. Stock-car racing had a name, it had a face, and it had *excitement*! Hollywood would love it. (It did, actually, making a grade C or D movie that wasn't a patch on the tail of Junior and his career, but that's another story....)

That was four decades ago, and the picture casual observers got, because they didn't bother to read the piece carefully, was that this was some sort of a backwards backwoodsman. What they missed was that his hill-country accent obscured the fact that he was a successful businessman with a very clear code of ethics.

But he was good for the stock-car racing image, so outsiders tended to overlook what was really there.

Junior drove for all of the Big Three, owned teams that ran cars for Ford and GM, had drivers who won six Winston Cup championships, and had a great deal of disappointment as well. In his day Junior Johnson *was* stock-car racing and now, living in his mansion located on a rise just a few miles from where he was born, with a young wife, two young children, 800 head of cattle and various other business interests, he too is complete.

He was one of The Guys, and he was also one of The Other Guys, depending on how he was treated by one manufacturer or another, but they all got their money's worth, because they were dealing with the heart and soul of the sport.

Robert Glenn Johnson Jr. is a large man, his shock of white hair sitting on top of a surprisingly youthful face, looking not too much different from when he made an impact on the Grand National scene in 1958, driving a 352-inch Ford. He went from that to Chevrolet's famous "Mystery engine" in 1963, then went to work for Chrysler when Chevrolet was shut down by its top management and found problems there.

Johnson and chief mechanic and car owner Ray Fox went to San Angelo, Texas, during that winter and took the Chevrolet, which Chrysler was using as a baseline car. "When we left San Angelo," Johnson says, "the Plymouth was about five miles an hour faster than the Chevrolet and the Dodge was about three. Me, Paul Goldsmith, Richard Petty, Jimmy Pardue, were all supposed to have Plymouths.

"When they delivered ours to Ray Fox's shop (in February 1964) it was Dodges. And I had done all the work on it. I won five races for them, but when I'd leave a short track, I'd get smoked off because of the extra two or three miles an hour.

"So I quit Dodge. They come in to tell me I couldn't quit, I had a contract, and I said I ain't drivin' no Dodge when I did all the work.... the reason they wouldn't let me have a Plymouth, they knew I'd blister their tail with it."

So he drove a Ford for Banjo Matthews in 1964, then formed his own team in 1965 with Holly Farms as his sponsor, won 13 races and retired from active driving. He was running a successful Ford team with LeeRoy Yarbrough as his driver when the company shut down at the end of 1970 and Ford came and took all the equipment even though he had a contract.

"Then in '71, simply because I didn't have no Ford cars or nothing, I started messing around with a Chevrolet for Richard Howard down at Charlotte."

Junior had his own knowledge and he had Holman-Moody's best engine builder, Robert Yates, who was working for him at night. Junior's teams won three titles with Cale Yarborough and three with Darrell Waltrip. In the mid-late '80s, the then-childless Johnson found someone who became a sort of surrogate son—Brent Kouthen, stepson of GM racing director Herb Fishel.

Kouthen was working for Johnson and was an engineering major at North Carolina State University in Raleigh, where GM had an arrangement. Junior: "In my deal with General Motors … I had them take $500,000 and do a grant with North Carolina State to study camshaft components and see what we could do to help the engine in that area. And they found like 40 horsepower just in the way they formulated all that stuff together…. Didn't know anything about it at the time, but Robert Yates' boy was in that class."

Kouthen and Douglas Yates in the same class, with Professor Joe David—who later went to work for Rick Hendrick's Chevrolet team.

In late 1989 Johnson discovered, more or less by accident, that Hendrick was getting considerably more money from GM than he was—and then found that cylinder heads he developed for GM were being slipped to Hendrick and that was enough. He came back to Ford for the 1990 season, which was a bad one before it really got started.

One night in late April of the year, Kouthen's car left the road. He was 24 years old. Those who know him well say a lot went out of Junior when Kouthen died.

He missed what would have been his seventh championship in 1992 when Bill Elliott lost the title to Alan Kulwicki in the last race of the season, had a triple bypass in 1993, kept the team until 1995 and then sold it. He hasn't been back since.

In the summer of 2000 Junior was invited to Britain's Goodwood Festival of Speed and was there along with his wife, children and dozens of other former and present drivers from practically every area of motorsports, everyone from Sir Stirling Moss, Jackie Stewart and John Surtees to Dan Gurney. Junior was busy signing autographs all weekend, somewhat surprised that British fans knew who he was. Then he was approached by a well-preserved, but somewhat older American.

"Mr. Johnson," he said, "we've never met, and I thought I should introduce myself ." It was Phil Hill, America's first world driving champion.

Two men from the same era, from opposite ends of the racing spectrum—meeting on a green lawn half a world away from home.

Glen Wood

Stuart, Virginia, was known as Taylorsville until after the Civil War, when it was renamed in honor of Confederate hero J.E.B. Stuart, who was born in surrounding Patrick County, which has as much of a right to be called the Deep South as any other

*Way back when—Glen Wood, 1958, at
Asheville-Weaverville.—Don Hunter*

place below the Mason-Dixon line. It is farming country and there is logging, and
there is a little bootlegging going on, but not enough to bother anyone, and it is one
of those places where stock-car racing has deep roots.

Stuart sits in the hills just above the Virginia-Carolina border, about 30 miles
west of Martinsville and a few miles below the Blue Ridge Parkway and it is peaceful
there, with the clock, figuratively anyway, turned back a few decades to a kinder,
gentler time. It is also not far from Floyd, which was Curtis Turner's hometown.
Turner was the Wood Brothers' hero, just as he was for many other young men in the
area when stock-car racing was in its infancy.

This is Wood Brothers' country, which has for more than half a century provided NASCAR with some of its most successful teams. Turner drove for them, as
did Junior Johnson, Joe Weatherly, Marvin Panch, Fred Lorenzen, Dan Gurney, A.J.
Foyt, Cale Yarborough, Parnelli Jones, David Pearson, Buddy Baker and Bobby
Rahal, among others, including family patriarch Glen.

The Woods never ran a large-scale operation on the level of a Holman-Moody
or a Jack Roush. It was almost always a one-car team, but it was one team that was
a contender in many years and remains a member of the NASCAR Establishment.

The best years were in the early '70s, when A.J. Foyt and David Pearson combined for eight wins in 20 starts in 1972—and led every race—and 1973 through '78, when Pearson won a total of 37 races in 124 starts, a mark hardly approached since by any other driver. But they're still going, and the number 21 is a fixture at Winston Cup events.

Wood is in his mid-70's now, still lean, almost angular, and the father of Eddie, Len and daughter Kim, who run the operation now. Glen himself is retired, but Leonard still puts in some time with the team.

When it all started he was part owner of a sawmill and in 1950, "Another friend of mine, Gifford Wood, he's no kin to me, he was driving a little bit at the time, and my brother in law, he says, 'Why don't we go down and watch Gifford run, he's going to practice some,' so we went down there [to a quarter-mile dirt track in Horse Pasture, a few miles east of Stuart] and I had a little '39 Ford coupe myself and had a new set of tires on it.... So he's runnin' around out there and things got a little dull, and I had my car inside the track so I just got out there with it, and it was geared exactly right to run it in second gear and I got to runnin' around out there and just kept getting a little faster and faster and I was runnin' about as good as he was—with my stock vehicle!"

The path from there was a typical one: Buy a flathead Ford, run it on dirt tracks in the area, then move up to NASCAR, which Glen and his brothers did in 1953. He was a factor in NASCAR's short-lived convertible division in 1956 and '57, but running the team became more important than driving for it, and by the time Tiny Lund won the 1963 Daytona 500 in their car Glen was about finished as a driver. The team was behind four of Dan Gurney's five Riverside road-course wins, plus one there with Parnelli Jones as the driver, and they became famous in a larger arena when they were the pit crew for Jimmy Clark's Indianapolis victory with a Lotus-Ford in 1965.

They survived Ford's shutdown years of the '70s, but at times it was a near thing, such as the adventure of 1975–76 that involved what were called the Australian Blocks. Special castings for race teams stopped when the company ceased supporting the sport in the U.S. in the fall of 1970, and a year later the situation was critical. Not only were there no castings, but the machining equipment had been shipped to Ford of Australia.

Don Tope, a retired vice-president of North American manufacturing planning and sympathetic to the race teams' plight, arranged to have a number of special castings made, shipped to Australia and returned to the U.S. There was, however, a catch:

"He said he knew the need for a good block," Wood says, "and if we could get so many together to say they would take so many blocks, he would do them himself.... Holman (Holman Automotive, not Holman-Moody, which was no longer in existence) might have taken 50 or 100, I had to take 20, and back then I didn't have that much money to do that with, but I knew if we were going to race ... so I agreed to take 20 ... I think it was $500 apiece.... And we weren't getting the blocks quick because they had to be shipped to Australia, so Don said if somebody would take five or six blocks, he would hand do 'em in Dearborn and get them to us in time for the Daytona 500, otherwise we wouldn't have gotten them back—but it would cost $1000 or $1500 to get it that way.... So I said well, there's no use goin' to Daytona without it, so fix me one at least, so he fixed the one, Tommy Turner at Holman's put it all together, we go down there and win the 500.... And that paid for the whole bunch of blocks, to say nothin' of winnin' the Daytona 500."

Daytona Beach 1976, on a wing and a prayer, David Pearson behind the wheel and one engine for practice, the preliminary races and the main event. No movie producer would ever buy the script. Especially the last lap, when Pearson and Petty collided within sight of the finish line and Pearson made it across on his starter motor while Petty watched, stalled in the infield.

Ned Jarrett

Ned Jarrett won his first NASCAR Grand National championship in 1961, and says, "I didn't know how to handle it.... I didn't know how to represent myself, my family, and the sport in the way that I felt I needed to, and I just wanted to do more for the sport than I was capable of doing. So I was looking around for ways to improve myself and I vowed that I'd win the championship again, and that I'd be better prepared for it the next time, so I took that Dale Carnegie course and of course that got a lot of attention.... Once you've taken that course you want to tell the world, and so they would seek me out for interviews, and when I announced my retirement ... The Universal Racing Network, the biggest racing network then, they came to me and asked me to sit in as an analyst, so that's how it really started.... it took a long long time to get to where it became a full-time job, because I started that in the latter part of 1966.... I didn't run all of the races in 1966, but it was about 1982 or '83 where it became full time, where I could make a living at it.... I had to do other things."

For Jarrett "other things" have gone by the wayside and he is now in his fourth decade as a NASCAR radio and television personality. He still lives in Newton, North Carolina, where he was born, but is long removed from the farming and sawmill labor of his youth. He was just 20 when, in 1952, he drove in the first race ever held at nearby Hickory Speedway, a half-mile dirt oval at the time, a place where Junior Johnson, Ralph Earnhardt and Gwyn Staley would be the heroes, and which, in later years, Jarrett would own.

His driving career meant working at the sawmill during the day and on the car at night, and by 1959 he was the two-time national sportsman champion, a title that was the '50s equivalent of today's Busch winner. Then it was time to move into the Grand National ranks. The first car was unreliable, but he found a 1957 Ford that had been driven by Johnson and was for sale for $2000.

The problem was he didn't have $2000. "So I told them," Jarrett says, "I'll go down there tomorrow morning and I'll buy that car, take it to Myrtle Beach—there was a race at Myrtle Beach Saturday night, a 100-miler, and then there was one at Charlotte on Sunday afternoon, on a half-mile track, and each of these races paid $950 to win.... And so I said I'll win those two races, that's $1900. They knew I didn't have any money so they asked how I was going to pay for it. I'd give the man a check and I'd cover that check before Monday morning.

"Anyway, I went down and bargained for that car on Saturday morning and got them to agree to let me take the truck, the crew chief and his helper, and an extra set of tires and the tools, all that I needed to go racing.... I didn't have anything but the desire and I got them to do all that for $2000, so we got through bargaining about 11 o'clock and I said, 'Well, I'll let you know.' Actually all I was waiting on was for the bank to close. Back then banks stayed open on Saturday until noon, and I knew they had their account in the same bank where I had mine, so I waited for the bank to close, and about five minutes after 12 I rushed back down there with the check and said, 'I'm set, let's go to Myrtle Beach!'

"So we managed to pull it off, we won both races, and that's how I really got started in Grand National. I ran that car in five races, won three of them, finished second in one and third in one. It was a good race car, and that set me up to run full time the next year.

"I ran Fords on my own, that I bought and paid for in 1960, and then Chevrolet came along and they were doing things under the table in 1961 and '62.... Vince Piggins is the guy I dealt with.... I couldn't make it on my own, I went in the hole in 1960—had mortgaged my soul, so when Chevrolet, through Rex White—he was running Chevrolets, he won the championship in 1960—said Chevrolet's interested in another young driver and I recommended you and they'd like to talk to you and so we did. They worked it out and all the parts and things came through Jim Rathmann down at Melbourne, Florida, that's where we went to pick up the cars.... I ran Chevrolet for two years simply because I got help from them and wasn't getting any from Ford and we lucked out and won the championship in '61.

"Then in September of 1963, Ford, Jacque Passino and I believe John Cowley, came to Darlington. They announced they were coming back into racing, they knew what Chevrolet had been doing under the table and, 'We're going to come out above the table and we're going to have four teams running under the Ford banner, that we would support,' and they came to me and asked if I would be interested in coming back to Ford and I jumped at the opportunity.... So that's when I went back to Ford and so that became the first time that I really became associated with Holman-Moody... The cars were built at Holman-Moody; they built the shell, the roll cages and put the bodies on them and then we took them to our shop and tailored them."

Jarrett won his second Grand National title in 1965. "I ran 54 races.... the majority of those races were 100-milers, you'd go in, practice, qualify and run the race.... There were times we might run Columbia on Thursday night, back at Charlotte on

Friday and maybe up at Hickory on Saturday! And maybe go up to Asheville and run on Sunday.... We'd run four races a week.

"You had Fireball Roberts and (Fred) Lorenzen who were driving for Holman-Moody, but Junior Johnson, he was on the deal, and the Wood Brothers were on the deal. We were given the cars and the parts and we were paid $2000 a race for every race 250 miles or longer.... There were 17 of those events, $34,000 a year, and that was a big deal, we were tickled to death to be on the Ford factory team."

Jarrett ran 59 races in 1964 and won 14 of them, did another 54 events in 1965, won 13 and was runner-up another 13 times and third ten times in a remarkable display of speed and consistency. He won a little over $77,000 in 1965. In the fall of that year he braved the flames while trying to pull Roberts out of his burning wreck at Charlotte, the next year he drove part of the season, and that was it. He'd won 50 Grand National races, the same as Johnson. "I set certain goals for myself and vowed however far up the ladder I got I'd quit while I was there, and I managed to reach those goals. I didn't retire because I had the money to retire."

He has spent the past few years watching his son Dale earn more for signing a contract than the entire NASCAR season paid in the early '60s—not for what he was paid personally, but what the entire circuit earned.

Times change.

Chapter 8

———●———

COMEBACK

The first cracks in the barrier to motorsports participation appeared in 1978, when the corporate policy and steering committee approved the expenditure of small sums for advertising that had performance-related cars in the background. Viewed from a distance of three decades this seems laughable, but it was an important step, because it was the first formal acknowledgement of a major marketing mistake. The next came in 1979 (actually begun in late 1978), when a Mustang was named as the pace car for the Indianapolis 500. At least now there was a Ford parked *next* to a racing car.

When Michael Kranefuss arrived in 1980, transferred from Europe with the assignment to return the North American arm to the racing arena, he found these first steps had already been taken. He also found places where the company had never left. He found the American motorsports scene a confusing agglomeration of sanctioning bodies, one on top of the other, at least several for each of the various forms of the sport, and people from each of these soon found him. They started calling for support as soon as they heard of Ford's return.

Kranefuss was from Muenster in what was then West Germany, and he was fascinated by motorsports to the point that he left his family's laundry business and got involved. This took him, in 1968, to be assistant to Jochen Neerpasch when the latter became Ford of Germany's first competition director. When Neerpasch left for the same job at BMW in 1972 Kranefuss took over, then became competition director of Ford of Europe in 1976, when that organization was given the responsibility for Germany and Britain.

His operation was derailed, to a degree, in 1974, when the energy crisis caused Ford to shut down his German racing effort, so he went looking for an outside team that would carry on. The result of the search was an organization called Zakspeed, which turned out, at least in Europe, to be successful. Rallying in Europe, less costly in those times, went on. Then Hayes moved to Dearborn and Bob Lutz, then chairman of Ford of Europe, brought in auto writer and ex-GM, ex-Fiat public relations man Karl Ludvigsen to fill Hayes' job, which included the motorsports oversight.

"Ludvigsen wanted to do the world sports car championship," says Kranefuss. "He wanted to do a brand-new rally car and he wanted to keep the thing going in

The debutante: Zakspeed Mustang, 1981 version.—Ford Motor Company

Germany, the touring car championship, for which we had no money, and within the company we had no support.... The times were completely wrong. So I talked to Walter and said, 'I'm not going to do this, and I can't get through to Lutz.'

"I need you to come over here for a couple of days," Hayes replied, "and tell me if we want to go back into racing [in the U.S.] what would you do." "I had been there a couple of times," Kranefuss says, "but I knew very little.... Jackie Stewart had taken me to one or two NASCAR races when he was with ABC Wide World of Sports, and I had been to Watkins Glen at some of the Formula One races, but that was about it.... So I came over in August and we talked, we talked with Red Poling (then executive vice president of North American Automotive Operations).... I love the man.... I always liked people who didn't give a damn about racing but who understood there's a business meaning behind it if you utilize it properly.

"After three days Walter took me to dinner and said, 'I'd like you to consider coming over here.'" The problem was that John Plant, a friend of Lutz's (who followed him from BMW to Ford of Europe), had already been chosen. This, however, was something Hayes would fix. Kranefuss called his wife, sold his new house in Germany, and was in America to stay. Plant became the marketing manager in the newly formed Special Vehicles Operation, or SVO, which for all practical purposes started work in January of 1981.

And there were restrictions, and problems. "So here I was," says Kranefuss, "and there were a lot of people from the old days who said, 'Why do they have to pick a ——— German? We could do the job 10 times better'.... There were three or four different philosophies within the company: We have to be in drag racing, we have to be in NASCAR, others said we have to be in road racing, we have to show what our new products are supposed to do.... Others said Indianapolis. I knew Walter wanted us to get back into road racing, and Poling wanted to stay away from NASCAR."

Now he was in Dearborn permanently, and he found things were different. He had Hayes as his sponsor, but he had no budget, he had few people in his department, and he found motorsports activities that were—for the moment, at least—outside his control. When Hayes got the go-ahead he informed the divisions and they had started looking for possibilities.

Motorcraft was first. The Parts and Service Division was struggling to make a name for itself after the Government's ten-year antitrust case again Autolite eliminated that brand name for the company in 1972. It was renamed Motorcraft, and sold filters, spark plugs, motor oil, wiring harnesses, shock absorbers and the like. It sold not only to the company dealer network, but also to independent garages, and Motorcraft needed whatever promotional help it could get.

Bob Glidden, in his day the Babe Ruth of the pro stock drag racers, had a Ford background, and was available since Chrysler's financial difficulties had caused that company to cancel Glidden's contract after one year. So he was signed—fortunately.

Then Ford Division found Lyn St. James to drive a Mustang in the IMSA Kelly American series. Company records of racing activity at this time have long since disappeared, but in all probability St. James' fall 1980 appearance at Road Atlanta was the first Ford-supported racing entry in a decade. Both of these were part of a joint effort with Firestone brokered by Gary Kohs, at the time a fringe player in Detroit promotional circles. Kohs also arranged for a U.S. team, using Escorts, to campaign in the Sports Car Club of America's national rally championship in 1982. In addition Kranefuss discovered that support for some of the off-road teams in Southern California had never stopped. Neither had Ford sponsorship of the Formula Atlantic series in Canada. They had simply been under the corporate radar.

All of these items led to months of turf battles unfortunately common in large companies, but they weren't the biggest problem. That was money, or the lack of it. Hayes and Kranefuss arrived in the middle of Ford's biggest financial crisis, one in which the company lost billions from 1979 through 1981. The average price of a share of Ford common stock dropped to $2.25 in 1981—a third of book value.

This was the atmosphere in the fall of 1980, when Hayes told Kranefuss to put a budget together. "And I asked if we had a limit," Kranefuss says, "and Walter said, 'No, just put together what you think. But keep in mind the company is really under a lot of stress right now.' So I arrived at, I think $7 million, and we presented it to Poling around October 15, and the only thing I knew was that when Red looked at the bottom line he went basically red. He didn't say a word."

Kranefuss waited for more than two weeks, then finally went to see Poling, whom he knew from their days in Europe. "He said," Kranefuss says, "'The maximum

I can spare for this is $2 million.' It was not that you didn't get anything for $2 million, but I said, 'I put a budget together as per instruction from Walter, I didn't know there's a limit, but let me tell you that for $2 million, you might as well save your $2 million.

"And he looked at me and said, 'I'll give you $4 million, and either you take it, or you can go back to Germany.' So I said, 'I'll take it,' and we struggled."

And so SVO was born.

Then there was the culture gap, both inside and outside the company. The many thousands of employees in the U.S. had not seen or heard anything about their company's involvement in motorsports for a decade, and now a campaign was needed to let them know what success in racing could do. Still other problems would come because of Ford's rotational system, in which people were supposed to move every three years or so in order to give them a better overview of their company. Kranefuss remembers his yearly interview with the personnel department, in which he was asked what he viewed as his next assignment. They never understood he was a racer, and that's where he wanted to stay.

The rotational system may have proven beneficial in other areas of the company, but it was a drawback to SVO (as the department would be known until 1999, when the name was changed to Ford Racing Technology, or FRT). Major manufacturer success in racing, on its higher levels, depends to a great degree on the maintaining of good relationships with sanctioning bodies and racing teams, relationships that take years to build. After Kranefuss left the company at the end of 1993, FRT would have three different leaders in the next five years. General Motors, on the other hand, has had two heads of its motorsports activities in 40 years. To the white-collar workers in the hundreds of departments in and around Dearborn, becoming a career racing person was considered "going native." It would put a dead-end sign on a career path. What most people didn't understand was that there were people—highly qualified, highly motivated people—who *wanted* to stay there.

All of that, relatively speaking, was the good news.

The bad news was that Ford, in 1980, had no product suitable for conversion to a competition car within the parameters established by budget and personnel limitations. SVO's mission was threefold: One part was to win races, another was to design limited-production, performance versions of Ford vehicles to make them more appealing. Finally, Ford needed to establish a high-performance parts catalog, a major task in itself.

There was also the problem of NASCAR, where Ford had pulled out in 1957, thanks to the AMA agreement, and again in 1970, and where there were still Ford-powered teams struggling, racing with outmoded equipment. Kranefuss knew Poling was against any involvement, he knew the primary objective was to, as he put it, "Emphasize agility, nimbleness, brakes. I supported the party line," he said, "but we knew we would have to be there eventually."

Because of this, and shortly after the department was created, Kranefuss and Len Pounds, a member of the 1960s racing group who would rejoin SVO, went to Daytona in November to pay a courtesy call on NASCAR, and were ushered in to Bill France the Elder. "I had met him a couple of times in Europe," Kranefuss said, "and we had a good discussion, then at the end he called his son in and told him what we were doing and Bill Junior said, 'Ford—that's all I need,' and walked out."

Whatever the attitude, an understandable one on the part of the Frances, the lack of suitable parts and funds meant NASCAR teams wouldn't be getting any help until at least the latter half of 1981.

And so it started. Special Vehicle Operations, at the outset, consisted of Kranefuss, Plant as the planning manager, Steve Lockwood in charge of finance, Glen Lyall as the engineering manager, Pounds in charge of performance operations, and Tom Rhoades as the public relations person. Moses (Mose) Nowland, another veteran of the '60s team, was brought back to assist with engineering duties, and his help would prove invaluable. Al Turner, also from the '60s, and Jerry Green were on board by the second quarter of 1981; Bill Westphal, who would eventually become performance parts manager, joined the team in late 1981, and the nucleus of an organization was formed. Bob Riley, possibly America's best racing car designer and a Ford employee early in his career, joined SVO in 1982 and spent time there before going on to other companies and finally to being a partner in Riley and Scott.

SVO even got help from Don Sullivan, the veteran engineer who joined the company in the late '20s (from Wills Sainte Claire) and who was one of the four men who conceived, designed and brought the flathead V8 to production in 18 months in the early '30s. Sullivan had been a vital part of the performance effort of the '60s,

The early staff: (left to right) Bob Riley, Michael Kranefuss, Glenn Lyall.
—Road and Track magazine

he was retired now, but eager to return. It was a disparate group, but they had one thing in common, and that was the desire to do well. Some of them, disdaining the "gone native" label, remained there for 20 years. Sullivan, even as a consultant, didn't leave until the early '90s, when he was in his '80s and troubled by a hip replacement that made it painful to stand.

For the moment, the Ford stock-car teams would have to wait. USAC single seaters of the Indianapolis variety were running with Cosworth engines, but this had nothing to do with Dearborn. Glidden, more or less on his own, was representing the company in drag racing, so what was left was road racing, where there could be opportunities in both International Motor Sports (IMSA) and Sports Car Club of America (SCCA) competition.

The quickest and cheapest way to become competitive, it was felt, was to bring Capris over from Germany, cars that were running in German events, cars that Kranefuss had shepherded through their development. IMSA was looking for new attractions, and Ford's return to competition would be the proverbial feather in IMSA's cap. All that was needed, basically, was to reskin the Capri tube frame with Mustang sheet metal. The SCCA's Trans Am series, for such as Mustangs and Camaros, required a car with a strong V8, one that could be developed into a racing powerplant, and there was nothing readily available. The engine in the St. James Mustang, for example, was put together from old blocks and even older heads.

Struggles and all, there was finally a program of sorts. But it would take time to be successful.

Chapter 9

FORMULA FORD—
THE WAY UP

There are many roads to a berth in major league motorsports, but the path to fame in single-seat, open-cockpit cars almost automatically goes through Formula Ford, a stepping-stone series popular in practically every country where there is racing.

Formula Ford was started—as was so much of the company's motorsports activity—in Britain, when the racing drivers school at the Brands Hatch circuit was running at a loss in 1967 due to the students' proclivity for crashing expensive rolling stock. Geoffrey Clarke, who ran the school, and John Webb, who ran Brands Hatch as well as three other circuits, came up with the specifications for a bargain-basement racing car that was nevertheless a real single seater.

They went to Bruce McLaren first, but the New Zealander was involved in his own projects and turned down the chance to build them on an assembly-line basis.

The first Formula Ford: Testing in 1967.—Ford Motor Company

Formula Ford, 1994 variety.—Ford Motor Company

The next port of call was Lotus, and the result was Model 51. It had a four-cylinder, 1.6-liter Cortina engine, with 86 horsepower in production form and about 105 after blueprinting, which was all the regulations allowed. Minimum weight, with driver, was 1135 pounds, and the cost was limited to £1000—about $2800 at 1967 rates of exchange. The ubiquitous Walter Hayes helped promote a club-racing category for the cars and gave it a name: Formula Ford.

This was a "real" racing car, looked remarkably similar to the Formula One cars of the time, and it behaved like one. You could get a lesson in vehicle behavior not possible in a sedan or sports car.

That was three decades ago. In the meantime, more than 190 different constructors have put together more than 6000 Formula Ford chassis and equipped them with Ford engines. There is some variance in engines, depending on the country and the series. In Britain the 1.8-liter Zetec engine is now standard, although there are still races for older, 1.6-liter cars. In the U.S. the professional series, known as the US F2000 series, employs a 2.0-liter engine formerly used in the Pinto, but is considering a move to the Zetec engine currently used in the Focus. Although practically every racing car builder of note has had a crack at doing one of these (tube frame only, no carbon fiber), the leader is Van Diemen, the British firm that has built more than 2500 of them, and which was taken over in 2000 by Don Panoz, the American pharmaceutical products manufacturer who has become in factor in sports-car racing (the American Le Mans series).

Two-time world champion and Indianapolis 500 winner Emerson Fittipaldi was the first star to graduate from Formula Ford to the Formula One ranks, winning the British Formula Ford title in 1969 and his first world championship three years later.

Nigel Mansell, Ayrton Senna, Michael Schumacher, Mika Hakkinen and Damon Hill were all graduates of the class on their way to world championships. So are Michael Andretti and even Winston Cup driver Jerry Nadeau.

The cost limit, as with practically every other price ceiling in the history of auto racing, soon proved unworkable and was abandoned in 1969, the second full year of Formula Ford activity. At present, a Formula Ford "roller" from one of the better manufacturers—a complete car with the exception of the engine—costs nearly $50,000. A racing engine of the Pinto variety costs $13,000 and has a life, before rebuild, of perhaps 800 miles. Running a full season on the pro circuit can run anywhere from $200,000 to more than $300,000, far more than the total purse or contingency money available for an individual car.

The first national run-offs in the U.S. were held in the fall of 1969 at Daytona and were won by Skip Barber, the Harvard-educated production manager for a small racing car builder who went on to become the owner of this country's largest group of competition driving schools. Today, the US F2000 national championship consists of a 14-race series, with each being run in conjunction with U.S. Auto Club midget races, or as preliminaries to Grand American sports-car events or CART races.

The US F2000 series is only the tip of the iceberg: The Sports Car Club of America runs dozens of races as part of its national championship program, and during the season there will be Formula Ford events almost every weekend, at road circuits in the U.S. Dan Anderson of Formula Motorsports, which runs the American professional series, estimates that there are now between 800 and 1000 Formula Ford cars in the United States, counting the ones in the hands of SCCA members. At present there are between 40 and 50 new-car sales per year, added to those built and sold since the late '60s.

Although the rate at which different drivers advance varies greatly—and some do not advance at all—Formula Ford, if we are not considering stock-car racing, is the first "real car" after go-karts. It is one of the steps on the way up to Formula One (which has room for only 24 drivers), to CART, to the IRL or other single-seat classes, including the midgets and sprint cars that are staples of American oval-track competition. US F2000 is considered the step just below Formula Atlantic, three steps below a CART car (otherwise known as a "Champ" car, this misnomer being left over from the days when the AAA single-seater program was considered the only true national championship series).

The way up through the various racing car classes, much of which is unintelligible to the non-fan, is based, more or less, on power-to-weight ratios. A typical American four-door sedan, a Taurus, for instance, weighs about 3350 pounds. Add a 175-pound driver and you have approximately 3530 pounds. Divide this by the car's 200 horsepower and the power-to-weight ratio is roughly 17.65 to 1.

Today's Formula One cars, have a weight (with driver) of approximately 1300 pounds and the better ones have, at a conservative estimate, 800 horsepower. This gives us a ratio of roughly 1.6 to 1, or about ten times more powerful than the Taurus. There is a long way from basic automotive transportation to the top of the racing pyramid, and there are many steps in between.

The rungs on the ladder vary from the U.S. to Europe and there are all sorts of fringe classes, but in general the pattern is the following (the horsepower figures are average ratings, not the maximum of the fastest cars):

Europe

- Formula Ford—1.8-liter Ford production engine, 130 hp, min. weight 1190 lbs. without driver.

- Formula Three—2.0-liter four-cylinder limit (non-production), 26 mm restrictor, 220 hp, min. weight 1190 lbs. without driver.

- Formula 3000—3.0-liter V8, 9000 rpm limit, 450 hp, min. weight 1190 lbs. without driver.

- Formula One—3.0-liter, 10 cylinders, 800 hp, min. weight 1320 lbs. with driver.

United States

- Formula Ford—2.0-liter modified Ford production engine, 150 hp, min. weight 1190 lbs. with driver.

- Formula Atlantic—2.0-liter Toyota 4-cylinder, 240 hp, min. weight 1265 lbs. without driver.

- Indy Lights—3.8-liter Buick V6, 450 hp, min. weight 1430 lbs. without driver.

- IRL—3.5-liter "production-derived" V8, 9500 rpm limit, 650 hp, min. weight 1550 lbs. without driver.

- CART—2.65-liter turbocharged 800 hp, min. weight 1550 lbs. without driver.

There are dozens of other "formulas," such as Formula Vee (Volkswagen based), Formula Palmer (Audi based), Formula Renault and so on, but those listed above are by far the most popular.

The vehicles designed for shorter oval tracks in the U.S. are midgets and sprint cars, and their specifications can vary from one sanctioning body to another, but a good general description is as follows:

- Midgets—2.0–3.0 liters, depending on engine type, approx. 340 hp on alcohol fuel, min. weight 900–1000 pounds, depending on engine type and without driver, wheelbases vary from 66 to 76 inches.

- Sprint cars—unlimited class has 410-inch pushrod engines, approx. 810 hp on alcohol fuel; those with no minimum weight are in the neighborhood of 1250 pounds without driver. Wheelbases vary but are in the neighborhood of 86 inches.

Both of these classes are purely American, created here and developed here over many years. They are strictly for ovals and comprise one of the toughest schools in all of racing. The top sprint cars, for example, have a power-to-weight ratio roughly the same as Formula One cars, and are considerably more difficult to handle. But they are another path to the top, and drivers from these ranks wind up everywhere in the racing firmament. Two of NASCAR's top attractions, Jeff Gordon and Tony Stewart, come from the midget and sprint-car circuits, and they drove Karts before that.

The other starting point, especially popular in Europe and Latin America, is through Karts, which have long since shed the name "go-kart" they carried when first developed in the 1930s, and when they became popular in Southern California in the early '50s. Karts now run in three competition classes: 80cc, 125cc, and 250cc, with the latter having six-speed transmissions, and they are fast. The 250cc two-stroke engines produce approximately 80 horsepower, and with a minimum weight limit of 400 pounds (driver and cart) that works out to a power-to-weight ratio of 5 lb/hp. They have a top speed of better than 120 mph. A NASCAR Winston Cup car, weighing about 3750 pounds with a full load of fuel and a 175-pound driver, has an engine that produces approximately 760 horsepower, and that gives us a power-to-weight ratio of 4.93, roughly the same as that of the 250cc Kart.

This is not to draw any comparison between the two, but rather to demonstrate the potency of Karts, which on short, tight courses would naturally be much faster than a Winston Cup car. Their steering is direct, and there is no better training ground for an aspiring driver. Mario Andretti remembers seeing his son Michael, at the age of nine, running over 100 mph in a Kart.

But much of it started with a Formula Ford, weighing about 1000 pounds and costing the same.

Chapter 10

◆

ALPHABET SOUP

The thoroughbreds of American racing have always been purpose-built single seaters, machines designed expressly for competition and with performance that makes ordinary passenger cars pale by comparison. These were the cars of Barney Oldfield and Ralph DePalma, of Frank Lockhart and Rex Mays, of Wilbur Shaw and Bill Vukovich and Parnelli Jones, of A.J. Foyt and Mario Andretti, and the Indianapolis Motor Speedway was their great stage.

These were the cars that competed for the so-called national championship, which since its inception in 1909 was sanctioned by the American Automobile Association, more commonly known as the AAA.

They ran at ovals scattered around the country, but the Indianapolis Motor Speedway, the colossus of the Midwest, was the nexus, and it was paid tribute by the manner in which the racing community referred to it. One spoke of DuQuoin, or Milwaukee, or Syracuse, but when discussing Indianapolis, "the Speedway," with a capital S, was enough. One knew what the speaker meant.

The post-World War II years saw the AAA act somewhat like the dog in the manger of Aesop's Fables, being more interested in building what had become a profitable insurance business than it was in sanctioning races. But it kept control of what was considered the championship and did not look kindly on upstart competing organizations.

In the early 1950s AAA Chief Steward Harry McQuinn had NASCAR President Bill France escorted from the Speedway garage area by uniformed officers. Any AAA driver who so much as bought a ticket to watch a NASCAR race could be punished, and no less than Bill Holland, winner of the 1949 Indianapolis 500, was banned after participating in a NASCAR event.

Then, in 1955, the AAA found the excuse that many of its officials had been seeking, and it was twofold: Bill Vukovich, the two-time winner of the 500, was killed on Memorial Day while seeking his third consecutive victory. Eleven days later, there was the Le Mans accident that killed driver Pierre Levegh and more than 80 spectators. With an eye toward the liability problems a similar incident could cause in the U.S., the AAA bowed out. The single-seat fraternity, with the Speedway ownership as godfather, formed the U.S. Auto Club, a Midwest-oriented organization that had the Speedway as the center of its solar system. Whatever the name of the sanctioning body, the Indianapolis 500 remained the same—the dream, however distant, of any American kid who ever drove a race car, and the sociological phenomena that attracted the country's notice every Memorial Day weekend.

The attention was directed at the winner, at the sight of the world's largest one-day sporting crowd, at the celebrities who attended—but not at the fact that the colorful, beautifully constructed "roadsters" of the 1950s and early '60s were examples of an outmoded design. Rear-engined cars had been successful in Europe since the mid-'30s and standard fare in grand prix and sports-car racing for several years, but somehow this message escaped the USAC community. Whether it was an isolationist streak, sheer thick-headedness or a lack of design skills (most probably the latter, which brought with it the first two), Indianapolis and its satellites had turned into a parade of high-speed dinosaurs, until Ford changed all that in 1963.

Ford engineers created the powerplants that Colin Chapman used in Jimmy Clark's Lotus, and the company financed the venture. By the late '60s the Ford Indianapolis engine was dominant and the Speedway was attracting more attention than ever before. The track was overseen by Anton (Tony) Hulman, the Ivy Leaguer from down-state Terre Haute who had been talked into buying the place by Shaw in 1945. The price was $750,000 (and a few days later he reportedly sold the concession rights for 10 years for the same sum).

Hulman invested millions in improving the Speedway, and he knew better than to fool with tradition. The facility and racing prospered, or at least prospered in what was accepted as the normal state of affairs, with the Speedway being the sun around which the planets—namely the smaller events counting for

Tony Hulman: The power in American single-seater racing.—Courtesy Indianapolis Motor Speedway

Jimmy Clark: The first Ford winner, 1965.—Ford Motor Company

the championship—would revolve. In the meantime, the alphabet-soup progression of acronyms was under way. The AAA had relinquished its position and USAC had taken over, and now, in the late '70s, the car owners were unhappy.

The attention boost Indianapolis had received in the mid-'60s, thanks to Ford's involvement and the accompanying new and different cars, plus the advent of television coverage, gave American open-cockpit racing another push away from the state-fair atmosphere in which it had survived for decades. Other sports were taking advantage of television exposure, most notably golf, and their purses were growing at a rapid rate. At the same time, despite phrases such as national championship, auto racing was for many who pursued it a hand-to-mouth existence. The successful car owners were by and large men who had made their fortunes in other endeavors and owned cars much as some of their peers owned race horses. For those who raced as a full-time occupation, however, it was not nearly as remunerative.

There were various reasons for the car owners' unhappiness, one of which was the fact that USAC was a "race-day" organization. The officials would arrive, conduct technical inspection, practice, the race, and then go home. They were professional in what they did, but promotion was left to the individual track owners, and this was, on a national basis, conspicuous by its absence. At the same time the NASCAR circuit was receiving the benefit of R.J. Reynolds' promotional dollars for the Winston Cup. In Europe Bernie Ecclestone was beginning to make better deals for the Formula One teams, even though they were still a long way from the millions they would command in the '90s. The comparisons, which were inevitable, were not good.

Then Hulman died unexpectedly in October of 1977, and this left a vacuum at the top. Although he held no administrative position in the U.S. Auto Club, there was no question Hulman was the decision maker if policies were to be changed. He was succeeded, for the interim, by family retainer Joe Cloutier, who was in a caretaker status at best. Then, in late April of the following year, eight USAC officials, including respected technical supervisor Frankie Delroy, were killed in a light-plane crash while returning to Indianapolis from a race at Trenton. It was perhaps more subconscious than anything else, but the car owners' confidence in USAC dropped to a new low.

The next step came later in 1978, when the car owners elected their representative to the USAC board. U.E. (Pat) Patrick, the Michigan oil man who was one of the wealthier owners and one of the more outspoken in the group, expected to be elected easily—and wasn't. The nod went to Rolla Vollstedt, the Oregon car owner respected for his ethical behavior, but far down the list when it came to net worth. Patrick took this as something of a personal insult, and this put him solidly in the ranks of those looking to form a new organization.

Al Unser Sr.: First Cosworth winner, 1978.—Ford Motor Company

Another push came in the form of a letter from Dan Gurney, now a team owner, to a number of the other owners, including Roger Penske and Patrick. It was written in the spring of the year and was a review of the state of open-wheel racing in the U.S., and it helped tip the scales. CART—Championship Auto Racing Teams—was established in the fall, and then in late November USAC turned down a proposal that would give CART equal representation on the USAC board.

By mid-December CART had made an agreement with the Sports Car Club of America to act as its sanctioning body, and the deed was done. In the spring of 1979 CART went to court to be allowed to race in the USAC-sanctioned Indianapolis 500 and won, but the relationship was never good after that. CART gave championship points for running in someone else's league, and a clash was inevitable.

What the CART owners had failed to realize was they didn't need a new organization, they needed a qualified promoter to run single-seat racing. NASCAR was run by a promoter—the France family, who were promoters first and track owners second. Formula One racing was being run by a promoter—Ecclestone. CART would be run by a junta of car owners with varied interests who treated the men they hired as operating heads as just that—hired hands.

Veteran racing executive John Cooper assumed the presidency of the Speedway after the 1979 race—too late to dissuade the CART car owners. When Cooper left in 1982 Cloutier once again assumed the presidency until grandson Anton Hulman (Tony) George took over in 1989 at the age of 30. By the time George assumed leadership major league open-wheel racing in the U.S. had undergone the AAA-USAC-CART metamorphosis, or alphabet soup in action.

Then George took the damage that had been done and added to it in a manner that ensured this most sophisticated level of American racing would take an apparently permanent back seat to stock cars when it came to attendance, television ratings and sponsor appeal. His family had been the caretaker of American racing's premier series for five decades, and in one step he disavowed his inheritance. His intentions were honorable, and for that matter a response to certain pressures from CART, but the split he created in the single-seat community gave NASCAR its best-ever opportunity to become the fans' primary choice.

The primacy of open-cockpit racing, taken for granted for the past nine decades, would disappear in a battle over turf.

Tony George: The successor.
—Courtesy Indianapolis Motor Speedway

In the fall of 1993 George began talking about an all oval-track series, and about lowering the cost of racing, and at first no one took him seriously. Then, in the fall of 1995, after months of listening to the pleas of Ford and other manufacturers—but with behind-the-scenes advice from GM, which wanted a series for itself, he announced the formation of IRL. Thus was born the Indy Racing League, and the split was official in time for the 1996 season. Most of the CART owners stayed with their organization, the principal exception being A.J. Foyt, who had a close relationship to the Hulman-George family. The IRL, in the eyes of the public, was relegated, almost immediately, to minor league status.

One of the results of the split was an ongoing series of secret negotiations designed to bring the two organizations back together, or to at least provide for a common engine formula. This would allow major manufacturers to participate in both series, if they desired, and would make it easier for CART teams to participate at Indianapolis. Most importantly for CART, it would give the organization a decent selling point in its search for major sponsorships and television money. A season-long advertising campaign can be built around one Indianapolis win. Hardly anything can be done with victories at Portland or Laguna Seca. Negotiations went on, and on, and on. The two sides were close in the summer of 1999, and were close again in January of 2000, but in each case, nothing happened. And Tony George, who was financing the money-losing IRL, more than made up for his losses with revenues from the Brickyard 400 and—beginning in 2000—the Grand Prix of the United States.

In the meantime NASCAR had built up a figurative two-lap lead in the contest for fan attention and sponsor dollars. NASCAR's Brickyard 400, inaugurated in 1994, would become the toughest ticket for any race at the Speedway.

All of this, however, came later. In the late 1960s USAC was supreme, and the Indianapolis 500 was the alpha and omega of a single-seat driver's existence.

1968

It is a year of revolts, with French students and New Leftists starting the movement that would unseat Charles de Gaulle.... Riots at the Democratic national convention in Chicago are instrumental in electing Republic Richard Nixon in the fall.... The "Prague Spring," which sees free thought rise up behind the Iron Curtain, is crushed by Soviet troops.

Mario Andretti was already established as the contender for A.J. Foyt's position as the top open-wheel driver in America, Parnelli Jones had retired to his business interests and part-time participation in Trans-Am racing and the like. USAC had made certain rules modifications that gave an advantage back to the turbocharged four-cylinder Offenhauser, with the impetus for this coming from the Champion spark plug company. Champion, for years dominant at Indianapolis, had been in the shadows ever since the Ford engines appeared, since Ford owned Autolite (at the time) and Autolite plugs were therefore in the majority. USAC had also modified its turbine rules so that Jones' almost-winning car of the previous year had a greater handicap. Nevertheless, Joe Leonard and 1966 winner Graham Hill managed to qualify 1-2 in STP-sponsored cars that were similar to Jones' 1967 mount. Art Pollard, in a third STP turbine, qualified eleventh.

The race itself went to Bobby Unser in an Eagle chassis equipped with a turbo Offy. Gurney himself finished second in a pushrod V8 Ford equipped with Weslake cylinder heads, but nine of the first eleven finishers had Offys. In 12th and 13th were Leonard and Pollard. Leonard had mechanical problems on the 190th lap when he was in the lead and at least figuratively in sight of the checkered flag, and Pollard was affected by the same fuel shaft problem three laps earlier. Hill crashed on his 111th lap.

The national championship, run over 28 races in 1968, went to Bobby Unser in the closest finish in USAC history, with Andretti second and brother Al Unser third. Bobby won five races, including four in a row; Al won five, and won them consecutively. Andretti and Foyt won four apiece, while Gurney, using his stock-block engine, won three—all on road courses. For Andretti, the runner-up finish was part of a five-year period in which he would win the championship three times (1965-66-69) and finish second twice (67-68).

The final point standings: Bobby Unser (Ford-Eagle, Drake/Offy Eagle) 4330, Mario Andretti (Ford-Brawner Hawk, Offy-Kuzma) 4319, Al Unser (Offy-Ward, Ford-Lola) 2895.

1969

> *"The Godfather" and "Ragtime" are two of the most popular new novels.... "Midnight Cowboy," starring Jon Voight and Dustin Hoffman, makes its debut.... Philip Morris purchases Miller Brewing.... ATM machines appear in New York City.*

The turbocharged Ford V8 was cured of most of its development problems by this year's "500," except for one problem which grew in importance as the race neared—the engine would overheat at high revs, and its life expectancy for what could be a three-hour race was questionable at best.

Andretti was driving for STP king Andy Granatelli, who had been trying to win for the past 20 years, and whose turbine cars had succumbed to minor engine malfunctions with victory in sight in the past two. He had been rookie of the year in 1965 and had already elevated himself to where he was one of the best drivers in the U.S., if not the world, and so it was assumed that before he was through he would win at Indianapolis at least several times. For the 1969 race he had one of Colin Chapman's newest Lotuses, a four-wheel drive creation.

Mario Andretti: Winning in 1969.—Ford Motor Company

Andretti: "It was so much more advanced than everything else.... I was loving it, but a blessing that happened was that the damn thing was so fragile that it broke a hub and the wheel came off. I know I would have been on pole ... but I would have been another DNF."

"So, all of a sudden, what do we have? We had this Brawner, this Hawk.... We won Hanford with that car but it was not even cleaned up, just stuck in a corner of the garage. Two days before qualifying we're relegated to that car, and I put that car in the middle of the front row.... To qualify fast enough we took off all the external radiators, but since we qualified without them they wouldn't let us put them back on for the race."

So 1969, despite qualifying second behind A.J. Foyt, was doubtful as long as the engine was running so hot. After qualifying crew chief Clint Brawner installed an extra oil cooler behind the roll bar, only to have it ruled out, as that constituted changing the configuration of the car from its qualifying trim. The night before the race Brawner and Ford's Dan Jones locked the garage door and installed another radiator under the driver's seat, where no one would see it. Mario won the race by two laps from Gurney's stock-block Ford, and won it without a tire change. The first five places were filled by four different engines, the two Ford varieties, two turbo Offys, and a Repco (GM-based) Brabham in fifth driven by first-time driver Peter Revson. It would be the only time he would win the Indianapolis 500.

The season encompassed 24 races, and Andretti was dominant, finishing with almost twice as many points as runner-up Al Unser. He won nine events, including the Pike's Peak hillclimb (which counted for the title in those years) and dirt-track races at hometown Nazareth, Pennsylvania, and Springfield, Illinois.

The final point standings: Mario Andretti (Ford-Brawner Hawk, Chevrolet-King, Offy-Kuzma) 5025, Al Unser (Ford-Lola, Ford-King) 2630, Bobby Unser (Drake-Offy Eagle), 2585.

1970

The New York Knickerbockers defeat the Los Angeles Lakers for the NBA title in a seven-game series.... Monday night football on television makes its debut.... 18-year-olds are given the vote in Federal elections.... Brazil wins the World Cup.

Parnelli Jones, now a car owner with Maurice Philippe as designer, a turbo-charged Ford in the tail of his PJ Colt chassis and Al Unser as his driver, won his first Indianapolis 500 as a team owner. Unser qualified fastest and led most of the way, including most of the last 100 laps, and did it on one set of tires. Ford turbos took five of the first six spots, with Gurney—who got Ford involved in Indianapolis in 1962—placing third with an Offenhauser engine in his Eagle. It was Unser's first win at Indianapolis, and Ford's fifth since coming back to Indiana in 1963.

It was Al's year. He won 10 of the 18 races, including all five of the dirt-track events as this phase of USAC championship competition came to a close with a 100-mile race at Sacramento in the fall. All of Unser's wins, including the dirt-track ones, were powered by a version of Ford's Indianapolis V8, turbocharged for the pavement races, naturally aspirated for the dirt tracks. It was the last year the company would have direct oversight. In the fall, Ford pulled out.

While Unser was dominant there was something else happening to single-seater championship racing. It was the performance of newcomers, including Mark Donohue in Roger Penske's Lola. They made their Indianapolis debut the year before and Donohue qualified fourth and finished seventh. Now he started fifth and finished second. The Penske-Donohue team had been successful in every type of racing they had entered and now they were fixing their attention on USAC and the Speedway, not only the most famous venue in America, but also the one with the biggest potential payoff in purses and sponsorship fees.

When Ford withdrew from racing in the fall, the entire Indianapolis engine inventory, parts and so on, was sold to A.J. Foyt for $1, which upset a number of other teams, including 1970 winner Vel's-Parnelli Jones. Dan Jones was dispatched to Houston and set up Foyt's engine business for him, down to making recommended shop layouts and designing ordering forms. Howard Gilbert, one of the country's better engine men, was hired to run the operation.

Although the engines were to be known as "Foyts" from then on, A.J. didn't get around to installing new valve covers for a year, so the 1971 results, in most record books, still list the engines as Fords.

The final point standings: Al Unser (Ford-Colt, Ford-King) 5130, Bobby Unser (Drake-Offy-Eagle) 2260, Jim McElreath (Ford-Coyote) 2060.

1971

Mariner 9 becomes the first spacecraft to orbit another planet—Mars. ... Bobby Jones dies after a long illness. ... Walt Disney World opens near Orlando, Florida. ... Loretta Lynn's "Coal Miner's Daughter" becomes her biggest hit.

Al Unser and Parnelli's team made it two in a row at the 500, and it was the third straight for the turbo version of Ford's Indianapolis engine and also for Firestone, the longtime dominator of American single-seater racing. Jones and Vel Miletich, his business partner in various ventures, had Unser and veteran Joe Leonard in their two cars, with the latter placing 19th in a race that saw Unser pull away from eventual runner-up Revson and Foyt in the closing stages.

The regular season saw Leonard win the national championship, now down to twelve races, including two in Rafaela, Argentina, on the same day. Leonard only won one race and Al Unser won five, but the points favored Leonard due to his reliability record. Ford-engined cars finished first in eight of the events.

The final point standings: Joe Leonard (Ford-Colt) 3016, A.J. Foyt (Foyt-Coyote) 2320, Bill Vukovich, Jr. (Brabham-Offy) 2250.

1972

President Nixon meets with Chinese leaders in Beijing. ... Federal Express is founded. ... Bobby Fischer defeats Boris Spassky for the chess championship. ... DDT is banned.

Rules changes that allowed bigger wings both front and rear, thus improving roadholding, led to the greatest increase in qualifying speeds in the history of the Indianapolis Motor Speedway. Whereas Revson sat his McLaren on the 1971 pole with an average of 178.7 mph, this year it was Bobby Unser, driving one of Gurney's Eagles with a turbocharged Offy that averaged 195.9—an improvement of 17 miles per hour.

There was only one car in the starting field that had "Ford" on its valve covers, and ten more that said "Foyt," with the rest being Offenhausers. Mark Donohue had one of the latter, which he put on the front row in qualifying and then won the race, leading only 13 laps and winning when his Penske teammate Gary Bettenhausen dropped out while in front with only 24 laps to go. This would prove to be the first of ten Indianapolis victories for Penske-led teams, as he built an organization that would bring new standards of professionalism to the sport.

The engine in Donohue's car had been purchased at the last minute from Parnelli Jones, as the Offys were suffering from reliability problems and Penske was short of powerplants. Donohue used a Garrett turbo in the race that was smaller than the ones originally employed in practice.

The regular season was down to ten events and Leonard won three of them, this time with the chassis named after team co-owner Jones. Bobby Unser won four times but points were awarded based on the length of a race. Leonard's trio included the 500-miler at Pocono; his reliability record was also much better, and so he wound up with the title.

Ford's domination of the series came to an end. All events were won by cars with the turbocharged four-cylinder Drake-Offenhauser.

The final point standings: Joe Leonard (Drake-Offy-Parnelli) 3460, Bill Vukovich, Jr. (Drake-Offy-Eagle) 2200, Roger McCluskey (Drake-Offy-McLaren) 1970.

1973

Eric Lindros, Monica Seles are born; Pablo Picasso, Eddie Rickenbacker die.... The new Sears Tower in Chicago becomes the world's tallest building—1454 feet.... Secretariat wins the Triple Crown.... Britain joins the European Economic Community.

———◆———

It rained at Indianapolis on Memorial Day, but after four hours the 500 finally started—and ended before the first lap was completed when Salt Walther crashed on the front straight, taking eleven other cars with him and injuring eleven spectators behind the protective fence. By the time everything was cleaned up, it rained again. It rained again Tuesday, and for the first time America's classic was postponed twice. On Wednesday it rained again, but only after 133 laps, so the race could be declared official, and given to leader Gordon Johncock.

By that time promising newcomer Swede Savage had been severely injured in one crash, and a crewman was killed in the pits, hit by a fire truck rushing to the Savage accident. Savage would hang on for 34 days before succumbing. The starting field of 33—if one counts Walther—included 25 turbocharged Offenhausers, six Foyts, and one turbocharged stock-block Chevrolet.

Roger McCluskey, a good but not outstanding driver and a veteran of the front-engined roadsters, wound up as the 1973 champion, a season that saw the schedule grow to 16 events. That number, however, included doubleheaders at Trenton in April, Ontario in August and Michigan in September. Wally Dallenbach, years later to be the chief steward for CART, won three races as Savage's replacement, as did Gordon Johncock. Foyt won two, equipped with the former Ford engines, now with "Foyt" on the cam covers. McCluskey had one victory, a 200-miler at Michigan Speedway.

The final point standings: Roger McCluskey (Drake-Offy-McLaren) 3705, Wally Dallenbach (Drake-Offy-Eagle) 2620, Johnny Rutherford (Drake-Offy-McLaren) 2595.

1974

The energy crisis brings with it a national speed limit of 55 mph. ... Congress passes the Freedom of Information Act over President Ford's veto. ... Multi-function, hand-held calculators replace the slide rule.

It was the summer of the year, and Vel Miletich and Jimmy Dilamarter, one a principal of Vel's-Parnelli Jones various racing teams and the other manager of the Formula One effort, were flying back to Britain from a race on the Continent. While en route they talked about the Cosworth DFV Formula One engine, and how it might be adapted for American oval-track racing.

"So we went to Northampton and saw [Cosworth founder] Keith Duckworth and told him what we wanted, and ... he looked at us like we had two heads," says Dilamarter.

So they went back home and talked about it some more, "and then," Dilamarter says, "we went back to see Duckworth and asked him to sell us some engine parts. We needed blocks and some other stuff, but we didn't need things like crankshafts, con rods or pistons." They were told you buy the entire engine or nothing. Eventually they bought three engines—disassembled—and shipped them back to California in 1975.

The USAC season saw the Offys again dominant, winning 12 of the 14 races, the only exceptions being the two Foyt won with his made-over Ford and benefitting from a change in USAC specifications for turbochargers. On the chassis side this was still the era of Dan Gurney's Eagles. They won eight events, McLarens took four and Foyt's Coyotes were involved in his two wins.

At the Indianapolis Motor Speedway the principal change was that for the first time the race would be run on the Sunday of Memorial Day weekend, rather than on Memorial Day itself. Johnny Rutherford, driving a McLaren chassis with Offy engine, survived a mid-race duel with Foyt (who had engine trouble on the 139th lap) and won handily, despite starting in 25th place. This was the first of his three victories and also the first for McLaren, now headed by American Teddy Mayer. There were 28 Offys in the starting field. Andretti, again one of the favorites, lasted just two laps before a broken piston sidelined him.

Bobby Unser, driving for Gurney, won three of the season's 14 events and the championship, which again included doubleheaders, this time at Ontario in March and Trenton in September. Rutherford won four, Foyt and Johncock two each.

The final point standings: Bobby Unser (Drake-Offy-Eagle) 4870, Johnny Rutherford (Drake-Offy-McLaren) 3650, Gordon Johncock (Drake-Offy-Eagle) 3050.

1975

*Lyme Disease is diagnosed in Lyme, Connecticut.... "A Chorus Line"
opens on Broadway and eventually runs for 15 years and more than 6000
performances.*

Firestone, which had won 43 races in a row at Indianapolis beginning in 1920
and which had now lost the last three to Goodyear, withdrew from racing as part of
its preparation for being sold to Japanese tire maker Bridgestone. Its crosstown
rival was now alone at the top of the heap in the U.S. The Firestone cutback was
also having a negative effect on the Vel's-Parnelli Jones efforts, with this team being
Firestone supported.

The team's adaptation of the Cosworth F1 engine was far enough along, however, to make its appearance at the 500, and was fitted into an F1 chassis used for the
grand prix effort. The engine ran well, but roadholding and handling problems with
the chassis caused Vel's-Parnelli drivers Andretti and Al Unser to qualify with Offy-
powered Eagles. Sixteen of them were in the 500, one in the hands of winner Bobby
Unser and entered by Gurney's All American racers, in an event that was stopped by
rain after 174 of the scheduled 200 laps. It was Unser's second win and the fourth
for his family, brother Al also having won twice at this juncture.

The season—13 events with only one doubleheader, at Ontario—saw the revival
of Foyt, the great veteran of American racing, who at the age of 42 won seven races
and his sixth national championship.

What didn't come out until several years later was the news that Foyt's Coyote
chassis had undergone a redesign by Bob Riley. He was a Ford engineer who would
take leaves of absence from time to time to work on racing projects—and who would
eventually become a partner in Riley and Scott and be this country's best racing
vehicle designer.

The final standings: A.J. Foyt (Foyt-Coyote) 4920, Johnny Rutherford (Drake-
Offy-McLaren) 2900, Bobby Unser (Drake-Offy-Eagle) 2480.

1976

*Cincinnati defeats the Yankees in four straight for the World Series
title.... Bjorn Borg wins at Wimbledon but loses to Jimmy Connors in the
U.S. Open.... CB radios become a national craze, with an average of more
than 650,000 license applications per month, and "10-4" becomes part of
the language.*

The good news for Vel's-Parnelli Jones Racing was that efforts to convert the
Formula One engine had been successful. They knew boost pressure for 1976 would

be limited to 80 inches for the race, so they got the Cosworth DFV blocks and went to work in 1975, with veteran Indianapolis technician—one of the last of the riding mechanics from the '30s—Chickie Hirashima doing the development, helped by Larry Slaughter.

Parnelli's turbocharged Cosworth was ready by Indianapolis time, and Al Unser qualified it fourth fastest—a performance that gave the assembled racing community a view of the future. Unser wound up seventh, a lap back. The race, however, went to Johnny Rutherford again, just ahead of Foyt, whose former Ford powerplant had a turbo fitted to it since 1971. The race itself was the shortest in Indianapolis history, lasting only 102 laps before the rains came for the third time in four years, and it would prove to be the last Offenhauser win in the 500.

A month later, at the Pocono 500, Unser recorded the first victory for the new engine, and Miletich and Jones had Keith Duckworth as their guest, watching what he had intimated couldn't be done.

Jones: "We went to Pocono, and we invited—because we knew that we were really competitive—we invited Duckworth, we got him over there because we wanted the distributorship for the engine. We deserved it, so we go over there, we win the race with the Cosworth, and he steals Larry Slaughter, who is under Chickie. He hires him and puts him in business down the street, because Larry Slaughter knew everything that we did, and that's where Cosworth of America came from."

Rutherford would win three times during the 13-event season, but the championship would go to Gordon Johncock, who won twice, by the narrowest of margins—20 points. Johncock was using an engine sometimes known as the "DGS-Offy" that he employed the previous year. The engine was the creation of Dale Drake (who was still designing, although his son John was running the Offenhauser business), Leo Goossen and Art Sparks, three of America's outstanding engine designers. Because it resembled, in many respects, the Offenhauser that Goossen had developed, the Offy nickname managed to attach itself. The DGS would win three more races in 1977 and one in 1978 (three of the four with Johncock driving) before disappearing under the onslaught of the Cosworths.

As a footnote, there was another engine present at Indianapolis, a stock-block American Motors powerplant, which would make the race—but not be a factor—in one car for each of the next three years.

The year also marked the debut of a woman driver at Indianapolis, Janet Guthrie, a veteran Sports Car Club of America contestant. She ran in practice, but did not attempt to qualify, saying she would be back next year.

The final point standings: Gordon Johncock (DGS-Offy-Wildcat) 4240, Johnny Rutherford (Cosworth-McLaren) 4220, Wally Dallenbach (DGS-Offy-Wildcat) 3105.

1977

The Concorde, finally passing a noise test, begins service between New York and London, New York and Paris.... The 800-mile Alaska pipeline starts pumping oil from the North Slope to Valdez.... Minimum wage is raised to $3.05 an hour.

———•———

Foyt, who so many times outran the field in all types of racing, was again the beneficiary of someone else's bad luck in 1977, winning his fourth Indianapolis 500 when Johncock was sidelined by engine trouble with 16 laps to go. It would prove to be the last win for the Ford double overhead cam V8 that was the spearhead of the company's Indianapolis effort, and that made its debut at the Speedway in 1964. Foyt, who was the beneficiary of the company's largesse when it withdrew from racing at the close of 1970, had persevered with the Ford—decorated with his own valve covers, saying "Foyt" for six years and "Coyote" in 1977—in the face of overwhelming Offenhauser opposition. Now it paid off.

It was the first year that someone—Tom Sneva, as it turned out—turned in a 200 mph lap in qualifying, and Guthrie qualified for the starting field. She started 26th and lasted 25 laps before being sidelined by a faulty fuel tank. It was also the first year the entire 2.5-mile track was resurfaced at the same time. The Cosworths, carrying a DFX model name, finished second and third as the new engine made its debut.

The full season, now up to 14 races, saw Sneva win the championship in a Penske-owned car, winning two races and finishing second at Indianapolis. Rutherford won four and Foyt three, but Sneva's consistency made the difference. Cosworths were in the cars of eight winners.

The final point standings: Tom Sneva (Cosworth-McLaren) 3965, Al Unser (Cosworth-Parnelli) 3030, A.J. Foyt (Foyt-Coyote) 2840.

1978

New Jersey legalizes gambling and Atlantic City is revived.... "Saturday Night Fever" gives disco dancing a big boost.... Dallas defeats Denver in the Super Bowl, 27-10.... Affirmed wins the Triple Crown.

———•———

Jim Hall, the creator (along with General Motors Advanced Engineering) of the great Chaparral sports cars, retired from driving in 1970 as the result of a serious accident in 1968. After that he owned Can-Am and Formula 5000 cars as a partner with Lola importer Carl Haas, but now he showed up at Indianapolis with a Lola chassis, a Cosworth engine and Al Unser as his driver.

Sneva, driving for Penske and also using a Cosworth DFX, became the pole sitter and the first man to qualify at more than 200 miles an hour, averaging 202 mph for the four-lap run. But Unser, who qualified in the third row, led 121 laps and finished eight seconds ahead of Sneva while fighting the effects of a bent front wing, damaged during his final pit stop on the 180th lap.

Both Hall and Penske had begun their racing careers in sports cars and Penske, after he retired from driving at the close of 1964, functioned as Hall's Chaparral team manager during the 1965 season. They won 16 events that year, including the 12 Hours of Sebring, which should have given others a message.

It would be the first of eleven consecutive years of winning at Indianapolis for the offspring—by now two generations removed—of Ford's $280,000 investment of the mid-'60s. It was also Unser's third win and put him one up on his brother Bobby, who would win again in 1981. Guthrie, driving with a cracked wrist that forced her to reach across and shift left-handed when accelerating out of the pits, finished ninth.

Unser also won the other two 500-milers that season, at Ontario and Pocono, to become the only Indy-car driver to win three 500-milers in the same year. But the championship eluded him, going instead to Sneva, the first man to win a national title without a victory since Tony Bettenhausen in 1958. It was an 18-event season that included two October races in Britain, at Silverstone and Brands Hatch, and then the year closed with the late-October event at Phoenix. This would be the last time leading teams and drivers would participate as members of the U.S. Auto Club.

The DGS engine, under the guidance of Johncock, scored the last four-cylinder victory in a national championship event at Trenton in April.

The final point standings: Tom Sneva (Penske-Cosworth) 4153, Al Unser (Lola-Cosworth) 4031, Gordon Johncock (Wildcat-DGS-Offy) 3548.

1979

> *The Sony Walkman is introduced.... Pittsburgh defeats Dallas in the Super Bowl, 35-31.... The Sandinistas assume power in Nicaragua.... 16-year-old Tracy Austin becomes the youngest woman to win the U.S. tennis championship.*

———•———

The winter of 1978–79 was one of intense activity for the new CART organization, putting together a staff, lining up a schedule, and the many other items necessary for a season. Penske, who owned Michigan Speedway, took a quick lease on the 1.5-mile oval at the New Jersey State Fairgrounds in Trenton to make sure CART had at least two more dates. A 13-race schedule covering ten dates—doubleheaders at Atlanta, Michigan and Trenton—included five races at Penske tracks. Then there was, of course, the Indianapolis 500, under the control of USAC.

Six CART teams made their entry for the 500, were turned down by USAC for "not being in good standing" on April 19, and went to court. The judge ruled in their favor and they were in, and for better or worse, CART was on its way, such as it was, and although Indianapolis was sanctioned by USAC, through some creative accounting CART decided it would count for its own title.

Penske had been a winner as a driver, as a car owner and most certainly in his various business ventures, but it had been seven years since Mark Donohue won the team's first Indianapolis 500 in 1972. In the meantime Penske's domination of Can Am racing with a Porsche 917 (and Donohue) had caused the cancellation of that series, and his Goodyear-financed Formula One invasion was given a terrible setback when Donohue was killed before the Austrian Grand Prix of 1975.

Since then he had kept his focus on American open-wheel racing, but he needed another driver. He had Mario Andretti for a while, Tom Sneva, Bobby Unser and some others, but he needed someone who was, like Donohue, *his* driver. He found him in Rick Mears, and Penske's success in the racing series he helped create became even more pronounced. Mears was a motorcycle and off-road racer from California and a good one, but his only trip to Indianapolis in 1977 had seen him fail to qualify. Then he met Penske at Wally Dallenbach's annual motorcycle ride in Colorado and Penske saw something he liked. It was the start of a successful relationship that saw Mears win three of CART's first four seasonal championships, 29 races in all, and win the Indianapolis 500 four times in twelve years.

The first of these came in Mears' second season with the team. Both Penske and Hall, following the latest Formula One practice, brought ground-effects vehicles to the season, cars with their undersides designed to create low-pressure areas and thus improve roadholding. Hall's car was done by well-known British Formula One designer John Barnard, Penske's car by his own company in Britain, Penske Cars Ltd.

Hall had Al Unser as his driver and at Indianapolis Unser disappeared from the field almost from the drop of the flag, and was comfortably ahead at the halfway point when his transmission failed due to a bad seal. Mears won when Foyt's car had engine trouble in the closing laps and A.J. coasted home in second. It was the second straight for the DFX at the Speedway.

Bobby Unser, driving Penske's other car, won six of the 14 championship races that year, but Mears nipped him for the title despite having only three wins due to CART adapting the USAC system of giving out points in direct proportion to the length of the event. To Mears' credit he never finished lower than seventh, was second four times and third twice. Mears, who switched to the ground-effects car for the second half of the season, and Bobby Unser were almost literally miles ahead of Johncock in third. Al Unser, whose Chaparral suffered from a lack of reliability, didn't win a race until the season-ending event at Phoenix. And Cosworth DFXs were in the engine bay of every winner.

Cosworths would win 108 of CART's first 109 races, in a stretch running from 1979 through 1986, interrupted only by Mike Mosley's stock-block Chevy win at Milwaukee in 1981.

Indicative of the "alphabet-soup-cum-acronym" battles that have persisted to this day, USAC ran a separate, seven-race championship schedule in 1979, with two events at Milwaukee and two at Texas Speedway near College Station. Foyt won five of the seven, Roger McCluskey one, and Mears took the seventh, since Indianapolis counted for both. Ontario was the only other track that staged a race sanctioned by both organizations, in Ontario's case one in March and the other in September. The March race at Ontario was part of one of the few doubleheaders in the sport's history. The single-seater event covered 200 miles and there was also a 200-mile USAC stock car race at Ontario on the same day. Jones, who had retired a number of years earlier, drove in the stock-car event.

The final CART point standings: Rick Mears (Penske PC6 and PC7-Cosworth) 4060, Bobby Unser (Penske PC7 Cosworth) 3780, Gordon Johncock (Penske PC6-Cosworth) 2211.

The final USAC point standings: A.J. Foyt (Cosworth-Parnelli, Foyt-Coyote) 3320, Bill Vukovich Jr. (Watson-Offy) 1770, Tom Bigelow (Lola-Cosworth) 1305.

1980

The 52 Americans held hostage in Iran since the previous November remain there throughout the year.... Shah Reza Pahlevi dies of cancer, in exile.... The U.S. boycotts the Moscow Olympics.... Mt. St. Helens erupts in the state of Washington.... Ted Turner's Cable News Network makes its debut.

———————•———————

Al Unser's unhappiness with the lack of Chaparral reliability turned out to be a blessing in disguise for Johnny Rutherford, who was at liberty when McLaren pulled out of CART racing. Unser left Hall's team at the close of 1979 and so Rutherford took over the seat in a car that had spent a season getting the bugs worked out.

Rutherford won five of the twelve races on the 1980 CART schedule, including the Indianapolis 500, finished second three times, made a runaway of the point standings, and also set a record for consecutive miles completed. He led 119 laps at Indianapolis and had no trouble pulling away from the field in the closing stages. It was also the last year an Offenhauser engine qualified for the 500, as three made it. The Offy, whose ancestry could be traced back to the Peugeot that won the 500 in 1913, was finished. Cosworth, for the moment, reigned supreme.

Rutherford also won at Ontario in the season opener, on Mid-Ohio's road course, at Michigan and Milwaukee. Unser, again second in the standings and still driving for Penske, won at Milwaukee, Pocono, Watkins Glen and the second race at Ontario. Pocono and the Ontario August race were both over the 500-mile distance, and the Ontario renewal proved to be the last open-wheel race held there, as the track closed after the 1980 season. The finale saw 37 cars at the start.

There was a brief period of reconciliation during the year as the internecine nonsense continued, and during this temporary honeymoon there was something called the Championship Racing League, or CRL—one more set of initials to confuse the public.

The dominance of Goodyear—Firestone was long gone—and Cosworth had one negative effect on the racing community. Both began charging for equipment previously handed out free in an effort to keep the teams concerned from accepting similar largesse from either Firestone or Drake.

The final point standings: Johnny Rutherford (Chaparral 2K-Cosworth) 4723; Bobby Unser (Penske PC9-Cosworth) 3714; Tom Sneva (McLaren M24-Cosworth, Phoenix-Cosworth) 2930.

1981

King Juan Carlos of Spain foils a radical right-wing group attempt to take over the government.... President Reagan is shot by John Hinckley, Jr., as he leaves a Washington hotel.... Reagan fires all 13,000 U.S. air traffic controllers.... Pope John Paul II is the victim of an attempted assassination, but survives.

———————•———————

When racing fans wonder why "their" sport doesn't gain the all-encompassing popularity they feel it deserves, they only have to look at the 1981 Indianapolis 500. The race took a little over three hours to run but several months to determine the winner, by which time the general (non-race fan) public had forgotten about it. Bobby Unser, driving for Penske again, and in the last of 19 appearances at Indianapolis, won on the track, and then lost—for a few months—when Andretti's car owner Pat Patrick protested his passing under the yellow flag in the closing stages. It was finally given back to Unser in October, and he was fined $40,000, a small portion of his car's prize money. Andretti, who started 32nd due to having someone else qualify his car while he was in Europe involved in a Formula One race, was second, then first—and after October, second again. There was even another unsuccessful appeal that was finally denied in the following year.

The sanctioning-body hostilities continued, with points earned at Indianapolis—the race was sanctioned by USAC, as usual—no longer counting for the CART championship. In the previous two years CART had simply assumed the points but USAC now objected to this. So the biggest race in America—still—was run for a non-existent championship.

It would be run under USAC sanction through 1983, although the CART teams would continue to participate. In 1981 and 1982 it did not count for the CART season championship, but it did in 1979, 1980 and 1983, and thereafter until the IRL reared its head in 1995. Pocono, also a USAC-sanctioned event, did not count for the CART title in 1981.

Alice in Wonderland could have sat on the pole.

The CART season covered eleven races and the Penske-Mears combination was dominant, with Mears winning six events and finishing with nearly twice as many points as runner-up Bill Alsup.

It would be Bobby Unser's last season, but there were replacements on the way, including his nephew Al Junior, who that year won the Sports Car Club of America's Super Vee championship.

The final point standings: Rick Mears (Penske PC9B-Cosworth) 304, Bill Alsup (Penske PC7/PC9B-Cosworth) 177, Pancho Carter (Lightning-Cosworth, Penske PC7-Cosworth) 168.

1982

Soviet leader Leonid Brezhnev dies after 18 years in office and his country in deep economic trouble. ... The Mexican economy comes close to collapse and inflation rates climb to 100 percent. ... Israel invades Lebanon. ... The Reverend Sun Myung Moon of the Unification Church marries 2075 couples at once in New York's Madison Square Garden.

———•———

The Old Guard was passing: Foyt drove five of the eleven CART (now called Indycar) events, plus Indianapolis. New names included Bobby Rahal, who had a sports-car upbringing, and who would finish second in the point standings. Danny Sullivan made his debut at Atlanta, Al Unser Jr. first appeared at Riverside in August, just a year out of Volkswagen-powered cars. Again, the USAC-CART split made the Indianapolis 500 a separate affair, this time won by Johncock as the total purse went over $2 million for the first time.

It was a race that put one of the favorites out before it ever started, when pole sitter Kevin Cogan, accelerating too hard on cold tires going for the green flag, spun on the straightway and was run into by Andretti, eliminating both. The 45-year-old Johncock won by the slimmest of margins, less than a car length in front of Mears, who tried to pass him three times on the last lap but was blocked by Johncock each time.

The split-second loss at the Speedway may have been frustration, but Mears had the satisfaction of winning CART's championship, taking four of the eleven races to finish comfortably in front of Rahal, who won in Cleveland and at Michigan International Speedway. Rahal was driving a March chassis, which was rapidly becoming the vehicle of choice.

The final point standings: Rick Mears (Penske PC10-Cosworth) 294, Bobby Rahal (March 82C-Cosworth) 242, Mario Andretti (Wildcat Mk. VIIIB-Cosworth) 188.

1983

The computer mouse, camcorders and compact discs appear on the scene.... Crack is added to the drug trade.... Argentina gets civilian rule after the military dictatorship steps down as the result of its defeat in the Falkland Islands.... The gross national product rises to $3.434 trillion.

Al Unser, now carrying a "Sr." after his name in race lineups due to his son's entry into CART racing, moved from the unsuccessful team financed by Texas millionaire Bobby Hillin to Roger Penske, and that made all the difference. Unser won the 13-event championship, which this time once again included Indianapolis, the various factions at USAC and CART having made up to the extent that one could at least count the points earned in the other's race.

Unser won only once during the year—in Cleveland—but he finished second three times, third once and fourth three times to pick up 151 points in CART's new scoring system. He finished just ahead of Italian Teo Fabi, driving for Gerry Forsythe. Fabi won four races, but dropped out of most of the others.

The Indianapolis 500, the linchpin of open-wheel racing in America, was won by Sneva, driving for veteran mechanic-car owner George Bignotti, just ahead of the Penske twosome of Unser Sr. and Mears. Fabi, who had the pole, was sidelined by a leaking gasket with fewer than 50 laps done.

One of life's truisms, especially evident in racing, is that if you are not getting better you are getting worse, and to a degree this was applicable to Cosworth in 1983. Since the DFX was dominant, there appeared to be an informal agreement between Cosworth and the car owners to freeze the design and thus save on development costs.

Keith Duckworth had sold his 85 percent share of the company to United Engineering Industries in 1980 and although he was still functioning as chairman and chief engineer, there was now a parent company looking at the bottom line and interested in maximizing financial return from this subsidiary. What no one realized at the moment was that there was a serious rival, not merely on the horizon, but on Cosworth's staff.

Two bright young engineers, Paul Morgan and Mario Illien, were not happy with what they perceived as a status quo operation and decided to go into business for themselves. By late November they had Penske as a partner.

There was one additional outside influence on single-seat racing: The death of the Sports Car Club of America's Can Am series left some car owners looking for a new arena, and CART was attractive. Among those moving over were Lola importer Carl Haas and actor Paul Newman, who were put together as a team by Andretti, who then became their driver. Road circuits, looking for more dates, also began making contact with CART, which would eventually be staging more races on roads than on ovals.

The final point standings: Al Unser Sr. (Penske PC10B/PC11-Cosworth) 151, Teo Fabi (March 83C-Cosworth) 146, Mario Andretti (Lola T700-Cosworth) 133.

1984

Geraldine Ferraro becomes the first woman nominated for vice president, running with ultimately unsuccessful Democratic presidential candidate Walter Mondale.... Vanessa Williams becomes the first black woman to be named Miss America.... I.M. Pei's pyramid addition to the Louvre opens in Paris.

Fifteen years after he won his third national championship of American open-wheel racing, Mario Andretti won another. Between 1969 and 1984 he spent considerable time on the Formula One circuit and won the world drivers' championship in 1978—but to win again in the U.S., even though the name of the game had changed to CART, this was a sort of homecoming. Driving for Newman-Haas, Andretti won six of the 16 races on the schedule, placed second in two more, and showed his speed by sitting on the pole eight times. What made his performance all the more remarkable was that he was now 44, considered retirement age for most drivers of sophisticated racing machinery, and that he was driving a Lola when the chassis/body/tub of choice was March.

At the Indianapolis 500, from which Mario eliminated himself when he ran into the back of another car while making a pit stop, 30 of the 33 starters were Marches—and so were the first 14 finishers, led by Mears in his Penske Pennzoil car. March was considered so superior that Penske gave up the cars built in his own factory. It was Mears' second Indianapolis win and he would eventually add two more, but his career suffered an enormous setback when he crashed at Sanair in Canada and incurred severe damage to his ankles. He would not be able to drive on a road course again until 1986. For Penske, Mears' victory was number four. This would grow to ten before CART left the Speedway in the schism of the mid-'90s.

Emerson Fittipaldi, the Brazilian who won the world championship in 1972 and 1974, came out of retirement to enter CART racing, and other new faces on the scene included Andretti's older son Michael. Although he appeared in three races the previous season, this was his first full year and he was competitive from the outset. Michael got his start in Formula Ford in 1980, and was SCCA Northeast Division Formula Ford champion with six wins in 1981. He was SCCA pro rookie of the year in 1982, moved to Formula Mondial (a mid-size European "training" series) in 1983 and also finished third in the Le Mans 24 Hours, driving with his father. Danny Sullivan, who made a brief appearance in CART events two years earlier, came back from Formula One for the full season, won three races and finished fourth.

The Penske-Morgan-Illien venture—by now called Ilmor—picked up a fourth and crucial partner in 1984 when Penske contacted then-GM President Jim McDonald. The announcement was made in October of the year. Time would pass before this new engine, which would carry the Chevrolet name on its valve covers, would be a factor, but it would be. At the outset there was little difference between the DFX and the Ilmor creation, which many at Cosworth considered to be nothing more than a copy. Interestingly, about the only feature not the same as on the DFX was the solution to the torsional problems in the gear train. It is believed that solving this cost Ilmor two years, and was the reason the engine wasn't a winner until 1986. Ownership of Ilmor was split four ways, with each party having 25 percent: Illien, Morgan, Penske and GM. In 1993 Penske would play a role in brokering GM's share to Daimler-Benz, and Ilmor would go on to build Mercedes engines for CART and for Formula One. Racing can put together some strange combinations.

The final point standings: Mario Andretti (Lola T800-Cosworth) 176, Tom Sneva (March 84C-Cosworth) 163, Bobby Rahal (March 84C-Cosworth) 137.

1985

Mikhail Gorbachev becomes the leader of the Soviet Union.... Enver Hoxha, the communist dictator of Albania for 40 years, dies at the age of 76.... Pete Rose breaks Ty Cobb's career record of 4191 hits.

Cosworth dominance on the track continued in 1985, but there was a momentary pause at the Indianapolis Motor Speedway in May: A stock-block Buick V6, driven by Pancho Carter, took the pole position for the 500 with a record average of better than 212 mph. One driven by Scott Brayton placed second. The Indianapolis rules allowed overhead camshaft engines a maximum displacement of 161 cubic inches and 47 inches of manifold boost pressure, and the stock-block engines, 209 inches of displacement and 57 inches of boost pressure. The advantage, clearly, was with the stock-block engines—providing someone cared to spend the development money.

In this case the development work was done by the Buick Division of General Motors, where Herb Fishel was in charge of the motorsports program. Fishel, who would take over what would eventually be called GM Racing in 1991, would appear on Ford's horizon again and again, especially in stock-car racing, but this was the first time anyone had seen him in the single-seater end of the sport. The Buicks never made a lasting impact on the upper levels of this discipline, but they have been long-lived: Today the engine, a derivative of the 3.8-liter production model (and without the turbocharger), is the 450-horsepower engine used by all entrants in CART's Indy Lights series. One question never answered to everyone's satisfaction is: What was Buick doing at Indianapolis when Chevrolet was going to be there in short order?

Danny Sullivan won the 500, narrowly avoiding hitting Andretti when spinning on the 120th lap but missing the wall and continuing on. His car owner was Penske, winning his fifth 500. Al Unser Sr., the 1985 season champion, was also driving Penske equipment as he managed to finish just one point ahead of his son at the close of the 15-race calendar. He passed a number of cars in the final laps of the season's last race in order to do so.

The final point standings: Al Unser Sr. (March 85C-Cosworth) 151, Al Unser Jr. (Lola T900-Cosworth) 150, Bobby Rahal (March 85C-Cosworth) 134.

1986

Ferdinand Marcos is deposed in the Philippines, along with wife Imelda, owner at the time of 1600 pairs of shoes.... Admiral Hyman Rickover, father of the nuclear submarine, dies.... Baby Doc Duvalier is deposed in Haiti.... Reagan and Gorbachev meet in Iceland.

This was the year of Bobby Rahal. He won the Indianapolis 500 with a daring 198th lap move on Kevin Cogan, and drove the fastest race lap in history—better than 209 mph—on the final tour around the oval to beat Cogan by 1.4 seconds. This was the first Indianapolis race to average over 170 mph, and therefore the first to finish in less than three hours. Rahal won six of the 17 races that comprised the season, and took the championship as well. The 500 was televised live for the first time, as Speedway management finally consented to apply the principle of immediacy to the event years after NASCAR had done so. The race had been telecast on a tape-delayed basis.

Rahal's victory at Indianapolis was his gift to Jim Trueman, his sponsor and a man who was suffering from incurable cancer and was almost literally at death's door. He managed to stay alive during the rain-induced one-week delay of the event, but succumbed eleven days later.

This was the first of three national championships amassed by Rahal, who would go on to be a successful team owner in addition to being a driver, and would eventually take over Ford's unsuccessful Jaguar Formula One team in the fall of 2000. He was also president of CART for some months in mid-2000 even though the word "interim" would be placed in front of his title. This took place while the organization was—once again—looking for a new leader.

The Ilmor-Chevrolet engine made its first appearance at the Speedway, was qualified in fifth position by Al Unser Sr., but dropped out of the event due to vibration problems. It is assumed the problems came as a result of not having Cosworth's vibration-dampening system for the gear train. Mears and Sullivan ran it in various other races but the teething troubles were still there, and aside from thirds at Elkhart Lake and Miami, it did little. Penske's exclusive-use contract expired at the end of the year, however, and other teams were ordering it for the coming season.

1987

More than 300 Mafioso are sentenced to a total of 2665 years in prison in Sicily's biggest trial, in a courthouse guarded by 3000 policemen.... Five years later, the chief judge, together with his wife and bodyguards, would be blown up.... Rudolf Hess, 93 and the last survivor of the Nazi hierarchy, strangles himself in his prison cell.

———•———

Cosworth's streak came to an end in the first race of the season, when Andretti won the street-circuit event at Long Beach with an Ilmor, but that was one of only five of 15 CART races the engine would win during the season. Its time would come in 1988. Andretti also put the world on notice, and his Lola on the pole, at the Indianapolis 500, which he dominated until there were less than 25 laps to go. Then an ignition problem sidelined him—again.

The Indianapolis victory, his fourth, went to Al Unser Sr., who was a late substitute for Danny Ongais, Penske's newest driver. Ongais crashed on May 7 and was ruled medically unfit to drive, so Penske found Unser and rescued one of his last year's cars, this one equipped with a Cosworth, which had been on display in a Pennsylvania hotel lobby, and had it brought back to the Speedway. Unser qualified 20th, but as the race progressed he worked his way through the field, and when Andretti retired it came down to a duel between Unser and Roberto Guerrero, who stalled his engine during his last pit stop. Unser, at 47 the oldest man ever to win there, finished 4.5 seconds in front, helped by a timely caution flag that lasted until there were four laps left.

Rahal won his second consecutive championship, comfortably in front of Michael Andretti. Rahal won three times—including an event in the parking lot of New Jersey's Meadowlands sports complex—finished second five times and third twice.

The final point standings: Bobby Rahal (Lola T87/00-Cosworth) 188, Michael Andretti (March 87C-Cosworth) 158, Al Unser Jr. (March 87C-Cosworth) 109.

1988

The U.S. imports grain for domestic use for the first time in its history, due to drought conditions.... The Dodgers defeat the Athletics in the World Series, 4-1.... Steffi Graf wins the grand slam of tennis.... Benazir Bhutto becomes the first woman to head a Muslim state, being elected prime minister of Pakistan.... She lasts 20 months.

———•———

It was Danny Sullivan's year, and Roger Penske's year. Sullivan, in his fourth season with the Penske team, won the championship and four of the 15 races, and no less than nine pole positions. His car was the new Penske PC17, designed by Nigel

Bennett, who was the chief designer on the Lolas that had been so competitive the past few years.

Penske's Indianapolis entry, composed of Sullivan, Rick Mears and Al Unser Sr., occupied the front row for the 500—the first time in history that drivers from one team had done so. In the race itself Sullivan led easily until sidelined by an accident after 91 laps, Mears won and Unser finished third. The threesome led 192 of the 200 laps, and it was Penske's fourth 500 win in five years.

The Ilmor engine, now known as a Chevrolet, finished 1-2-3 at the Speedway and won 14 of the year's events, the lone interruption coming at the Pocono 500 when Rahal won a flag-strewn race with a British Judd powerplant in his Lola. Cosworth's ten-year run at Indianapolis, and its streak of 95 consecutive wins in CART races, had come to an end.

The final point standings: Danny Sullivan (Penske PC17-Chevrolet) 182, Al Unser Jr. (March 88C-Chevrolet) 149, Bobby Rahal (Lola T88-Judd) 136.

1989

> *The Stealth bomber becomes known to the public, along with Teenage Mutant Ninja Turtles. ... Time Warner is created by a merger of Time, Inc., and Warner Brothers. ... Colin Powell is named chairman of the Joint Chiefs of Staff. ... Pete Rozelle retires after 29 years as NFL commissioner.*

For four years, beginning with the 1972 season, Emerson Fittipaldi was the hottest driver on the world championship circuit. The smiling Brazilian won the title twice (1972 and 1974) and was second twice, in 1973 and 1975—all before he was 29. Then he left the McLaren team, where he had been in the last two years, to start his own Formula One effort with Brazilian funding for a grand prix entry called the Copersucar, named after his sugar company sponsor.

The car was conspicuous only by its lack of success and Fittipaldi faded into the background, retiring from world championship competition after the 1980 season. He returned to competition by joining a CART team in 1984 at the age of 38, and worked his way through a succession of cars and an oval-track learning process. By 1989 he had the experience, was ready to move to the front and did, winning the Indianapolis 500, four other races on the 15-event calendar, and the championship as well.

Fittipaldi's Indianapolis win came after a series of closing laps in which he and Al Unser Jr. went wheel to wheel until the 199th lap, when the two cars touched in the third turn and Unser spun out, unhurt, but finished for the day. "Little Al" finished second, still a lap ahead of Brazilian Raul Boesel in third.

An event that would shape the future of racing, but at the time attracted little attention outside the racing community took placed in December of the year, when

Joe Cloutier, the caretaker president of the Hulman family-owned Indianapolis Motor Speedway, died and was succeeded by Tony George.

The final point standings: Emerson Fittipaldi (Penske PC17/18-Chevrolet) 196, Rick Mears (Penske PC18-Chevrolet) 186, Michael Andretti (Lola T89-Chevrolet) 150.

Chapter 11

THE GREAT ONES

The line of great, charismatic open-cockpit drivers in the modern era of American racing, at least those involved with Ford, came to an end with the retirement of Mario Andretti and A.J. Foyt in the mid-'90s. By then Dan Gurney and Parnelli Jones were decades away from competing and were full-time team owners, and Foyt had been an owner and driver for some time. It is possible that those who followed had their stature diminished by the CART-IRL split and the resultant flood of publicity for NASCAR people, but this cannot be the only reason. Michael Andretti, the fastest over the past decade, has never resonated with the fans or the media. Neither, for that matter, had any of the Unsers, or even Rick Mears, after they retired.

Andretti the Elder, Foyt, Jones, Gurney, are still the ones with the flair, in large part because they were not only successful in open-cockpit machines, but also in stock cars, sports cars, and off-road vehicles. If you had a race, they would be there. It did not matter what was being driven, and perhaps that is the problem with today's crop. The place in this spotlight, as the 21st century gets under way, is empty.

Dan Gurney (left) and Parnelli Jones at Daytona.
—Don Hunter

A.J. Foyt: *Four times at Indianapolis.*—Ford Motor Company

Mario Andretti: *The face of American racing, 1969 (left) and 1994.*
—*Ford Motor Company*

Gurney, after Phil Hill (1961) and before Andretti (1978) the best American Formula One driver, was always a threat at Indianapolis, was a winner in long-distance sports-car racing, and was practically untouchable in NASCAR road-racing events. Foyt, the four-time Indianapolis winner, an artist on an oval track with a single seater, was a winner in NASCAR's major events when he had the time, was a threat in sports cars and also won the Le Mans 24 Hours with Gurney in 1967.

Dan Gurney: He never won the 500, but he was a force there.—Ford/Dave Friedman

Jones got out faster than the rest of them—got out, that is, of open-cockpit racing—went on for another 30 years in Trans-Am Mustangs and off-road vehicles, and went on to a successful business career, partly racing oriented, mostly not. If the four have one thing in common, aside from their talents, it is that all have sons who became racing drivers.

Mario Andretti

Nazareth is located on the northeastern fringe of Pennsylvania, on the edge of the Lehigh Valley, and for the most part it is a gray town, dominated by a giant cement plant to the east and with a large speedway on its south side. The cement factory is one of several in the valley, since the indigenous rock formation is one of the basic elements in the making of this product.

It is also in the heart of Northeastern short-track country, where racing put down roots shortly after the birth of the Model T, and the sport has flourished ever since. Nothing fancy, but it has a long-term racing history with its own set of heroes and traditions. If you owned a midget or a modified and lived here, in the summer you could hook up the trailer and tow your race car to a different oval almost every night, across the river to Jersey, north to New York, or head south toward Philadelphia and Maryland.

Nazareth is a working man's town, with about 5000 in the city limits and perhaps 15,000 in the area, and it is basically unchanged from Eisenhower times, which is when the 15-year-old Andretti twins, Aldo and Mario, arrived with the their family after spending seven years in a displaced persons' camp in Italy.

That was more than four decades ago; the dirt track has been replaced by a one-mile paved oval that has the latest spectator amenities, there are various shopping centers in and out of town, and various racing drivers have come and gone, some well-known for a while, many of them little noted and not remembered for long.

North of the city, located on a hill and facing east is Villa Montona, an impressive Italianate structure that is the present home of Mario, about whom many make the argument that he was the best racing driver of the 20th century—which means, since the sport is roughly 100 years old, the best ever.

Whether Andretti is or is not—some like Juan Manuel Fangio, others prefer Tazio Nuvolari or Ayrton Senna, or Foyt—is academic. It makes little sense to compare drivers from different eras, and it doesn't make any difference. He was one of the great ones, in any sense of the word.

Andretti is in his early 60s, and the short, skinny kid, who was replaced by a slim young man, is now stocky—not fat, but stocky—crowned by a full, hardly gray, carefully combed head of hair, and is the archetype of racing's elder statesman. He is articulate, personable, and has become a one-man industry, fronting for any number of corporations, most notably Texaco. And the wonder of it, of all the championships, of Indianapolis and Monza and Sebring and the rest is not that he won, but that he was there at all. He came out of postwar Europe, out of a childhood in a DP camp, with an incredible drive to make himself the best at his way of life, and to do so even when his brother suffered a career-ending injury soon after they started. It is hard to conceive of that kind of determination, even harder to find it in combination with a great natural talent.

He is a presence, and has been one almost since the spring of 1965, when he burst upon the American racing consciousness by finishing a strong third in his inaugural Indianapolis 500. It wasn't only a matter of being fast—it was how he handled himself, how he dealt with the media, how the skinny kid's personality stacked up against those of Jones, Foyt and the rest. Even then he was articulate, he was quotable, and he was available.

Combined with his driving he thus became a winner in more ways than one, and as a result, also thanks in part to his years, he has become The Face of American Racing.

With apologies to Richard Petty, who never saw an autograph collector he didn't like, Andretti is the one. Petty is regional, Andretti is international. Dale Earnhardt, despite all of his obvious talents, was a regional hero and was not elevated past this until his death.

The postwar flood of immigrants gave this country everything from Nobel prize winners to tennis players, millions coming across the water, looking for a better life, looking to leave a still badly damaged Europe, and among them were these two kids whose heroes were Fangio, Alberto Ascari and Stirling Moss, and who heard the sound of racing engines somewhere near their first home on Whitfield Street.

The noise came from the Fairgrounds, ".... And that's where we discovered motor racing in America.... A couple of days after we arrived—it was June so the season was going—come Sunday we hear this noise ... so we went where the noise was, and we see all this dust and everything else, so we go over and we get close and we see these cars.... Weird-looking, these modified stock cars, but they looked very approachable, very do-able, it didn't look sophisticated; you know, the last race we saw, of any consequence, which was really quite impressive, was the 1954 Italian Grand Prix in Monza."

"Almost immediately we started working on the idea.... This is where we're going to start racing.... We had school and all that, but three, four years later we were on our way to building a car."

In the summer of 1959 it was ready, a 1948 Hudson the Andrettis had turned into something suitable for the dirt oval in their hometown. Aldo drove it first.

Mario: "We went in there and we had no idea we were going to be a factor and then Aldo's out there, starting dead last.... If you had no points you had to start from the back, so he started in the back in a heat race, and he's going through the pack, it was like watching Fangio, and then he goes and wins the heat, starts last in the feature, he just bolts through.... We must have done something right along the way ... and he wins the damn race...."

There was a downside: "I don't know why, but we won right away, and that was a huge problem also because we thought we'd have to win every race and we started crashing.... And then reality sets in and you're not winning and then you start figuring out why...."

The idea of winning every race stayed with Andretti for years: "That sort of concept, of approaching this business, remained with me.... Because you look at the really smart career, you know, 'Finish if you can.' I could care less about finishing second for the longest time, and that's why I was always going for broke, and I admit, that's not always the smartest way to go.... The sense of pride, the sense of whatever, was detrimental in some ways because I was just driven to win—that's the only thing that matters, basically."

He did it in 1963, when he won three midget races on Labor Day, one in Flemington, New Jersey, across the river from his home, and then two at Hatfield, back in Pennsylvania. The next year he was into sprint cars, the toughest and most dangerous form of oval-track racing, a validation process for anyone looking to move up in single seaters.

A force in oval-track racing almost from the day he made it to America's major leagues, he won the Indianapolis 500 only once, but was the man to beat at the Speedway for more than two decades. He was a winner in sports-car racing when he had time for it, won the Daytona 500 in a Fairlane, and most important for this segment of history, was one of only two Americans to win the World Driver's Championship, and the only one to be driving a Ford-powered car. He was as much of a force on the grand prix circuit as he was in any other discipline, even though he combined efforts in this arena with all of his others. He had a four-decade career going back to a start on the dirt ovals near his home.

With most drivers it is reasonably easy to enumerate their successes, because they are all in one area of the sport. With Andretti the list covers most everything, and goes on, seemingly, for pages: World champion, four-time USAC/CART champion, Daytona 500 winner, three-time Sebring winner, Indianapolis 500 winner, USAC national dirt track champion, and so on. He drove for 35 years, and it is doubtful if anyone knows how many races. There were 407 starts in USAC-CART racing alone—staggering.

Somewhere back there, almost forgotten in the flood of statistics, is the fact that in 1972 he won four major long-distance events in a Ferrari, sharing the seat with Jacky Ickx. He got another offer from Ferrari after the close of the 1977 season, one that had him close to leaving Colin Chapman after a frustrating year in which he had the fastest car, but was set back by mechanical breakdowns (that was also a year in which he made 18 round trips between the U.S. and Europe). It was good thing Lotus came up with the money to keep him, as Andretti won the world championship the following year.

At the age of 60 he was still trying to win the one major race that had eluded him—Le Mans. Some people drive, others are driven, a few are both.

Dan Gurney

Daniel Sexton Gurney, the opera singer's son who became one of the mid-20th century icons of American racing, was one of the great drivers of his time, and another one of those who drove most anything on wheels, rather than stick to just one of the racing disciplines. He is a tall man, still handsome at 70, a hero to the sports-car populace of California and then the country starting in the late 1950s; he is someone who made an immediate impact when he got to Europe and what were the major leagues for those who wanted to turn right as well as left.

That was in 1958, and by the next year he was on the Ferrari Formula One team. He is also a man whose biggest contributions to the sport lie not so much in what he won, but in what he precipitated:

- Although it would have come to pass eventually, the rear-engine revolution in American open-cockpit racing was brought to full scale by Gurney's getting the Ford Motor Company together with Chapman in 1962. Jack Brabham had run the Indianapolis 500 in a 2.7-liter unblown Cooper in 1961 and Harry Miller had presented an undeveloped and unsuccessful rear-engined car in 1939, but Gurney's introducing Ford to Chapman, and Ford's investment in an Indianapolis program, were what made it happen.

- He showed NASCAR that a "road racer" could drive a stock car as well as a sports car, winning the Riverside 500 five times between 1963 and 1968.

- He was, right after Hill, the American who made the greatest impact in Europe in the late '50s and 1960s. He never won the world championship, but he was as fast, if not faster, than anyone else in his era, and if he had not persisted in ceaseless re-engineering of his cars, or jumping from one team to another, there is no telling what he might have done.

- In 1967, driving an Eagle designed and built in his own shops and equipped with an engine designed specifically for him, Gurney won the Grand Prix of Belgium in his Eagle, marking the first victory for an American car in a grand prix race since Jimmy Murphy won the Grand Prix of the Automobile Club of France in a Duesenberg in 1921.

- In the mid-'70s his company's chassis designs were the dominant ones in American oval-track racing, with their high point probably being the 1973-'74-'75 Indianapolis 500s. Twenty of the 33 starters were equipped with Eagles that first year, 18 the second and 16 the third, and the 1973 and '75 winners were in Eagles, including Bobby Unser driving for Gurney in 1975.

- He was, along with Andretti, the most versatile driver this country has ever seen, being successful in Formula One, sports cars, the Trans-Am series, NASCAR, and in USAC/CART.

- He was one of the leaders of the car owners' revolt that saw this country's better open-cockpit teams split with the U.S. Auto Club and form CART in time for the 1979 season. Although the move was a logical one (and some say necessary) at the time, what it also did was continue the ongoing war between racing organizations. In the end, these are successful in only one thing: Confusing that segment of the public who are not die-hard fans, and as a consequence making sure they will remain interested in another type of racing, or turn away from racing altogether.

"Here we were," said Gurney, "being led by an outfit that was happy to have one race a year and then let this façade of USAC, which looked like an independent sanctioning body but was a wholly owned child of the Indianapolis Motor Speedway, but the reality was that as long as it stayed that way everybody was going to be hand to mouth except for that one race a year and that's no way to have anything more than a hobby, so those of us who wanted to continue racing, but have it be a profession, said, 'Well, let's try and do something about it.'"

Gurney's driving career ended in 1970, just before his 39th birthday, and he won his last race, a USAC national championship event at Sears Point, and became a full-time team owner and chassis constructor. But as racing moved into the '80s, other constructors, March and Lola, for example, became dominant in single-seater racing, and Gurney's All American Racers moved on to running Toyota entries in IMSA. At first it was with the then-new Supra in GT under two liters, and a few years later he was dominant in GTP, running Toyota prototypes with Jones' son P.J. and Fangio's nephew Juan Manuel II. They won 17 races in a row at one time and then Toyota moved into CART racing in 1996, with Gurney, Jones and Fangio.

It didn't work out well, either with Jones and Fangio, or with those who came afterwards. After the 1999 season Toyota moved to Ganassi Racing, and Gurney was left without a race team.

The only Gurney left racing is son Alex, who after spending time in Formula Atlantic, a CART stepping-stone series, moved to Britain this year to gain more experience in a another series.

His father is developing a motorcycle.

Parnelli Jones

Troy Ruttman, the great young talent of the 1940s and early '50s, was a hero to Parnelli Jones, just as he was to dozens of other aspiring race drivers in Southern California, and that is where Ruttman made his mark before winning the Indianapolis 500 in J.C. Agajanian's dirt-track car in 1952, at 22 years of age.

Ruttman took his share of the Indianapolis purse and threw it away, in a figurative sense. He spent it on all manner of things, including alcohol, and despite trying to make a comeback, remains little more than the leader, perhaps, on the list of great talents gone astray.

Jones also drove for Agajanian, the wealthy Los Angeles owner of a large garbage collection service ("I deal in used food," he would joke) and other business interests. When Jones won the Indianapolis 500 in 1963 he didn't make the same mistake. "Aggie told me all these Ruttman stories and then I'd raced a couple of times with Troy ... when he came out of retirement ... and I was so impressed with him, and he said, 'Parnelli, don't do like I did,' so I had both sides of the story; I had Aggie's side and Troy's side and they were the same, basically. He said, 'You get a good accountant and a good attorney and you take care of your money.'"

Agajanian got Jones into his first real estate investment in the early '60s, a 19-acre orange grove in Cucamonga, and it turned out well. It was the first of many for someone who grew up poor, left high school early, and scratched for a living as a cement finisher. He taught himself how to be a successful driver, and perhaps more than any driver of his era, used racing as a stepping stone and stepped down when he achieved his goals.

His contemporaries were Foyt and for a few years Andretti, and although he could run with them—and faster—he was not possessed of the same blind ambition as the others, men who drove until they were pushing 60, icons of the sport who couldn't quit. The decision to leave open-cockpit racing was made during the 1967 Indianapolis 500, when Jones was cruising along in the closing stages, a few laps from his second win at the Speedway:

"I was thinking, you know, winning again was not going to be that big thrill ... I'd done that, right? And so after the race, I was thinking if it's not going to be that thrilling, why are you doing it? I knew that my real future financially was in my business, and I was single and that's when I got married. Judy and I got married in '67 and I always wanted kids and stuff...."

Jones was already a car owner—he even owned one he raced against in the 1967 500—and by 1970 he and partner Vel Miletich were the owners of the 500 winner, with Al Unser as the driver. They won the 500 again the next year; Vel and Parnelli had a Formula One team in the mid-'70s; Jones was busy with his tire business; he was busy winning the Baja 500 and the Baja 1000—he was busy being a business-man, and he was busy having fun. At the high point of one business venture, he had 45 Firestone stores in Southern California.

Once, about 20 years ago, he was outlining his workday schedule to someone, and explaining that he usually arrived in the office in the late morning, and left after two or three hours. When he was asked how someone could run his enterprises in that manner, his answer was simple: If you're not smart enough to tell people what to do in two or three hours, you shouldn't be the boss.

He is almost exclusively in real estate now, the icon either in repose or on the golf course, the man who first hit the national headlines when he won the 1963 Indianapolis 500 ahead of Jimmy Clark in the first Lotus-Ford. At that time he was the bad guy in the eyes of Ford, but that would change. He won stock-car races for Ford and Mercury, he won sports-car races with a Ford engine, he won USAC races with a Lotus-Ford, he won Trans-Am races with a Mustang and his off-road vehicles, prepared by Bill Stroppe, were all Fords.

His two boys were both racing drivers and good ones, and then Page, the younger, was injured in a sprint car race and will never drive again. PJ, successful with Gurney's Toyota team, has never been able to hook up with a successful CART or NASCAR organization. What he needs, possibly, is an Agajanian or a Miletich.

A.J. Foyt

The end-of-century polls that attempted to name the best driver of the past 100 years had Mario Andretti tied with A.J. Foyt, more formally known as Anthony Joseph Foyt, Junior, who drove for more than 40 years and never quit trying.

One of his contemporaries, one of the two or three qualified to pass judgement, once said that Foyt's driving skills were not his strength. That came from his incredible competitive nature.

He is a big man and looks even bigger, partly because of his intimidating manner, one that has made him larger than life in the eyes of not only fans on the other side of the fences, but also those in the racing fraternity. He started driving in his teens—midgets on Texas dirt tracks in 1953, and kept at it until 1995, when a Craftsman truck event was his last. In between he drove at least 1000 races, but there are records of only—only?—about 910. The rest were on the dusty fairgrounds ovals, in places where record-keeping was unknown, but the ones that are known are remarkable: 690 USAC-sanctioned starts, 127 in NASCAR, another 20 in IMSA, just for openers.

He was the first man to win the Indianapolis 500 four times; he won at Le Mans, Sebring and the Daytona 24 Hours, won the Daytona 500, and won 67 USAC national championship races in open-cockpit competition—more than anyone. The price for all of this was injury, perhaps more than any other first-quality driver. In 1965 a doctor thought he was dead after a stock-car crash at Riverside, but Jones and Ralph Moody pulled him out of the car when they saw he was still breathing. He had a broken back, a fractured ankle and thoracic injuries. He won three of the season's last four races. The next year he suffered second ands third-degree burns at Milwaukee, in 1972 he was burned again at DuQuoin and broke a leg and an ankle to boot. In 1981 he almost tore his right arm off in a crash at Michigan, and in 1990 he suffered crippling foot and leg injuries in a crash at Elkhart Lake.

The next Memorial Day saw the 56-year-old Foyt start from the middle of the front row. It was his 34th consecutive race at the Speedway.

Some people are more determined than others.

Chapter 12

THE HOLY GRAIL

The Holy Grail of racing, if such exists, is the World Driver's Championship, a title which has been with us since 1950 and which is supposed to mean, obviously, that the holder is the best in the world. This is not necessarily true, and also possibly not true, but it is the only one of literally hundreds of driver's championships contested for around the globe that has "world" as an integral part of its description.

It is a championship that employs the most sophisticated of racing cars, built of aerospace-quality materials and weighing, with driver, slightly over 1300 pounds, and with engines, in the better ones, producing more than 800 horsepower without turbocharging. These are the most agile racing machines ever built.

The championship is conducted at races in Europe, Asia, Oceania and in the U.S., it involves some of the world's major auto manufacturers, and it has, in recent years, produced some of the most boring events imaginable. Despite the sophistication of the cars and the unquestioned skill of the better drivers, there is more passing in ten laps of any NASCAR race than in the entire world championship season.

Whether or not the emperor is wearing any clothes,[1] however, seems to be, at the outset of the 21st century, academic. The championship is something like Mount Everest. It exists, and people are interested in it. Perhaps more important, some automakers and producers of major consumer goods use it as a marketing tool, four decades after racing was done for racing's sake. As it has with many other things in our society, television brought about the changes. It has transformed what is commonly called Formula One racing (the name comes from the title of the regulations under which the cars are built) into a business so successful that leading teams can show a profit despite annual budgets in excess of $200 million for a 17-race season.

In the first half century of the championship there were 635 races. Twenty-seven men won this title, one of them five times, one four times and six three times. Thirty-two different engine makes were used by the various competitors, and 17 of these were able to propel a winner at least once. The most successful of these, by far, were those designed by Cosworth at Ford's behest and with Ford financing (and eventually Ford ownership.) They won 176 world championship events and were behind the seats of 13 world champions—more than any other make.

---

[1] With apologies to Hans Christian Andersen's "Fairy Tales."

The chase for the title has attracted many, but few have even made it into a championship race; the number of drivers who took the starter's flag in the first 50 years was 670. They ranged from Argentina's Juan Manuel Fangio, who drove in 51 and won 24 of them, to Italian Riccardo Patrese, who drove in 256 and won six, to Italian Luca Badoer, who started 52 grands prix and never scored a point.

Cars with Ford engines, beginning with the Lotus introduction of the Cosworth DFV in the spring of 1967, won one-third of all championship races held through the end of the century. In the 15 years from 1968 through 1981, Ford-engined cars powered twelve world champions, and then were not a factor again until the mid-'90s, when the company took the first serious steps toward regaining what many regarded as their rightful place.

The organization founded by Keith Duckworth and Mike Costin was responsible for Ford's engine, and powered practically the entire British grand prix industry for more than a decade. This Northampton group, located slightly over an hour north of London, went through several changes of ownership after Duckworth and Costin retired and was eventually—and long overdue—purchased by Ford in 1998.

The first DFV: Graham Hill in the Lotus 49, 1967.—Ford Motor Company

In 1996 Ford underwrote the creation of former world champion Jackie Stewart's team, then bought him out in 1999 and changed the name to Jaguar for the 2000 season in order to give one of its new marques a needed image boost.

The Stewart Racing-Jaguar effort, which saw the Stewart tartan on the cars for 1997-98-99 and British Racing Green the dominant color beginning in 2000, was less than successful, especially the latter year, in which neither of the two-car team was competitive, and which revealed personnel and organizational shortcomings. The agonizing reappraisal included plans for an expansion of Jaguar Racing and Cosworth Racing facilities.

Now: The Jaguar R2 at the Grand Prix of Australia, 2001.—Jaguar

So by the start of the new century the company was fully engaged, with its name and reputation, in an area of motorsports that it originally neither knew nor cared about. But it was one that more than any other kind held the possibilities of enhancing a Ford subsidiary's reputation. The principal question was When?

Those are the bare facts. There is much more, and not just a recitation of who won and who lost. The last three-plus decades of world championship racing is as interesting for the story of how it became a business as it is for its sporting aspects or engineering development.

For example:

- While the British auto industry was falling into the hands of foreign companies—although Ford had been there almost from the beginning—Britain was assuming dominance in racing car design. Even Italian teams had to have British designers, as did American open-cockpit teams. But the British near-monopoly on design stops, for the most part, at the firewall. The engines usually come from auto manufacturers. The exceptions are the Fords designed by Cosworth and the Mercedes-Benz engines from Ilmor, which was founded by former Cosworth employees in the early '80s, and even these were eventually "factory" owned as well as financed in their early stages. The bulk of the Formula One engines of the first half century came from the Continent (Porsche, Renault, Ferrari, Mercedes, BMW, Peugeot) or Japan (Honda and for a while Yamaha, with Toyota expected in 2002).

- The principal sponsors of the world driver's championship teams, by the close of the 20th century, were cigarette manufacturers forced away from many of their traditional advertising mediums due to government concerns over tobacco's cancer-causing potential. Instead, they paid to have their names painted on the flanks of racing cars, and thus took advantage of the ever-increasing exposure provided by televised races. The first cigarette maker to sponsor a world championship car did so in Europe in 1968, four years before Reynolds took the step in the U.S. With increasing governmental pressure on tobacco-related advertising, and with most European nations already enforcing a ban, by 2006 this type of advertising is expected to disappear from the grand prix circuit. Replacing this income stream will be difficult. At least two tobacco companies are currently paying Formula One teams more than $80 million annually.

- The most important technical advancement in the history of auto racing—and for all sports—was the development of television. It transformed racing into a major marketing medium, and made it more pressing for the principal automakers to somehow get involved. It raised the price of participation to levels undreamed of in the 1950s, and it moved drivers into the ranks of the world's wealthier athletes.

- Despite all this, the level of competition in world championship racing suffered badly by comparison with other, less sophisticated forms of the sport. In 1999 and 2000, for example, only two, and sometimes three, of the 22 cars admitted to championship races were capable of winning. The other 19 or 20 could only finish first if the leaders had mechanical difficulties or crashed. This was in stark contrast to a Winston Cup race, for example, where a dozen drivers in any of the 43-car fields were capable of outrunning the rest on a given day. More interesting, perhaps, was the fact that none of the millions of Formula One adherents seemed to mind.

- The last two decades of the century saw Englishman Bernard Charles (Bernie) Ecclestone, who recognized the basic scientific principle that nature abhors a vacuum, take control of the world championship and be responsible for its financial success. A motorcycle dealer, sometime racer in his youth, manager of drivers and team owner, he realized that the acknowledged authority, namely the International Automobile Federation, had no concept of the financial potential of the series. As a consequence, through a series of maneuvers he took over the running of the championship. When he began selling off pieces in 1999, the total value of Formula One Holdings was several billion dollars. What the France family did in America with NASCAR and the International Speedway Corporation, Ecclestone did on a worldwide basis, and did it quicker and more profitably, although the two situations are not exactly comparable.

- Because of the marketing possibilities, more major manufacturers than ever became involved, primarily as engine suppliers. These are the nine mentioned earlier. As an addendum it should be noted that Ferrari has for years been financed (and owned since 1988) by Fiat, which uses the Prancing Horse as a sort of public relations-cum-sales promotion icon for Italian products in general. It should also be noted that Ferrari probably earns more from licensing its logo than it does from the sale of its passenger cars.

- In Britain, the business home of grand prix racing, the sport has been one of many factors that have moved the country from its pre-World War II quasi-feudal state towards being more of a meritocracy. A socially acceptable hobby at its beginnings, racing provided the opportunity for persons allied with it to somehow move up the social ladder, at least to a degree, and even to be knighted. An anachronism in American eyes, perhaps, but the social structure of Britain has been changed by the country's involvement in the sport. When Stirling Moss, Jack Brabham and Frank Williams have a "Sir" in front of their names, and when Jackie Stewart, a garage owner's son, was added to this group in June, someone in government has to be paying attention.

- And towards the close of the century, thanks to television and the increased coverage in print media, Americans began to develop a greater interest in grand prix racing. Most of them found it boring but there is a certain appeal, even to those fans whose tastes run to oval tracks and stock cars.

- In America, Ford's ongoing successes in the (Europe-oriented) world championship races of the late '60s, the '70s and early '80s went begging for want of anyone to advertise or otherwise promote them. The Ford racing ban, instituted in late 1970 and lasting for about a decade, did not apply to Europe and, for some reason or other never verbalized, no one in the U.S. cared to look this gift horse in its mouth.

Because of the use of "world" before "championship," and because of the tacit acceptance by the public that the person who wins this must be the fastest driver on the planet—NASCAR, CART and drivers in other series notwithstanding—a certain mystique usually attaches itself to the holders of this title.

Whether justified or not, that is the case, and it has been so since the middle of the past century. At that time 8000 rpm was considered extreme and racing cars bore a faint resemblance to what was driven on the street. Today engines can run at 18,000 rpm and the cars act more like giant Karts than anything else. They are the fastest racing machines (when on a circuit that bears at least some resemblance to the true road courses of earlier times) competing in any form of the sport. In either case, and that has been one of the great attractions, there is a certain visceral thrill created by the sight and sound of a thoroughbred racing car streaking through the sunlight at 200 miles an hour.

It is what attracts the crowds, the sponsors and the television cameras, and is the basis for the aura that surrounds grand prix racing. It no doubt was there at the very first event of this type, long before there was a world championship per se, the 1906 Grand Prix of the Automobile Club of France. And it has been there ever since.

In today's environment, where consumer electronic devices provide instantaneous response to the most mundane requests, it is difficult to realize that something mechanical, namely, a V10 Formula One engine operating at maximum rpm, has its pistons coming to a full stop and reversing direction more than 600 times per second.

At outset of the 21st century the Otto-cycle engine, a basically inefficient arrangement in which only one fourth of the piston movement provides power, and which has to transform reciprocating motion into rotary, was 124 years old, and had undergone a remarkable degree of development. In 1906 the 13-liter winner of the French Grand Prix operated at 1200 rpm. The ongoing development of the four-stroke principle has pushed even lawn mower engines well past this, but the Formula One powerplant has always been the showpiece of the engine engineer. It is ironic, but the men who create these, with rare exception, are unknown to the world at large. The ones the public knows are the drivers. And they, not the engineers or the designers, are the ones who carry the title of champion. There is a Constructor's Cup but even that is awarded to the team, not to any individual on the technical staff.

The romance of the series has been provided by the drivers, by five-time champion Juan Manuel Fangio; four-time winner Alain Prost; by Stewart, Ayrton Senna, Niki Lauda, Brabham, and Michael Schumacher, all of whom won three times; by Americans Phil Hill and Mario Andretti; by Moss; and by dozens of others.

Romance needs a face, not a horsepower rating.

At its birth, shortly after World War II, the series was little more than what in the 1930s had been the European championship, with the Indianapolis 500 added to the list. This was a bow to the American Automobile Association, which at that time was the principal sanctioning body for racing in this country, and to justify the use of "world." (With the notable exception of world champion Alberto Ascari of Italy in 1952, no one who competed in the European races took part in the 500 during this period. As a consequence this review of the half century does not include the 1950–60 Indianapolis results; the 500 was dropped after 1960. With these added, the total number of races rises to 646.)

This new competition attracted little notice outside the Continent, least of all in Dearborn. For that matter, it attracted little notice anywhere in the U.S., except for the small group of road-racing enthusiasts who felt that oval-track racing, with little or no use of brakes and gearboxes, was in the dark ages compared to what was common practice in Europe.

At first the fields—and they varied from 13 to as many as 31—were composed principally of "factory" entries from Alfa Romeo, Ferrari, Maserati, Lancia, Talbot, Gordini, ERA, HWM, Connaught and the like. All have become history, or in the case of Ferrari remained alive by being supported through Fiat. Added to these were so-called private entries, wealthy amateurs who had purchased a car from one of the factories and were welcomed by race organizers as fillers. The great exception to the privateers-at-the back situation was Moss, who in the last three years of his Formula One career drove for Johnnie Walker whiskey heir R.R.C. Walker because he could make more money that way. Walker bought the cars, usually Lotuses or Coopers, and Moss drove them.

The basic change started in the late 1950s, when British teams whose business was racing, but who used engines built by others, began dominating the grids. Cooper, which introduced the mid-engined racing car to the postwar era, was first; Lotus was next; and the others, including Brabham, McLaren, Tyrrell and Williams, came after.

The reasons were economic: Most of the British teams were small and couldn't afford engine development programs of their own. For a while their powerplant of choice was built by Coventry Climax, and when that company ceased being a supplier at the close of 1966, the door was open for Ford and Cosworth. The 1967 debut of the DFV engine (DFV stands for double four valve) was covered in Volume I. A look at the engine more than three decades later shows that Ford's $280,000 investment, coaxed, cajoled and politicked past Dearborn by Ford of Britain's Walter Hayes, is the best business decision ever made regarding a racing project. Not only did Ford pave the way for Lotus' success, it also provided, through the DFV, the basic building block for most of the others.

There were a few exceptions to the model established by Cooper, Lotus and others in similar circumstances. These were Vanwall and BRM, which stood for British Racing Motors. Each had its own purpose-built engine. Vanwall, the racing arm of Vandervell Products, a major supplier of bearings and bushings and once an investor in BRM, had the fastest Formula One cars in 1957 and 1958 and won six of the nine races in which the team participated in the latter year. It was the last of the successful front-engined grand prix cars, but owner Tony Vandervell withdrew after winning the first of the FIA Constructor's Cups—and realizing his dream of beating Ferrari.

BRM, originally designed as an effort to bring racing prestige to the United Kingdom, is perhaps most noted for a supercharged 1.5-liter V16 engine that was remarkably unsuccessful in the early 1950s. The team, for much of its life funded by the Rubery Owen industrial empire and run in its later years by Sir Alfred Owen's brother-in-law, was at its best in the early 1960s. It finally succumbed after the 1974 season when Sir Alfred died and the financial tap was turned off. In the end, both teams ceased operations not so much because of what happened on the circuits, but because they were money losers rather than moneymakers. In the new era of world championship racing there was little room for benevolent owners.

At first Formula One entrants—and cars in any internationally sanctioned racing—were required to wear their FIA-assigned colors (red for Italian cars, green for British, blue for French, etc.). This ceased abruptly in 1968, when Lotus, after team leader and owner Colin Chapman had taken a look at the commercial aspects of American racing, obtained Gold Leaf cigarettes as a sponsor and decked his cars out in that livery. The rest followed soon afterward, and by the last decade of the century the most difficult thing to find on a Formula One car was a national color, advertising having long since replaced such quaint ideas. Even Ferrari, which can be considered the great exception to the rule, as it has been to many of F1's folkways and mores, has its red color very close to that of sponsor Marlboro.

Chapman, the brilliant designer and team owner, was a key figure in the history of Formula One racing. His designs kept Lotus ahead of the pack in the '60s and '70s, his teams won six FIA Constructor's Cups and his drivers six championships, and he was responsible for bringing European road racing into the realm of commercialism. Chapman's alliance with Gold Leaf, and the FIA's acceptance of advertising on cars as a fact of life, provoked a sea change in the way F1 racing was conducted. It enabled the Tyrrells, the Williamses, the McLarens and the rest to become financially stable and in later years wealthy.

One unforeseen result of Ford's bringing Chapman to America and paying him to educate Americans about the virtues of rear-engined cars was to educate him in the ways sponsorship could be achieved. He imported that concept to Europe, so in one sense was partly responsible for the rise of Ecclestone. When Ford laid out large sums to put Stewart Grand Prix in business, to buy Cosworth Racing and data acquisition specialists Pi, and later to buy out Stewart, the seed for the exponential growth of the money involved had been planted by one of its own vendors.

At the outset—again, without Indianapolis—there were only six races counting for the title, and this number finally reached ten in 1958. It grew to 15 by 1973, and was either 16 or 17 (the latter twice) beginning in 1984. In 1950 a driver's best four finishes out of the seven races counted, and this number varied by year and by the FIA's indecision (10 out of 12, 12 of 14, 11 of 16, etc.). It finally stabilized in 1991 and since then all results have counted, with the points being awarded on a 10-6-4-3-2-1-basis to the first six finishers. The number of races grew for a simple reason: There was money to be made, and so new countries—and in some cases new circuits in "old" countries—were added to the schedule.

In the 1950s numerous grand prix races were run over distances of roughly 300 miles, but by the close of the century that had shrunk to an FIA-imposed limit of

190 miles or two hours, for television packaging purposes. The circuits had also shrunk, with the only three close to their original dimensions being Silverstone in Britain, Monza in Italy and the street layout in Monaco. The greatest of the circuits—the 14.2-mile Nürburgring in Germany and 8.5-mile Spa-Francorchamps in Belgium—were now truncated versions of their former selves. The German grand prix left the Eifel region for a more accessible Hockenheim Ring after the 1976 race, and it has been held there, with only two exceptions, ever since, returning to the "new" Ring twice. The "new" Nürburgring has also been the venue for various other championship events, such as the Ecclestone-organized Grand Prix of Luxembourg (the country is practically next door to the Ring) and the Grand Prix of Europe in several years—in other words, another TV date.

The term Formula One comes from the French, the mother tongue of the Europe-oriented *Federation Internationale de l'Automobile*, or International Automobile Federation (FIA), which writes the rules and conducts both the driver's championship and the constructor's championship. By the end of the century the term "formula" was in common use for many national classes of racing car in addition to international classes, with such as Formula Ford, Formula Vee, Formula Nissan, Formula Atlantic, Formula 3000 and the like having proliferated.

The ones with manufacturer's names attached are sometimes called "marketing formulas," because of financial or engineering support from the eponymous automaker, although Formula Ford has for many years grown well past being company-supported. In either case what is meant is that these are racing cars, designed for that purpose with no need for headlights, horns, turn indicators, passenger seats or anything else not contributing to speed.

Language and cultural differences being what they are, the U.S. sanctioning bodies, especially those in the oval-track community, don't use the term "formula," but whatever the specifications, for everything from quarter-midgets driven by five-year-olds through sprint cars running on half-mile dirt ovals, up to the close-to-F1-regulation CART machines, the idea is the same: Formula One cars are merely more sophisticated in design and in the materials used.

At the birth of the world championship a private entrant could buy a complete car for less than $10,000. After 50 years the price has increased somewhat. A "rolling chassis," which means the carbon-fiber tub with all suspension pieces, steering, brakes and transmission—in other words everything but the engine—costs in the millions. It is not possible to put a dollar figure on this, because each team has its own designers, development engineers and the like, and spends the entire season and off-season (if there is such a thing in modern racing) improving what they already have.

By way of comparison, the rolling chassis currently in use in CART, which are roughly comparable to those used in F1 and which are bought off the shelf from suppliers such as Reynard, cost approximately $500,000. Private drivers, with any size pocketbook, are a thing of the past insofar as owning cars is concerned, although there are some who buy their way onto the lesser teams for sums that can be as high as $10 million, usually by way of bringing sponsorship money with them. Or they go to another variety of the sport where the price of admission is not so steep.

Although the regulations have become increasingly complicated over the years, the basics are still the same: maximum allowable engine displacement, sometimes with supercharger or turbocharger, sometimes without, and minimum allowable weight. The rest, with the exception of details that assure a measure of safety for the driver, is up to the designer.

The basic regulations for Formula One cars were changed 19 times in those first 50 years, with nine involving power limitation, which in the end served to prove something known all along: Engineers can usually outsmart the rules makers. The current limitation of ten cylinders and five valves per cylinder has done little to slow the cars, which means the problem of the vehicles being too fast for their circuits is an ongoing one.

By way of illustration: The 1951 Alfa Romeos had 1.5-liter supercharged engines that produced, at best, an unsubstantiated 420 horsepower on alcohol-based fuel and weighed roughly 1550 pounds (with oil and water, but without fuel or driver) in an era when there was no minimum weight limit.

The 2000 Jaguars, McLaren-Mercedes and Ferraris weighed in at the current minimum limit of 600 kilograms (approximately 1325 pounds) with driver, oil and water, but no fuel, and produced a little more than 800 horsepower on 105-octane gasoline from 3.0-liter normally aspirated engines. The power-to-weight ratios, if we add 175 pounds for the 1950 driver, are 4.1 pounds per horsepower in 1950 and

*Then: Juan Manuel Fangio in his Alfa Romeo Tipo 159,
the Grand Prix of Switzerland, 1951.—Robson Collection*

1.66 pounds per horsepower in 1999. This works out, for the 2000 engines, to about 4.5 horsepower per cubic inch. It should also be noted that the current cars are brought in under the minimum weight, and therefore have the advantage of adding ballast where it is needed to lower the car's center of gravity even more. In some cases there is as much as 100 pounds of ballast, sometimes depleted uranium, one of the heaviest substances on the periodic table.

The FIA was based at birth and for many years thereafter in Paris, and is composed of the national automobile clubs of the various countries that belong. The FIA and its members at first owed their influential position to the fact that in Europe they controlled the *Carnets de Passage*, the documents drivers needed to travel from one country to another in the pre- and immediate post-World War II eras.

Once the carnets were surpassed in importance by a simple international insurance card in the late 1950s, the influence of the national clubs waned, and the only practical purpose served by the FIA was to oversee auto racing. Its byzantine arrangements with all the various elements of racing, including television networks, caused the organization to move to Geneva in 1999 in order to avoid European Community scrutiny of some relationships that appeared to be in restraint of trade.

The series, organized at the outset by the blue-blazered and blue-blooded FIA, has been run by Ecclestone since 1980, the first man to view the championship as a business opportunity. But in the late 1960s and 1970s it was still masquerading as a sport, and was, had Dearborn wanted to take advantage of it on the west side of the Atlantic, a ready-made image builder.

From the spring of 1967, when Clark and Graham Hill drove DFV-Lotuses in the engine's debut at Zandvoort, practically every great grand prix driver sat behind the wheel of a Ford-engined Formula One car at one point in his career. Ten of them won the title using Ford power, but there are two who are more closely identified with the blue oval, when it comes to driving grand prix machinery, than any of the rest:

Stewart and Andretti.

They came from different backgrounds and performed, for the most part, in different arenas, but they were both key figures for Ford in the last four decades of the century.

Stewart won the world championship three times, in 1969, 1971 and 1973, all with Ford engines. He was second in 1968 despite missing two races due to a broken wrist suffered in a non-championship event, and also second in 1972 despite being hampered for a great part of the year by an ulcer. With a bit of luck he could have been the second five-time champion. He came within a hair of winning the Indianapolis 500 in his first of only two attempts and retired in 1973, after only 99 world championship starts, as the ruler of his era. When his racing career ended he became a consultant to Ford, first in a public relations function and later in an engineering development role, and spent a good part of the next 30 years on test tracks, helping to elevate the roadholding standards of the company's products.

Jackie Stewart: Winning at Monaco, 1973.—Ford Motor Company

Andretti was discussed in the previous chapter. He has become an American icon who has evolved into a distinguished elder statesman of the sport.

After its debut the DFV engine won 151 of the 221 races held in that span, or better than two-thirds. Lotus had the engine to itself for the first season, but it was clear to Hayes, Duckworth and Chapman that the latter would have exclusive rights for 1967 only, and the next year Matra and McLaren used it as well. By 1969 it was also in the hands of Brabham, and it was clear this was The Engine if one wanted to win.

The drivers who succeeded with the DFV were a disparate group:

- Graham Hill, the archetypical Englishman with a helmet carrying the colors of his rowing club, who won the second his of championships in 1968 with a Lotus.

- Stewart, who led European drivers into the high-income bracket and won three times with Matra and Tyrrell chassis.

- Jochen Rindt, the Austrian who was Stewart's neighbor in Switzerland and who had enough of a points lead in 1970 that he won despite being killed at Monza late in the season.

- Brazilian Emerson Fittipaldi, who won in 1972 and 1974, first with a Lotus and then with a McLaren.

- James Hunt, the Englishman who won in 1976 with a McLaren.

- Andretti, who managed to be a trans-Atlantic commuter and win for Lotus in 1978 while still competing in American events.

- Australia's Alan Jones, who won in 1980 for the Williams team's first championship.

- Nelson Piquet, the initial three-time winner from Brazil, who won his first title in 1981 with a Brabham.

- Finn Keke Rosberg, the 1982 winner, the last of the DFV-powered titleholders, for the second of Williams' titles.

At the beginning of the DFV era Denis Hulme of New Zealand won the 1967 world championship driving a Repco-Brabham, using an Australian engine based on a GM aluminum block and with only one camshaft per cylinder bank. But that was the end of winning with reliability rather than torque and horsepower.

There are seven different disciplines in the realm of major-league motorsports, if one counts rallying, and if there were to be a true world champion he would have to participate in at least several of these. Today, with the amount of money involved and with schedule demands, there is practically no in-season crossing over from one type of racing to another such as practiced in the 1960s and '70s by Andretti, Dan Gurney, Parnelli Jones, A.J. Foyt and a few others.

Others who came close were Fittipaldi and Britain's Nigel Mansell, both of whom were winners on the American single-seater circuit after their grand prix careers. Earlier there was Clark, a two-time champion who was the first post-World War II foreigner to win the Indianapolis 500, and Stewart, who had a comfortable lead at Indianapolis when engine trouble sidelined him eight laps before the end. The DNF, as it turned out, was a gift to Graham Hill, who wound up the winner.

Stock-car drivers are conspicuous by their absence from the all-around list, either because their schedule never permitted time for other types of racing or because they didn't have the desire. Whether Richard Petty, David Pearson, Cale Yarborough, Dale Earnhardt or Jeff Gordon would have been world class in another type of vehicle is speculation and can only be discussed, never proven one way or the other. The same is true for Ayrton Senna, Michael Schumacher or any other first-rank grand prix driver.

The debate over who *would* have been better, or *could* have been better, had he moved from one kind of racing to another, is one that can have no end, because until someone has actually done it in all forms of competition, there can only be speculation. Britain's Moss, for example, was the fastest driver in Formula One when he had his career-ending accident, and was untouchable in long-distance sports-car racing. But he never drove stock cars, and his only oval-track appearance was a brief one in an unsuitable vehicle. These observations are made to point out that there is no true "world" champion in automobile racing, only one that has been created for some sort of marketing purpose, just as it has in many other forms of sport.

Year by year, once the DFV appeared the Formula One picture looked like this:

1967—Reliability Over Speed and Innovation

In the second year of the 3.0-liter unsupercharged/1.5-liter supercharged formula, many expected Ferrari's V12 to be dominant. But after the Ford-Cosworth V8 made its debut in the Netherlands on June 4, there was little question of what was fastest: It was the Lotus 49, complete with the new V8 plus Clark and Hill as drivers. But something happened on the way to the championship, which was won by New Zealander Denis Hulme in his tube-frame Brabham equipped with the Repco V8.

There were eleven races counting for the title and the new Ford engine, which appeared in the third, won four of the last nine, all by Clark. But both Hulme and team owner Jack Brabham won two, and both earned points in nine of the eleven events. Clark finished six races with points, Hill only three. Chapman's brilliance as the designer of the 49, in which the engine became a stressed chassis member, was once again diminished by the Lotus' lack of reliability, something Ford had experienced a few years earlier in its Indianapolis campaigns. In addition, despite its obvious superiority, the DFV also had to suffer through a maturation process. The nine races in which DFV-powered Lotuses competed saw either Clark or Hill put them on the pole, so the rest of the field knew if the Lotuses stayed together they would in all probability win. Clark won in Holland, Britain, Watkins Glen and Mexico. Clark and Hill were the only drivers to hold the lead in the latter three events.

The Brabhams also won the FIA Constructor's Cup, 67-50, over Lotus. But that would change in the years to come. The DFV was producing approximately 405 horsepower in its first season, a figure that would grow to more than 500 before the engine saw its last world championship in 1982.

1968—Clark Dies, Hill Wins, DFV Dominant

The addition of the Spanish Grand Prix in May increased the world championship season to twelve races, eleven of which were won by Ford-engined cars. The biggest story of the season came in April, when Clark, who became the most successful grand prix driver of all time when he won his 25th in January's Grand Prix of South Africa, was killed. His Lotus went straight off the road in a high-speed bend at Hockenheim in a Formula Two race, and the cause of the accident was never determined. Clark was running well back in the pack at the time of the mishap.

Hill won his second championship in a season-long struggle with Stewart and Hulme that was not decided until the Mexican Grand Prix, the last race of the season.

Hill won three races, including two when Stewart was sidelined with his fractured wrist—incurred in a Formula Two event early in the year—and spent much of the season driving with a cast on one arm. Stewart, in a Matra with Ford engine as the French aerospace company entered the Formula One circus, competed in ten events. He finished eight of them, an 80 percent mark in a year in which roughly 44 percent of the starting fields dropped out for one reason or another, and earned points in seven.

Matra and McLaren were added to the ranks of Ford engine customers in 1968, and a private entry, Rob Walker, also got one when he was able to purchase the first Lotus 49 sold to anyone outside Chapman's organization. The car, with Swiss Jo Siffert driving, won the British Grand Prix at Brands Hatch the week it was delivered. Lotus won the Constructor's Cup with 62 points to 51 for McLaren and 45 for Matra.

This was also the first year of wings, with the aerodynamic assists being made popular by the GM-backed Chaparral, 1967's fastest racing sports car, which was on full view for British designers when it won at Brands Hatch in the fall of that year. Almost everyone tried them in 1968, sometimes with good results, sometimes with disastrous ones. Almost all were add-ons done by rule-of-thumb engineering. But it was the start of aerodynamic research on the part of Formula One teams. It was also a year in which Cosworth spent some serious research time, with Ford financial backing, looking into the possibility of building a four-wheel drive grand prix car carrying its own name. Robin Herd, later the McLaren designer responsible for the team's Can-Am Series sports cars, was brought in to do this one, and spent two years with Cosworth. In the end nothing came of the project, but it was interesting to note.

As a footnote to the season Andretti, already a star on the USAC circuit and the 1967 winner of the Daytona 500, made his Formula One debut at Watkins Glen—and sat his Lotus on the pole. He only lasted 33 of the 108 laps until his clutch let go, but Europe had been served notice that one of their own would be coming back, the immigrant American no longer a boy wondering what the future held, but now someone who would determine it for himself.

1969—Stewart Drives Away with It

He had been a threat ever since first appearing in a grand prix race in 1965 and almost took the title in 1968, but this would be Jackie Stewart's year. By the time six of the eleven races were over he had clinched the championship, having won five. The Matra team, its funding commensurate with what one would expect from a major defense contractor and with its cars built by technicians used to aircraft standards, were untouchable until late in the season. In their first nine races—a total of 18 starts—Stewart and teammate Jean-Pierre Beltoise were running at the finish 15 times. Only one design flaw came to light, when both cars were forced out of the Monte Carlo Grand Prix by broken half-axles, these being too light to handle the constant demand for low-speed acceleration characteristic of the Monegasque event. The Constructor's Cup was almost an afterthought, with 66 points to Brabham's 51.

DFV engines finished at least 1-2 in every world championship race, as they were the choice of every team except Ferrari and BRM. The engine now produced approximately 430 hp at 9500 rpm, with better reliability. The Ferrari V12 was also reputed to have 430 hp, but at 11,000 rpm, and with torque characteristics not nearly as good as the Ford's. In certain quarters the Ferrari figure was dismissed as referring to ponies rather than full-size horses.

Stewart's principal opposition came from two brilliant young men, Belgian Jacky Ickx, who drove for Brabham, and Jochen Rindt, the fiery Austrian who was now number one for Lotus. Ickx, later to share the seat of a Le Mans winner a total of six times, won the German Grand Prix, running nose-to-tail with Stewart in the early stages, then moving ahead when the Scotsman had gearbox problems. Rindt was the pole sitter five times during the season and won the U.S. Grand Prix at Watkins Glen, which carried what one publication called the "stupendous" first prize of $50,000. Since the engines were the same the difference between chassis placed greater importance on the difference between drivers. As a consequence the prices paid to them rose and then rose again, a trend that has continued. Andretti, busy with his USAC campaign and winning the Indianapolis 500, drove only three events for Lotus and failed to finish any, including the U.S. GP, where he was the pilot of Chapman's experimental four-wheel drive vehicle.

The European Formula Two championship was also a Ford-Matra affair, as Frenchman Johnny Servoz-Gavin won with this combination. Fifteen of the first 18 cars in the F2 point standings were powered by Ford 1.6-liter FVA engines—the ancestor of the DFV.

1970—The Carriage Is As Important As the Horse

At the beginning of 1969 Stewart and Tyrrell knew Matra was building a V12 engine and would want to use it for 1970. They wanted to stay with the Ford V8, and as a consequence began the search for a new car. The first choice was March, a new vehicle designed by Herd, who left Cosworth to form a team with former drivers Alan Rees and Max Mosley, the latter better known, in non-racing circles, as the son of pre-World War II British Fascist Sir Oswald Mosley. The son would go on to become the president of the FIA. As an indication of just how small the Formula One community had become, at the same time Herd was entertaining an offer from Jochen Rindt's manager to start another team. The manager was Bernie Ecclestone.

March not only built cars for others, it also had its own drivers, Chris Amon and Jo Siffert, with even Andretti available for five races. The net result was that 1970 was a down year for Stewart and for Ford as well, winning "only" eight of the 13 races. The March was not equal to the Matra of 1969, much less the new Lotus 72, which was viewed as a quantum leap in racing car design. In addition, the new Ferrari flat-12 cylinder engine was producing more horsepower than the Ford, and there were also Matra and BRM V12s to consider. Finally, with 15 drivers using Ford engines, Cosworth's maintenance facilities were strained. At times the quality of the rebuilds—especially in the middle of the season—was not up to previous standards.

It was a year marked more by controversy and tragedy than anything else, with three drivers killed, including Rindt, who died during practice for the Italian Grand Prix in September. The others were Piers Courage, in the Grand Prix of the Netherlands, and Bruce McLaren, who died at Goodwood while testing a new Can Am car. The drive for safer circuits, led by Stewart, resulted in the German Grand Prix being transferred from the Eifel Mountains to Hockenheim, a relatively featureless circuit not in the class of the Nürburgring but with better safety features. The issue was prominent throughout the year, necessitating the French GP being transferred from Albi to Clermont-Ferrand, and the Belgian race threatened with a boycott—which never took place—before being held at Spa.

Rindt won five of the first eight races in 1970, including four in a row: the grands prix of Holland, France, Britain and Germany. Ickx, driving the new flat-12 Ferrari, won in Austria, Canada and Mexico. Clay Regazzoni, a Swiss from the Italian-speaking part of that country, won the Italian Grand Prix and a newcomer, in his fourth F1 event, won at Watkins Glen. His name was Emerson Fittipaldi.

Stewart won only in Spain and finished tied for fifth behind Rindt (45), Ickx (40), Regazzoni (33) and Hulme (27), and even with Brabham (25). The Tyrrell team's recognition of March's limited future caused it to head in another direction even before its first race. In late February of the year Tyrrell and Stewart were discussing building their own chassis. Tyrrell had already contracted with Derek Gardner to design the first Tyrrell and Stewart didn't find out until a month later. The budget money was provided by Walter Hayes, and the finished car was presented in Ford's London showroom in mid-August.

Jochen Rindt: The 1970 champion in a Lotus 72.—Ford Motor Company

*Early wings: Graham Hill leads Jochen Rindt and Jack Brabham
at Brands Hatch, 1970.—Ford Motor Company*

It participated in the last three events of the year and Stewart was the pole sitter twice and second fastest once. Engine trouble once, collapsed suspension once, and bad steering the third time wound up the year. The Constructor's Cup went to Lotus, just ahead of Ferrari.

1971—Stewart Again—and Again

Paul Frere, the journalist, engineer, former grand prix driver and Le Mans winner, in reviewing the season, wrote: "… it is improper to pick out a single driver as world champion in a form of competition in which so much depends on factors which have nothing in common with the ability of the driver. The best driver in the world cannot possibly become a world champion if he happens to sit in an inferior car.… even if his car is fully up to the task so many trivial things can happen which have nothing to do with the driver's ability (an electrical fault, a puncture, and so on), that you cannot really separate the performance of a driver from all sorts of technical aspects. But if we *must* have a world championship … then surely the title could not have crowned a more undisputed champion than Jackie Stewart.…"

It was Stewart's busiest year, combining a full championship season with an almost full-time effort in the SCCA's Can Am series. This necessitated his crossing the Atlantic on a weekly basis from June through October, and no doubt contributed to the ulcer he acquired the following year. Stewart and Tyrrell had the latest Cosworth, producing 450 horsepower with a maximum rev limit of 10,500—1700 more than in 1967. Although the Ferrari twelve-cylinder could be taken to 12,500 rpm and the logical assumption is that it produced more top-end power, it was no match for the Ford. In road racing acceleration out of corners is more important than top speed, which is reached few times on any lap. And mid-range torque was the strong point of Keith Duckworth's creation.

Stewart finished nine of the season's eleven grand prix races, as before a remarkable record for consistency and car preparation as well as for speed. He finished second to Andretti's Ferrari in the season opener in South Africa, in what was Mario's first Ferrari drive and first grand prix win. Stewart led almost from start to finish in Spain, went wire-to-wire in Monte Carlo, then had a bad race in the rain in Holland when his tires weren't competitive. He led from start to finish in France, led all but three laps in the British Grand Prix and led from the start to the flag in Germany. By the close of the year he had 62 points, almost double Lotus driver Ronnie Peterson's runner-up 33. The Constructor's Cup was a runaway: Tyrrell 73, BRM 36.

Three more drivers died during the season: Siffert in a non-championship F1 race at Brands Hatch, Pedro Rodriguez in a sports-car race in Germany, and Italian Ignazio Giunti in an Argentine sports-car event. Among the drivers making their debuts was Austrian Niki Lauda, who rented a March to participate in his country's grand prix. He lasted 20 of the 54 laps, an inauspicious beginning to a career that would see him win three world championships.

Chapter 13

———•———

TURNING LEFT—AND RIGHT

Grand-scale racing for what can be termed sports or prototype cars has been in danger of extinction for some time. In the U.S. it has become a footnote, albeit a large one, to NASCAR stock-car and CART single-seater competition, and although it has its fans, they are few in number compared to the more popular forms of the sport. On a worldwide basis there is one notable exception to this decline and that is the 24 Hours of Le Mans, which has become as much of an institution as an automotive event, and which prospers because it has managed to rise above the restrictions and mistakes of the International Automobile Federation. A testimonial to its stature is the fact that it is televised live in the U.S. from start to finish. It may be on cable, but 24 hours is a long time for one program in any form of broadcasting.

What is called sports-car racing, prototype racing or simply road racing, has European roots, and the reasons for this are found in the history of the automobile. Roads in Europe pre-dated the automobile by hundreds, even thousands of years, and as a consequence cars had to be designed to fit the roads. In addition, it has been traditional in Europe to tax by engine displacement or horsepower. Add high taxes on fuel, and the design path for the automaker was clear. It led down the road to light, maneuverable vehicles, especially in Britain, where a straight road was an anomaly (and still is, except for the motorways). There were always large ones owned by the wealthy, but neither these cars nor their owners were representative of the basic economic condition.

In the U.S. the automobile and a large portion of the road system grew up more or less in tandem. In many places towns could be designed around roads rather than vice versa, there was no tax on displacement or horsepower, and fuel was cheap. The result, after the Model T put America on wheels, was a trend toward large, low-revving engines and big cars. The performance cars of the '20s and '30s were vehicles such as the Stutz Bearcat or a number of different Duesenbergs: They looked sporting, but they weren't very maneuverable. Although few realized it at the time, the few Model Ts, when made over with the many speed-equipment chassis and engine parts available, were what passed for a sports car in the 'teens and '20s. In the '30s, with the exception of an insignificant number of European models, a V8 Ford roadster was as sporting a vehicle as you could find here. There were Cords and the like, but again, they were not the mainstream.

In the U.S. the sport moved in the direction of ovals—horse tracks at country fairgrounds at the start—for a simple economic reason: There was a fence, and a turnstile. You could charge admission, and so racing became a business as well as a sport. As a consequence racing car design took the oval tracks into account, and moved farther away from that of series production cars.

In the early days of the automobile there were some road races in the U.S. The pre-World War I Vanderbilt Cup events on Long Island, the Grand Prize races at Savannah, Milwaukee and San Francisco, the Vanderbilt Cup and Grand Prize races at Santa Monica before and after the war were the outstanding ones, but the ovals then took over. It would be decades before a major American event would be held on a road course again.

In pre-World War I Europe automobiles were the playthings of the aristocracy. They had connections to (or were) the rulers, and it was a relatively simple matter to close roads for competitions. And although racing car design may have become sophisticated, in those days it never lost the connection to the "real" world. Ferdinand Porsche may have designed the Auto Unions, for example, but he also did the Volkswagen.

To understand what has happened to this variety of competition one has to first go back to the 30-year period following World War II, which was the best time for road racing. Europe was recovering from six years of conflict, the auto industry was profitable due to pent-up demand for cars, and there was a tradition of racing on roads that went back to the birth of the automobile. There was money to build competition cars, readily available labor, and the national automobile clubs were looking to return to racing.

Although they had such prewar ancestors as two-seater Bentleys, Delages, Delahayes, Alfa Romeos and Mercedes, grand touring cars came into "official" being in the late 1940s. Grand touring comes from the French *Grand Tourisme*, which was the FIA name given to high-performance two-seater cars at that time so that race and rally organizers could fit them into a class. These were series production cars, usually well appointed, and intended for touring in what was supposed to be the grand manner. And if you wanted to take your helmet instead of a wallet and toothbrush, that was OK.

They first came to America after the war in the form of the MG TC and other British creations, such as Austin Healeys and Triumph TR2's (which may have looked appealing, but which should have given observers a clue as to what would eventually happen to the UK's auto industry). This genre included the Mercedes 300SL, Porsches, Jaguars, Aston Martins, Lancias, Alfas, Maseratis and Ferraris. Some were convertibles, although the vast majority of those competing in Europe were coupes.

There were events for these and for their (almost inevitable) children, such as the C-Type Jaguar, which came from the XK120 production model. Called racing sports cars, and known later on as sports prototypes, these were the next step—

lower, lighter, faster. They had to have two seats, a windshield of sorts, head-lights, fenders, and other accoutrements to show their relationship to standard production, and in theory at least they could be licensed for the road if anyone put mufflers on them (in the '50s many of them did carry license numbers—even without the mufflers).

The races in which they competed, especially those counting for the new (in 1953) World Manufacturer's Championship, were long-distance events, designed to test a car's all-around performance and endurance. These included Le Mans, Italy's Mille Miglia (which ran around the country for 1000 miles), the Sicilian Targa Florio, the Mexican Carrera Panamericana, the 1000-kilometer race at Germany's Nürburgring, and the Tourist Trophy on the Isle of Man and later at the Dundrod circuit in Northern Ireland. Some of these had been in existence for decades—the Targa since 1906, the Mille Miglia since 1927, Le Mans since 1923.

There were others, too: 1000-kilometer events in Argentina and at Monza in Italy; Spa's 1000-kilometer and 24-hour races in Belgium; another 1000-kilometer race in Venezuela; and starting in the early 1950s, a twelve-hour event on an airport made into a circuit near the orange groves in Sebring, Florida.

They provided much of the romance that went with racing in the '40s-'50s-'60s era. The big names were all there, the Juan Manuel Fangios, Alberto Ascaris, Phil Hills and Stirling Mosses, but since many of the events needed large fields (the Mille Miglia attracted hundreds of competitors), amateurs were welcome. In Europe, in fact, there was no distinction between amateur and professional in the literal sense. Professional meant only that you drove as a means of earning a living.

The way road racing was: Juan Manuel Fangio at the start of the Mille Miglia, 1955.—Daimler-Benz

In theory at least, this type of racing should be the best, most entertaining form of the sport. One has to turn both left and right, go through fast bends and slow ones, make constant use of brakes and transmission, and so on. It requires a better-balanced automobile than does oval-track racing, and as such should be best suited for a manufacturer to use for sales promotion, since the cars carry names that are the same as those of production models. Racing cars with brand names, after all, has been the secret of NASCAR's success.

But it hasn't worked out that way:

- Open-road racing bowed to safety considerations years ago. The last major event of this type in North and Central America was the Carrera Panamericana of 1950–54, and the problems involved with keeping spectators, not to mention cows and chickens, off the road were the reason for its demise. The last point-to-point race in the United States, as far as anyone can attest, was the pre-World War I Los Angeles–Phoenix. Point-to-point racing stopped in Europe as a result of the disastrous Paris–Madrid contest of 1903, which was canceled when the leaders reached Bordeaux after a number of onlookers, unfamiliar with these new automotive creations, were killed. (Among the drivers who died was Marcel Renault, a founder of the firm carrying his name.)

    The Mille Miglia was cancelled after the 1957 accident in which the Marquis de Portago lost his own life, plus that of his co-driver and took more than a dozen spectators with him. The Targa Florio, run on a 45-mile circuit of Sicilian roads closed for the occasion, lasted through 1973. Even the *Gran Premio Standard,* or production-car grand prix of Argentina, run for years on the country's public highways, is now part of history. The various events of America's off-road racers—if "off road" can be construed as "open" road—are all that is left.

- The closed-circuit facilities, including those using highways transformed for the occasion, have shrunk to where the 8.5-mile Le Mans circuit is the only one left that resembles its former self. The "old" 14.2-mile Nürburgring, now an extension of the shorter circuit that opened in 1984, is used only for some longer production-car events, including a 24-hour race once a year, but those have become more of an anomaly than anything else.

    There are few of any stature in the U.S. that are "road" courses—Laguna Seca, Watkins Glen, Road Atlanta, Road America, Sebring and Sears Point. There are numerous smaller ones, probably led by Lime Rock, and many ovals that have makeshift road circuits in their infields, with Daytona being by far the best of these. None of these, however, have the dimensions of the Ring or Le Mans, or Spa.

- The economics of racing: It is difficult to put a fence around a road circuit of any length. And those who watch without paying do not help a promoter's financial statement. In Europe in the "golden" days, the races were organized (as opposed to promoted) by the national auto clubs, who at the time were more interested in tradition than in making money, until Ecclestone showed them how.

- In Europe the FIA and its member clubs managed to sublimate sports-car racing to Formula One because of the increased emphasis on the latter and the profits to be derived from F1. This began in the mid-1970s, or about the time Ecclestone became a person of influence.

- The FIA was incapable of consistency. In the 48 years since the World Manufacturer's Championship was inaugurated, the top level of sports-car/prototype racing has counted for more than 20 different championships. Most of the public has never been quite clear about what constitutes the championship. And once they became accustomed to something called Group 5, or Group C, or Group Whatever, the FIA could be depended upon to change the name again. Imagine the reaction of fans (or sponsors) if the World Series, or soccer World Cup, changed its name on a more or less regular basis.

- With the growth of television coverage, events held on big circuits, much less open roads, needed larger production budgets, and their running time made putting together live television packages impractical (Formula One races are limited to two hours because of this). Le Mans is the exception. The growth of cable television and its need for programming has changed this to a degree, but it remains to be seen if long-distance races on television, using current production technology, will be successful.

- The inability of sanctioning bodies to promote this segment of the sport. In the U.S. this refers primarily to the Sports Car Club of America, or SCCA, and also to IMSA, or International Motor Sports Association. The SCCA was founded in 1945 as an Eastern Establishment amateurs-only group, and after five decades of up-and-down success with professional series, has now become a successful club racing organization. IMSA was created in 1969 by John Bishop, a former SCCA executive who felt his original club had not achieved its potential, and he did this with the backing of NASCAR's Bill France. In the last few years the SCCA has been joined by Grand American Road Racing Association (Grand Am), financed by the France family and their associates, and by the ALMS, or American Le Mans Series. This group has been created and financed by pharmaceuticals manufacturer Don Panoz, a businessman who is a relative newcomer to motorsports. Whether or not he will be successful in bringing back what has become a more or less minor-league form remains to be seen. IMSA, which went through some bad times and various ownerships, has survived as Professional Sports Car Racing, which is the sanctioning and organizing body for the Panoz series.

As a consequence, what passes for major long-distance racing, on an international basis, has boiled down to the 24-hour race at Daytona in early February, Sebring's twelve-hour event, and Le Mans. The latter, run on highways just south of town and with almost 80 years of history behind it, has become more than just an auto race. It is an institution, as is the Indianapolis 500, and one which has been able to write its own rules whenever the FIA made regulations the Automobile Club de l'Ouest felt would be detrimental to it.

That being said, Ford's efforts in sports-car or prototype road racing never again approached the triumphs at Le Mans of the 1960s. Those were the great days for the company, defeating Ferrari in 1966 and 1967 and setting records in the process. Le Mans became a story in the U.S., and of all the company's successes in the 1960s "Total Performance" campaign, the Le Mans victories were equaled only by the invasion of the Indianapolis and the Lotus-Ford's changing the basic engineering of American oval-track cars.

When Ford decided that twice was enough, and other events moved up on the list of priorities, Le Mans was left to the private-entry GT40's. These were a story unto themselves, and were a redemption for John Wyer, who managed the best GT40 team for the Gulf Oil Company. Wyer had been the first choice to manage the factory team in 1963, but was removed from his job in the fall of 1964 when one failure followed another. It was a blow to the former Aston Martin director, whose reputation as a racing tactician had been impeccable. He was moved over to Ford Advanced Vehicles, to oversee the building of the "production" GT40's.

In mid-April 1966, while Le Mans preparations were in full swing, a road-specification GT40 was delivered to Gulf executive Grady Davis. This was one of the production versions (if one can call a total GT40 run of 134 cars "production"), with a 289-inch V8 rather than the 427's carried by the factory cars. Davis soon convinced Gulf that long-distance racing would be good for the Gulf image, and a team was formed in time for the 1967 season, the cars being built by JWA, short for John Wyer Automotive, the new name for Ford Advanced Vehicles, located just west of London.

The three cars would be basically GT40's, but would be of lightweight construction, and would have a slightly different body contour done by Len Bailey, who had also been a part of the original design team. They were called Mirages instead of Fords, and they won two races in 1967, helped by the addition of Belgian star Jacky Ickx for the 1000-kilometer event at his home circuit, Spa. The other win was at Monthlery, a French circuit then in use but on its way into history.

The day after Le Mans: The FIA, either concerned about the top speeds of 7-liter Fords or hoping to pave the way for French manufacturer Matra, announced a rules change for 1968. Prototype cars (called Group 6) would be limited to 3 liters, while Group 4 (a minimum of 50 examples) would be allowed 5 liters, but would have their minimum weight limit raised from 650 kilograms to 800 (approximately 1430 pounds to 1765). None of the 1967 teams that competed for the title were consulted, and as a consequence Ferrari pulled out of sports-car racing for 1968.

First of two: The GT40 on its way to winning at Le Mans, 1968. The same car did it again the following year.—Ford Motor Company

The Gulf Oil GT40's, once again with "standard" bodywork as the Mirage name was removed, then went ahead and won the 1968 manufacturer's championship for Ford. After a shaky start at both Daytona and Sebring, with the cars failing to finish, the Gulf team won six of its next seven races: Brands Hatch in Britain (the BOAC 500), Monza in Italy (1000 km.), Spa in Belgium (1000 km.), the Watkins Glen Six Hours, Le Mans—run in September rather than its normal June date—and Kyalami in South Africa (9 hours).

Mexican Pedro Rodriguez and Belgian Lucien Bianchi were the drivers of the Le Mans winner, which finished in front by five laps, or more than 40 miles. This same car was also the winner at Brands Hatch, Spa and Watkins Glen, a remarkable achievement.

In 1969, with the Porsche 917 making its debut, and with the Wyer team having an all-new Mirage in addition to the GT40, the old cars' days were numbered, and they were entered in only a few races. A cracked block put the previous year's Le Mans winner out of Daytona, but the car came back to win at Sebring, with Ickx and Jackie Oliver beating a new Ferrari driven by Mario Andretti and Chris Amon. The car was then rested until Le Mans. There, in the closest "non-arranged" finish in the history of the race, Ickx edged Porsche star Hans Herrmann, driving a 3-liter 908, by about 100 yards after 24 hours.

That was the end of the GT40 in major competition, and the last hurrah in this arena for Ford's pushrod V8. The car, and the engine, had been involved in both the start and the finish of a remarkable chapter in Ford's racing history. Wyer, seeing the handwriting, moved his team over to the new Porsche 917 for 1970.

The remaining attempts—by Ford and by people using Ford engines—never came close to the success achieved by the pushrod-powered GT40's and their cousins, the Mark II's and Mark IV's. The reason for this was the mistaken belief that the Cosworth DFV, undoubtedly the finest Formula One engine in history of racing, could have its displacement increased by a substantial amount.

Spectators at the roadside: Jo Siffert in a Porsche 908 on his way to victory in the Targa Florio of 1970.—Porsche AG

The DFV had been adapted for American oval-track racing, complete with turbocharger, in the mid-'70s and *that* had worked, so why not for long-distance races as well? It would take several years, and a number of failures, before people realized the DFV could not be all things to all cars. It could, perhaps, in its original 3-liter form, but not when it was enlarged.

The FIA continued its policy of changing the championship around and in 1972 inaugurated a new Group 5, limited to 3-liter cars, and the 5-liter Group 4 cars were banned. The upshot of this, in 1972, was that the Ferrari won the nine races the factory entered, and finished 1-2 in seven of them. Wyer had new Mirages designed and used a detuned version of the DFV, but the cars were late in development and missed most of the season. This would be Ferrari's 14th and last sports-car championship.

The Mirages, complete with Cosworth power, were improved for 1973, but the battle for the title was between Ferrari and Matra, using a version of its Formula One engine. Matra took the championship as it won the last event of the season at Watkins Glen, while Wyer's Mirages, with Cosworths, finished 1-2 in the 1000 Kilometers of Spa. The team would go on to finish second in 1974, a year dominated by Matra (nine wins in ten events). The Mirages occupied the runner-up spot, ahead of Porsche and Alfa Romeo, and it came through with a number of second-, third- and fourth-place finishes.

Le Mans didn't count for the sports-car championship in 1975, due to the organizers coming up with a new fuel-efficiency formula that resulted in many manufacturers boycotting the race. The consumption formula resulted in eliminating most of the detuned Formula One engines used in sports prototypes at this time, but the DFV, still in its 3-liter form, was not as affected. Wyer's Mirages placed 1-3, and a French-built Ligier, using the same powerplant, was second. The DFV, seemingly immortal, was carrying on as long as the regulations limited sports cars to this displacement. In 1976 DFV-powered cars finished second and third at Le Mans, even though the winning Porsche was almost 100 miles ahead at the finish.

A Mirage was second, and Alain De Cadenet, a wealthy Englishman who was a Le Mans regular at the time, financed and co-drove the third-place Lola. One of the smaller constructors using the DFV was Jean Rondeau, who was located in Le Mans and whose cars made their debut on the Sarthe circuit in 1976 when they were known

The 1975 winner: The Gulf Mirage that won at Le Mans in 1975.—Ford Motor Company

as Inalteras, that being the name of their sponsor. A Rondeau creation finished fourth in 1977, with De Cadenet fifth. Rondeau and his cars would be an interesting, even heartwarming episode in the long history of the 24 Hours before he was killed in a railroad-crossing mishap not far from Le Mans.

By 1978 the World Sports Car Championship was abandoned, but the World Championship for Manufacturers continued, and the casual fan was even more confused. Porsches, usually in private hands, made the running at most long-distance events, and without competition from other manufacturers this form of racing was becoming less attractive.

It was one of the small teams, however, that upset the Porsches in 1980, gave the DFV its second win at Le Mans, and gave encouragement to race-car constructors of limited means.

The team and the car were the creation of Rondeau, 34 at the time and in his fifth year of chasing his dream of winning the 24 Hours. This time it worked. It did so after a thrilling late-race battle with one of the Porsches, and with Rondeau himself as one of the drivers, and another Rondeau entry finished third. Rondeau, although he had access to consulting aerodynamicists, was reported as having a staff of only eight men. As in the past few years, Le Mans did not count for either of the FIA manufacturer's titles.

De Cadenet gave Cosworth, not to mention himself, two other wins in the World Championship of Makes in 1980. He shared the wheel of a car carrying his name (and powered by a DFV) that ran first in the six-hour races at Monza and Silverstone, held only two weeks apart.

Rondeau's cars finished second and third in 1981, now with some sponsorship from Ford-France. But he would soon run into the same engine problems as others. While Rondeau was surprising everyone, and especially Porsche, Ford of Europe was making plans to return to major sports-car competition.

The year was 1981, the name of the vehicle was C100, and the program was the brainchild of Karl Ludvigsen, Ford of Europe's new vice president for public and governmental affairs. Ludvigsen, an auto writer and former public relations man for General Motors and Fiat, was friendly with Ford of Europe Chairman Bob Lutz, and when Walter Hayes moved to Dearborn Ludvigsen got the job in early 1980 despite having no prior experience with the company. He picked up most of Hayes' responsibilities, including the European motorsports oversight. Successful director Stuart Turner, who had moved on to other jobs in the company, was out of the picture, and Michael Kranefuss, the current director, would be gone to the U.S. in a matter of months.

At the same time the FIA was showing concern—finally—over the decline in long-distance racing. While it was making the Faustian bargain of the Concorde Agreement with the Formula One Constructor's Association, the FIA also made new rules for what was still called the World Championship of Makes.

Porsches had dominated at Le Mans for several years, the Ferraris were concentrating on Formula One, and the Renault Alpine-Alfa Romeo battles of the mid-'70s had not revived any interest. So the FIA came up with a consumption formula for 1982, called Group C.

Cars would be limited in their width (2 meters—79 inches), length (4.8 meters—189 inches) and dry weight (800 kg—1760 pounds). Engine size would be free, however, but there was a catch: Cars would receive a limited amount of fuel for a race, and if you ran out—too bad. So engine type and displacement became a guessing game, and many independent constructors opted for the long-distance version of the DFV. Since Group C left engine size up to the manufacturers, as opposed to the previous 3-liter limit, there were plans to stretch the DFV to 3.3 and even 3.9 liters, with the larger one (called the DFL) expected to produce 540 hp.

There was one other important stipulation: Engines had to carry the name of an auto manufacturer. So Duckworth, in order to make his Group C effort commercially successful, approached Ford, and the DFV and DFL engines used for Group C racing would carry a Ford oval on their valve covers. Although Ford had been responsible for much of Cosworth's success, and the two had been entwined ever since the mid-'60s, this was the first time engines from Northampton had ever "officially" been dubbed a Ford.

Part of the arrangement was a 100,000-pound payment to Cosworth for development costs, as the engine was to be enlarged to 3.3 and to 3.9 liters. And this is where it all came apart—or better said, vibrated apart.

Ludvigsen was also contacted by De Cadenet, who had hired Bailey to design a Group 6 coupe. Bailey had been one of the design team on the GT40 and had also designed, at the behest of Hayes, a lightweight sports car equipped with a Cosworth engine known as the F3L. This latter vehicle, which made its debut in 1968 and lasted through 1969, was known to some as "Hayes' love child." It was built and campaigned by Alan Mann Racing and was fast but fragile, and disappeared quickly.

Ludvigsen liked the De Cadenet project, and the upshot was that Ford of Europe would take it over, build one car for De Cadenet, use the C100 in Group C world championship events, and also use it for the German national racing championship. The name came from the car's height in centimeters, and it was almost exactly a half inch lower than the old GT40, which got its name—in inches—from the same kind of thinking.

The project was given to Ford of Germany, the De Cadenet chassis was taken over, another was scheduled to be built in Cologne, and all was to be ready for two races at the end of 1981, to be run as part of a development program for the 1982 championship season. The cars, it was decided, would be run by Zakspeed.

From the start, it was not a happy affair. Kranefuss, now in the U.S., couldn't stop the program, which had approval of the chairman of Ford of Europe. Peter Ashcroft, who took over in Europe from Kranefuss, was saddled with the supervisory role, but he was in Britain, and the Germans had their own viewpoint.

Zakspeed now had contracts to run its turbo Capris in Europe, to do the same with the Mustang in American IMSA racing, and to build, develop and race the C100. It didn't work.

*The idea was better than the execution: The C100 in cutaway drawing
and in its first win in Germany, 1982.—Ford Motor Company*

After various delays the original car, now modified, finally got to a 1000-kilometer race at Brands Hatch in late September. It sat on the pole and led for an hour or so until the gearbox broke. That was it for 1981.

In 1982 the situation was worse. The vibrations from the larger version of the DFL were shaking the cars apart, and Zakspeed was not doing a good job with vehicle preparation. There were five races counting for what was then known as the

World Championship of Makes, with the best four results counting for a manufacturer. Porsche won, thanks to some poorly worded rules; finishing second was Rondeau.

The factory C100's were nowhere to be seen. The 3.9-liter Cosworths were shaking the cars (Rondeau used the 3-liter version), there was considerable tension between Britain and Germany, and management was unable to cure this. In defense of the C100, almost every constructor using the 3.9-liter had vibration problems. The original engine size was the only one that would work in long-distance events. But it took Cosworth some time to admit this and to work on a solution.

There were plans to reconfigure the engine for 1983, and even to install a turbocharger. There was also a new designer, Tony Southgate, who produced a much-improved C100.

But Lutz moved to Dearborn in the fall of 1982, Ed Blanch took over as chairman, and in February of 1983 Ludvigsen was gone, back to his career as an auto writer. Ashcroft, who had suffered through the program, had the new car at the Paul Ricard circuit in Southern France for some pre-season development work when he got the word. The car was turning in record lap times with no trouble when the call came.

It was too late.

Klaus Ludwig, the triple Le Mans winner and one of Germany's best drivers for over three decades, did much of the testing work and drove the C100 in 14 races in 1981–82. He failed to finish eleven of them.

The verdict was, according to Ludwig, with several expletives deleted, "The worst car I ever drove."

It would take nearly two decades, another private entrant, and another version of Ford's pushrod engine, before the company's products would be successful in another major long-distance event.

All of this was done without factory support. The GT40's, Mark II's and Mark IV's were still looking for a successor, but Ford was looking in other directions.

Chapter 14

---◆---

THE LAST GREAT ADVENTURE

In the early 1960s Baja California wasn't much different than it had been at the end of the 19th century. To most Americans, even those in neighboring Southern California, it was just a place on a map, the modern-day version of *Terra Incognita*, filled with desert scrub, some forest, some mountainous country, a scattering of poverty-stricken inhabitants and a few fishing camps. What passed for roads in the region were hardly deserving of the name, and if you wanted to go to La Paz, on the eastern shore near the foot of the peninsula, you flew or went by boat.

Ensenada, located about 60 miles south of the border town of Tijuana, was the jumping-off point for adventure. After Ensenada there was pavement of sorts for 110 miles, then about 600 miles of wilderness, and finally another 130 miles of hard surface on the way into La Paz. One simply didn't go there in a land vehicle.

This is where off-road racing came of age, where it became organized, to a greater or lesser degree, and where it became something companies could sponsor and the media could cover. It became the newest variety of motorsports—in Baja, with people from Southern California. If it had started in other parts of the country that would have been surprising, because no other area has ever approached the Los Angeles Basin for its automotive innovation.

Southern California produced the first hot-rodders, going back to Ed Winfield, the pre-World War I patriarch. It was where kids were running on the dry lakes in the '30s, it was the birthplace of organized drag racing, it provided American racing with much of its design, construction and driver talent, and people from here were the ones who reopened the Bonneville Salt Flats for record runs. America no doubt would have wound up with just as many cars if Southern California had never existed, but they wouldn't have been as much fun.

There was some racing in riverbeds prior to the 1960s but nothing of consequence, just courses of a mile or so in length. The step up from that to the Baja 1000 was a quantum leap, and the run from Ensenada to La Paz was in the grand tradition of the old point-to-point events such as the Mille Miglia and the Carrera Panamericana of the '50s.

In the case of off-road racing, best known through the Baja 1000 but encompassing a number of other events in the U.S. as well as Mexico, it began with Ed Pearlman. What he and his friends did, in effect, is give us what was, and is, the Last Frontier of automobile racing.

Pearlman tried to join the Marines the day after Pearl Harbor but he wasn't old enough and his mother wouldn't sign the papers, so he had to wait until he turned 18 in the late fall of 1942. More than three years later, after having fought through the Pacific with the 3rd Marine Division, he was discharged in April of 1946. His parents had moved to Los Angeles in the meantime so he went there too, and wound up as a florist, because that was the family business. Later on, in the '60s, he had one of the earlier Toyota SUVs and started taking part in Jeep Club river-bottom events, usually organized by Brian Chuchua, a local dealer and enthusiast.

Ed Pearlman: He was the founder and organizer.—Pearlman Collection

In May of 1967 Pearlman and a few of his friends went after the 1962 mark established by Dave Ekins, a motorcycle dealer from the San Fernando Valley, who had driven a Honda 250 Scrambler from Tijuana to La Paz in slightly over 39 hours. It was part of a promotion to introduce the new model, and confirmation came in the form of time stamps from telegraph offices in the cities at the start and finish.

Pearlman and his friends made the trip, Los Angeles Times auto writer Bob Thomas went along and did a piece on it, and in no time at all off-road racing's cast of characters would include many Southern Californians who were Ford driving stars in other forms of the sport. They would eventually be joined by a whole new set who grew up "playing in the dirt," as one veteran observer termed it. Finally, the off-road activity would become a training ground for drivers who went on to the other disciplines.

The National Off Road Racing Association, better known as NORRA, was born as a result of that May trip. The first race, after the usual struggle with permits, sponsorship and the like, saw 57 cars, trucks and dune buggies, plus eleven motorcycles, leave Ensenada on November 1, heading south through what were in some places, trackless wastes. And among them was the Ford Ranchero of Ak Miller and Ray Brock, which finished 13th over-all. The Ranchero was basically a passenger car—with that kind of ground clearance—with a new body to make it look vaguely like a pickup truck.

The original race was done without any pre-running, or reconnaissance, except for that first trip to La Paz. Everyone got in their cars, drove from Tijuana to Ensenada, waited for dawn on November 1 and then took off at one-minute intervals. No pit crews, scarcely a map ("A compass was no good," Miller says), and either carry fuel or buy it at one of the stations in the few villages.

They wound up winning their class despite the vehicle's obvious unsuitability for Baja, but they learned, and in the process would make pickups the feared competitors of Buggies, bikes and the rest. First was the move to the pickup truck itself (an F100), then a V8, then the first automatic transmission (better for deep sand), and then power steering (easier on the driver). Miller and Brock won their class and were in the lead group the next two years, even fifth over-all in 1970. Then Brock employer Petersen Publishing didn't want to chance losing an executive so he had to drop out and Miller went ahead with others.

*1967: Ak Miller and Ray Brock arriving at Santa Ynez
in the Baja 1000.—Brock Collection*

1970: Ray Brock (left), Ak Miller and their F150 at the Baja 500.—Brock Collection

The Baja 1000—it was usually somewhere in the 800-mile range—was the prototype, and others followed: There was the Baja 500, events in Parker, Arizona, and around Las Vegas, and soon there were four or five per year. NORRA was attracting sponsors, celebrities, and a Ford team led by Bill Stroppe.

And Stroppe would soon have his old friend, Parnelli Jones.

Jones had already become an icon of American racing, and not only for his Indianapolis win of 1963. He had a lock on his second 500 in 1967 when his turbine-powered car quit with just a few laps to go, he had been a winner in everything from stock cars to sports cars, he was the owner of the winning cars at Indianapolis in 1970 and '71, and at the time he was the owner of a chain of Firestone tire stores in the Los Angeles area.

So when Parnelli went off-road racing it was news. It all started in Las Vegas at an event sponsored by the Stardust Hotel, where Stroppe was running a few cars.

Jones: "Stroppe says, 'Why don't you come and drive an off-road deal,' and I said, 'Nah, it wasn't my bag,' but he knew how to get to me and so later on he said, 'You're probably not man enough to do it anyway,' or something like that. That was like throwing the red flag, so I said, 'Get that son of a bitch out there, I'll go in it.'

"I never did a pre-run, which was stupid on my part ... And then they put this kid in with me and I told him, you know, tap me on the leg if I'm running too fast or you want me to slow down.... The guy about beat me to death before we got out of town.... Well anyway, I hit a couple of holes and blew the front tires off of it, and finally I ran it out of gas, because it got to running so rich because of all the dust clogging it up."

That was the start. Later on Jones not only won the Baja 1000 in 1971 and '72, but the Baja 500 and some others as well, and he did a lot of it in Big Oly, the tube-frame off-road racer with a Bronco skin on it that was sponsored by the Olympia Brewing Company. One of the jokes of the Stroppe operation was that it was still funded, to a degree, by Ford. The ban on racing, initiated in the fall of 1970, never did reach as far as the off-road activities.

Big Oly was Jones' idea, and he got Dick Russell, one of Stroppe's mechanics, to start building it at home, then Stroppe found out and took the project in-house and finally wound up as Jones' co-driver for a few races.

The winning Baja 1000 time of 1967, set at 27:38 by a Meyers Manx with Volkswagen engine, took a beating as the vehicles became more sophisticated. In 1970 Drino Miller, one of off-road racing's early heroes, shared time with Vic Wilson in a single-seat tube-frame Volkswagen specially constructed for Baja, and they covered the distance in 16:07. He won by more than an hour with a time that was thought unbeatable. The next year Jones teamed with Stroppe in their 351 cubic-inch, 400-horsepower creation and covered the distance in 14:59. What made their performance all the more impressive was that Jones and Stroppe ran the last 129 miles with brakes functioning on only three wheels, and one of the front radius rods loose from its moorings. Stroppe's team included ten vehicles, ranging from Big Oly to a Van, and nine of them made it to the finish.

Jones would win it again in 1972, a feat all the more remarkable when one considers that VW (and later Porsche) specials, with engines in the rear, had a built-in design advantage. He was even running in off-road events in the early '90s, part of Parnelli's "playing in the dirt."

The Baja, and the mystique it created, drew not only the hard-core off-road racers of California, Nevada and Arizona, but others as well. Gunnar Nilsson, the Swedish grand prix driver, competed on a motorcycle, actors James Garner and Steve McQueen were part of the scene, as was George Plimpton, the author of *Paper Lion* and other books, who got a taste of the off-road world. European rally champion Erik Carlsson and his wife Pat, Stirling Moss' sister, were there, and the organizers of Paris-Dakar, the great European endurance event, came over to look at the Baja before putting their own event together.

In one sense it was like a pro-am golf tournament. Only 33 drivers could start at Indianapolis, only 43 in a NASCAR Winston Cup event, and in both cases everyone was a professional. Here, in the Baja, or in the other off-road events that sprung up, there was always a class for your vehicle, and as long as you had the desire, you could enter. If you finished, regardless of how many hours behind the stars, it was still great—and if you wound up with your shock mounts ripped off the chassis by some rocks in the Mexican wilderness, well, you still had stories to tell....

The end of the springtime of the Baja, and the end of NORRA, came in 1973, when Mickey Thompson moved in on Pearlman and his partner, Don Francisco. There was perhaps nothing illegal about it, but many of those who were involved are clear there was much that was unethical. Thompson, who was promoting various and sundry "off-road" races in stadiums such as the Los Angeles Coliseum, wanted to take over and he did. Those who were witnesses to the deed say Thompson went to the Mexican authorities and told them Pearlman couldn't get a permit and thus got one for his own organization. It was named SCORE, although for probably the first time in the history of auto racing the initials were not an acronym, just Thompson's idea of a name.

SCORE has run it ever since, with Thompson and with Sal Fish, who came on board from Petersen Publishing in 1973, and who bought out Thompson a few years before Mickey and his wife were assassinated in 1988. SCORE's primacy in staging off-road events in Mexico has been constant, but other groups have cropped up from time to time, with the most successful one being the Best in the Desert Racing Association, which has become the leader in off-road events in the U.S. Another of the perhaps ten organizing bodies in this country is CORR, which operates on short, man-made courses in Wisconsin, Michigan, Indiana and Kansas. The Baja, thanks to its relationship with Mexican officialdom, is run by SCORE.

But regardless of who runs it, the magic is still there.

Chapter 15

---•---

QUICKER IS BETTER

When the National Hot Rod Association was formed in 1951 its principal task was to impress The Establishment (whatever that was) with the fact that the NHRA was a legitimate, safety-oriented organization. Half a century later it *was* The Establishment as far as drag racing was concerned.

By 2000 it had more than 80,000 members, its sanctioned tracks held thousands of races each year, and there was a championship schedule of 24 national events. The NHRA paid out more than $45 million in prize money, was the subject of regular television coverage, and attracted 2.4 million spectators to its major promotions. The organization that Wally Parks founded 50 years ago benefited considerably from R.J. Reynolds' 1974 decision to place NHRA under the Winston motorsports sponsorship umbrella. But whatever Reynolds may have done for the NHRA, its investment was returned many times over.

There are other drag-racing groups among the many sanctioning bodies populating America's racing landscape, but the NHRA is the one with tradition, and with the best television package. From the standpoint of an automaker, it is the one to support if you want to reach a large segment of the youth market.

Although the organizations are different, the NHRA and its adherents were also part of the group that organized the Speed Equipment Manufacturers Association in 1966, a group that has changed its name from "Speed" to "Specialty" and "Manufacturers" to "Marketing," but has kept the acronym. SEMA members make go-faster pieces and look-faster pieces, and if you are a racer, would-be racer, or are simply trying to recapture your youth, they have something for you. SEMA held its first show at Dodger Stadium in 1967 and there were 98 booths in the hallways of the ballpark. In the fall of 2000 the SEMA show, located in Las Vegas since 1974, covered 1.5 million square feet and attendance was mandatory for every leading auto industry executive. The 4200 SEMA members did a gross sales volume of $23.2 billion in 1999, the latest year for which figures are available.

The third member of the triumvirate, if there was one, was the Petersen publishing empire, which was founded on the basis of *Hot Rod* magazine in 1949. Petersen would eventually publish more than 30 titles, including *Motor Trend*, *Car Craft* and others, but *Hot Rod*—the first salaried editor was Parks—was the pied piper of drag racing and along with its sister publications was a principal medium for speed-equipment advertising. One helped the other, and still does.

Adherents of other forms of motorsports sometimes look down on drag racing as being too simplistic, forgetting that doing something better than anyone else is difficult regardless of the activity. For example:

To walk 100 yards is easy.

To run 100 yards is not hard.

To run 100 yards faster than anyone in the world is most difficult.

It is the same with the quarter mile and an automobile. Harder perhaps, because it involves not only human beings, but mechanical equipment as well.

And as a result there is a certain mystique that surrounds those who do this better than anyone else, and it is a mystique that automakers have tried to adapt to their own purposes. No one has done this better than General Motors. GM, with its "small-block" Chevrolet V8, introduced as a 1955 model-year engine, took steps to ensure that performance-equipment manufacturers were provided with the information and the opportunity to make as many parts as possible for it. When the Chevrolet V8 became a so-called "corporate" engine in the mid-'70s, there was an additional opportunity.

The GM campaign to get its engines in the hands of the speed-equipment manufacturers came from an action plan put forward by Zora Arkus-Duntov, best known as the chief engineer of the Corvette line. A former speed-equipment manufacturer himself ("Ardun" heads for flathead Fords), his work with the Corvettes gave GM a boost in the image department. But his work with the speed-equipment manufacturers, while not known to the general public and perhaps little known on the management floor of GM headquarters, was more important to the company's earnings report.

Ford, which lost the youth market when the Chevrolet engine became the successor to Dearborn's flathead of the '30s and '40s, had no comparable V8 in 1955, and it took until the mid-'60s, when the V8 (now a 351-inch engine in standard cars) became a factor. But it became popular in sports-car and stock-car racing. In the science of running the quarter mile, the Chevy V8 was still ahead.

One of the secrets of drag racing's success, NHRA style, is that there are more than 220 classifications for vehicles—which means, in simpler terms, if you bring a car, NHRA will find a class in which it can run. Most of these are for amateurs, people for whom drag racing is a hobby, and they are called Sportsman classes. There are three classes that attract the headlines, the television coverage, the crowds and the sponsors, and in recent years two more have gained in popularity.

They are: Top Fuel, Funny Car and Pro Stock, and the recent additions of Pro Stock Motorcycle and Pro Stock Truck. These are all marvelous examples of mechanical excess and creativity, and none so much as the Fuelers and the Funny Cars, the latter being a creation that first took form in the 1960s in the mind of Ford's Fran Hernandez.

They are purpose-built creations, in recent years with the engines mounted behind the drivers in Fuelers but in front of the driver in Funny Cars. The engines, limited to 500 cubic inches and with a giant supercharger on top, produce somewhere in the neighborhood of 6000 horsepower for the less than five seconds it takes to complete the standing-start quarter mile, with terminal speeds on the best runs being in excess of 320 mph. A run consumes approximately eleven gallons of special racing fuel for the time it takes to "stage" the vehicle, warm up the tires with a burnout, and do the run itself, which resembles nothing so much as a giant mechanical orgasm. If a car running 100 mph passed the start line at the same time as the Top Fuel car got under way, it would be passed at the end of the first second.

Pro Stock, the class that has direct promotional value for an automaker, was dominated for years by Ford, dominated, basically, because of one man—Bob Glidden. He was the successor to the early '70s Pro Stock team of Ford engineers Wayne Gapp and Jack Roush, and he came out of central Indiana while the company was deep into its no-racing mode of the 1970s.

Pro Stock specifications today limit the cars to 500 cubic inches' worth of engine and two four-barrel carburetors. They run on 118-octane gasoline, and produce between 1300 and 1400 horsepower. Minimum weight is 2350 pounds with driver, and this means elapsed times of between 6.90 and 7.00 seconds, with a trap speed between 195 and 200 mph.

Winners: (Left to right) Jack Roush, NHRA boss Wally Parks and Wayne Gapp.
—Roush Museum

Glidden would go on to be a record-setting winner of NHRA national champion-ships, and in the fall of 1980 he was—next to NASCAR's Bobby Allison—about the only successful Ford driver in any form of American motorsport.

By the time the company was taking the first steps back to formal involvement in the fall of 1980, two Ford drivers, namely Don Nicholson and Glidden, had won the NHRA's Pro Stock national championship four of the past six years without any help from Dearborn.

Now, even before new racing director Michael Kranefuss arrived from Europe, Ford's Motorcraft division aligned itself with Kenny Bernstein, one of the kings of the sport, a driver/team owner who perhaps more than any other knew how to pro-mote himself and his sponsors. It all started in mid-1980, when Walter Hayes called a meeting of the various divisions and told everyone to start looking for opportuni-ties. The division that had already been actively seeking an alliance was Parts and Service, which in addition to its intra-company activities sold parts, plugs and the like to independent garages, under the Motorcraft label. Motorcraft became the successor to Autolite in 1979, when the latter name was taken away from Ford after a ten-year antitrust case.

Kenny Bernstein: The leader of the Motorcraft Super Team.
—Ford Motor Company

"It was Labor Day weekend of 1980," Bernstein says, "at the NHRA nationals in Indianapolis and I met Gene Dicola in an elevator, and a few weeks later Gene contacted me and we got together again."

The Motorcraft Division needed exposure, and Bernstein was the man to do it. He became the Motorcraft standard bearer, as did Raymond Beadle for the Ford Division, both in Funny Cars, with the latter being a sort of support for Glidden, who was the king of the Pro Stock class.

Then, in 1984, when Ford decided to become more deeply involved, Bernstein was called in, a meeting was held with Motorcraft, since this division was designated as the title sponsor, and the Super Team was born. It would include Bernstein in a Tempo Funny Car, Frank Iaconio in a Pro Stock Thunderbird, plus three drivers in Sportsman, or amateur, categories. These were Jim Van Cleve in a B/Gas Mustang, Glen Tinsley in a SS/GTB Mustang, and Larry Cummings in a Super Gas Thunderbird—all classes that have disappeared in the meantime.

Glidden was less than happy with this, but he responded by winning the Pro Stock title in both 1985 and 1986, two of the ten he would collect as NHRA's all-time winningest driver at the time of his retirement.

The team itself was "fairly successful," as Bernstein puts it. "It was one of those things that needed to be done at the time, but the lower classes weren't getting the television exposure and after a while it didn't make sense, so we stopped," he adds.

That left Glidden, and he left after the 1996 season, when the then-management of SVO decided that drag racing was not important. Ford, which had not really embraced this motorsports discipline since the overhead-cam Top Fuel days of the late '60s, when Connie Kalitta and Don Prudhomme were the standard bearers, now had just one champion.

His name was John Force, he was the king of the Funny Car drivers, and he came over from GM.

Chapter 16

GLIDDEN AND NICHOLSON

About 20 miles south of Indianapolis, in the cornfields that border Interstate 65, is Whiteland, Indiana, and just outside town is a faded sign that says Whiteland is the home of Bob Glidden.

Until last year no other driver in the history of the National Hot Rod Association had won as many national championship races as Glidden, who for more than a decade was Ford's principal standard bearer in America's most grassroots form of racing.

The sometimes irascible Glidden won 85 NHRA championship events in 22 years, 78 of them driving Fords when hardly anyone else on a major-league level—or for that matter a minor one—was running anything other than a GM engine. He was the ten-time NHRA Winston Pro Stock points champion, and he got out after the 1996 season, in his early 50s at the time but through with Ford, when the company decided to withdraw funding from this motorsports discipline.

Bob Glidden: The man to beat for two decades.—Ford Motor Company

It took John Force another four years and about 150 races to catch up, and eventually pass, Glidden's total. When he finally did his Funny Car was carrying a Ford decal on its nose, but that and the contract he had with the company to run his two-car team were about the only things Ford had in the deal. Force, however, had the personality to carry the message, and Glidden sometimes did not.

An early one: Don Nicholson and one of the first Funny Cars.—Ford Motor Company

That being said, if there was ever a drag racer who was a one-man band—driver, mechanic and whatever else—it was Glidden. Even after he had his multiple bypass in 1995. The bypass was on a Friday, he was back to work Monday.

"You've got to get past the pain sometime, so why not early," he says.

Glidden was working as a mechanic for Ed Martin Ford up the road in Indianapolis when, at the age of 18, he bought a 1962 Galaxie with a 406-inch engine and started a career that would span more than 30 years. It was one that saw him battle everyone from Bill (Grumpy) Jenkins in the early '70s to Warren Johnson in the '90s. When Glidden first met him Jenkins was the legend of the Pro Stock class. When he left Johnson was the legend. In the middle Glidden became the legend—and still is, to many.

It was a loss to the Chevrolet-equipped Jenkins in the 1972 NHRA Supernationals meet at Ontario that proved to him he could run with the best.

Glidden arrived at Ontario with a teen-age assistant (his wife—and crew chief—Etta was about to give birth and couldn't make it) and the Super Stock Pinto he had bought from Wayne Gapp and Jack Roush, with Gapp the driver and Roush the man on his way to making his racing involvement into a company with more than 2000 employees by the turn of the century.

"They blew the thing up at a race in Louisville, Kentucky, and that was probably the best thing that could have happened to me," he says, "because I got it in a basket and had to start using my own ability to figure out what to do next and we won our first [NHRA] national championship race with that car."

At Ontario, "We get out there and the next thing you know we're in the final.... If I'd have written the damn script it wouldn't have been nearly like that—and should have won. I'd been two thousandths quicker than Jenkins and lost by two or three thousandths. That was in the fall of '72.... When I got home from there I knew we could be competitive."

Some drivers get interested in engines and automobiles as a hobby; in Glidden's case it happened when he was twelve, and it was a matter of necessity: "My dad was a real poor sharecropper and he had horrible equipment and our biggest tractor broke down, right when we were in the middle of trying to get the crops out.... Every place that did that type of work was booked up, so I ended up splitting that tractor and opening up the engine and it was pretty interesting.... I'd never even taken a lawn mower engine apart, so that was where I started."

Glidden got his start with a Ford and made his name with a Ford, but one of the keys in his professional career with Ford was Chrysler's financial implosion of 1980.

"In mid-'78 Chrysler came down and I went to a couple of tests they had with a new engine, the 340, and there really wasn't anything to decide. I didn't get a nut or bolt from Ford and Chrysler comes to me with—for those days—a really nice contract, so I worked the winter of '78 on the engine program and in 1979, with the Plymouth, won all but two races during the season and should have won those. I red-lighted in the finals in the ones I didn't win."

"The following year Chrysler filed bankruptcy and one of the first things to go was the program, then Mickey Matus came here with a proposal from Ford."

The rest, including the national championship wins, is history.

Glidden and Ford parted company after the 1996 season, and there were several reasons for the split, none of which took anything away from Glidden's performance over more than two decades. In an era of increased technological sophistication, where computers are as necessary for some as the car itself, Glidden would be a throwback—but no one doubts he would still be a winner.

Now he does "Whatever I feel like," which most of the time means working on his golf game. He's still trying to keep it under 90 on a consistent basis, only two years after taking it up.

There's golf, and there are still two parrots, left over from the high of 19 he had a few years ago, complete with a large building he made into a tropical rain forest so that the birds would have a suitable home. They're almost all in Florida at the Parrot Jungle but the two remain, one red, the other blue, down there next to the cornfields, just west of Interstate 65.

Dyno Don

Men who were racing drivers usually wind up in some auto-related activity after hanging up their helmets, some more successfully than others. The majority of the better-known ones, especially those who have been active in the last decade, are well off, thanks to quantum increases in salaries, purses, sponsorship moneys and the like. Many of the older ones, most of whom had other jobs to support their racing activities, have gone back to work.

To them, retirement means no longer driving race cars; it doesn't mean living on the beach in Maui or playing golf in Palm Springs.

Don Nicholson, better known as Dyno Don in his racing days, is in his mid-70s now and still lives in Orange, one of the many municipalities forming the amorphous mass known as Greater Los Angeles. He still works as a mechanic, running a backyard shop that is light years removed from when he was the National Hot Rod Association's Pro Stock champion and one of Ford's headliners.

Nicholson grew up in Missouri, raised on a farm ("We didn't wear shoes to school in the summertime"). His father was a carpenter who made annual trips to Southern California to work and send the money home and then finally, in 1940, the entire family moved west, part of the great prewar migration to a place where the Dust Bowl would be only a memory. "The farm was just a few miles off Route 66 and when they finally stopped in Pasadena they got a place even closer to the famous highway," Nicholson says.

A 1934 Chevy Six came with them and when his brother gave it to him soon after they got to California ("There was only street racing then"), Nicholson started beating all the flatheads. "Overhead valves were better than flatheads," he says with a laugh.

He ran some sprint cars in the California Racing Association, but when organized drag racing started at the Santa Ana strip in 1949 Nicholson was there, running and working and building a reputation. He got a 409 Chevrolet in 1961, was in Atlanta by then, working for a Chevrolet dealer and had "Dyno Tuned by Don Nicholson" on its flanks, "and the announcers down South started calling me Dyno Don because of it," he says. Nicholson won the 1961 and 1962 Winternationals at Pomona with the Chevy, then moved over to Ford when General Motors shut down its performance activities in 1963.

"Never got any money, just parts," but that was enough, what with all the match racing that was going on: "We used to run for $1000 a race—that was big money then," he laughs. Match racing, to many in that era, was more profitable than running NHRA championship events.

Ford got its first Pro Stock national championship win from Nicholson when he took the class at Englishtown, N.J., in 1971, driving a Maverick modified to take a single overhead cam engine. Nicholson pre-dated Bob Glidden by a few years and then spent a number of years running against Ford's all-time top drag racer. Nicholson was the NHRA Pro Stock national champion in 1977, "and I had to beat Glidden a few times to do it," he says with a smile.

The subject of John Force comes up, and the discussion turns to how Force, at the turn of the century, is the uncrowned king of drag racing, the biggest winner, the best interview, and all the rest. "What's Force making now?," he asks, and when told, he shrugs his shoulders. "Well, he gets the job done." There's no hint of envy, just one of admiration. Everyone has his time and his place, and he knows that.

Dyno Don's was long ago. He knows that, too.

Pro Stock special: Bob Glidden's 1994 Mustang.—Ford Motor Company

Chapter 17

———◆———

THE "OTHER" SPORTS CAR CLUB

For three decades after World War II American road racing lay mostly in the realm of the Sports Car Club of America, an organization whose spiritual roots were in Britain. There, between the two great wars, drivers drank champagne in the pits, wore neckties and Herbert Johnson helmets, and made annual excursions to Le Mans. That's where the Bentley Boys, a group of wealthy Englishmen, won four in a row, beginning in 1927. They didn't have any trouble getting the cars, since one of them owned the company.

The SCCA was founded in 1945 as the successor to the prewar Automobile Racing Club of America, and had a distinct Northeastern, Ivy League orientation. It also had its Bentley Boys equivalent: The group gathered around Briggs Cunningham, the wealthy sportsman who mounted his own Le Mans campaigns in the early '50s, and was reasonably successful at it, although he never won. Later it merged with the California Sports Car Club, which brought with it such drivers as Phil Hill and Ken Miles (the latter refused to take a driver's test because he maintained no one in the SCCA could drive as well as he, and so there could be no one capable of passing judgement).

The SCCA was mocked by the oval-track mainstream, but it soon became apparent that its better drivers were as good as anyone. World champion Hill, Dan Gurney, John Fitch, Miles and Carroll Shelby all came from its ranks, and so did Roger Penske, who was not only an excellent driver, but would end up as the most successful American team owner in history. One of the early struggles within the SCCA concerned the problem of amateurism, and whether or not you were a true sportsman if you accepted money. When viewed from a distance of five decades this seems laughable, but at the outset it was a problem, and there were some with sham jobs, carried on the books of their patron's business, so they could afford to drive.

By the 1960s these worries had vanished, sports-car racing was flourishing, led by the twelve-hour race at Sebring, and international teams and drivers were coming to the U.S. In the mid-'60s Fords were battling with Ferraris and Chaparrals at Sebring and Daytona, the Trans-Am series was formed and so was the Can-Am racing prototype sports-car series, which was a high-water mark for the SCCA. The Trans-Am and the Can-Am were inaugurated in 1966, so was Formula 5000 for single seaters, and the SCCA was becoming a sanctioning body of international importance.

At that time the SCCA was alternating its national championship run-offs—the end-of-season races for the various minor classes—between Daytona in Florida and Riverside in California, and Bill France liked having the amateurs at his speedway. It wasn't a very profitable date, but it was worthwhile for France, who used the SCCA to sanction his 24-hour race and who liked the international connection it gave him, a connection he later expanded on his own.

Then, in early 1969, France was walking through the Atlanta airport when he picked up a paper at a newsstand and read that the SCCA would be moving its championship finale to Road Atlanta. He had not been given the courtesy of advance notification.

That was the genesis of the International Motor Sports Association, which thus added its acronym to the many already populating the ranks of American sanctioning organizations. IMSA would survive as a promotional organization for 27 years and for a substantial portion of that it provided racing as good as one could find with the SCCA. But it eventually failed as a promotional group, due to a lack of a principal sponsor and the actions of one of its later owners. Since the late fall of 1997, now called Professional Sports Car Racing, it has been owned by some of its former employees and in the past two years has done a workmanlike job as the sanctioning and organizing body for the American Le Mans Series.

In 1969, although he had done a good job as executive director, John Bishop had left the SCCA after a policy disagreement, and was available. He was contacted by France, and the head of NASCAR not only became IMSA's principal backer, but even the designer of its logo. The International Motor Sports Association was incorporated in July of 1969, with Bishop as president. Its first event was a Formula Ford race at Pocono Speedway in October, with 23 entries and 348 spectators, who paid $3 apiece.

But it grew, and moved up from Formula Ford. In order to simplify matters there were two classes, GTO (over 2.5 liters) and GTU (under). There was also a support series, called the Kelly American Challenge, for American grand touring cars, that was more or less an alternative for the SCCA's Trans-Am series. There was a six-race season for GTO and GTU in 1971, and ten races in 1972, the year that IMSA—thanks to France—secured R.J. Reynolds' Camel cigarettes as its principal sponsor (at the same time NASCAR signed with Reynolds for Winston).

The first year of annual championships was 1971, with Dave Heinz winning the GTO class in a Corvette and Peter Gregg and Hurley Haywood, who would be IMSA regulars, splitting the GTU title with a Porsche. For the next 15 years, with only two exceptions, Porsche drivers would be the over-all IMSA titleholders. Haywood won in 1972, then Gregg took it the next three years. Al Holbert won in 1976–77, Gregg again in 1978–79, and Englishman John Fitzpatrick in 1980. The last three championships were won with Porsche 935's, which meant that by the time Ford arrived with its rediscovered racing ambitions in 1981, the opposition had a proven product.

Ford's European Capri, complete with turbocharger and Mustang sheet metal, was the fastest and least expensive way Special Vehicle Operations could start racing, and at the same time fulfill management's idea of showing the flag for some of its more sporting models. IMSA had usually been receptive to manufacturer requests, such as allowing turbochargers in 1977 when Porsche introduced the 935, and now, for 1981, there was a new class for prototypes, called GTP, which would overshadow the GTOs and GTUs.

The Mustang driver would be Klaus Ludwig, the smiling German who became an instant hit with his American sponsors. He was good, he was fast, and he could drive the nervous beast that would be entered and maintained by Zakspeed, the organization that had been running Ford of Europe's race cars since the mid-'70s, and with whom Kranefuss was very close. Ludwig came within an ace of winning in the car's debut at Road Atlanta, finishing second to Fitzpatrick, and was the only non-935 among the first nine finishers.

It was a good beginning, but it was also the beginning of a losing streak—a crash at Laguna Seca, then engine trouble at Lime Rock and Mid-Ohio, troubles that would haunt Ford as long as the turbocharged 1.7-liter engine was being used (and being maintained) by Zakspeed. Ludwig came back to win at Brainerd and Sears Point in June and July, taking the latter when he bumped Brian Redman's Lola out of the way with two laps to go. Then the car began missing races.

It missed Portland, Road America and Mid-Ohio in August, Road Atlanta and Pocono in September—five races before two of them showed up for the season-ending 250-miler at Daytona. Neither ran well and neither lasted, the only item of note being that (eventual) four-time Indianapolis 500 winner Rick Mears shared a seat with Ludwig.

Zakspeed, which had its original U.S. headquarters at Summit Point Raceway in West Virginia, would be moved to the Detroit suburb of Livonia for 1982 and Jack Roush, the former Ford employee who was building up an engineering business there, was asked to form a partnership with Erich Zakowski. The arrangement, unfortunately, gave Zakowski 51 percent.

The partnership would eventually fail, as did the Zakspeed Mustang more than once, but Roush would form his own team, and would be the first man to give Ford's new performance program some credibility.

Ford's factory-supported history with IMSA, which would run through the 1993 season, was a mixed one. At the more sophisticated end of the spectrum it was unsuccessful, which means that the GT40's, Mark II's and Mark IV's of the late 1960s were the last world-class cars of this type that were designed and built at the behest of the company.

That was too bad, because there was an opportunity there. But the Mustangs imported from Germany, the front-engined GTP's and the Probes, all of which were IMSA competitors in the mid-'80s, were never a match for the Porsches, and neither was much else until the factory teams from first Nissan and then Toyota arrived, beginning with the 1988 season.

The Zakspeed Mustang, regardless of what sort of success it had in Europe, was unreliable in the U.S., and problems associated with its highly stressed engine kept the team from entering long-distance events such as the Daytona 24 Hours or the Sebring 12 Hours. That first year, it turned out, was the best the Zakspeed car would do. In 1982 it appeared in only four of the 18 events on the schedule and Ludwig's win at Sears Point marked the only time it was competitive for an entire race.

In 1983, before it was replaced by a new model, it appeared only three times. Thirds by Ludwig (Miami) and Bobby Rahal (Laguna Seca) were its best showing, and it didn't suffer from a lack of driving talent: In addition to Ludwig and Rahal, Mears, Kevin Cogan and Geoff Brabham started at one time or another.

The GTP, which came next, was an anomaly in modern-day sports-prototype construction, having its engine in front of the driver. Even 20 years later, no one wants to admit that the engine location was the victim of some misguided notion of brand identification. The thinking (or lack of it) said that since the production Mustang had its engine up front, the GTP Mustang had to likewise. A look at the rest of the world, or for that matter at the GT40, was all that was needed. Designer Bob Riley, at that time still a member of the SVO team, did the job as best he could and he did well, considering the directive he had regarding engine placement. The GTP entry was designed around a version of the four-cylinder turbocharged engine that had proven unreliable in the Zakspeed Mustang, and despite being mounted in the front, location was not the principal reason for its downfall.

The GTP Mustang: It didn't work.—Ford Motor Company

Its debut, however, was something else. The GTP's maiden voyage was at the Road America 500 in late August, an event that was stopped after 460 miles due to a sudden rainstorm. When the checkered flag dropped, the car driven by Ludwig and Tim Coconis was two laps in front. The engine was on its last legs at the time, so the storm was fortuitous, and few outside the team ever knew. The second Mustang GTP, with Rahal and Brabham, placed third. No one suspected this would not only be the first, but also the last.

Riley, who earlier in his career took leaves of absence from Ford to design Indianapolis cars for A.J. Foyt and Gordon Johncock, was (at least publicly) pleased with the aerodynamic qualities built into the new GTP, which benefited from the ground-effects "tunnel" on the underside of the vehicle. But the GTP—due to the engine and the team management—was little short of a disaster.

During the 1983 and '84 seasons, there were 18 cars that started in a total of 14 races. Only four managed to finish, and only one—that first, at Road America—managed to win.

Riley would retire in 1985 and then join Roush's growing business. Before he left Ford he did the tube frame for the V8-engined Mustang, as both IMSA and SCCA rules allowed this type of non-production design, and also started the design for the 1986 Trans-Am XR4TI Merkur. Riley would go on to be a partner in Riley & Scott, and by the mid-'90s was generally considered America's finest racing-car designer.

In the overdue reappraisal of the GTP situation, Roush gave up his 49 percent of Zakspeed and decided to mount his own efforts in both IMSA and SCCA, and this proved to be the best thing for both Roush and the Ford performance program. Zakowski, in the meantime, engaged his own designer, Paul Brown, and came up with the Mustang Probe in time for the May, 1985 feature at Laguna Seca. The Probe was a more conventional car, in the racing sense of the word, as it had the engine mounted behind the driver. This car was designed for a V8, most probably the Cosworth DFV, but it wound up with Zakspeed's 2.1-liter turbocharged four. Zakowski wanted something of his own in the vehicle.

It didn't make much difference. The Probe suffered from a lack of downforce, had a convoluted cooling system, and worst of all, had its fuel pumps mounted in the wrong position—too high. As soon the fuel level went down the pumps started sucking air along with gasoline, and the result was a blown engine. The performance of the car was predictable—fast at first, and when the tank emptied the engine would go. The long-suffering Ludwig was its principal driver, the Probe started in nine races during the remainder of the season. It showed speed in qualifying, managed to finish only four times and did not win. It finished second twice to Porsche 962's, the latest in a long line from this make that dominated road racing on both sides of the Atlantic.

Preston Miller, who was Ford's program manager for the Probe, tried to convince Zakowski to try a V8, and Miller eventually installed a destroked Cosworth DFX—the Indianapolis version—in one car. This engine was of 2.1 liters displacement and with twin turbos produced between 850 and 865 horsepower—and Zakowski wasn't interested. The V8 car made its debut at Watkins Glen in September and managed to finish far behind. It was a DNF at Columbus and Daytona, and then the season was over and Miller was transferred to the management of Ford's NASCAR program, to which he moved, he said, "as fast as I could."

The Probe's 1986 record: 23 cars started in twelve races, eight finished, and there was one win. There were two more entries at the outset of 1987, one at Daytona for the 24 Hours, and at Miami a month later. The only noteworthy item was that Emerson Fittipaldi was one of the two drivers of the Miami cars. The one shared by Halsmer and Pruett finished third, Fittipaldi and Roberto Guerrero were a DNF, and the Probe was consigned to history, along with Zakspeed. The latter entered the Probes in a few events the next year, with the same lack of success.

The first factory-supported GTO entries in IMSA did not come from Special Vehicle Operations, but were the result of the promotion the Marketing Corporation of America put together with Firestone and the Parts and Service Division. This was done at roughly the same time MCA made a similar deal for drag-racing star Bob Glidden. In most cases the Mustangs were entered by Firestone.

The result was two Mustangs at the Daytona 24 Hours in the winter of 1981, with John Morton and Tom Klausler doing the driving of the more successful one, which finished 191 laps behind the winner, and then failed to finish at Sebring. They were back in 1982, this time only 150 laps down at Daytona, with a second car running on street-version tires and retiring midway through the event. Morton and Klausler did better at Sebring (to the discomfiture of SVO), placing ninth, with the other car 15th. The Morton-Klausler car also ran in a six-hour event at Riverside (18th) and in the Road America 500 (12th). The second Firestone Mustang, driven as before by Milt Minter and John Bauer, was 16th at Road America. Klausler and Minter shared the wheel in the six-hour event at Mid-Ohio (21st).

They were back again in 1983, unsuccessful at Daytona, but with Morton and Klausler ninth again at Sebring, and that was about the end of the Firestone promotion.

Ford's GTO entries built and operated by Roush Racing were much better. The company-sponsored effort began in 1985 and remained active through 1993, when IMSA stopped being attractive from a marketing standpoint. It should be noted that to the casual racing fan the difference between IMSA racing and SCCA racing, and therefore the difference between one marketing campaign and another by two automakers fighting for the same piece of the pie, could be confusing.

Year by year, it looked like this:

1985

Roush Racing, using a tube-frame chassis Mustang with V8 engine, came away with 13 class wins in 16 attempts, and the GTO individual title for 19-year-old Canadian John Jones, who won eight races, including some in which he shared the seat with other drivers. Jones, Wally Dallenbach Jr., and Darin Brassfield, the latter spending most of his time in an IMSA-spec Thunderbird, gave Ford a sweep of the top three places. It was also Roush's first class win in the Daytona 24 Hours, with Jones, Dallenbach and Doc Bundy sharing a car that finished eighth over-all. This would start Roush on a ten-year string of class wins in America's longest event. Jones and Dallenbach were also sixth over-all at Sebring, despite the presence of numerous GTP cars.

Lee White, who would go on to be vice president of Toyota Racing Development, joined Roush in the fall and would be primarily responsible for both the IMSA and Trans-Am campaigns for the next seven years.

1986

Scott Pruett, who got his start as a karting champion, and would go on to single seaters and then NASCAR, emerged as Ford's most successful driver as Roush Mustangs took eight of the 17 scheduled races and won the GTO championship again. Pruett was a class winner seven times, and won the driver's title, in a year that other automakers showed up with sponsored teams: Chevrolet had several Camaros (with chassis designed by Riley, who was now with Protofab), and there were turbocharged Toyota Celicas, Mazda RX7s and Pontiac Firebirds that had factory fingerprints all over them.

One of the season's surprises came in the opening race, the Daytona 24 Hours, in which a Roush "customer" Mustang, shared by Tennesseans Lanny Hester and Maurice Hassey and Californian Lee Mueller placed fourth over-all. Roush prepared the car and handled the pit work, and as a result Hester, Hassey and Muller finished eight laps in front of the Roush "team" car in fifth, driven by Pruett, former Olympic decathlon champion Bruce Jenner and Ludwig.

1987

Porsche 962's won 13 of the 16 events in the GTP category, and in GTO, the Toyota Celicas, a factory-backed effort run by Dan Gurney's All American Racers, were the best. Aside from class wins at Daytona and Sebring, and Tom Gloy's win on the Palm Beach street circuit, the Mustangs never stood a chance.

The Roush Mustang at Daytona, which finished seventh over-all behind six Porsche 962's, was co-driven by Gloy, Pruett, Lyn St. James and stock-car headliner Bill Elliott. At Sebring the Mustang was eighth over-all, with Dallenbach, Jenner and Bobby Akin sharing the driving. They were, however, second in class to a Protofab Camaro. The Probe, now a pure Zakspeed project, made an appearance at Daytona and lasted about half the race. Roush tried to resurrect the Ford GTP car and that also disappeared before too many laps were run.

The Ford Probe: Not much better than the GTP Mustang.—Ford Motor Company

1988

The emphasis on IMSA racing switched from Ford to Mercury for 1988, as a result of the Lincoln-Mercury Division's decision to build, hopefully, a sporting image for the turbocharged Merkur XR4Ti. This was an import from Ford of Europe designed to perk up the division with a car that appealed to the youth market, which it did not do. The production model accounted for approximately 9000 sales in 1985, the year of its introduction, peaked at 14,500 the next year then dropped steadily until it was phased out at the close of 1990.

The racing version, which was first entered in the SCCA's Trans-Am series in 1986 and 1987, turned out to be more successful, thanks in no small part to Roush's 2.5-liter version of the production 2.3-liter. The regulations allowed considerable leeway in engine building as long as a few of the original specifications were maintained, and White managed to put together a series of between 25 and 30 engines that lasted for all the years the company was running them in both SCCA and IMSA. White, who credits technical advice from Roush for making the new construction work as well as it did, says the 2.5's were producing between 720 and 740 horsepower at the final stage of their development.

In 1988 the result was a return to championship status in the GTO category, with Roush running four Merkurs, with the exception of a few erstwhile Mustangs reskinned as Merkurs that still carried V8's for Daytona and Sebring. The Merkurs had competition from the turbocharged Toyotas that won the previous year, and from the Protofab Corvette team, and kept the Roush Daytona 24-hour string alive—but just barely—in the opening race of the season. The car driven by Pruett, Pete Halsmer, Paul Miller and Bobby Akin passed a faltering Camaro in the last half hour.

The Roush team won four of the twelve events on the schedule while Toyota won five and Corvette two, but consistency took the title. Pruett, who won the individual championship, won twice, but also managed to finish in all twelve events, and placed second four times.

The GTP class went to Nissan, which was led by Geoff Brabham, son of three-time world driving champion Sir Jack. He won nine of the twelve events, including eight in a row.

1989

The turbocharger remained, the horsepower was 690 at this stage, the name was changed from XR4Ti to Mercury Cougar, and there was a new and serious opponent in IMSA GTO racing. This latest entry was Audi, complete with the four-wheel drive Quattro and drivers Hans Stuck and Hurley Haywood.

The result was the same—the Roush Mercurys won seven races and the championship, but it came down to the final event of the 15-race season, held on a makeshift road course on the grounds of the horse track at Del Mar, California. This was also the second straight year of Nissan dominance of the GTP category, with Brabham winning nine races. For the organization as a whole, 1989 marked the start of a downturn in the fortunes of IMSA, and the reason was the retirement of founder John Bishop. He sold the organization to Tampa businessman Mike Cone in the spring and retired in June, and IMSA would never again have the kind of leadership that Bishop provided.

The Mercurys got their edge over Audi right at the start of the year, when the Roush team finished sixth and seventh over-all in the Daytona 24 Hours, and the Audis were not even there. This gave Lincoln-Mercury a points lead that could not be overcome, despite a massive effort, in both manpower and money, from Audi. The Daytona success, which was Roush's fifth straight in the event, saw Pete Halsmer, Bob Earl and NASCAR's Mark Martin divide the driving time, with Jackie Stewart's son Paul also given a short stint. The second Mercury was handled by Dallenbach, returned from his year with the Corvette team, Dorsey Schroeder and Martin.

Halsmer and Stuck battled through much of the year, with Halsmer winning four times and Stuck seven, but the 45-year-old Halsmer finished in the top five in all but one event. Dallenbach, his teammate, won three races and placed second in the standings.

1990

Dorsey Schroeder, new to the Roush team, won the GTO championship with his Cougar, taking three of the 15 events on the schedule and finishing sixth or better in every event. He thus edged his new teammate, the mercurial off-road racer Robby Gordon, who won five times but was not able to produce the same consistency.

Among those they defeated for the points title was Halsmer, now driving an RX7 for the Mazda factory team.

Brabham won five events for Nissan, and as a consequence took this third consecutive GTP championship. This was also the last racing effort for the Lincoln-Mercury Division. From now on, the entries in both IMSA and SCCA would be Mustangs.

1991

This time it was a three-way battle among the Roush Mustangs, the RX7 Mazdas led by Halsmer, and a strong Nissan GTO team with Steve Millen and 300ZX's. The Roush team won at Daytona again, this time with a Mustang finishing fourth over-all

Lyn St. James.
—Ford Motor Company

Klaus Ludwig.
—Ford Motor Company

Pete Halsmer.
—Ford Motor Company

Wally Dallenbach Jr.
—Ford Motor Company

and being shared by Gordon, Martin and Dallenbach, and another placing sixth with Max Jones, Schroeder and John Fergus driving.

The Mustangs won five of the 15 events on the calendar, Gordon finished second in the point standings, but the manufacturer's title went to Mazda and individual honors were won by Halsmer. The problem lay in some defective electronic control units, which weren't discovered and fixed until late in the season. The GTO honors, for the fourth consecutive year, went to Brabham and Nissan. Brabham won only one race, but managed to finish in the top five twelve times.

That was, for all intents, the end of Ford's full-scale GTO activity, which by this time was called the Exxon GT series. The Roush team won again at Daytona in 1992, this time with Gordon, Dallenbach and Dorsey Schroeder, but that was one of just a few appearances.

Robby Gordon ran two of the nine GTO events held that year, winning at Del Mar and placing fourth at Portland in a Mustang. Nissan withdrew from IMSA at the end of the year, possibly because it was losing its promotional value, and also possibly because the Toyota Eagle Mark III, driven by Juan Manuel Fangio II, won seven of the 13 races held in this division. It was also the first time a Porsche failed to win a race since IMSA started its GT class 31 years earlier.

Daytona winner: Roush Racing's 1992 class winner in the Daytona 24 Hours, driven by Wally Dallenbach Jr., Robby Gordon and Dorsey Schroeder.—Ford Motor Company

In 1993, with GTO having morphed into GTS, there were only nine races in a year that saw Camel drop its sponsorship at the end of the season. This effectively spelled the end of IMSA, even though it would hang on for another four years. Tommy Kendall won the GTS title, thanks in part to a best-ever performance by Jack Roush's entry at Daytona. Roush Mustangs finished second and third over-all behind a Prototype Toyota Eagle, with the runner-up car piloted by Kendall, Dallenbach, Gordon and Robbie Buhl. The third-place entry had Mark Martin, Jim Stevens and John Fergus sharing seat time.

Roush took another crack at the 24 Hours in 1995 and finished third over-all, this time with Martin, Kendall, Mike Brockman and Paul Newman in the car. But that was the end of it. He was too busy with his NASCAR teams, and IMSA was not providing a reasonable platform for marketing purposes.

As IMSA shut down, by this time with its name changed (in 1997) to Professional Sports Car Racing, the running in the prototype class was being made by a private-entry Ford-powered vehicle, the Riley & Scott chassis being mated to a 351-inch V8. The operation belonged to Rob Dyson, a successful broadcasting entrepreneur who had been a fixture in U.S. road racing for nearly two decades. Dyson's team won the makes championship in 1997, and won the Daytona 24 Hours in 1997 and 1999. They could have won it easily the next two years as well, but were slowed by a cracked head in 2000 and sidelined by engine failure in 2001 when they had a lead of more than half an hour.

The Fast One

Klaus Ludwig grew up in Roisdorf, which is practically a suburb of Bonn, located on the west bank of the Rhine and about an hour from Germany's Nürburgring, considered the greatest racing circuit ever built. Klaus' father was friendly with the son-in-law of the Ring's managing director and about once a week, in the late 1950s and early '60s, he would drive over there for a card game. Klaus went along, and there was usually a lap of the Ring as part of the trip, even though Klaus was scarcely tall enough to see out of the windows.

By the time Dearborn imported Ludwig, along with the turbocharged Capri reskinned as a Mustang for the company's return in 1981, he was one of Germany's best drivers, and had won (with a Porsche 935) the first of what would eventually be three Le Mans victories.

The racing Capri of the early 1980s had little to do with the street version, producing in the neighborhood of 650 horsepower from its 1.7-liter turbocharged engine, and it was not an easy car to drive.

But Ludwig could, and did, as he did most everything else he drove in a 25-year career that included 123 victories. But the Capri of 1981 was like some wines—it didn't travel well. Ludwig drove it, under the Capri name in Europe and as a Mustang in IMSA events, 21 times in 1981, won twelve races, was second in two and was sidelined by mechanical failure in seven. The European record was 10-1-3. The American mark was 2-1-4.

The American debut of the racing Capri was at Road Atlanta in April and Ludwig finished second to John Fitzpatrick in a Porsche: "When we came to Atlanta they looked at us and said, 'Aaaah, little shit car,' but it was very close…. I still think racing in America was much better than here because it's more on the sunny side of life, everybody knows everybody, everybody's friendly and helpful, and the fans, they are totally enthusiastic."

Ludwig was less than enthusiastic about the C100, Ford's early '80s effort to return to racing sports-car dominance, which he had the misfortune to drive. "This hopeless situation," he said, "is best described by the statistics. I started 24 times with the C100 and dropped out 17 times." (Note: These numbers include the German national events in 1983-84-85 after Ford Corporate gave up on the project.)

The U.S. part of his career saw Ludwig sharing rides with Bobby Rahal, Tom Gloy, Scott Pruett, Bruce Jenner, Rick Mears, and he even drove a Thunderbird with Darrin Brassfield when they won their class in the 1985 three-hour race at Watkins Glen. The Ford part of his career ended after the 1988 season and then he drove Mercedes coupes and sedans almost exclusively, the only exception being the 1995–96 season, when he drove for Opel in the German Touring Car Championship.

He retired after the 1998 season, in which he won the FIA's GT championship by winning five of the ten races and placing second in four, but it wasn't over, despite the public pronouncement. The next year he was talked into driving a Viper in the 24-hour race on the full circuit at the Nürburgring, which he won for the third time, and in 2000 he came back with the Mercedes team in sedan racing. After that season, he retired again.

Walking away can be difficult.

Chapter 18

---•---

"WHAT ARE YOU GUYS UP TO?"

"About 10 seconds after the decision was made," said veteran public relations man Tom Rhoades, "everyone in NASCAR got the word." And the word was no. Ford's return to motorsports, when the corporation was in the worst financial condition of its life as a public company, would revolve around road racing in the IMSA and SCCA series.

Harold (Red) Poling was now executive vice president in charge of corporate staffs, but he had been the point man of the shutdown in 1970. He was wary of getting involved with NASCAR teams, and he was very aware of his company's financial condition. The year 1981 saw Ford post its second consecutive loss, this time for $1.06 billion.

Charlie Gray, who was Ford's NASCAR program manager in the '60s, was still with the company, and showed up looking to rejoin the effort. Kranefuss told him there would be no NASCAR program. "I told them," Gray says, "that one of these days someone in the company, and it would be someone near the top, would come in and tell them to get back into NASCAR." Gray was right and Kranefuss knew this, but he had no money, and for the time being he had no management support for a NASCAR effort. Ironically, when he retired 13 years later, Kranefuss would wind up as the owner of a NASCAR team.

And their phones were ringing. Regardless of Kranefuss' immediate objectives, the NASCAR contingent, abandoned a decade earlier, was desperate for parts, and there was no money to design or make them. Nevertheless, car owners Bud Moore, George Elliott, Glen and Leonard Wood and Junie Donlavey showed up in Dearborn one day, Rhoades says, "and Moore pulled out a sheaf of paper with part numbers on it, and said, 'We've got to have this if we're going racing.' Now understand there's an evolution going on here, which started with Michael saying, 'We're not going NASCAR racing,' to Michael being besieged by phone calls from former Ford racers still in the company. So it wasn't like Michael didn't know about NASCAR, he knew he had a problem, because here was this 'other' race series and he had no money for it. What it finally came down to—the horse trading—was, 'Well, what do you really need, worse than anything else?,' and they said two things: 'We've got to have blocks, and we've got to have heads.'

"I can remember one of the guys saying, 'We've got to go to junkyards and pull blocks out of old cars, and we are literally down to our last blocks.' They had to find blocks to go racing, or they were going to pack it in."

The upshot was Australian Block Story number two, since the tooling for machining the 351-inch blocks had been there since the early '70s. This was much the same as in 1975–76, except this time the blocks were both cast and machined Down Under, and shipment was fast. But it had been a close-run thing. NASCAR had considered letting all makes run with GM engines, regardless of the sheet-metal exteriors.

Next came the problem of heads. A new one was needed, but the design and the tooling would cost $400,000, which did not exist in the SVO budget. Kranefuss: "On one hand you're trying to convince the teams, 'We need you, hang in there,' and on the other Poling was telling me, 'We're not going back into this'.... I finally got the money from Red after he threw me out seven times, but we lost a year."

Don Sullivan, the legend of the engineering department dating back to the '20s and now long retired but back as a consultant, designed the new heads, assisted by Mose Nowland. One more problem solved, even if a bit late.

In February Rhoades was sent to Daytona Speed Weeks to look around and report on the situation, and it was a return after 30 years. In 1951, when he was a small boy, Rhoades' father was in charge of the Hudson performance program and took his son along to Daytona for the race that in those days was run half on the beach, half on the road running parallel to the sand.

Things were different then. "We stayed at a hotel on the beach, and I was there with my mother and my dad, I was 10 years old, and Marshall Teague picked us up at the hotel in his race car, his Hudson Hornet, that at the time had a back seat in it. He put us in the back seat, he drove us to the track, let us out, took the seat out of the car, taped the headlamps and the grille with masking tape to protect them from the sand, won the race, put the seat back in the car and drove us back to the hotel."

Now, three decades later, Rhoades was walking behind the Daytona pits when a NASCAR official sought him out and said Bill France wanted to see him. "And I said you mean Bill France Junior," Rhoades says, "and he said, 'No, the old man.' I said something like, 'What does he want to see me for?,' and he said, 'I don't know, but he wants to see you right now.' He drives me through the tunnel, and I'm thinking it's got to have something to do with my dad.... He probably wants to see me to talk about the old days.

"So I walk into the office and Mr. France is sitting looking out the window with his back to me in this big high-backed leather chair, and I walked in, and I felt like I was back in the Army, as Private Rhoades reporting to some general.... So I said, 'Yes sir, Mr. France, you wanted to see me,' so he turned around in his swivel chair, motioned for me to sit down, so I sat down in front of him, and then he leaned across his desk and he said, 'What are you guys up to?'

"I said, 'Sir?,' and he said, 'Ford. What are you doing?' And I suddenly realized he is asking me what our involvement is, and of course I'm not the guy to talk to, he should have picked up the phone and called Harold Poling, or at least Michael, but fortunately I'm already dealing with the media on stuff like this, so I give him the party line, and he pointed at me and he said, 'Let me tell you something. We are NOT in the racing business. We are in the entertainment business.'

The Kranefuss courtesy call of the previous November was not enough. This was Bill France the Elder, a decade after he turned the day-to-day operation over to his son, and he wanted to know more.

"It was NASCAR's way of saying they remembered being abandoned by Ford for more than a decade while General Motors stayed, and they have long memories. There was a great deal of suspicion," Rhoades says, "that here we come, and we're going to buy our way back in, and they wanted to let us know that it's not going to be that easy."

1981

The first public announcement of what would eventually become the AIDS epidemic appears in mid-June.... Crown Prince Charles marries Lady Diana Spencer.... Sandra Day O'Connor becomes the first woman member of the Supreme Court.... IBM introduces its first model of the PC and sells 25,000.

The word was out—Ford was back. But there was little evidence of this in 1981-vintage Winston Cup. There were 31 events in 1980, with an average of 36 starters per race. Of this number, 32 were General Motors cars and four were Fords (Chrysler products were absent).

Again, the basic Ford representatives were Moore (Benny Parsons), the Woods (Neil Bonnett, running a limited schedule of 22 races), Elmo Langley (Tommy Gale) and Donlavey (Jody Ridley), with the latter two unfortunately being non-competitive. Bill Elliott, still a few years away from being a star, ran 13 events in a car owned by his father and prepared by brother Ernie.

Finally, on November 8 a group of Ford executives flew down to see the season's penultimate event, the Atlanta Journal 500. Neil Bonnett, driving the Wood Brothers Ford, won by a car length over Darrell Waltrip. It was, coincidentally, the first start-to-finish NASCAR event ever televised live by ESPN but at the time few realized the impact this all-sports cable channel would have on racing.

This was the first year of 110-inch wheelbases, and as usual when a major rules change was instituted, the teams had early problems coming to grips with it. Handling characteristics were changed considerably by the five-inch decrease in wheelbase. Some didn't work at all, and one of these was the Dodge Mirada Richard Petty tried in pre-season testing before switching to Buick. NASCAR was also among those having problems with the regulations, but once again demonstrated its proclivity for changing rules whenever it was convenient. At the Daytona 500 Bobby Allison demonstrated that his Pontiac LeMans was clearly faster than anyone else—he finished second to Petty only because of more time in the pits—so a month later the Pontiac's rear spoiler size was reduced to 1-1/2 inches—then given an increase to 2-1/2 inches before the race, and a week later given a 3-inch allowance for what later would be called "downforce" tracks. At the same time the Fords were allowed 3-1/8 inches and all other GM cars had 3-1/2 inch spoilers. Allison had the only Pontiac in NASCAR.

Parsons won three times—Nashville, at the old Texas Speedway (reopened for this event) and Richmond—but was hurt by engine weakness all season. He started all 31 races and managed to finish in the top ten only twelve times. Bonnett won three events for the Woods, all at the end of the season when better parts were available—the Southern 500 at Darlington, Dover, and the Atlanta race viewed by the Dearborn contingent. The other Ford victory in 1981 went to Jody Ridley and car owner Donlavey, one of the more beloved NASCAR regulars, someone who began entering cars in 1950. Ridley won the season's first race at Dover, and it would turn out to be the only win for a Donlavey-owned vehicle in the first 50 years of his participation.

Darrell Waltrip, still driving for Junior Johnson and like most GM-oriented people with a Buick skin over their tube frames during 1981, won the championship by just a few points over Bobby Allison thanks to NASCAR's peculiar point system. Both drove in all 31 events; Waltrip won twelve and Allison five. Both finished in the top five 21 times; Allison was in the top ten no less than 26 times, Waltrip 25.

Among the little-noticed events of the 1981 season was the Winston Cup debut of a small, almost tiny 22-year-old from Batesville, Arkansas, who had been American Speed Association champion. Driving his own Pontiac, Mark Martin took part in five events and actually sat on the pole twice. He would be heard from in the future.

The final point standings: Darrell Waltrip (Buick) 4880, Bobby Allison (Pontiac, Buick) 4827, Harry Gant (Buick) 4210, Terry Labonte (Buick) 4052.

Wins: Buick 22, Ford 7, Pontiac 1, Chevrolet 1.

Manufacturer's Trophy: Buick 240, Pontiac 103.

1982

The Vietnam Memorial is dedicated in Washington. ... Argentina invades the Falkland Islands and is kicked out by the British two months later. ... Madonna's first hit record, "Everybody," is issued. ... USA Today, the first national newspaper, makes its debut.

The big hope for the season was Dale Earnhardt, now driving for Bud Moore and with factory support. He was already the owner of one Winston Cup title, he was acknowledged as one of the best—but something happened. He won only one race, the Rebel 500 at Darlington in April, and was hampered by mechanical problems

Brief interlude: Dale Earnhardt drove for Bud Moore in 1982 and 1983.
—Ford Motor Company

and crashes all season, including a serious accident at Pocono in late July that resulted in a broken kneecap. He finished in the top ten only twelve times during the 30-race season.

In the meantime Waltrip, still in Johnson's Buick, won his second consecutive Winston Cup championship, and Bobby Allison was the runner-up again. Waltrip won twelve races and Allison eight, so they accounted for two-thirds of the 30 events on the schedule. Cale Yarborough, driving a limited schedule (16 races), won three in his Buick and Tim Richmond added a pair in still another Buick. Richmond, the talented son of wealthy parents, came from single-seat racing and brought a certain flair to the South. His career would be brief, but spectacular.

The final point standings: Darrell Waltrip (Buick) 4489, Bobby Allison (Buick, Chevrolet) 4417, Terry Labonte (Buick) 4211, Harry Gant (Buick) 3877.

Wins: Buick 25, Chevrolet 3, Ford 2.

Manufacturer's Trophy: Buick 243, Pontiac 93.

1983

The U.S. invades Grenada.... Korean Airlines Flight 007 is shot down when it ventures into Russian airspace.... Australia wins the America's Cup, taking the trophy home after it sat in the U.S. for 132 years.

The Earnhardt-Moore-Thunderbird saga continued for its second year, and the combination was no more successful than previously. This time the bottom line was two wins in 30 starts, only nine top-five finishes, and eighth place in the point standings. At the end of the season Earnhardt would move to former driver Richard Childress' Chevrolet team. There he would spend the next two decades and become not only NASCAR's second seven-time champion, but would also turn into a one-man industry with total earnings from racing and other business interests in excess of $50 million. When he died in February of 2001, as the result of a crash in the Daytona 500, the sport lost an icon, someone who had reached almost mythic status.

But in the meantime, despite an increase in support from Dearborn, the Chevrolet-powered cars were dominant. Masquerading as Chevys, Buicks or Pontiacs—some being reskinned for each race depending on whether streamlining or downforce was primary, GM cars won 26 of the 30 races and Bobby Allison finally won his first Winston Cup championship, with Robert Yates as the engine builder on his Chevrolet-cum-Buick.

Allison and Darrell Waltrip each won six events while running a full season. Cale Yarborough, still sticking to his limited schedule, won four times in only 16 appearances. The news, for Ford fans, was the excitement provided by Bill Elliott, in his second year as Harry Melling's driver. Elliott gained his first victory in the season-ending event at Riverside's road circuit and his Thunderbird was reliable enough that he finished in the top ten a total of 22 times during the year. Earnhardt won at Nashville and Talladega. Buddy Baker, now driving for the Wood Brothers, picked up the other Ford victory at Daytona in July. It ended a 13-month drought for cars carrying the blue oval.

Near the close of the year, in the October 500-miler at Charlotte, Richard Petty won when he put on a suspicious burst of speed in the closing laps, which led to an examination. He was using left-side tires on the right, which give better grip for short periods of time, and had an engine almost 23 cubic inches bigger than the maximum. Typical of NASCAR, he was allowed to keep the victory—his 198th—but was stripped of 104 points and fined $35,000. His prize money was $40,400. Some drivers were more equal than others.

The final point standings: Bobby Allison (Chevrolet, Buick) 4667, Darrell Waltrip (Chevrolet) 4620, Bill Elliott (Ford) 4279, Richard Petty (Pontiac) 4042.

Wins: Chevrolet 15, Buick 6, Pontiac 5, Ford 4.

Manufacturer's Trophy: Chevrolet 211, Buick 139.

1984

> *The Los Angeles Olympics become the first to show a profit, thanks to greatly increased television revenues.... Ronald Reagan is reelected, defeating Walter Mondale.... The New York Stock Exchange volume exceeds 200 million shares per day for the first time.... Detroit defeats San Diego in the World Series.*

The closing ceremonies of the 1984 Winter Olympics in Sarajevo, always a dependable television attraction, were held on February 19, the same date as the Daytona 500. The telecast of the race drew a larger viewing audience than did the Olympics and for the next few days the telephone in the office of Chris Economaki, owner, editor, columnist and resident sage of *National Speed Sport News*, was busy.

The typical conversation went something like this: "I don't know who you are, but everybody tells me you're the man to see and my client wants to get into all this stock car stuff." The major advertising agencies were being told by the Nielsen ratings and their clients it was time to become sponsors. They weren't quite sure what to do, but anyone who had ever spent more than a few minutes involved with any segment of motorsports knew Economaki, and knew he would be able to point someone in the right direction.

The GM dominance of stock-car racing continued, this time primarily in Chevrolets. Terry Labonte, driving a Chevy, was the beneficiary of NASCAR's point system, winning only two of the 30 races but taking home the championship just ahead of Harry Gant and Bill Elliott, each of whom won three. Waltrip, who won seven events and was the dominant factor all season long, somehow managed to wind up fifth. Waltrip was still driving for Johnson's team, which at the time was co-owned by California contractor Warner Hodgdon. The latter first appeared on the scene in 1979 as a Bud Moore sponsor, but bought into Johnson's operation in 1982. By this time he also had substantial interests in the tracks at Nashville, Phoenix and North Wilkesboro, and later bought into Bristol and the International Hot Rod Association. His NASCAR career would end with the 1984 season, as he was forced to file for bankruptcy early the next year.

One other car owner made his debut this season, a bright young man from Charlotte who already had eleven car dealerships and would eventually wind up with 89, making him the largest individual dealer in the nation's history. This was Rick Hendrick, who appeared on the scene with a first-class operation composed of Geoff Bodine as the driver and Harry Hyde as crew chief. Bodine won three times that year and Hendrick was on his way to being one of the most successful car owners in NASCAR at a time when purses, rights fees, sponsorship prices, ancillary income and the like would grow far beyond the dreams of those involved at this stage.

The Ford contribution to the season consisted, basically, of Elliott, who won at Michigan, Rockingham and Charlotte. The only other Ford win was achieved by Ricky

Rudd, now driving for Moore, at Richmond in the spring. Kyle Petty was now driving a Ford, with indifferent success, and Buddy Baker was in the Wood Brothers' car.

The final point standings: Terry Labonte (Chevrolet) 4508, Harry Gant (Chevrolet) 4443, Bill Elliott (Ford) 4377, Dale Earnhardt (Chevrolet) 4265.

Wins: Chevrolet 21, Ford 4, Pontiac 3, Buick 2.

Manufacturer's Trophy: Chevrolet 238, Ford 105.

1985

> *The "Rainbow Warrior," flagship of the environmental group Greenpeace, is bombed and sunk in Auckland harbor.... Investigation proves it was sabotaged by French intelligence agents, which leads to a public scandal in France.... TWA Flight 847 is hijacked and forced to land in Beirut.*

The years of frustration finally came to an end as Elliott won eleven super-speedway races to break David Pearson's old record of ten, won the first Winston million-dollar bonus, won more than $2.4 million for the year—an unheard-of sum at the time—and didn't win the championship. Had Elliott run under the Formula One system, he could have headed for the golf course right after Labor Day, which is when he won the Southern 500 and the big bonus. As it was, a transmission problem in the last race of the season at Riverside cost him the title.

The winner: Bill Elliott after the Atlanta 500, 1985.—Don Hunter

Thundering Bird: Bill Elliott's Thunderbird was dominant in 1985.
—Ford Motor Company

There were several reasons for Elliott's dominance, one of which, obviously, was his ability to keep his foot on the floor longer than most. One of the others was the fact that his team, led by brother Ernie, had developed a "thin" race car. At the time NASCAR did not have regulations regarding track or body width—there were no "cross" templates—and the Elliotts knew how to read the rule book. They were also among the first to start using Bilstein gas-pressure shock absorbers, which maintained their efficiency longer than those filled with conventional fluid.

The upshot was that Elliott qualified at more than 205 mph for the Daytona 500 and at better than 209 for the spring race at Talladega. In Alabama there was a four-mile gap between Elliott and Cale Yarborough, who was second fastest. This was practically speaking an eternity in the world of NASCAR qualifying, where tenths of miles per hour, or even less, are the usual margins at the front of the pack. Even more impressive was Elliott's win at Talladega, coming from two laps down after a lengthy green-flag pit stop, running consistent laps at 204 and 205 mph, to charge back into the lead without the benefit of a caution flag. The race average was 186.3 mph, still a NASCAR record.

It was a remarkable performance, made even more so by the fact that Elliott fractured his leg March 3 at Rockingham and yet came back to win at Atlanta two weeks later, driving with a cast. He won ten of the first 20 races and only one of the last eight, but that made little difference. His year was already more than successful after gaining the million-dollar bonus at Darlington. It was also the first year since 1969 that Ford was able to at least draw even with Chevrolet. Each won 14 events, with Yarborough adding two and Rudd one for the blue oval. Yarborough, still on a limited schedule for the Ranier-Lundy team, was in 16 events. Rudd was driving for Moore.

The final point standings: Darrell Waltrip (Chevrolet) 4292, Bill Elliott (Ford) 4191, Harry Gant (Chevrolet) 4033, Neil Bonnett (Chevrolet) 3902.

Wins: Ford 14, Chevrolet 14.

Manufacturer's Trophy: Chevrolet 196, Ford 168.

1986

The Chernobyl nuclear plant experiences a full-scale meltdown.... The space shuttle Challenger explodes minutes after launch.... Willie Shoemaker, 54, becomes the oldest jockey ever to win the Kentucky Derby.... The Iran-Contra scandal becomes public.... Oprah Winfrey's talk show goes national.... Argentina defeats Germany in the World Cup final, 3-2.

Like a flame that burns brightest just before it dies, 1986 was Tim Richmond's banner year in stock-car racing. He was first successful driving super-modifieds on Midwestern ovals, then got his big break. In 1979 he won a Super Vee event at Phoenix that was the preliminary race to one featuring Indianapolis single seaters, was thus on display in front of all the CART teams, and soon got a ride. He was rookie of the year at the 1980 Indianapolis 500, finishing ninth, drove there again in 1981 and by that time was involved in NASCAR. In 1986 he had a ride with Hendrick's team and became a star, winning seven of the year's 29 races driving a Chevrolet. Dale Earnhardt won the championship, his second, but the last half of the season belonged to Richmond. His wins all came in the last 17 races after he and veteran crew chief Harry Hyde learned how to communicate with each other—too late to displace Earnhardt, but enough to endear him to the fans. He was among the first to have an expensive motor home at the tracks, he was handsome, charismatic, and he was quick.

He became ill in the late fall of the year, and eventually had to inform Hendrick that he would not be available for the early part of the 1987 season. He eventually came back to drive in eight races and actually won two, but his health was failing and he never drove again. He died of an infection caused by AIDS on August 13, 1989, as the disease that was ravaging other segments of society made its presence known in a place where it would hardly be expected.

Elliott was not able to repeat his performance of the previous year although he did win twice, both times at Michigan. Rudd added two for Bud Moore's team, at Martinsville and Dover, while the fifth Ford win went to Kyle Petty, now driving for the Woods, when he managed to maneuver through a late-race crash involving Waltrip and Earnhardt at Richmond. The man who would eventually bring Ford its next Winston Cup championship was in his first full Winston Cup season in 1986, after having tried it for five races the year before. His name was Alan Kulwicki, he was from the north, which made him an outsider in this southern-oriented sport, he had an engineering degree, and he was his own team owner and crew chief. If there was a market in racing futures you could have gotten long odds betting on his chances.

The final point standings: Dale Earnhardt (Chevrolet) 4468, Darrell Waltrip (Chevrolet) 4180, Tim Richmond (Chevrolet) 4174, Bill Elliott (Ford) 3844.

Wins: Chevrolet 18, Ford 5, Buick 3, Pontiac 2, Oldsmobile 1.

Manufacturer's Trophy: Chevrolet 220, Ford 146.

1987

> *The Dow-Jones Industrial average drops 22 percent on October 19, to 1738. ... Japan becomes the world's leading producer of manufactured goods and the world's number one creditor. ... More than 200,000 farmers leave the land as the result of poor agricultural prices. ... Women are admitted to Rotary clubs. ... Condoms are advertised on television.*

On March 1 Lou Ross was executive vice president in charge of Ford's North American Automotive Operations, known internally as NAAO. He had inherited the oversight of the performance program in 1985, when Red Poling moved up to the presidency of the company, and now Ross wanted out. He walked into Bob Rewey's office and said, "Here, you take it." Rewey was Ford Division general manager at the time, on his way to eventually being group vice president in charge of worldwide sales, service and marketing, and he was someone who believed success in motorsports was a useful marketing tool.

Rewey was located in Cleveland in the mid '60s, working his way up through the field organization when he saw the benefits that resulted from Ford's (at the time) aggressive sales promotion efforts centered around drag racing and he became a convert. The program would stay with Rewey until he retired in 2001.

That was the major change in Dearborn. In the field, Ford picked up a potential new star: Davey Allison, the 26-year-old son of stock-car legend Bobby. Davey had worked his way up through the minor leagues, he had been a winner, and now he stepped into Cale Yarborough's seat on Harry Ranier's team. Yarborough, another member of the NASCAR hall of fame, had been running a limited schedule for a number of years, and now he wanted to run his own team. This would turn out to be a mistake. In the two years before he retired Yarborough did not win a race, and in the 13 seasons before he finally shut down in 2000, his organization managed but one Winston Cup victory.

Allison had a seat in a good car, with Robert Yates as the team manager and engine builder, and Joe Knuckles as crew chief. Yates got his start in the mid-'60s with Holman-Moody, staying there until the company dissolved in 1972. In the intervening years he had developed a reputation as one of the premier engine builders in NASCAR, having worked for Johnson.

Now he also had the opportunity to manage the team and this brought Yates closer to owning one. Allison ran 22 events during the 29-event season and won twice, at Talladega and Dover, and was a contender in various other races. He was a good second fiddle to Elliott, who won six times and finished as the runner-up in the point standings to Earnhardt, who won eleven races and was an easy winner of the season championship. It was his second in a row and third over-all, and there would be more.

There was one other remarkable development in 1987, this coming at the start of the season and being noticed, at the outset, more by Madison Avenue than anyone else: Tide, America's leading laundry detergent, became the primary sponsor of Darrell Waltrip's car. This was a milestone in the development of stock-car racing, which had started life with the names of garages on the sides of its cars, graduated to new-car dealers and then to auto-related products before attracting what could be called minor-league consumer goods.

Now the world's premier package-goods marketers, led by R.J. Reynolds, were learning that you could sell things other than oil and tires through NASCAR, and this provided a certain comfort level to other marketing managers. Kodak had become a sponsor the year before, Kellogg cereals would follow in 1992, and McDonald's in 1993. By the year 2000 even Viagra decals could be seen on stock cars.

Speeds were becoming even more of a potential problem than before. Elliott, seemingly always at the head of the pack when it came to the ultra-fast tracks, ran 210.3 mph for the pole at Daytona in February, and 212.8 at Talladega in May. He also won both events, but this would be the last time speeds reached these levels. Bobby Allison had a major accident during the spring race at Talladega, one that included his taking out a large section of the fence protecting the spectators—several of whom were injured, fortunately not seriously. The restrictor plates introduced for Talladega and Daytona in 1970 were obviously outdated, and a new series was introduced. Speeds at Talladega were down nearly 10 miles per hour for the July event.

The final point standings: Dale Earnhardt (Chevrolet) 4696, Bill Elliott (Ford) 4207, Terry Labonte (Chevrolet) 4007, Darrell Waltrip (Chevrolet) 3911.

Wins: Chevrolet 15, Ford 11, Pontiac 2, Buick 1.

Manufacturer's Trophy: Chevrolet 209, Ford 184.

1988

Pan Am Flight 103 is blown up over Scotland, killing 269 people.... Kohlberg, Kravis and Roberts assume control of RJR Nabisco in the largest corporate takeover in history.... Fax machines become standard equipment, even at home.

Bill Elliott, who was victimized by the point system in 1985, was the beneficiary of it this time as he won his only Winston Cup championship, albeit by the narrowest of margins over Pontiac—later to be Ford—driver Rusty Wallace. Each won six times during the 29-race season, one in which the competition between Goodyear and the Hoosier Tire Company led to a number of failures and the resultant crashes as each pushed the development envelope as far as it would go. Elliott edged Wallace by four points and Fords—for the first time in 19 years—were the biggest winners on the circuit. Elliott's half-dozen, plus two for Davey Allison and one for the oncoming Kulwicki gave the company nine, one more than Chevrolet or Pontiac.

It was a year of transition for Ford and for NASCAR. The former saw the debut of a team that would become a major factor in stock-car racing in the years to come, and the latter saw several of its longtime headliners reach the end of the road. Yarborough retired after 31 years, as did Benny Parsons after 24. Buddy Baker, who had driven for 29 years, was sidelined by a blood clot and announced his retirement. He would change his mind in 1990, but drove in just a few events over the next three years before hanging it up for good. A surprise retirement announcement came from David Pearson, who hadn't driven for three years, and an enforced retirement, due to a horrific early season crash, was handed to Bobby Allison. The 50-year-old and his son Davey had finished 1-2 in February's Daytona 500, but the first-lap collision on June 19 at Pocono left him with head injuries that precluded any further activity. The elder Allison competed in NASCAR for 24 years, and left with the third highest number of Winston Cup and Grand National victories—85. Pearson was second with 105, Yarborough fourth at the time with 83. Only Richard Petty, no longer a factor but still grinding away and looking for win number 201, was left from the Old Guard.

The newest addition to the ranks of car owners—and fortunately Ford team owners—was Jack Roush. Roush had been part of a national championship drag racing effort, he had been instrumental in helping the company when it returned to SCCA and IMSA racing in 1981, then he formed his own Trans-Am team and dominated that series for a number of years. Now it was time to move up, which was a longtime goal, and he chose Mark Martin as his first driver. The diminutive Martin was a graduate of the hard-knocks school of auto racing, starting out at the age of 15 on Arkansas dirt tracks, and being successful on every level as he worked his way up to Winston Cup. Martin was a four-time American Speed Association champion. He had been successful driving for Roush in several 24-hour races at Daytona, but he was having a hard time cracking the major leagues, where funding and engineering expertise are as important as driving talent. What impressed Roush the most, he would say later, was that when he interviewed prospective drivers Martin was more interested in how the program would be run than he was in how much his salary would be.

In the year 2000 Martin would still be Roush's number one driver, but the team had grown to where it was NASCAR's largest: Five cars in the Winston Cup series, two more running in the Busch series, and with two trucks as regular entrants in the Craftsman series that was inaugurated in 1995. But 1988 was a learning experience, and the team finished 15th in the season standings. The Elliotts, the Ranier team led by Robert Yates, and the Wood Brothers were the mainstays.

Elliott won at Bristol in April, Dover in June, the Firecracker 400 on July 4 weekend, Pocono at the end of July, the Southern 500 at Darlington on Labor Day, and Dover again at the end of September. Wallace won four of the season's last five races, but Elliott's lead was too much to overcome. Kulwicki won his first Cup race, a 500-kilometer event at Phoenix in the fall, while Davey Allison won at Michigan in August and Richmond in September.

The final point standings: Bill Elliott (Ford) 4488, Rusty Wallace (Pontiac) 4484, Dale Earnhardt (Chevrolet) 4256, Terry Labonte (Chevrolet) 4007.

Wins: Ford 9, Pontiac 8, Chevrolet 8, Buick 2, Oldsmobile 2.

Manufacturer's Trophy: Chevrolet 165, Ford 163.

1989

The Berlin Wall comes down as East and West Germany are reunited. ... Communist leaders are removed from power throughout Europe's eastern region. ... George Herbert Walker Bush is elected President. ... San Francisco is hit with a major earthquake. ... American Greg LeMond wins the Tour de France. ... Pete Rose is banned from baseball.

From NASCAR's standpoint it was an excellent year. Eleven different drivers won races during the 29-event season, and purses, plus bonus money, were up to where Ken Schrader, who finished sixth in the standings, won more than $1 million for his car owner. It was an even better year for Rusty Wallace, who won six races, the points championship, and more than $2 million for his team.

Wallace just managed to get past Earnhardt in what was practically a season-long struggle for the points leadership, a struggle in which the Fords became competitive too late in the season. No Ford driver was able to win a race until May 7, when Davey Allison won at Talladega in an event where the restrictor plates reduced speeds another 10 mph from what they were in the second event of 1988. Fords finished 1-2-3 at Talladega, and it was Robert Yates' first win as an owner.

The other Ford team owner to record his first victory was Roush, who saw Martin come home first at Rockingham in October. Martin nearly won two more—the Firecracker 400 at Daytona and the fall race at Charlotte. He ran out of gas at Daytona and lost air in a tire in the closing stages at Charlotte. He finished third in the point standings, and everyone knew he would be a contender in the future. Elliott won three events, Terry Labonte two and Davey Allison two.

It was also the year in which Goodyear introduced radial tires for major league stock-car racing. They were withdrawn after accidents during Daytona practice in February, but would eventually return and be standard equipment for all.

The final point standings: Rusty Wallace (Pontiac) 4176, Dale Earnhardt (Chevrolet) 4164, Mark Martin (Ford) 4053, Darrell Waltrip (Chevrolet) 3971.

Wins: Chevrolet 13, Ford 8, Pontiac 6, Oldsmobile 1, Buick 1.

Manufacturer's Trophy: Chevrolet 186, Ford 166.

1990

The world population reaches 5.3 billion, a nearly 18 percent increase in the past decade.... Australia has ten deaths by handgun in 1990, Britain 22, the U.S. 10,567.... The Fresh Kills landfill on Staten Island is the world's largest man-made construction.... The world's six biggest banks are all Japanese.... A decade earlier none were in the top ten.

If you were a Chevrolet fan, this was Earnhardt's well-deserved fourth Winston Cup championship, deserved for many reasons, among them being the fact that he won nine of the year's 29 events.

If you were a Ford fan, looking for the second Cup championship in two years, Mark Martin lost the title because NASCAR chose to interpret certain rules in favor of The Establishment rather than relative newcomer Roush Racing. After Martin won the season's second event at Richmond the post-race inspection found a 2-1/2-inch spacer bolted to his carburetor—a half-inch taller than the regulations allowed. Had the spacer been welded to the intake manifold, directly underneath, there would have been no substantive difference in engine efficiency—and no penalty. Martin kept the win but lost the 46 points he had earned, and Roush was fined $40,000.

At Charlotte in October, Earnhardt's car left a pit stop with loose lug nuts, and spun into the first turn. Despite stringent rules against crews working on cars anywhere but in the pits, and despite an official attempting to wave them back, his team ran down to the infield and tightened the nuts. There was no penalty. Earnhardt's margin of victory at the end of the season was 26 points—less than the 46 Martin lost at Richmond.

Going into the last race of the season at Atlanta, Martin still stood a mathematical chance. He would have to win the race and Earnhardt finish far down. Kranefuss and company arranged for a pre-race private practice session in which Martin tried several different cars, and wound up picking one prepared by Yates. It didn't help: Earnhardt finished third, Martin was sixth.

It was also the season in which Junior Johnson returned to the Ford fold after many years with General Motors. Johnson, a man of principle, had discovered that GM Racing was giving his secrets to other Chevrolet teams.

Despite the controversy, and despite the championship that might have been, Ford was becoming more of a presence. Earnhardt may have won, but Ford drivers were 2-3-4-5 in the standings, something that had not happened before. Geoff Bodine, driving his last season for Johnson, was third; Bill Elliott was fourth and Morgan Shepherd, in Bud Moore's car, placed fifth. Alan Kulwicki, still soldiering on as a one-man team owner, driver, crew chief and all the rest, was eighth. Bodine was driving for Johnson after Junior was turned down by Kulwicki, which caused some amazement in the NASCAR community. But Kulwicki, while voicing his respect for Johnson and his operation, was determined to go it alone. Kulwicki's contract offer had been for three years; Bodine signed for one.

The young man tabbed as the next star of the circuit, Davey Allison, won two events but was having his problems. The Yates team driver ran all 29 events but managed to finish in the top five only five times, in the top ten only ten times. He dropped out twice because of engine failures but was running at the end every other time.

Martin and Bodine won three times, Elliott won once, as did Kulwicki and Shepherd. The total enabled Ford to equal Chevrolet, but Earnhardt was the one who walked off with the prize.

The final point standings: Dale Earnhardt (Chevrolet) 4430, Mark Martin (Ford) 4404, Geoff Bodine (Ford) 4017, Bill Elliott (Ford) 3999.

Wins: Ford 12, Chevrolet 12, Pontiac 3, Buick 1, Oldsmobile 1.

Manufacturer's Trophy: Chevrolet 194, Ford 194.

1991

Desert Storm, in which the actual ground war lasts only 100 hours, sees more than 200,000 Iraqi troops killed and Kuwait liberated. American casualties total 148.... The Church of England ordains women priests.... The Dow-Jones Industrial Average tops 3000 for the first time.... Earvin (Magic) Johnson announces he has tested positive for the HIV virus and retires from the National Basketball Association.

Davey Allison, making a comeback from the previous year, and veteran Harry Gant, who dominated in the fall, each won five of the season's 29 races.

But Earnhardt won his fifth Winston Cup championship.

Again, it was the point system, which awards consistency, and Earnhardt finished in the top ten no less than 21 times, more than anyone else. Greg Fielden, in the fifth volume of his monumental *40 Years of Stock Car Racing*, points out that it is mathematically possible for a driver to win 28 of 29 races, finish second in the other—and lose the championship. Someone who piled up bonus points by leading races at one point or another, and finishing second in all the events, could win. The current system has been in place since 1975, and there is no prospect of it being changed.

No Ford crossed the finish line first until the 10th race of the season on May 26, when Davey Allison won the 600-miler at Charlotte, and by that time Earnhardt was far ahead on points. Allison won again at Sears Point when Ricky Rudd was penalized for his actions on the last lap, he won again at Michigan International Speedway at the end of June, at Rockingham in October and Phoenix in November.

Davey had become the most successful member of the Ford contingent, which now included Elliott driving for Melling, Martin for Roush, Morgan Shepherd for Moore, Geoff Bodine and Sterling Marlin for Johnson, Dale Jarrett now with the Wood Brothers, and Kulwicki driving for his own team. Donlavey, the eternal optimist, used Wally Dallenbach Jr. for eleven races during the year.

Sometimes it didn't make any difference how many Fords were out there. At Talladega in July Earnhardt was trapped among a group of Fords in the closing stages but when they wouldn't work together he got away and got the win, with Elliott and Martin right on his bumper.

The final point standings: Dale Earnhardt (Chevrolet) 4287, Ricky Rudd (Chevrolet) 4092, Davey Allison (Ford) 4088, Harry Gant (Oldsmobile) 3985.

Wins: Chevrolet 11, Ford 10, Oldsmobile 5, Pontiac 3.

Manufacturer's Trophy: Chevrolet 184, Ford 181.

1992

William Jefferson Clinton is elected President of the United States.... The Serbs lay siege to Sarajevo as the Yugoslav republic comes apart at the seams and thousands die.... The breakup of the Soviet Union into dozens of republics allows old ethnic rivalries to explode and chaos rules.... GM announces a $4.45 billion loss, the largest in U.S. corporate history.

Although he had not been the titular head of NASCAR for 20 years, the shadow of Bill France the Elder was always present, whether the races were being run in Daytona, his adopted hometown, or any other venue. When he stepped down in 1972 he devoted his energy to building the International Speedway Corporation until he was sidelined by Alzheimer's disease, which made the closing years of his life unfortunate ones. He died on June 7 at the age of 82 and left an empire behind, one that was built by the force of his personality and vision, and by his making sure that whatever success he achieved, he took others along with him.

The good news for the year was the Horatio Alger story provided by Kulwicki, who won the championship in the closing race of the season, edging Elliott by the narrowest of margins. Kulwicki sent a message to every small, low-budget team in stock-car racing: If you are focused enough, if you try hard enough, you will get backing, and you will win. He showed up on the Winston Cup circuit in 1986 with a car and a dream, and six years later it came true, in a year in which Fords were dominant. Kulwicki, Elliott and Davey Allison finished 1-2-3 for the championship, and Fords won 16 of the 29 events, including the first ten in a row.

France's death was one of the major events of a transitional year, even though he had long since given the reins of the organization to his son Bill. Among the others was the retirement of Richard Petty from active driving after a 34-year career which saw him win 200 races and become, to stock-car racing, what Arnold Palmer was to golf. Both carried the nickname "The King," and in Petty's case it was appropriate. No other driver ever came close to 200, and no driver was ever more accessible to the fans. Years after his retirement, when NASCAR was holding its December banquets at New York's Waldorf-Astoria, when the stars of the day were sliding in the side doors on their way up to their suites, Petty would stand in the lobby and sign autographs by the hour. He may not have been competitive for the last decade of his career, but neither was Palmer—and no one cared.

There were also new arrivals, one owner who was strictly a neophyte at the start but who would soon become a mainstay of the series, and one driver, who didn't look old enough to have a license.

The new team owner was Joe Gibbs, the three-time Super Bowl-winning coach of the Washington Redskins, who had decided that despite all the media attention attracted by the National Football League, being an owner was better than working for one. He started with one car—a Chevrolet—hired Dale Jarrett, who had done little of note, as his driver, and wouldn't win a race until his second year on the circuit. The rookie on the scene, who was actually winning races—hundreds of them—before he was old enough for a regular driver's license was Jeff Gordon, who appeared in one Winston Cup event, the season finale at Atlanta, and crashed halfway through the race. Jeff had been a boy wonder—practically an infant wonder—winning races from the time he was five in every conceivable class from quarter midgets to go-karts to midgets to sprint cars. He had been driving for owner Bill Davis in the Busch series and was doing well—driving a Ford.

Then Rick Hendrick saw him drive one day and soon after Ford lost the next great stock-car pilot to the opposition. It would take three more years, but it would happen.

Davey Allison won the Daytona 500 as Fords ran 1-2-3-4 but Elliott, now driving for Johnson, won the next four events, at Rockingham, Richmond, Hampton and Darlington. Kulwicki, then Allison, then Martin won the next three in what was beginning to look like a Ford commercial, and then Allison won again at Talladega, just ahead of Elliott. The streak finally stopped there, as Earnhardt won the May race at Charlotte. Earnhardt got a late-race advantage by exceeding the pit lane speed limit on his last stop. That gave him enough to stay in front the rest of the way; no official said anything. Kulwicki won the first event at Pocono, followed by Allison's win at Michigan.

Allison had not only been winning, he had also been crashing, at Bristol, Martinsville and Charlotte, and now he had a big one at Pocono, the scene of his father's last big accident. He wound up with a broken wrist, arm and collarbone. A week later, with cast and shoulder brace, he managed to qualify third fastest and was relieved after the start by Bobby Hillin, who brought the car home third and gave Allison enough points to take over the lead in the standings. Allison needed a relief driver two weeks later at Watkins Glen; this time Dorsey Schroeder gave him help. A week later, at Michigan International Speedway, Davey's brother Cliff was killed during practice for the Busch preliminary event. There should have been some sort of a message in all this, but whatever it was, Allison didn't get it.

Davey actually drove in the Michigan 400-miler and finished fifth before going home for the funeral. Going into the last event of the season, at Atlanta, he needed a fifth-place finish for the championship and was in that position when Ernie Irvan

Jeff Gordon: He got away.
—Don Hunter

Alan Kulwicki: He did it on
his own.—Don Hunter

Davey Allison: The star-crossed family.—Don Hunter

spun in front of him and there was no place to go. He wound up in 27th place, 43 laps back, and after the accident that left the title fight between Elliott and Kulwicki. Elliott won the race, Kulwicki was second—but Kulwicki led 103 laps, Elliott 102, and that gave Kulwicki the five bonus points for leading most laps. His margin of victory for the season was the slimmest in NASCAR history.

Elliott and Allison each won five races; Kulwicki, Mark Martin and Geoff Bodine, driving for Moore, each won two in the most successful season the blue oval had in stock car racing in years.

Final point standings: Alan Kulwicki (Ford) 4078, Bill Elliott (Ford) 4068, Davey Allison (Ford) 4015, Harry Gant (Oldsmobile) 3955.

Wins: Ford 16, Chevrolet 8, Pontiac 3, Oldsmobile 2.

Manufacturer's Trophy: Ford 207, Chevrolet 173.

1993

The U.S. National Science Foundation, the first financier of the Internet, adopts the T3 system, and the Internet becomes available to all. ... The term "cyberspace" becomes part of the everyday vocabulary. ... 49 consecutive days of rain cause the Mississippi River to flood the Midwest. ... Michael Jordan retires for the first time, to play baseball.

Whatever satisfaction Ford gained from its winning season of the previous year vanished on April 1, when Alan Kulwicki was killed along with three others when his sponsor's plane crashed en route to Bristol, Tennessee, the site of his next race. Kulwicki was the first shock of the season for Ford, and the second came on July 12, when Davey Allison, their bright young star, crashed his helicopter while attempting to land at Talladega. Allison died the next morning.

The season itself saw Earnhardt win six races and Rusty Wallace win ten, but the peculiarities of the point system gave Earnhardt his sixth season championship. The final race of the year saw Ricky Rudd finish second to Wallace's Pontiac in a Chevrolet, and that gave Chevy the Manufacturer's Trophy by one point over Ford. It was ironic: Rudd, unhappy with the way he was treated by GM, had already announced that he was switching to Ford for the 1994 season.

Kranefuss retired at the end of the season after 20 years with Ford of Germany, Ford of Europe and SVO in Dearborn. Dan Rivard, a veteran Ford engineer who was already retired but was active running special projects for the company, was given the job for what he was told would be six months—until someone was chosen to take the position on a permanent basis. Six months turned out to be three years.

The final point standings: Dale Earnhardt (Chevrolet) 4526, Rusty Wallace (Pontiac) 4446, Mark Martin (Ford) 4150, Dale Jarrett (Chevrolet) 4000.

Wins: Pontiac 11, Ford 10, Chevrolet 9.

Manufacturer's Trophy: Chevrolet 191, Ford 190.

Chapter 19

◆

THE ASCENT OF BERNIE

The groundwork for the great changes in the organization of Formula One racing was laid early in the 1970s, when Bernie Ecclestone became a team owner. Although he had been involved for more than 15 years in one way or another, he had always been on the periphery. Now he would be an integral part, and as such would have a fulcrum with which to exercise leverage. There would be struggles with the International Automobile Federation, there would be disagreements and agreements. In the end he would control it down to the last detail, to a point where the manner in which team trucks were parked at races had to be approved by him.

1972—Fittipaldi Wins, Ecclestone Buys In

Although it created only a nominal amount of attention when it happened, Ecclestone bought out Jack Brabham's interest in his team, and soon took over Ron Tauranac's share as well. Tauranac went to join Frank Williams, as that group was looking to join the F1 ranks the following season.

Fittipaldi, at the age of 25, won the championship in his Lotus 72, which now lost its real name and took on the appellation of John Player Special—again, a cigarette

Emerson Fittipaldi: Two-time champion.—Ford Motor Company

manufacturer. Stewart wound up second despite missing one race due to his ulcer and being less than 100 percent physically for much of the season. Fittipaldi won five races and was second in two; Stewart won four, including the U.S. and Canadian grands prix at the end of the year. Hulme won one and so did Ickx in his Ferrari, once again showing his mastery of the Nürburgring.

BRM, in its declining years and without Siffert or Rodriguez, made the ill-advised attempt to maintain five cars, three for its own team and two for cars sponsored by Marlboro for Austrian Helmut Marko and Spaniard Alex Soler-Roig. Jean-Pierre Beltoise won in Monte Carlo, and aside from that, there were only two other placings in the top six for the entire 13-race season. Beltoise's win, accomplished in the rain, was the last in BRM's 20-plus year history. The minimum weight limit, which had been increased from 500 kg to 530 for the 1970 season, was bumped again, this time to 550 kg. Despite this, the heavier continentals (meaning Ferrari) didn't fare any better. Among those joining a team was Lauda, who brought with him financing from an Austrian bank to the STP-March equipe. Andretti drove five races for Ferrari, still splitting his time between both sides of the Atlantic. The Constructor's Cup went to Lotus with 61 points to 51 for Tyrrell and 47 for McLaren.

1973—Stewart: Hail and Farewell

Stewart won his third title in this, his final year. It was one in which the world championship season was expanded to 15 races, and one in which a record was set that will probably never be equaled: Ford-engined cars finished 1-2-3 in all 15 events.

The Cosworth-designed engine, now in its seventh season, was still untouchable, and was used by practically every team except Ferrari and BRM. Why no one else attempted to build a competitor has never been answered properly, but there are several possible explanations: For one, there wasn't that kind of talent around in the private, or cottage industry, sector. And at this juncture none of the major auto manufacturers cared to invest the time and money. The payoff for them would have been in an image-building campaign but none were so inclined. The fact that the formula of the time (3.0 liters normally aspirated or 1.5 with a blower) gave a considerable advantage to the turbocharged engine, seems to have escaped everyone who could afford it, at least for the moment.

Stewart had decided before the season it would be his last, but kept this a secret from everyone except Tyrrell so as not to divert attention from the racing. The competition was perhaps greater than in any of the first 22 championship seasons: Fittipaldi won three of the first four races, but the year wound up with Stewart winning five, Fittipaldi stuck at three and finishing second in the championship.

Third place went to Ronnie Peterson, Fittipaldi's Lotus teammate, while Francois Cevert, Stewart's teammate, was fourth. Neither Stewart, who scored points in twelve of the 14 races he drove, nor Cevert took part in the final event of the year at Watkins

Glen. Cevert was killed in a practice accident, and the Tyrrell team withdrew as a result. Stewart wound up with 27 grand prix victories in 99 starts, and general acknowledgement as the successor to Fangio, Moss and Clark.

Fifth in the 1973 points race, and now considered a legitimate threat was Peter Revson, who had taken Hulme's place as the lead McLaren driver. It was to be his last season as well. Revson died in an accident while testing in South Africa the following spring. The Constructor's Cup saw Lotus with 92 points and Tyrrell with 82.

1974—The Changing of the Guard

Fittipaldi won the championship, his second; for Ferrari, Clay Regazzoni finished second and Lauda fourth as the red cars were competitive again. Jody Scheckter, the young South African driving his first full season, was third with a Ford-powered Tyrrell. Minimum weights, which had been increased to 575 kilograms (approximately 1265 pounds, without driver) the year before due to more mandated safety equipment, would remain at that figure through 1980.

Fittipaldi, now driving for McLaren and with Marlboro and Texaco money behind the team, edged Regazzoni in the last race of the season—the U.S. Grand Prix at Watkins Glen—finishing a solid fourth there while the Ferrari team had two engine failures and handling difficulties. The final point total was 55-52. Fittipaldi won three races, Regazzoni only one, but had four seconds to Fittipaldi's two. The end of the season saw two American teams make their debuts:

One was Roger Penske's, led by Mark Donohue (who came out of retirement), and the other was the Vel's-Parnelli Jones team with Andretti as driver. Both used Ford engines, and Parnelli's car resembled a Lotus 72, which was no surprise since both had Maurice Phillippe as designer. Both ran the last two events of the season in the U.S. to gain experience for 1975. For the year, with 15 races scheduled, Fords won twelve, Ferraris the other three. The Constructor's Cup standings read McLaren 73, Ferrari 65.

1975—Lauda to the Front

Lauda, only 26 but by now a veteran and finally equipped with a Ferrari that was superior, had the title practically clinched by the time the year was two-thirds done. He had one of the outstanding seasons of the first 50 years of F1 racing, scoring points in twelve of the 14 races and leading Ferrari to its first driver's and constructor's championships since the Cosworth-designed Ford engine appeared. Fittipaldi was second, this time driving a McLaren, with Argentine Carlos Reutemann third in a Brabham. Aside from the two Ferraris, which won six races, all others were powered by Ford.

The "flat" twelve-cylinder Ferrari engine was particularly well suited to the new F1 regulation that changed the location of the rear wing. This disturbed the airflow over the intake trumpets of the Cosworth V8, and was one of the main reasons

*Niki Lauda: Three-time
winner.—Ford Motor Company*

for Lauda's success, and also for the design of the new "flat" Alfa Romeo engine, which would appear in the following season. This was another indication of the increasing awareness of aerodynamics.

Safety considerations led to a driver boycott—and therefore the cancellation—of the Canadian Grand Prix, and almost did the same to the Spanish event, which was held only when the organizers threatened to sue the team owners for breach of contract—in Spanish courts. The drivers' complaint had to do with inadequate safety precautions, which unfortunately proved prophetic when German Rolf Stommelen left the road on the 26th lap, killing two marshals and two reporters who were located behind the safety barriers. The race was stopped after three more laps.

The American entries had little success and one tragedy in 1975. Penske was financed by First National City Bank and Goodyear, Parnelli by Viceroy and Firestone. The latter company, however, was on its way out of racing—and into the hands of Bridgestone—before the season started. Neither was ever in contention, Parnelli's F1 money was running out and this was to be the last year for his team, save for two races in 1976. Penske would run one more full season, but the heart went out of the effort when Donohue was killed in pre-race warm-ups before the Austrian Grand Prix. Two more fatalities occurred after the close of the season, as Graham Hill and Tony Brise were killed in a plane crash at the end of November. It was Hill's private aircraft, and he was attempting a night landing at Elstree, outside London. Hill had retired as an active driver earlier in the year.

1976—Lauda Leaves, Hunt Wins

Cars with six wheels won races and the season was filled with protests and counter-protests, but when all was said and done Englishman James Hunt, driving a

McLaren ever since Lord Hesketh ran short of money and sold his team, won the championship in the last event of the season. He edged the favored Lauda by one point as the 16-race series that began in Brazil in January ended in Japan in October.

The great drama of the year, which was marked by the drivers and constructors associations becoming more and more estranged from the FIA, was provided by the Grand Prix of Germany at the beginning of August. Lauda was trapped in his burning Ferrari, was rescued by four other drivers, was given the last rites but made a remarkable recovery and was able to drive in the Italian Grand Prix six weeks later.

The championship came down to the Japanese race, which was run in the rain. Lauda, third fastest in practice, pulled in to the pits after the second lap saying conditions were too dangerous. Hunt went on to finish third, giving him 69 points to 68 for Lauda. Andretti, now fully committed to F1, won in a Lotus. The Tyrrells, complete with six wheels (two sets at the front, one behind the other), finished third (Scheckter) and fourth (Patrick Depailler) in the championship. Scheckter won the GP of Sweden, with Depailler right behind. Fittipaldi, who left McLaren to drive a Brazilian-built and sponsored car, was reduced to being an also-ran. As a final note, a new engine appeared in the Brabhams—a twelve-cylinder Alfa Romeo designed by former Ferrari engineer Carlo Chiti, to go along with the V12 Matra as powerplants for the back markers. The Constructor's Cup standings: Ferrari 83, McLaren 74, Tyrrell 71, and the rest far behind.

America's second titleholder: Mario Andretti with Lotus head Colin Chapman the year after he won the world championship.—Ford Motor Company

James Hunt: Win in 1976.
—Ford Motor Company

Last-race winner: James Hunt in the 1976 Grand Prix of Japan. He won
the world championship by finishing third.—Ford Motor Company

Although his world championship was still two years in the future, the partnership that made it possible started on March 29, 1976, at breakfast the morning after the U.S. Grand Prix at Long Beach. Andretti had been well back on the starting grid a day earlier when he was informed that the Vel's-Parnelli Jones Formula One effort was at an end, and as he said years later, "I was so upset I even forgot to put the damn thing in gear."

The next morning Andretti saw Colin Chapman at breakfast and joined him. Chapman's Lotus organization was at low ebb, and so was Mario. He had been in and out of grand prix racing for eight years, everyone knew he was fast, but he had never made the right connection.

Andretti: "I was really, really down, because I said, 'Man, I want to pursue Formula One,' I made up my mind, and I'm not getting any younger, I was 36 already.... I see Colin across the room by himself so we waved, and we somehow agreed to join each other, and he said, 'Yes, bugger all, it was really terrible,' they missed the show with one car, and this and that and the other, and I said, 'I have some unfinished business here.... How are you set with drivers?'

"'Not at all,' he said, 'I'm not set with anything.' I said, 'What if we join forces?' And I said the only way I'll join forces with you is if I'm number one, if I'm the leader of the team, and I have your undivided, unqualified attention. You become my engineer. Somehow we kept talking and he said, 'Right.' And that's the deal we made, and we started. In '77, we said, we're going to win, that's how we set our goals.... We're going to win with this car, and then next year we're going to do something different.

"We won in Japan ... and by the end of 1976 Colin says, 'Next year's car—you wait and see.'"

1977—Lauda Steals One—and Leaves Again

There were 17 races in the season, Andretti and the ground-effects Lotus, otherwise known as Model 78, were the quickest, Scheckter in his newly christened Wolf (nee Williams) was his principal competition—but Lauda won his second championship in as many years.

Had it not been for the lack of reliability Andretti would have practically walked home the winner, because Chapman's ground-effects car design was particularly well suited to the profile of the Cosworth V8. Conversely, the Ferrari flat 12 was the wrong engine for a ground effects vehicle. Ten years after its debut, the DFV had a new lease on life. But ...

Still driving for Ferrari, Lauda took advantage of various mechanical problems that struck the others, plus a few accidents here and there, and won three races and scored points in twelve of the 15 events in which he competed. After clinching the title at the U.S. Grand Prix in early October, and ostensibly because his personal mechanic was fired by Ferrari, Lauda refused to drive in the last two events. He would return the next year, but in a Brabham powered by Alfa engines.

Andretti won four races, Scheckter three, Hunt picked up two, Carlos Reutemann won one for Ferrari, Gunnar Nilsson added one for Lotus, and Jacques Lafitte gave Ligier, complete with a Matra V12, its first victory by winning in Sweden. Ford-powered cars won 13 of the 17 events, and when Scheckter won in Monte Carlo that marked the 100th world championship win for the Duckworth-designed engine in less than ten years. His creations, however, lost some of their reliability during the 1977 season. Andretti alone lost three probable victories, plus two other in-points finishes, due to engine failures. It was also the year that Michelin returned to GP racing with radial tires, which proved to be at least a match for the entrenched Goodyears. Ferrari won the Constructor's Cup, 95-62 over Lotus, with McLaren third at 60.

This was also the year in which the first turbocharged Formula One engine appeared, a Renault V6 that made its debut on July 14 at practice for the British Grand Prix. A decade after the F1 regulations gave this alternative the clear-cut advantage, somebody finally had one in a racing car.

But there was little doubt about who and what were the fastest: Andretti and the new Lotus 78, the ground-breaking ground-effects car. Mario on Chapman: "I was one of those guys that was destined to be another champion that he made.... He made champions, he had the ability to do that. When Colin was at his best he was able to demonstrate and show his enthusiasm at the right time, and put it into technical terms and make it happen.... He was a genius.... He was a very ruthless man, very cold, but you would never know it. You do things the right way, you accomplish what he wants accomplished, and he's the warmest man alive."

1978—Andretti on Top

He was the fastest driver, he had the best car, and with three races to go Andretti had already clinched the world championship he had dreamed of ever since he was a boy in Italy. Andretti drove five of the year's 16 events in the Lotus 78, then switched to the newer 79, an improved version of the 78. He won six of the season's championship events and managed to squeeze in the Indianapolis 500 as well, even though he had someone else qualify his car and was forced to start at the back of the grid. Teammate Ronnie Peterson won two and finished second four times to place second in the standings, but never saw the end of the season, dying after being involved in a first-lap crash in the Italian Grand Prix.

In addition to the best car, Andretti also brought a few tricks from oval-track racing with him, including the use of "stagger," which in simple terms means having tires on one side of the vehicle bigger (as little as a quarter inch is fine) than on the other. In oval racing the larger tires are put on the right, which makes turning left easier. This can also be done, to a degree, by putting more pressure in the tires on one side. Andretti: "If the track had eleven turns, had seven turns to the right, four turns to the left, I worked on the seven turns to the right; I threw away the others. I knew I had an advantage until some of the others caught on to the setup."

The reign of the Cosworth V8 went into its second decade, but there was little question the engine now had serious competition. Ferraris won four events, cars with the twelve-cylinder Alfa Romeo engines took two. The Renault V6 turbo, which made an inauspicious debut the year before, never challenged but was getting better, and was winning long-distance sports-car events in a somewhat milder configuration. The tire scene was also changing, with Michelin's radials mounted on five winners, including Ferrari, and giving Goodyear cause for concern. The most interesting on-track episode took place at the Grand Prix of Sweden, where Ecclestone's Brabham-Alfa team, with Lauda driving, came equipped with an auxiliary fan at the rear. This device, somewhat similar to the one on the Chaparrals of a decade earlier, sucked the car down to the road and Lauda won as a result. The ensuing screams caused the device to be banned, but Lauda was able to keep his points.

Off the track, the progress of Ecclestone toward controlling the industry continued. He had the Formula One Constructor's Association, known as FOCA, take over the running of the German Grand Prix, a major step toward direct control of all the championship events. Late in the year Frenchman Jean-Marie Balestre was elected president of the International Sporting Commission of the FIA. He and Ecclestone would fight for control over the next 2½ years, but Ecclestone would win. The Constructor's Cup leaders were Lotus, with 86, and Ferrari with 58.

The dominant one: Colin Chapman and his Lotus 78, the best Formula One car of the second half of the 1977 season and for all of 1978.—Ford Motor Company

1979—The Changing of the Guard

Colin Chapman's Lotus 80, supposed to be even better than the 79 of the previous season, turned out to be worse, and as a result Andretti was an also-ran after two seasons of dominance, and Scheckter won the championship for Ferrari, more on reliability than anything else. The South African scored points in twelve of the

15 events counting for the title, but under a new system designed to make the closing races of the season interesting he received credit for only eight of these.

Scheckter won three races, as did teammate Gilles Villeneuve, who was runner-up for the title, but most of the excitement during the latter half of the season was provided by the Williams team and Australian driver Alan Jones. Frank Williams, for years the owner of an organization that had to scratch for its existence, finally found a wealthy sponsor in Saudia Airways and the results were impressive. Jones won four of the last six races and placed third in the championship, while teammate Regazzoni won one and placed fifth. Perhaps more significant, the Renault powered by its V6 turbo, won the French Grand Prix with Jean-Pierre Jabouille driving. A Renault engine was in the pole sitter's car at eight of the 15 events. Ford-powered cars won eight of the races.

Alan Jones: Another Australian
champion.—Ford Motor Company

Hunt, Ickx and Lauda retired, the latter simply walking away from his car during practice for the Canadian Grand Prix without a word to anyone. The Constructor's Cup went to Ferrari, with 113 points to 75 for Williams, coming back from its unsuccessful relationship of 1976 with Walter Wolf. Williams would be a major player in the years to come, with Middle East money and with cars created by Patrick Head.

1980—Controversy Above All

Jones won the championship, still another for Cosworth's design but one more important for Williams, whose team solidified its ranking at the top of the pyramid. Jones, with his Head-designed car, won the last two races of the season to defeat young Brazilian Nelson Piquet, driving for Ecclestone's Brabham team, now equipped with Ford engines.

The season was marked more by controversy and the ongoing FIA-FOCA fight than anything else, and the Spanish Grand Prix, which Jones won, wound up not counting because of the political struggles. The race in Spain was run without Ferrari, Alfa and Renault and was called by some a "Formula DFV" event. It was later wiped off the championship table as part of what could charitably be termed the political process. Jones won five of the 14 events that did count, while Piquet won three. Carlos Reutemann, Jones' Argentine teammate, placed third and finished in the top six in eleven of the events, including the last ten.

Andretti earned one point, Scheckter two, as both Lotus and Ferrari had their worst seasons in years. Scheckter retired at the end of the season. Also retiring, in a different sense, was the Shadows team run by American Don Nichols, which had taken part in F1 racing, with indifferent success, since 1973. Nichols managed to make only one race in this, his last year. The team won only one event, the Austrian GP of 1977, with Jones as the driver. The Constructor's Cup went to Williams in a runaway, 120 points to 66 for the French Ligier team, for what would be the first of nine titles through the end of the century.

1981—The Skirts and the Concorde Agreement

Nelson Piquet won the world championship in the U.S. Grand Prix in a parking lot, where the last of the season's 15 events was held. The Brazilian, driving a Brabham with Ford engine, picked up two points for placing fifth and thus edged Reutemann and his Williams by one point, 50-49, as the latter went without points in the last two races.

Going into Las Vegas, where a ridiculous artificial circuit of 2.26 miles was created next to the Caesar's Palace Hotel, Ligier driver Jacques Lafitte also had a mathematical chance to win, but his sixth place was not enough. Jones, who won in Las Vegas, placed third in the championship and together with Reutemann gave Williams a decisive victory in the Constructor's Cup. Jones then retired.

There were actually 16 events, but the South African GP, devised by Ecclestone and FOCA, was declared void after Ecclestone and Balestre met in mid-January and declared a truce, referred to as the Concorde Agreement, because Paris' Place de la Concorde was the address of the International Automobile Federation. What the FIA thought was a truce was in reality a victory for Ecclestone: FIA retained the right to set the rules for competition, but Bernie got the TV negotiating rights—the keys to the vault.

Andretti, driving for Alfa Romeo, had his last full season without a single point. Ferrari produced a turbocharged V6 engine which won the Monte Carlo Grand Prix, the one pundits said couldn't be won by a turbo. And a new young driver, Frenchman Alain Prost, won three races for Renault, as many as Piquet. Before he retired at the close of 1993, Prost would win 51 world championship events, more than Fangio, Stewart, or anyone else. Ford-powered cars won eight events. The minimum weight went up from 575 kilos, the limit since 1973, to 585—adding 22 pounds. The driver's championship point standings were the closest ever, with Jones having 46 in third; Lafitte, 44 in fourth; and Prost 43 in fifth. In the Constructor's Cup standings, Williams had 95 points to 61 for Brabham.

The season also was also marked by American Teddy Mayer's selling a share of the McLaren team to Ron Dennis, laying the foundation for an organization that would challenge Williams for supremacy. Dennis brought in designer John Barnard and the latter produced the carbon-fiber MP4 chassis, one of the milestones of Formula One engineering and one that would pay dividends in the future.

1982—The First Finn Is First

Sixteen years after the DFV was introduced, it was still capable of powering the world champion, as Keke Rosberg's Williams-Ford won the 1982 title despite finishing first in only one of the 16 races. For the first time since 1967, however, the engine did not win a majority of the events, taking only seven. The turbocharged opposition was clearly faster, which led one to wonder what took them so long.

Keke Rosberg: The last DFV winner.—Ford Motor Company

Williams' engines had undergone the team's own development program over the winter and were thought to be producing 20 horsepower more than the rest. Whatever the power readings, Rosberg's title was to be the last one taken by a driver in a Ford-engined car until 1994.

Canadian Gilles Villeneuve, the fastest driver of the year, was killed in practice for the Belgian Grand Prix in early May. Ferrari struggled for leadership thereafter although Frenchman Didier Pironi tied for second in the standings despite missing the last five races—and ending his career—due to a practice crash before the German Grand Prix. Nevertheless, Ferrari won the Constructor's Cup, 74-69 over McLaren. Prost, who won the first two races, was handicapped by an unreliable turbo in his Renault and placed fourth behind Pironi and veteran McLaren pilot John Watson, while fifth went to Lauda, now with McLaren as he made a comeback.

No less than five drivers won their first grand prix event: Rosberg, Riccardo Patrese, Patrick Tambay, Elio DeAngelis and Michele Alboreto—none of whom would go down in history as anything but a run-of-the-mill competitor. Ecclestone, still wheeling and dealing, contracted with BMW to install its four-cylinder turbo in his Brabhams and was criticized in some quarters for letting money get in the way of winning. He had done the same in 1975, when he made a deal with Alfa Romeo that was profitable but did not lead to a winning car. Piquet and Patrese each won a race with the BMW-Brabham and would do considerably better the next year.

Three of the 16 events were held in the U.S., all on circuits that were poor excuses for true road courses: Long Beach, Detroit and Las Vegas. Walter Hayes was in part responsible for arranging the downtown Detroit event as he attempted to show Ford management what Formula One was all about. He even got the company to lend the organizers $200,000 to help them get off the ground. He couldn't have picked a worse place even though a Ford-powered car (Watson's McLaren) won.

The U.S. Grand Prix—or at least one of them—would be run on an unsuitable Detroit street circuit for the next six years, and if anything, it would lower the domestic auto industry's opinion of Formula One. Here were these fancy cars from Europe, everyone was saying they were better than "our" Indianapolis cars, and all they were doing was averaging about 85 miles an hour around a lot of city streets and most of them never even finished the race.... Detroit had not yet developed the worldwide view it would have later on.

CART had the Indianapolis Motor Speedway as its center stage, NASCAR had Daytona, and Formula One had a lot of bumpy Detroit streets. That would change too, but it would take more than a decade.

Andretti drove his last three grands prix in 1982, one for Williams (Long Beach) and two for Ferrari (Monza and Vegas). Lauda's return with McLaren saw him win two races and place fifth in the championship. FISA dropped the minimum weight limit by five kilos, or eleven pounds.

(After the season Duckworth was clear as to why the DFV had won again: "It was not because we were competitive, it was due to the unreliability of the opposition.... winning is a matter of finishing—first.")

1983—Turbos and Pit Stops

The missing man in the 1983 season was Colin Chapman, the Lotus owner, designer and intellectual impetus behind much of single-seater racing worldwide. Chapman, 54, died in his sleep on December 16, 1982, reportedly of a heart attack.

The Ford-Cosworth had its last hurrah, winning the U.S. Grand Prix—this time one of two held in America—in the hands of Michele Alboreto and his Tyrrell. By now the engine was the DFY, the latest development of the original DFV. But it was the season in which the turbocharged cars finally caught up with the 16-year-old, normally aspirated engine. Nelson Piquet, driving a Brabham with the four-cylinder BMW turbo, edged Prost, with the Renault V6 turbo, 59-57. Piquet won three races and scored points in ten. The closing events of the 15-race season saw him win two of the last three and place third in the finale. Prost won four, but managed only a second place over the final three events.

The rules changed for 1983, with flat bottoms and no skirts eliminating the downforce layouts pioneered by Chapman, and mandatory pit stops being the order of the day. These were designed to add a little spice and uncertainty to races that were turning into processions.

Honda returned to F1 for the first time since 1968, at first quietly with the short-lived Spirit team before moving to Williams at the end of the season, a precursor to backing this organization in 1984. Porsche turbos, carrying the TAG label because of financing coming from Saudi businessman Mansour Ojjeh, who owned a company called Techniques d'Avant Garde, made their debut in McLarens in the last four events. The minimum weight limit was dropped 40 kilos, to 540 kg (approximately 1190 pounds). Ken Tyrrell's team picked up a new sponsor, Italian clothing manufacturer Benetton, which would be heard from in the future. Alboreto's win on June 5 would be the last Ford-powered F1 victory for six years.

The need for a new engine was pressing, and Hayes started working on Duckworth, who was no longer the owner of his company, having sold it to United Engineering Industries, but who was still its head. He was also philosophically opposed to turbocharged engines in Formula One—despite their presence. Hayes got Duckworth to agree to building one, and in November SVO presented a paper to the Policy and Strategy Committee proposing a five-year development program for a 1.5-liter turbocharged powerplant to be developed by Cosworth and to carry the Ford name. The program would cost $4.7 million, and was the first step toward the engine. But much would transpire between that November meeting and the engine's debut.

1984—McLaren, Lauda, Prost and Porsche

Ron Dennis, a McLaren mechanic of the '60s who operated Formula Two and Three teams in the '70s, scraped together financing to rebuild the McLaren team in 1981, and became one of the competitive and business success stories of Formula One.

The underfunded Dennis convinced ex-McLaren engineer John Barnard to design a car, then got Marlboro as principal sponsor. He went to Ojjeh, who was a Williams sponsor, and persuaded him to finance Porsche's building of a turbo V6 that would carry TAG on its valve covers and be advertised as such. Porsche would build a total of 17 engines for this effort.

Dennis also got Niki Lauda and Alain Prost as his drivers: The result was that Lauda won his third championship, defeating teammate Prost by half a point in the last race of the year. The two of them won twelve of the 16 events on the calendar, Prost seven and Lauda five. But Lauda had three second places and Prost one. The Frenchman outqualified Lauda before every race, but was forced to retire from three events when he was leading. In the last race of the year Lauda needed a second place to clinch, and got it in the closing laps: He was running third behind Nigel Mansell when the latter suddenly dropped back with failing brakes.

Lauda had 72 points, Prost 71.5—more than double that of third-place Lotus-Renault driver Elio De Angelis. In the Constructor's Cup it was McLaren 143.5, Ferrari 43.5, and Dennis has remained a major factor in F1 racing ever since. For the first time the races were run with a fuel-consumption limit—220 liters, or approximately 57 gallons. One newcomer made himself visible: Young Brazilian Ayrton Senna da Silva, who had dominated the Formula Two and Three classes in Britain in previous years. Driving a non-competitive Toleman with four-cylinder Hart engine, Senna finished the season with one fourth place and two thirds.

1985—McLaren, Prost and Porsche

After two years of just missing, Prost won the first of his four championships, once again driving a McLaren with TAG-Porsche engine. He won six of the 16 races but was disqualified after the Grand Prix of San Marino (run at the nearby Imola circuit in Italy) when the post-race inspection showed oil consumption of nearly two gallons put his car under the minimum weight. Prost managed to score points in all but three of the events. McLaren once again won the Constructor's Cup, 90-82, over a disorganized Ferrari team. Prost had 73 points for the title, while runner-up Michele Alboreto of Ferrari had 53 and Rosberg, now with Williams, had 40.

Senna, now with Lotus-Renault, fulfilled the promise he showed the previous year, being fastest qualifier seven times and placing fourth in the point standings—the lowest he would finish until the sudden end of his career a decade hence. Cause for concern was voiced by many due to the steady increase in horsepower, now that the mysteries of turbos had been solved. Qualifying engines were reputed to be close to 1200 horsepower, race engines between 900 and 1000. Renault withdrew its team, but continued to function as an engine supplier. Lauda, who had an unsuccessful season, retired for good at its end.

Work on Cosworth's new engine started with a four-cylinder, then was changed to a V6, and in the fall of the year Ford made a further appropriation, this time another $7.7 million. While all this was going on Ford was negotiating with a team that was a potential partner—a team that would use the new engine.

The team was Brabham, the lead driver was (already) two-time world champion Nelson Piquet, and the owner was Ecclestone.

The deal was never consummated for a variety of reasons, and before long Ford would wind up with a team of a different stripe.

1986—Haas and Beatrice and ...

It was the first week of August, 1984. Carl Haas and Paul Newman were at CART's Road America event complete with Mario on his way to another pole position, another win and what would eventually be another championship, when Jim Dutt appeared. He was a racing fan, and also a man with an impressive budget.

Dutt was chairman of Beatrice, a worldwide diversified food corporation (which also owned Avis rental cars, Airstream trailers and Samsonite luggage) based in Chicago. He was busy transforming Beatrice from a company, which one insider says, "had its executives taking taxis and flying coach to where everybody had a limo and the company had its own jets." Beatrice was old, it was traditional, and it was profitable—until Dutt came along. He lasted as chairman from 1979 until mid-August, 1985, and when he was ousted the company stock made an upturn.

In the meantime Dutt indulged himself by sponsoring Haas, both in CART and Formula One. The F1 agreement was for five years, the CART deal for three. Haas—who was also the Lola importer—thus put together the Beatrice Lola team, and Dutt was the one who made Ford an offer it couldn't refuse. As the owner of the world's second largest car-rental firm, Dutt could determine who sold Avis the many thousands of new cars it needed each year. It was a convincing argument, and one that was also made to Goodyear.

Ford Chairman Don Petersen made the formal announcement of the new relationship on June 20, and nine weeks later the Beatrice board of directors ousted Dutt. Since the new Cosworth V6 was not ready, Haas, as a stopgap, equipped his cars with four-cylinder turbocharged Hart engines, hired retired world champion Alan Jones, and managed to get in three races before the season closed—without success.

For 1986 Jones, Frenchman Patrick Tambay and expatriate American Eddie Cheever split the driving duties, Haas picked up the Ford V6's after the opening two races, and ran the entire 16-event season. The engines turned out to be a case of too little, too late. By the time they were competitive the rest of the grand prix teams had gone past them, and the rest of the operation was not up to championship level. Jones' fourth place in Austria was the team's greatest achievement. Dutt's ego demanded the team be advertised as Beatrice, but you couldn't buy a "Beatrice," so insofar as promotional measures were concerned, the venture was a total loss. After Dutt departed Haas and the company settled the remainder of the contract for a sum reported to be anywhere from $20 to $65 million, the number depending on whether one read the auto magazines or knew someone inside the company.

As a final nail in the coffin, although Ford and Cosworth had been assured the turbocharged-engine formula would remain in effect for some time, this would not be the case. This would be the last American team effort in grand prix racing until Ford sponsored Stewart a decade later.

While Haas was struggling the rest of the Formula One world proceeded with its business and Prost won again, and again by the narrowest of margins. Prost and his McLaren-TAG Porsche edged Nigel Mansell, driving for Williams with Honda turbos that were now over their teething problems, 72-70, with Mansell losing the championship at the season-ending Australian Grand Prix when a tire blew on the closing laps. Mansell was running third at the time, which would have given him enough points to win it.

Prost won three of the 16 events and earned points in 13, while Mansell won five and scored points in eleven. Piquet, now driving for Williams, placed third. As a result Williams finished far ahead of McLaren for the Constructor's Cup, 141-96. Maximum consumption was lowered to 195 liters per car, approximately 51 gallons.

1987—Times Change But Piquet Wins 3rd

The turbocharged formula, in effect since 1966, with some turbos in use since 1977 and dominant since 1982, was coming to an end. Beginning in 1989 Formula One entries would be limited to 3.5 liters unblown, with a minimum weight of 500 kilograms (approximately 1100 pounds) with oil and water, but no fuel or driver, and no limit on fuel consumption. This was announced before the 1987 season in order to give teams two years' notice.

The cars were becoming too fast for the circuits, which had been obvious for a number of years, and the engines were becoming too expensive, not only for the also-ran teams that had to buy them, but also for the companies that made them.

As an additional incentive for normally aspirated engines, two trophies, the Jim Clark Cup for drivers and the Colin Chapman Cup for constructors, were there to sweeten the pot for the poorer (a relative term) teams. For 1987 the turbocharged cars had a minimum weight limit of 540 kilos (about 1190 pounds) versus 500 kilos, giving those with less horsepower a decided weight advantage. But the Clark and Chapman trophies were for the back markers.

Up front the Honda and Porsche turbos dominated, with Honda leading and propelling the Williams team to a runaway win for the Constructor's Cup, 137-76 over McLaren. Piquet, who won three of the 16 races and placed second in seven of them, finished just ahead of teammate Mansell, who won six and had no seconds. Mansell, still with a chance to beat Piquet, was injured in a practice accident at the Japanese Grand Prix and as a consequence missed the last two races.

Turbos were limited to a boost pressure of four atmospheres, which meant roughly 120 inches, or more than any team was actually running except possibly during qualifying. Fuel consumption was still 51 gallons per 190-mile event. Honda, it was reported, was getting close to 900 horsepower in race tune and using little more than 40 gallons for the distance. Honda, after using Williams as a development team for several seasons, announced in September it would switch to supporting Lotus and McLaren. The real reason—never publicly admitted—was its disapproval of the manner in which Williams allowed its two drivers to fight it out for the title rather than insuring that Honda had an opportunity to advertise its engines as world champions. Honda-powered cars actually finished 1-2-3-4 at the British Grand Prix. Piquet left Williams for Lotus at the end of the season.

Ecclestone managed to find another way of raising money, charging grand prix drivers a minimum of 5000 French francs (about $1000) for their "super license," plus 100 francs for every point they earned the previous year. In the case of Alain Prost, the 1986 champion, this meant he had to pay 12,400 francs for the right to work. And Ecclestone made it stick.

Ford was scarcely a factor, but the new regulations brought with them the DFZ, a Cosworth 3.5-liter V8 that produced about 560 horsepower at the start. The principal step in the return to a competitive state was taken when Benetton was signed to a three-year deal. It was one that would eventually bear fruit—but it would take more than three years. The only others using Ford power in 87 were the also-rans, Tyrrell, Lola and March, although Tyrrell did win the Chapman Cup.

1988—Senna and Prost, Prost and Senna

Whatever the prospects were for 1988, any doubts disappeared after the first race of the 16-event season, which Prost, Senna and their McLaren-Hondas dominated. The pair wound up winning 15 times and ran 1-2 in nine events. Senna won the championship, which in 1988 was based on the best eleven results for any one driver. He won eight, Prost had seven. The points that counted wound up 90-87 in favor of Senna, but the former had a "total" point total of 94 to 105 for Prost. Senna placed in 13 races and was disqualified from one, Prost scored points in 14 events. McLaren won the Constructor's Cup with almost three times the number of points for runner-up Ferrari, 199-65.

Boost pressure in this, the last year of the turbocharged alternative, was limited to 2.5 atmospheres (about 75 inches of mercury), and fuel was limited to 150 liters (approximately 39 gallons) per race.

The Cosworth DFR, now the "factory" engine for Benetton, worked well enough for the team to come in third in Constructor's Cup standings and for Belgian Thierry Boutsen to finish fourth in the chase—what there was of it—for the driver's title. Seven of the 18 teams competing in 1988 used Ford-financed engines, all but Benetton with the DFZ version, now available as a "customer" engine. The DFZ's were producing about 560 horsepower, the DFR approximately 600.

Enzo Ferrari, ailing for several years, died in April, and soon thereafter control of all of his empire—small, perhaps, but nevertheless worldwide—was assumed by Fiat.

1989—The More Things Change …

The return to normally aspirated engines, now limited to 3.5 liters and a maximum of twelve cylinders, brought new entries into Formula One, attracted by the lower costs. A total of 20 teams appeared at one time or another during 1989, with the result being "pre-qualifying" necessary to determine the 26 cars that would form the starting grids, now limited to this size.

The net result was the same as the previous year: McLaren, with Prost and Senna driving, won ten of the 16 races and waltzed off with the Constructor's Cup, almost doubling runner-up Williams' point total, 141-77. Prost won the driver's championship ahead of Senna, 76-60, and thus became the seventh man to win at least three championships. He won four races and finished second in five, while Senna won six, placed second in one—and scored no other points. Prost placed in the top six in 13 events. The fact that the McLarens were now using a Honda V10 instead of the previous turbo V6 made a difference only in the noise from the exhaust pipes.

The hoped-for Ford comeback registered its first victory since 1982, when Benetton pilot Alessandro Nannini inherited the winner's wreath in the Japanese Grand Prix, next to last event of the year, when Senna was disqualified. (The Brazilian had crashed with teammate Prost while trying to pass him with six laps to go, Prost was eliminated, Senna was push-started by course marshals and rejoined the circuit at a point other than where he left it, and although he finished first, was ruled out of the results.)

Benetton got the use of the Cosworth HB late in the season, with this unit producing between 600 and 630 horsepower at the outset. The DFR, exclusive to Benetton in 1988, was now used by ten teams, including many little noticed and not long remembered, such as Rial, Onyx, Osella and Coloni. Eight different engine manufacturers were represented during the year: Renault, Judd, Yamaha, Lamborghini and Hart, plus Ford, Honda and old standby Ferrari.

On the driver's side the principal news was the rise of Mansell, now with Ferrari. He won two events and showed he could be as quick as either Prost or Senna—the latter two hardly speaking to each other despite being on the same team—and the championship being decided when one crashed into the other in Japan. Senna was fined $100,000 by FISA for the Japan incident plus various and sundry other examples of dangerous behavior, and was also placed on "probation" for twelve months. Prost left for Ferrari at the end of the year. It should be noted that Lamborghini was a subsidiary of Chrysler during 1989, although no one made any connection between Auburn Hills and the Formula One project.

1990—Senna Again—and Again

Senna, still with McLaren, won three of the 16-event season's first five races and that gave him a lead that he never lost as he edged Prost for his second championship.

McLaren, complete with its Honda V10's, also won the Constructor's Cup for the third consecutive year, but Ferrari, with Prost, Mansell and its V12's, made it closer than before, the final being 121-110.

The Ford effort, still with Benetton as the factory-supported team, was stronger than before and Benetton was third in the Cup standings with 71 points, thanks in great part to Nelson Piquet's return to being competitive. Piquet, back from the purgatory that was Lotus, placed third in the driver's championship standings and won the two closing races of the season in Japan and Australia.

It was clear, however, that if Senna or Prost stayed out of trouble there was little chance to beat them. Their cars were better and their engines were stronger and between them they won eleven races, six by Senna. The Honda V10 was estimated at a little more than 700 horsepower in racing (as opposed to qualifying) trim, while Ferrari, by the end of the year, had 712 for qualifying and 684 for the race. The Ford-Cosworth engines that Benetton used had, at best, 680 horsepower. The "customer" DFR engines used by nine of the 19 teams that competed during the year—a direct descendant of the 1967 DFV—had 650 at most.

When FIA made the decision to return to normally aspirated engines, one of the factors in the decision was safety, the feeling being that the turbocharged cars were too fast. In the second year of the non-turbo rules the better cars were beating the lap times established by the turbos, and specific power outputs topped 200 hp per liter.

So much for delaying progress.

The engines were only part of the equation: Faster lap speeds also came as the result of great cornering power generated by new and better car designs, which brought with them greater G-loads for the drivers. The FIA was preparing to do something about this in the years ahead, but the Europe-oriented organization wasn't quite sure what to do about the Japanese. The economic boom in that country had fueled, among other things, Japanese interest in F1: In addition to Honda's McLaren relationship, costing in excess of $100 million per year, Japanese firms had sponsorship interests in six other teams. Ford power was used by ten teams, but it was not competitive.

1991—Still Senna—But Closer

The Brazilian, threatened with a year-long suspension because of his criticism of FIA official Jean-Marie Balestre in 1990, nevertheless was in the seat of his McLaren-Honda when the season opened on the makeshift road circuit in Phoenix in early March. It was, fortunately, the last time an American world championship race would be held in such an unsuitable setting, and the last time an F1 event would be held in this country until 2000.

This time the Hondas were V12's instead of the previous ten-cylinder models and both Senna and teammate Gerhard Berger complained about their performance all year. But Senna won the first four events of the 16-race season, and Mansell, driving a Williams chassis with Renault V10 engine, could never catch up although he was as fast on the track. Senna won the title, 96-72, and as events in the next few years would dictate, it was to be his last championship. For the first time all points-earning finishes counted, and the allocation went from the 9-6-4-3-2-1 of the past three decades to 10-6-4-3-2-1, where it has remained. Senna wound up earning points in 14 races, winning six; Mansell won five, including three in a row, finished only ten, and lost a few through mechanical failures almost literally in sight of the finish line. McLaren also won the Constructor's Cup for the fourth consecutive time, 139-125, with Williams second.

The engine capacity remained at 3.5 liters unblown, active suspensions were still allowed, consumption was free but pit stops for fuel were forbidden, and there were 18 teams taking part, some with little chance of success, including the eight using Ford engines. Honda or Renault engines powered the winner in 15 of the events, with the only Ford win coming when Nelson Piquet, driving for Benetton in the twilight of his career, inherited the Grand Prix of Canada when Mansell's Williams stopped within 900 yards of the checker.

Among the greater failures of the year was the Ferrari team, which was disorganized and unsuccessful and fired newcomer Prost before the final race of the year, probably to Prost's satisfaction. That final race, the Australian Grand Prix, was started in a downpour to satisfy a television commitment and lasted only 14 of its scheduled 81 laps. Porsche, which had a new V12 for rent, made a deal with the Japanese Footwork team, but the engine proved unsatisfactory.

Among the more interesting—and more secretive—competitions in 1991 was the battle among the fuel companies, Shell, Mobil, BP, Elf and Agip. With special brews still allowed, all were busy mixing up whatever they could to help the teams with which they were allied. It was reliably reported that one company had 50 different mixtures during the season, track tested more than 20 of them, and actually had three or four in use during practice for one race. Many of the cars had a different look to them, with the "high-nose" configuration now common being introduced by Tyrrell and followed soon afterward by others.

New to the scene and making their debuts in F1 were German Michael Schumacher and Finn Mika Hakkinen, the former with Jordan, the latter with Lotus. Schumacher was so impressive in practice at Spa that a week later Benetton managed to entice him away from Jordan.

At the end of the season one more Formula One fixture passed into history: Balestre, the ill-tempered, erratic president of the FIA's sporting arm, was defeated in an election by Max Mosley, Ecclestone's right-hand man. Mosley was not yet president of FIA—that would come later—but insofar as racing was concerned, this was more than enough. Controversy was now, for all practical purposes, as good as illegal.

Before the switch: Michael Schumacher won the 1994 world championship with his Benetton-Ford, then moved over to Ferrari.—Ford Motor Company

1992—Mansell, Nine Times Over and Quits

The season was 16 races long, but for most of the drivers it was over before the first event was run. Nigel Mansell's practice performance at Kyalami's South African Grand Prix showed the other 16 teams involved in the chase for the championship the only way they could win would be if Mansell—or possibly even teammate Riccardo Patrese—had mechanical problems and/or dropped out.

The Williams team still had the Renault V10's, which were probably superior to Honda's V12 the previous year, and also had an active suspension system working properly. The result was that Mansell was fastest qualifier 14 times, won the first five races of the year, eight of the first ten, and almost doubled runner-up Patrese's point total in the chase for the championship, 108-56. As a consequence Williams also won the Constructor's Cup for the first time since 1987, 164-99, ahead of McLaren. The latter still had Senna, who recorded three wins although he finished fourth in points behind the meteoric Schumacher, who won one race and placed in nine as the Ford-engined Benettons became a contender. Mansell's nine wins were a record, since tied, and his five in a row are still unmatched. Now world champion, Mansell had participated in 72 grand prix races, starting in 1980, before winning his first one, five years later.

The Williams cars not only had an active suspension, but traction control, which was coming into vogue with many teams. The Williams version, which operated in the lower gears, would temporarily—very temporarily—cut off a few cylinders, thus reducing power and therefore wheelspin while accelerating out of slow corners. Williams also had French national oil company Elf as a fuel sponsor and supplier, and their special formulas were better than anyone else's. This advantage was lessened somewhat before the Hungarian Grand Prix, the ninth race of the year, when more stringent controls were put on what could be fed to engines.

The joke of the season came on the political side, when Senna was busy trying to switch to Williams for the 1993 season, and Mansell got wind of this. His relationship with Williams was already strained despite being on the way to a title, so he left after the season and moved to CART. Senna, in the meantime, found that Prost, on a year's sabbatical after being dropped by Ferrari, had already secured the lead spot at Williams for 1993.

Schumacher continued to impress, the win at Spa was the first of his career, and the Benettons were obviously the class of the field after one discounted the Williams and Senna's McLaren. Only three teams used Ford engines. The rest were powered by a group that included Lamborghini, Judd, Ilmor, Mugen (a Honda derivative), Yamaha and Ferrari, with the latter having its worst season in many years.

1993—Prost Wins—and Goes
Andretti Comes—and Goes
Controversy Stays

Honda once again departed the grand prix scene and this left Renault with a clear field and McLaren without an engine, so the team had to pay for its motive power for the first time in many years, the supplier being Ford. Since the company had an agreement with Benetton this meant McLaren would not get the latest pneumatic-valve HB's, but those with steel springs instead. This made for a strained relationship and also ensured that 1993 would be the only year that McLaren was aligned with Ford, the team moving to Peugeot for the next season. Senna, who spent the winter in Brazil, showed up a few weeks before the opening event and joined McLaren on a "per race" basis, which was a new way of leaning on sponsors to come up with more money for the driver. Senna was paired with Michael Andretti, CART's top driver and although a newcomer to Formula One racing, someone with impeccable credentials.

Senna would wind up winning five races; Andretti would wind up back home.

Prost was the favorite to win the world championship even before the year started. He didn't disappoint anyone, except possibly the twelve teams that were competing with Williams and its V10 Renaults. It was again a 16-race season; Prost sat on the pole 13 times, won seven of the first ten and was never headed for the title, which he won with two races to go. Driving conservatively, he finished second in the last three and took his fourth championship, more than anyone except Fangio some 40 years earlier. He then retired, which was announced two days before he clinched the championship, and through 2000 his records stand.

He achieved 51 victories, ten ahead of runner-up (at the time) Senna, in 199 races (fifth most active) for a winning percentage of 25.6; an average of 4.01 points per start, better than anyone except Fangio's 5.44; and 798.5 points in all, well ahead of anyone else.

Prost and Schumacher, who had matured to where he was as fast as anyone when his Ford-powered Benetton was competitive, were the good news. The bad news came in several forms, one being the Andretti situation and the other, the FIA's turning the development clock back and banning what were classified as "driver aids." What this meant was that all the advances of the past several years—active suspension, ABS brakes, traction control—would be ruled out for the next season. The reason given was to lower costs for less well-funded teams, and to return the driver's championship to the drivers, rather than give a trophy to some software engineer.

The bomb was dropped during practice for the Canadian Grand Prix midway through the season, when a sudden announcement said that these items were in violation of the current rules, and it took a threatened owner's strike to keep the cars as they were until the end of the year. Although no one wanted to admit it, the move was made due to the lack of competition, causing the races to become parades, the telecasts to lose rating points, and the sponsors to question the wisdom of their investment.

Andretti had several factors working against him from the start. Although he came to the Europe-oriented F1 community with a great reputation, his decision to commute from Pennsylvania rather than take up residence in Britain caused a negative reaction from the start, and he had trouble being accepted. A new FIA rule— again, an attempt to lower costs for the smaller teams—limited each team to practice and qualifying laps only, except on circuits in their own countries. This came at a time when a new driver, regardless of his previous experience, needed as many familiarization laps as possible. He was also involved in a series of early-season crashes, and his confidence suffered as a result. Finally, being on the same team with Senna meant the bulk of the attention was given to the Brazilian.

To make things worse Mansell had taken his seat with the Newman-Haas team in the CART series, and was on his way to that championship in his first season. Andretti finally placed third in the Italian Grand Prix, the 13th race of the year, and returned to the U.S. for good.

Despite Benetton being entitled to a year's exclusive use of the latest Ford V8, McLaren eventually managed to get the same engines, first the HB Series VII, and later Series VIII, complete with pneumatic valves, which could be turned to 13,500 rpm, and which produced more than 700 horsepower.

In the end it didn't make any difference. Prost was untouchable and teammate Damon Hill also was hard to beat, Senna winning the last two races of the season to squeeze Hill back to third place in the driver's championship. The Constructor's Cup was all Williams, 168 to half that amount for McLaren. The FIA, now firmly in the hands of Ecclestone and Mosley, sent a message early in the year when Prost, who had made statements criticizing the sanctioning body, was called on the carpet to explain why he should not lose his license. The message was clear: Drive fast, keep quiet, get paid and fly home in your private jet.

1994—Senna Dies, Schumacher Wins, Ford Loses Him

Although there was little advance notice, 1994 turned out to be the last year of the 3.5-liter limit. As a result the new Zetec-R engine, its name coming from a new Ford of Europe passenger car powerplant and therefore designed to do duty as an image builder as well as a racing tool, only had one good season in the sun. The same can be said for Ford's Formula One aspirations.

Work on the engine, still a V8 as opposed to Renault's V10, began in the fall of 1992, and it was installed in the Benettons in January of 1994, two months before the season opener. They could be turned to 14,500 rpm, not quite what the Renaults could do but with excellent mid-range torque, and produced slightly better than 215 horsepower per liter.

The problem, however, was not with the engine, car or driver, but with the budget: In spring Ford had to inform Benetton that there was no money available for 1995. By summer, when Dearborn had found enough funds for the next season, Benetton had already made an arrangement with Renault, which was planning a comeback, and the chance for two titles in a row was gone.

Ford power was behind the seat of the champion for the first time in twelve years, but the fact that Schumacher was now the most successful driver was obscured, to a degree, by Senna's death.

The mercurial Brazilian, who had developed a worldwide following, died on the seventh lap of the third race of the season. It was the Grand Prix of San Marino, run on Italy's Imola circuit, and his Williams-Renault went straight into the barriers outside one of the fastest corners on the course. His death was the second of the weekend, newcomer Roland Ratzenberger being killed in a crash of his Simtek during practice, the first grand prix fatality in a dozen seasons.

Schumacher, with his Benetton-Ford better than ever and with Senna gone, was now The Man. He won eight of the 16 scheduled races and placed second twice, but was banned from two of them and disqualified from two more, so his points were achieved in just twelve events. The manner in which he won the title, however, left a bad taste in many mouths. He was leading Williams-Renault's Damon Hill by one point, 92-91, in Adelaide's season-ending Grand Prix of Australia when Hill attempted to pass him for the lead on the 36th of 81 laps. Schumacher's car was already damaged and no longer competitive, so instead of letting Hill by he ran him off the road, taking both cars out of the event but ensuring the title.

Schumacher had six wins and one second in the first seven events of the year, but then was disqualified after placing second in the British Grand Prix when he first passed Hill during the warm-up lap. This should have placed him at the back of the grid, but the stewards were not clear on the rules, and by the time they realized what should be done the event was under way. After they decided on a five-second stop-and-go penalty, Schumacher was shown the black flag three times, and he ignored it. At first the FIA fined him $50,000, but a few days later this was increased to disqualification from the race, the fine boosted to $500,000, and a ban from two more races was added.

Schumacher won in Hungary with Hill second, then won in Belgium but was thrown out on the smallest of technicalities. In midseason the FIA had introduced a wooden plank to the underside of all cars to ensure a minimum amount of ground clearance. After the Belgian race an inspection of the board showed an excessive amount had been ground off by contact with the road. So Hill won that race and the next two when Schumacher's two-event ban was implemented. Schumacher returned to win the Grand Prix of Europe at Jerez, and Hill returned the favor in the Japanese Grand Prix, setting the stage for Australia.

The FIA instituted rules changes announced in 1993 were supposed to give the series back to the drivers, but all they did was to make Formula One racing more affordable for the smaller (read: less wealthy) teams that made up the bulk of the fields. They did not affect the balance of power. In certain instances, most prominently traction control, enforcing the rules was difficult as these systems were easy to disguise and in certain cases the officials turned a blind eye toward them.

Only semi-automatic gearboxes remained: They lessened the danger of someone over-revving an engine and thus kept rebuild costs down. Other changes, introduced after Monaco, included aerodynamic modifications to reduce cornering forces. At the Canadian Grand Prix in June, pump fuel replaced special mixtures and the air boxes had to be removed from engines in an attempt to reduce horsepower. In addition, 25 kilos (55 pounds) were added to the minimum weight.

With the season turning into a Schumacher-Benetton runaway, Ecclestone saw to it that Nigel Mansell was brought out of retirement for the French Grand Prix in July, driving for Williams in this and three other races to help fill the gap left by Senna's death. He would drive two more events for McLaren in the following year as his F1 career came to an end. There were 14 teams competing during 1994, four with Ford power, the "other" three—Footwork, Minardi and Larrousse, all in the spear-carrier category—using HB engines with an estimated 720 horsepower in this model's final configuration. Williams won the 1994 Constructor's Cup, 118-103, with Benetton next.

Chapter 20

———————●———————

"YOU JUST SHOW UP"

Ford was more or less pulled into off-road racing by the fact that Ak Miller, and Bill Stroppe and his Long Beach-based operation, were in it up to their hubcaps before Ford really knew what was going on, and because certain Southern California dealers were off-roaders and knew whom to call in Dearborn.

One of these was Dick Landfield, in the late 1960s a freshly minted dealer in Yorba Linda, as he put it, "out in the orange groves, with no road through." Slide-in campers were becoming popular, and Landfield did well by making packages of the truck and camper unit so customers were offered one-stop shopping and financing: "I started advertising and I was pulling people from San Diego and Santa Barbara ... and we were selling more trucks and campers then we were cars.... We'd sell 60 trucks and campers a month...."

Trucks, campers and the Baja peninsula were also part of Landfield's avocation and he was a fan of the region before racing ever started there, so when Irv Hanks talked him into entering the initial Baja 500 in 1968, he was game.

"So that was my first race. Do I need a competition license? No, you just show up. You got to have a helmet. So I went and bought a Bell helmet. We went first class—we even bought driver suits—they were more like coveralls, but we had driver suits."

Hanks and Landfield drove a Bronco, and it did not go well. "We kept losing the rear axle, and we'd stop, and knock things back in, and stop again. There was one guy who had pits, and that was Bill Stroppe—this was an organized effort and he had people out there and he was wonderful. We stopped in Stroppe's pits and got fixed.

"Well, the Bronco finally expired and I left Irv there with a tube of honey, a stick of salami and a canteen of water. And I hitchhiked into Calexico, bought the parts to fix the thing, bought an old four-wheel drive pickup and drove back and got there five days later. I got back five days late and I know he's gonna be dead, right? So I come back there and he's sitting on the side of the road and he's drunk, and he's got this cache of canned ham, sardines, cheese, canned fruit.

"Everybody that came along would see him there.

"'Are you OK?' 'No, I'm not OK, I'm starving.'

"And they'd give him food and water. And he'd amused himself for five days building these mazes and watching the ants—putting a piece of cheese in the center

Bill Stroppe.—Ford Motor Company

of the maze and watching the ants try and find their way through to get this piece of cheese."

That was off-road racing, Baja style, in the early days.

The next year Landfield and his friends formed FAIR—the First Association of Independent Racers. They got $10,000 from the light truck manager in Dearborn and were able to assemble their own service crews.

Dealers who are either fans or find that participation helps sales are involved in several motorsports disciplines, but when racing or rallying becomes major league, dealers normally drop out due lack of major-league budgets and lack of the required level of technical sophistication. One of the few exceptions to this is off-road racing, where dealer-sponsored efforts, helped by the manufacturer, have been an important part of the scene since the beginning.

Off-road racing was on its way with the impetus provided by the events in Baja, and Ford's withdrawal from motorsports in the U.S. at the close of 1970 had little effect on what was happening in the desert. The off-roaders still knew people in Dearborn and the ban on participation never really affected them. They were independents to begin with, and there was always the Back Door....

Landfield: "In '72 Ford came out with the Courier and somebody in Dearborn called me up and said, 'Hey, we've got this little truck and we want to prove how tough it is. We want you to race it in Baja,' and I said, 'There's no class for it, there's just a pickup class and you race against the big pickups, against Drino Miller and Walker Evans and all those hot dogs.' So he said, 'Well, why don't you see if they'll make another class?'"

"So I went to Ed Pearlman and said, 'Ed, the big thing coming is these mini-trucks,' and he said, 'No more classes,' and I said, 'Well, Ford is willing to fund this and they realize it's going to cost you time and money to write up the rules and all that,' and he said, 'Fund?'

"And I said, 'Yes, they want to put up contingency money and this and that.'

"'Tell me more about the fund,' he said, and I said, 'There's ten grand in it for you,' and he said, 'Just what I was saying. We need another class for mini-trucks.'"

There was no Baja 1000 in 1974, as it was cancelled because of the energy crisis, but the event has run every year since, for a total of 32 in all. La Paz has been the finish for 14 of them while 15 have wound up back in Ensenada, due to the Mexican government's desire to keep the course in certain areas of the state. It has even started and/or finished in Mexicali and in Ojos Negro, but the classic route is considered to be Ensenada-La Paz, which in recent times has been run every third year. The 2000 event was the first to finish in Cabo San Lucas, at the foot of the peninsula.

Off-road promoter Mickey Thompson was expanding, running events in such places as the Los Angeles Coliseum and Anaheim Stadium, where thousands of tons of dirt were brought in and artificial courses were laid out where admission could be charged. He even installed an off-road circuit at Riverside Raceway, when that venue was still in existence, so there were more opportunities for off-roaders and their sponsors.

As a consequence, as with any other form of the sport, new heroes were made—or better said made themselves—and more manufacturers became involved. Dodge was involved for a while in the '70s, and Toyota has been a high-budget operation for several decades, spending a good percentage of it on Ivan (Ironman) Stewart, who at last count had won 17 Baja 500's and dozens of other events.

Stewart runs in the Trophy Truck class, something that was created in 1994 as the result of a suggestion from Kranefuss. He was seeking to find something more marketable than the proliferation of classes that made it possible for practically every automaker to claim victory, and asked SCORE for a class that would be comparable to NASCAR's Winston Cup. Trophy Trucks were the result.

In brief, Trophy Truck means a tube-frame racing chassis with an engine mounted behind the driver and a vestigial body draped over everything. Horsepower is somewhere around 600, and total weight is normally right on the 3500-pound limit that both SCORE and Best in the Desert use for this class. Suspension travel approaches two feet, and trophy trucks can run at close to 140 mph when they are on level pavement.

Stroppe's lead driver, when Parnelli Jones was not involved, was Manny Esquerra, a Native American out of Parker, Arizona, who won dozens of events. Driving a Ranger, he won his class in SCORE races seven times in the ten-year stretch from 1981 through 1990, and added High Desert Racing Association class wins in 1982 and 1984, before HDRA merged with SCORE.

Toyota had Stewart, Evans was the star driver for Dodge and Larry Ragland was one of the Chevrolet mainstays and suddenly, in 1987, 18-year-old Robbie Gordon popped up on the off-road horizon, and on Ford's as well.

Robby was the son of Bob Gordon, a veteran off-road racer and a good one from the greater Los Angeles area. When Robby was in his early teens his father would take him along as co-driver, providing the sight, as one veteran observer says, of "watching this little kid's helmet bobbing up and down in the car because they couldn't find one small enough to fit him."

Robby Gordon.—Ford Motor Company

At speed: Robby Gordon, the wunderkind of off-road racing.
—Ford Motor Company

When he was in his late teens Robby was beating established veterans almost everywhere and anywhere. He was voted rookie of the year when he was 18, and in 1989, when he was 20, he won the Baja 1000 in a Ford, coming back the next year to do it again in a Porsche-powered Baja special co-driven by his father. He won the Mickey Thompson Stadium series in 1988 and 1989, and should have been on his way.

Robby was to be the next great American driver, everyone thought, and he went from off-road to sports-car racing and single seaters, and everywhere he went, the talent was apparent after a few laps. So, unfortunately, was the lack of discipline. Gordon drove for Jack Roush in IMSA, and was part of the winning team at the Daytona 24 Hours for four straight years (1993–96) in a Mustang. In 1996 he became the first driver ever to win three straight off-road events in the SCORE series in his trophy truck, and won the season championship comfortably even though he only participated in six of the seven races. In 1998 he came within two laps of winning the Indianapolis 500, having to pit for fuel with five miles left and finishing fourth as a result. By 2000 he had drifted from one Winston Cup team to another, no longer a factor, a talent seemingly gone adrift, while contemporaries such as Jeff Gordon and Tony Stewart had become major winners.

The next big step in Ford's off-road efforts came in 1990, and again, the impetus came from the Southern California dealers and from Landfield and Ashley, and the idea was to combine all the various Ford teams that were getting support. Landfield sold the concept to the Special Vehicles Operation, it went up through the marketing department and the Rough Riders were born.

They wore the same uniforms, the race trucks and chase trucks all had the same paint jobs, same tire and oil sponsorships and so on, and it worked. In 1991, the first year of operation, the team included Esquerra, Ashley, Chuck Johnson, Rob MacCachren, Paul and Dave Simon, John Swift and Dan Smith, in his rookie year on four wheels.

They ran an eight-race SCORE/HDRA schedule, plus there were ten stadium races on Mickey Thompson's slate, all of them in either baseball or football stadiums, including the Rose Bowl, the Los Angeles Coliseum, Texas Stadium and the Kingdome in Seattle. Ashley moved from his winning Bronco of the year before to an F150, Smith took over the Bronco, Esquerra was in a Ranger with two-wheel drive, Johnson had a 7S Ranger, MacCachren was in a Class 8 F150, the Simons in a 4x4 Ranger, and Swift in an Explorer.

They brought Ford seven season titles that first year, including Johnson with the Spirit Racing Ranger, Swift with the Explorer in Class 6, Ashley with the F150 in Class 4, the Simons in Class 7 4x4 with their Ranger. Ford also won what back then was known as the Heavy Metal (full-size) and Mini-Metal (compact) classes, manufacturer's trophies, in effect, and Smith was the SCORE/HDRA rookie of the year.

Although the composition of the Rough Riders varied slightly from one year to the next, the mainstays were the same: MacCachren, the Simon Brothers, Ashley,

Winner: John Swift of the Rough Riders in the 1991 Baja 500.
—Ford Motor Company

John Swift.
—Ford Motor Company

Chuck Johnson.
—Ford Motor Company

Dave Ashley.
—Ford Motor Company

Rob MacCachren.
—Ford Motor Company

Smith, Johnson and Swift. They won a host of class championships during the years they were functioning as a group, both in SCORE events and in Thompson's stadium competitions.

The Rough Riders, as a more-or-less team and as a marketing tool, lasted through the 1996 season, when the lack of sufficient exposure—certainly not the lack of success—was the reason given. There were many who felt the program was canceled because Bruce Cambern, who was the director of SVO from October 1996 through the following October, didn't care for it. Support for individual teams has continued through the truck and power train departments, which have used them for engine and transmission development work.

Off-road racing, even though better organized than it was in the '60s and '70s, has always managed to maintain a certain *laissez faire* attitude, brought about, perhaps, by the very nature of the sport. At the beginning it was a case of "Run what you brung." Even in 2000, although there are classes, there was plenty of choice of vehicle for anyone who wants to compete. At present there are 23 classes in SCORE events and 18 car and truck classes in the Best in the Desert Racing Association. The latter started life in 1984 as a motorcycle-oriented group and began including four-wheeled vehicles in 1996, and has done well organizing and promoting races in Nevada.

Best in The Desert was conceived and is operated by Las Vegas native and veteran off-road motorcycle racer Casey Folks, who brought cars and trucks into the mix at the request of Ford, as the company was becoming increasingly concerned about safety—or the lack of same—in Mexican events. Deaths and serious injuries—involving both drivers and spectators—were becoming a regular part of the scene in

Baja, and a particularly unfortunate 1995 accident, which left John Swift co-driver Dino Pugeda in a vegetative state when better medical care might have saved him, prompted Ford to take action. Dan Rivard, in charge of Ford motorsports then, had been unhappy with the situation for some time, so as off-road program manager Dan Stuczynski put it, "I picked up the phone and called Casey."

Folks runs a tight ship. As an example the Nevada 2000 "road book," which includes detailed directions, maps, mileages, etc., for every one of the event's 1468 racing miles, covers 101 pages. Because his events are run inside the Nevada state border, relations with state officials, Native American tribes who are resident there, police, Bureau of Land Management, etc., are simplified. "When we got to the first race and found a registered medical technician at every pit stop we knew this was a different ballgame," Stuczynski says.

Direct Ford sponsorship of vehicles racing in Mexico ceased at that time, although the magic of the name and the traditions that go with it continue to attract big fields, and parts and pieces intended for use in Best in the Desert events wind up in vehicles running south of the border. Best in the Desert now promotes six events per year, two for motorcycles and four for bikes and four-wheeled vehicles. There are ten different organizations promoting off-road races somewhere in the U.S., Canada and Mexico, but Best in the Desert and SCORE are by far the most prominent. SCORE also runs six events annually, three in Mexico, two in Nevada and one in California. Championship Off-Road Racing (CORR) attracts some West Coast participants, including Evans and MacCachren, but for all intents and purposes, off-road racing is a Southwestern sport.

That's where the deserts are, and that's where one can run wide open, where you can see the horizon—not to mention some boulders, sinkholes, gila monsters and dry washes.

The key to off-road racing's future success, or lack of same, is television exposure—which has been spotty. The reasons for lack of adequate coverage have been twofold, a sort of chicken-and-egg situation: Until coverage is better, major sponsors won't get involved in a major manner. And until major sponsors get involved, coverage won't improve. Recent developments involving satellite pickup from miniature cameras have made this not only possible, but much simpler as well. In this respect off-road racing is in the same developmental stage as international rallying. Until someone takes the first big step, what could be excellent television, as well as an effective marketing tool, will stay at its current level.

Chapter 21

BACK TO THE SPEEDWAY

There were several reasons for Ford's rejoining American open-cockpit racing in 1992, and the best one of all was that Indianapolis, and all of its attendant exposure, was the place to be if you were a major manufacturer. NASCAR was fine, but single-seater cars were the sophisticated ones, and the Indianapolis was still the ground zero of American motorsport.

There was another reason, and a good one: Cosworth was looking to get back into the game. Cosworth was owned by arms manufacturer Vickers at the time, and its CART business had represented a large part of its profits in the days before fixed-price rebuilds. Steve Miller, then in charge of Cosworth's CART activity, talked Vickers into financing a new engine before he had a customer. The next two items on the agenda were to find an auto manufacturer as sponsor, and to find a team with championship potential.

The team was Newman-Haas, and the drivers were the Andrettis, father and son. In the spring of 1991 Miller spoke with Mario Andretti and showed him the early reports: The engine was smaller, lighter and more powerful than the Ilmor-Chevrolet and Andretti pushed Carl Haas to get them for the team. Contractual agreements, plus needed testing time, would keep them from dropping the Ilmor-Chevrolet engine until the 1992 season. Cosworth's manufacturer of choice, and it was a natural one, was Ford, which had financed Cosworth projects since the firm's inception.

There was some reluctance at first, but the lure of getting to Indianapolis, of going head to head with Chevrolet—and the possibility that Cosworth would find another sponsor—proved irresistible. Development costs had already been absorbed by Vickers, and all engine deals were arranged by Cosworth directly with the individual teams. Engines would be leased, not sold, and a Cosworth technician would go with each one. Haas, says then-Ford racing director Michael Kranefuss, would receive Ford subsidies down the road, but at the outset the arrangements were between Cosworth and Newman-Haas.

The design for what was called the XB engine was started in the late summer of 1989, with Miller as the head of the team, Stuart Groove doing most of the work, and Bruce Wood as Groove's right hand. Wood, who came to Cosworth right out of college, would stay with the CART program and its ensuing development. When

Groove left for Ferrari in 1993 Wood became senior designer; when Miller went to Ilmor in 1997 he became chief engineer—and later would add the responsibility for Cosworth's NASCAR involvement. The engine was first run on a dynamometer on July 30, 1990, was expected to be in cars for the fall and winter track testing, and be ready for the 1991 season. The postponement until 1992, however, delayed the testing, and as Wood says, "Just shows that only racing really galvanizes a project into action, since despite the huge development period all through 1991, when we were not racing we still weren't ready for the first race in '92."

The choice of Newman-Haas was an interesting step from Ford's viewpoint, because five years earlier Haas and Kranefuss had been at odds over their failed Formula One program. But Cosworth had already chosen Newman-Haas, Ford was now in line to sponsor the engine, and both Haas and Kranefuss were pragmatists. On September 23, 1991, the Monday after the CART race at Elkhart Lake, the Andrettis were testing the new XB.

The engine showed itself to be approximately 40 horsepower stronger than the Ilmor-Chevy, and the first track test went well. The next on-track step was to run an extensive series at the old Texas Motor Speedway, a two-mile oval near College Station, using Michael Andretti and Eddie Cheever of the Ganassi team, which would also get XB's.

Until this point, and for decades, American championship car racing had usually been dominated by one powerplant. At various times it had been Offenhauser, or Ford, or Cosworth, or for the past few years, the Ilmor-Chevrolet. There were usually one or more "other" engines making a cameo appearance, but they seldom stood a chance.

Now, the return of Ford would set off a flurry of activity that would—within four years—see four of the world's major automakers competing at the same time in an all-American racing series. Mercedes-Benz would take over GM's interest in Ilmor after the 1993 season, Honda would appear in 1995, and Toyota would come in the next year.

Racing had become more and more popular, fueled by the growth of cable television and the general bull market economic conditions, and the Germans and Japanese were viewing CART as a means of sales promotion for their U.S. efforts. Ironically, just as they were all helping CART to undreamed-of prosperity, in the late winter of 1994 Tony George pulled the rug out with his creation of the Indy Racing League. And CART, ruled by a group of modern-day feudal barons, each with his own self-interest blocking any sort of a long-range view, wasn't smart enough to convince George otherwise.

In the meantime, however, CART racing went on, with the later developments not picked up by the sport's distant early warning system.

Table 1 Cosworth USAC/CART Engine Development

Year	Engine	Size, liters	Boost Level, inches	Power, hp	RPM
1976	Cos./Parnelli	2.65	80	795	9500
1977	Cos./Parnelli	2.65	80	840	9500
1978	Cos./Parnelli	2.65	80	840	9500
1979	Cos./Parnelli	2.65	80	840	9500
1980	DFX	2.65	48	600	10,000
1981	DFX	2.65	48	658	10,500
1982	DFX	2.65	48	695	10,500
1983	DFX	2.65	48	700	11,000
1984	DFX	2.65	48	705	11,000
1985	DFX	2.65	48	710	11,000
1986	DFX	2.65	48	720	11,200
1987	DFX	2.65	48	725	11,200
1988	DFX	2.65	45	695	11,200
1989	DFS	2.65	45	710	11,500
1990	DFS	2.65	45	720	11,500
1991	DFS	2.65	45	720	11,800
1992	XB	2.65	45	755	13,000
1993	XB	2.65	45	780	13,000
1994	XB	2.65	45	800	13,250
1995	XB	2.65	45	810	13,250
1996	XB/XD	2.65	45	830	14,000
1997	XD	2.65	40	800	14,200
1998	XD	2.65	40	815	14,500
1999	XD	2.65	40	830	14,700
2000	XF	2.65	40	850	15,300

Source: Cosworth Racing, Parnelli Jones

1990

Smoking is banned on all domestic airline flights. ... McDonald's opens a store in Moscow. ... East and West Germany undergo their formal reunification on October 3. ... Gene therapy becomes a reality.

Arie Luyendyk, the transplanted Dutchman who had never previously been a factor, won the fastest Indianapolis 500 in history, averaging 185.9 mph in defeating runner-up Bobby Rahal and longtime race leader Emerson Fittipaldi. The average was more than 15 mph quicker than Rahal's record of 1986, and to do it—and beat Rahal—Luyendyk had to circulate at averages above 216 in the closing stages. Fittipaldi led 128 laps, but was slowed by extra pit stops made necessary by tire trouble.

Al Unser Jr. won his first season championship, placing first in six of the 16 events, including a streak of four straight that stretched from Toronto in late July to Vancouver in early December. All the winners were equipped with Ilmor-Chevrolet power.

It was also the year in which xenophobia reared its head in American racing, and not for the first time. In fact, in Porsche's case it was for the second time. The German manufacturer, which perhaps more than any other depended on a racing image for sales success, was foiled in its 1979 attempt to compete at Indianapolis when USAC insisted Porsche run its V6 at the same turbo boost levels as the V8's everyone else was using. Now, in 1990, after two full years of middling success, Porsche showed up with CART's first full carbon-fiber chassis, designed by March. It was lighter, it was stiffer, and it was safer for the driver. CART, acting in the best Luddite tradition, promptly made it ineligible. What the CART owners were afraid of was a factory team with Porsche's credentials coming in to compete against teams that were privately owned.

The Porsche chassis banning did little to improve CART's image in other parts of the world, but the various team owners, most of them Midwest oriented, didn't care. For 1991, once Porsche was gone, the board voted to allow carbon-fiber chassis, which have been standard ever since. When the next German manufacturer arrived a few years later it made sure Roger Penske was its partner.

The final point standings: Al Unser Jr. (Lola T90-Chevrolet) 210, Michael Andretti (Lola T90-Chevrolet) 181, Rick Mears (Penske PC19-Chevrolet) 168.

1991

A cholera epidemic in Peru is the first since the 19th century. ... Clarence Thomas is confirmed as a justice of the Supreme Court after surviving accusations of sexual harassment. ... The Giants win the Super Bowl, defeating Buffalo, 21-19, when a field goal attempt misses in the closing minutes.

Michael Andretti, following in his father's footsteps just as Al Unser Jr. did the year before, ascended to the throne in 1991, winning the CART championship and setting a record by finishing first in eight of the 17 races. His cousin John, who would later move over to NASCAR, also won one, giving the family the majority of the season's trophies. In addition the Andrettis achieved something never seen before in early June, when Michael won the 200-miler at Milwaukee, with John second and father Mario third. Mario's younger son, Jeff, placed eleventh.

Michael Andretti: Like father, like son.
—Ford Motor Company

But the Indianapolis 500, which for a sponsor has more promotional value than the rest of the CART series combined, went to Rick Mears for the fourth time—and again in a Penske car. Mears, the pole sitter, was the winner of a late-race duel with Michael.

The big news of the season, from a Ford standpoint, came in September at Elkhart Lake, when the Newman-Haas team stayed behind to test with the new engine. They had the best car and the best driver, so it was easy to establish a baseline.

Now all they had to do was get ready for next season.

That was the good news. The dubious news came at CART's year-end board meeting, which was attended by Tony George, who proposed Goodyear racing director and personal friend Leo Mehl for the chairman's job. This was rejected, and the split between the industry barons who owned CART and the young man who owned the world's most famous venue became greater.

The final point standings: Michael Andretti (Lola-Chevrolet) 234, Bobby Rahal (Lola-Chevrolet) 200, Al Unser Jr. (Lola-Chevrolet) 197.

1992

*The Mall of America, the largest ever, opens outside Minneapolis. ...
The Nicoderm patch is approved by the Food and Drug Administration. ...
Riddick Bowe defeats Evander Holyfield for the heavyweight title.*

Michael Andretti and his new engine were fast right from the start of the year, but it was not until the sixth event of the 16-race season that he managed to win, this coming at Portland on a road course. Michael was the leading winner of the season, taking five events, but he lost the championship to four-race winner Rahal by the narrow margin of 196-192.

The Newman-Haas team, with Andretti father and son, and Ganassi, with Cheever and Robby Gordon, were the only ones with the new Ford powerplant, which proved fast, but had teething problems early in the season. The most obvious of these came in the Indianapolis 500, where Michael was well in front, had made his last pit stop, and was on his way to victory when a broken timing belt sidelined him with eleven laps to go. (Ford engineer Don Hayward: "The cause lay in the vibrations induced by the new transmission, which was different than the one used for testing a year earlier.") The race was not only an emotional setback for Michael, it was a physical one for his father and brother Jeffrey. Mario crashed on a restart on the 78th lap and fractured numerous toes, while Jeff had more serious injuries when his right rear hub carrier broke on the 115th lap and he ran into the wall on turn two. He incurred multiple injuries to his feet and legs that required extensive surgery.

The race itself was won by Al Unser Jr., with one of the first-generation Ilmor-Chevrolet engines, in the closest finish in the history of the 500. Unser edged Scott Goodyear, who had started in 33rd and last position, by less than a car length—.043 seconds. It was the eighth victory for a member of the Unser clan (four for his father, three for Uncle Bobby), and a race that saw four former winners appear for the last time: A.J. Foyt, after 35 years; Rick Mears; Gordon Johncock; and Tom Sneva.

The final point standings: Bobby Rahal (Lola-Chevrolet) 196, Michael Andretti (Lola-Ford) 192, Al Unser Jr. (Galmer-Chevrolet) 169.

1993

*The Czech and Slovak Federal Republic is dissolved after 74 years. ...
Each becomes an independent nation, complete with its own language
and set of problems. ... The North American Free Trade Agreement (NAFTA)
is ratified and, despite many warnings, is an aid to the economy.*

Nigel Mansell, the Englishman who was the clear-cut world champion in 1992, had a disagreement over his 1993 compensation from the Williams Formula One team and as a result wound up with Newman-Haas for the next season. He replaced Michael Andretti, who went off to join McLaren in an attempt to replicate his father's feats on the grand prix circuit.

The 1993 champion: Nigel Mansell, who won the 1992 Formula One title, took the 1993 CART championship as well. Car owner Carl Haas is at right.—Ford Motor Company

Mansell was the reigning world champion, and although there were other former champions in CART, namely Mario Andretti (1978) and Emerson Fittipaldi (1972, 74), he was the freshly baked one, and as such attracted an inordinate amount of attention. He lived up to it, winning the title in his first year, and coming within an ace of winning the Indianapolis 500 as well.

He was leading the 500 with 15 laps to go when a yellow flag slowed the field, and he was outgunned when the green came on because of a lack of experience, and as a result Fittipaldi won his second 500 and Mansell was third. He wasn't the only one who had second thoughts afterward: Mario Andretti was in contention for almost the entire race, was given the wrong set of tires at the end and dropped back to sixth as a consequence.

The season, which again included 16 races, saw Mansell fastest qualifier seven times and finish with five wins, the same as Paul Tracy, who finished third in the season standings behind Fittipaldi. He even won his first event, the street race at Australia's Surfer's Paradise, and was a help to CART's worldwide television ambitions, since he was better known around the globe than most of the other drivers.

Mario Andretti, who finished sixth in the season standings, nevertheless managed to pull off one of the feats of this or any other season: At the age of 53 he won a race against America's finest open-wheel opposition. And, almost parenthetically, he did it while most of his Newman-Haas crew was fascinated by their newest addition from the Formula One ranks and was devoting less and less attention to him.

This would be the last year for the Ilmor-Chevrolet, but the Penske team and Rahal-Hogan were still using them, and doing well. In addition to Tracy's five wins Fittipaldi had three, so half the season went to Penske drivers. Chevrolet drivers wound up with ten wins, Ford with six.

The final point standings: Nigel Mansell (Lola-Ford) 191, Emerson Fittipaldi (Penske-Chevrolet) 183, Paul Tracy (Penske-Chevrolet) 157.

1994

The U.S. restores Jean-Bertrand Aristide to the presidency of Haiti. ...
A midsummer earthquake in the Los Angeles area kills 57 and causes an
estimated $15 billion in damage.

This was the year of The Split, in which George announced his plans for the formation of the Indy Racing League, and the year of Roger Penske.

George's motivation has never been explained to everyone's satisfaction, or at least not accepted. Wealthy from birth, he inherited command of the world's best-known racing facility five years earlier, when he was just 30, and it is entirely possible that he felt the older members of the racing community, many of whom were self-made men, were not showing him enough respect. They were the backbone of CART, and they were pressuring George to run the 500 under CART sanction rather than USAC, and he was concerned that if they ever boycotted the 500 he would not be able to fill the field. It is also possible that his Midwest orientation made him sensitive to the fact that "his" race, and "his" racing series, was becoming increasingly dominated by foreigners who had not worked their way through the traditional ranks of midget and sprint car racing.

They had come from the increasingly popular Karting series staged in the Latin American countries, or had their open-wheel experience in one of Europe's many different formulas. In addition, many of the Brazilians and Mexicans were bringing millions of dollars in sponsorship money, and this meant they were buying their rides, not "earning" them. When Jeff Gordon, a local hero from just up the road in

Roger Penske: The most successful team owner
in history.—Penske Archives

Pittsboro, won two single-seat titles in 1991, he couldn't get a test drive with a CART team. So he went to NASCAR, became a star, and came back to win the Brickyard 400. But open-wheel racing—and Indianapolis—had lost another gate attraction.

On March 11 he announced plans for the IRL, which would begin competition in 1996. Now he would have his own race track and his own series. Most of the racing world, which had been hearing these rumors for several months, felt he would fail. Six years later they were still wrong.

It was a Pyrrhic victory, however, and helped no one.

Penske had been a dominant force in single-seater racing—in fact in many facets of American racing—for three decades. Now the indefinite article would be replaced by the definite: He was The Dominant Force in 1994.

His drivers finished 1-2-3 in five races, and were also 1-2-3 in the season standings, with titleholder Al Unser Jr. taking eight firsts and three seconds in the 16 races. And Unser won the Indianapolis 500 in what proved to be a master stroke for Penske as his Mercedes pushrod engine came, saw and ran away from the field in its only appearance.

Penske's formal relationship with the Daimler-Benz AG began in 1988, when he bought control of the Detroit Diesel corporation from General Motors, and saw to it that Daimler wound up with a substantial share of the new company. Freightliner, America's largest heavy truck manufacturer, was a subsidiary of Daimler-Benz, and was also an excellent customer for Penske's diesel engines. Penske Truck Leasing was also a good customer for Freightliner products. Penske also saw to it that all his diesel engines were delivered with Mobil oil, which was the recommended brand. Mobil was a sponsor of Penske Racing. It was good for everyone concerned.

Through his association with Daimler-Benz Penske met Helmut Werner, who at the beginning of the '90s was the chairman of Mercedes-Benz, the car and truck-making subsidiary of DBAG, and they became friendly. Penske had Werner as his guest at the 1992 Indianapolis 500, and at the season-ending event at Laguna Seca.

When, in 1993, General Motors informed Penske that it wanted to sell its share of Ilmor, he had a ready buyer in the wings. And at the same time, he was working on an idea.

The story of Mercedes' pushrod-engine walkover at Indianapolis started a year earlier, and its genesis took place at the Speedway during the month before the 1993 race. Penske had read the rules carefully and knew the regulations for so-called stock-block engines gave them a considerable advantage over the overhead-camshaft engines considered standard for high-level racing. The loophole, if it can be called that, came about because the terms "pushrod" or "stock block" carried with them the connotation of some low-budget operation attempting to take a basically inferior engine design and redo it to compete with the more sophisticated overhead cam variety.

The specifications permitted overhead-camshaft engines, when turbocharged, to have a maximum displacement of 2.65 liters and a boost of 45 inches. The pushrod engines could have a 3.43-liter maximum displacement and 55 inches of boost.

What it did not take into account was that someone could come up with a purpose-built pushrod engine that would be, from birth, superior. Nowhere was it written that the pushrod engine had to have a production ancestry. It merely needed someone with the budget and the engineering capability.

But it would be expensive, Penske thought. He discussed this with Mario Illien, the "Il" in Ilmor, and Illien said it could be done relatively inexpensively. He sketched what he was talking about on a napkin, and the groundwork for the 1994 victory was laid. Penske financed the project out of his own pocket, and the effort, from day one, was undertaken with the tightest security. Penske would blindside the entire racing community.

About the only thing that changed was the name on the valve covers, which went from Chevrolet to Mercedes-Benz when the GM division decided to back out of the partnership in the fall of 1993. Thus Penske not only brought the world's oldest automakers back to Indianapolis for the first time since 1922, but also made them a factor in American open-wheel racing.

When the engine appeared at Indianapolis in May there was a storm of protest but it was legal, it stayed, and the Penske team was doing its best to disguise the power advantage. But while they were practicing, Hayward was watching the times recorded over the various track segments, and soon realized what was happening: The three cars, driven by Unser, Fittipaldi and Tracy, were sandbagging. On every practice lap they were backing off on one corner or another to hide their true capabilities.

They had so much power (reported at 1076 hp) that when Tracy had an accident on the Friday before the first qualifying day, film analysis of the crash showed it was caused by his accelerating and breaking the rear wheels loose—at 225 mph. The race itself was a walkover, with Unser winning because of Fittipaldi's ill-considered attempt to lap his teammate while well in the lead with 15 laps to go. If it were not for that, they would have been 1-2.

After the race:

The U.S. Auto Club, which was still the sanctioning body for the 500, lowered the boost for pushrod engines to 52 inches at a June 28 meeting. Ford felt it wasn't enough, and there was another meeting on August 1, which also happened to be three weeks after George announced the engine specifications for the IRL—which spelled the end of Cosworths, Mercedes, Hondas and the rest.

Veteran Ford engineer Dan Rivard (who took over SVO when Kranefuss retired) was accompanied by Hayward and Cosworth's Miller when he met with USAC and IRL officials, the goal being a common (with CART) engine formula, and to renew discussion on reducing the boost on pushrod engines. The IRL-CART part of the discussion proved fruitless—as it would many other times—and for a while so did the talks regarding boost pressure. Then, when the meeting was about to end, Miller gave them the news that Cosworth had initiated the design of a pushrod engine, opened his briefcase and showed USAC President John Capels and his associates a few of the parts.

That did it. A short time later, the reduction in boost for "purpose-built" pushrod engines, as opposed to "production" pushrod engines, was announced, being lowered to 48 inches. The Cosworth engine was never seen, and any hopes Penske had of making his Mercedes version commercially available went with it. The projections for the Cosworth pushrod, at 55 inches of boost, were from 1088 to 1099 horsepower, and at 52 inches of boost were still over 1000 hp. (At that time the XB Cosworth was producing just under 800 hp. The turbocharged Buick V6 had about 865, but suffered from reliability problems.)

It was Mario Andretti's last year as a single-seat driver although he would continue in his quest for a victory at Le Mans. It also proved to be the last year in CART for Mansell, who was nothing more than a shadow of his championship-winning performance of 1993. He seemed to have no interest, and by the end of the season was involved in Formula One racing again. Williams, the team that had propelled him to the 1992 world championship, was in need of a driver and he did four races, at a reported fee of $1 million each.

Honda made its debut in CART with the Rahal-Hogan team and was not impressive, but Honda's history of producing power was known, and the racing community knew Honda would be back, and would be competitive. The name Mercedes was carried only on the valve covers of the Penske pushrod engines. The new overhead-camshaft engines, which would be called Mercedes in 1995, carried the Ilmor designation for this season.

Ironically, Penske's defeat of the Ford forces in CART came at the same time he was switching his NASCAR team, Penske Racing South, from Pontiacs to Thunderbirds.

The final point standings: Al Unser Jr. (Penske-Ilmor, Penske-Mercedes) 225, Emerson Fittipaldi (Penske-Ilmor, Penske-Mercedes) 178, Paul Tracy (Penske-Ilmor, Penske-Mercedes) 152.

1995

The U.S. sends 20,000 troops to Bosnia to enforce the Dayton Peace Agreements and end the war in the Balkans... John Daly wins the British Open in a playoff with Constantino Rocca of Italy.

The season, which in many respects took second billing to the year-long wrangling that went on, saw Jacques Villeneuve, the little Canadian whose late father Gilles had been a star of the Ferrari Formula One team, win the Indianapolis 500 and the CART championship. And his Reynard was equipped with a Cosworth. Reynard was becoming the new chassis of choice in CART, succeeding Penskes (he built those, too) and being used by as many teams as were Lolas.

Villeneuve would spend only two years with CART before moving on to Formula One and the world championship in 1997. He sat on six poles in 17 events and won four of them, the same as Al Unser Jr. (who had no poles), still with Penske and now using the Ilmor-developed Mercedes overhead cam engine.

The Penske news, however, was that he and his team were human. After their dominance of 1994, this time they could not even qualify for the 500. The reason, many observers felt, was that the roadholding of the 1994 cars was not good—but there was so much power that no one noticed. And the team, more concerned with hiding its horsepower advantage, did not pay sufficient attention to chassis setup. When they came back in 1995, they had no departure point for adjustments, and it cost them.

In the meantime Ford was among those still talking with George and his people and attempting to devise some engine specifications that would allow the company to participate in both series—unsuccessfully. During one of the discussions, after much time and little progress, USAC's Capels pulled out a set of papers that outlined what the specs would be—a 4.0-liter stock-block formula. There was no heading on the papers, but the specifications matched General Motors' Oldsmobile engine.

No one ever admitted it, but this was obviously GM's way of getting back to Indianapolis after having been blown out of it by Ford and Mercedes. Without this kind of backing for an engine supply, it is questionable if the IRL would have gotten off the ground. In its first year of operation, Ford made the Cosworth engines available, a generous gesture that achieved nothing insofar as a reunification was concerned.

What few persons outside of IRL knew was that Ford gave serious consideration to undertaking an engine development program for the new series. Although the term "stock block" was in common use, it was obvious that the engines did not need to be anything related to stock, and that they would be expensive. The company could afford to subsidize the Cosworth CART program, but any IRL engine venture would have to carry itself, and that was not financially feasible. The money available for IRL engine development was moved, in the summer of 1995, to supporting the new Formula One program. Cosworth would get the funding to develop an engine for Jackie Stewart.

One of the side issues of the year was the appearance of Firestone in CART for the first time in the organization's relatively brief history. Firestone, which had dominated Indianapolis and oval-track racing for most of its early years, recorded its first win at Michigan Speedway in late summer. Scott Pruett was the driver, Lola was the chassis, Ford was the engine.

The final point standings: Jacques Villeneuve (Reynard-Ford) 172, Al Unser Jr. (Penske-Mercedes, Lola-Mercedes) 161, Bobby Rahal (Lola-Mercedes) 128.

Manufacturer's Championship (inaugural year): Ford-Cosworth 310, Mercedes-Benz 272, Honda 40.

Constructor's Championship (inaugural year): Reynard 286, Lola 264, Penske 197.

1996

TWA Flight 800 explodes in midair shortly after takeoff from New York and dives into the Atlantic.... Welfare reform legislation is enacted.... The Colorado Avalanche wins the Stanley Cup.

The general feeling, at the beginning of the year, was that the true professionals had stayed with CART and the lesser lights (plus A.J. Foyt) had gone to the IRL. Then came the day of the Indianapolis 500 and the U.S. 500, the latter staged at Penske's Michigan International Speedway as a challenge to Indianapolis. The older race, despite being populated by a group of little-known drivers, went off without a hitch. The U.S. 500 was enlivened by a parade-lap accident that took the edge off the day, and the race required a restart with numerous backup cars.

Although no one was happy with the situation, one thing was clear: The IRL was not going to go away, and George was willing to finance it. The finances were a private matter, but the income from the Indianapolis 500 and NASCAR's increasingly popular Brickyard 400 should have been enough to cover any losses.

Jimmy Vasser, who was driving for Chip Ganassi and who had the benefit of the new and powerful Honda engine, wound up as the champion of the 16-race season, one in which four of the events were in foreign countries—two in Canada, one in Brazil, one in Australia. The Rio de Janeiro race was new; the Australian event had been on the calendar since 1991. No fewer than eleven of the races were on road circuits, or city streets converted to road courses.

Vasser won four of the first six races and as a consequence Michael Andretti spent the rest of the season trying to catch him, but never quite made it. Andretti won five races, including two of the last three, but that wasn't enough, even though he was helped toward the end of the season by the new Cosworth XD engine. Andretti and third-place finisher Alex Zanardi wound up tied in points, but Andretti was awarded second place due to his greater number of wins, five to Zanardi's three. Zanardi, coming from Europe, was an instant success in American racing. Hondas were in the winner's circle eleven times during the year, Andretti being the only one to beat them. Ganassi's cars were also equipped with Firestone tires, as that company was making a success of its reentry into open-wheel racing.

It was also the year of Toyota's debut. Japan's largest automaker, which had been successful in IMSA racing with Dan Gurney's team, financed Gurney's return to CART. It was not successful, with Juan Fangio II (Juan Manuel's nephew) and P.J. Jones (Parnelli's son) finishing far down the standings.

For the first time the series had serious efforts from no fewer than four of the world's major manufacturers—Ford, Mercedes, Honda and Toyota. But Indianapolis, the sun at the center of the CART solar system, was missing.

The final point standings: Jimmy Vasser (Reynard-Honda) 154, Michael Andretti (Lola-Ford) 132, Alex Zanardi (Reynard-Honda) 132.

Manufacturer's Championship: Honda 271, Ford 234, Mercedes-Benz 218.

Constructor's Championship: Reynard 276, Lola 260, Penske 139.

1997

The Dow-Jones Industrial Average climbs past 7000, then 8000.... 30 of Wall Street's largest brokerage firms agree to pay $900 million to end a civil suit contending that it conspired for years to fix prices on the Nasdaq market.

Floyd (Chip) Ganassi Jr. came to Indianapolis as a driver in 1982 and retired after the 1986 season as a result of family pressure. He then moved into team ownership, and in 1996 proved that he was a better owner than a driver, being the man behind the first- and third-place finishers in the season standings. In 1997 he did it again, and would continue to do so for the next two years—the new main man of the series.

In 1997 he had the same drivers as the previous year, but this time Zanardi won the championship and Vasser finished third. Zanardi won five of the 17 events, including five on road courses, while Vasser won only once, at Laguna Seca. Eleven of the races were on road circuits, and there were two new ovals: Gateway, just outside St. Louis, and Fontana, east of Los Angeles.

The latter was a Penske creation, just a few miles from the site of the unsuccessful Ontario Speedway of the 1970s, was two miles in length, and was an example of what a modern sports facility should be. It was a success right from the start, but unfortunately more for stock cars than for CART, still suffering from the loss of Indianapolis.

It was not a good year for Ford, which won only two events, Michael Andretti at season-opening Homestead and Scott Pruett in the next event, Surfer's Paradise. After that it was all Honda and Mercedes, with the latter winning nine events and the manufacturer's trophy, and Honda taking the other six.

The IRL series finally got its "own" engines, as practically all of the teams opted for Oldsmobile Auroras. A few chose Infinitis from Nissan, but the series was dominated by the GM powerplant. The irony was provided by the fact that after all of GM's maneuvering to shut out the other manufacturers, the Oldsmobile Division did practically nothing to merchandise its racing success and would, eventually, go out of business. Olds was America's oldest automotive nameplate.

The final point standings: Alex Zanardi (Reynard-Honda) 195, Gil de Ferran (Reynard-Honda) 162, Jimmy Vasser (Reynard-Honda) 144.

Manufacturer's Championship: Mercedes-Benz 316, Honda 290, Ford 230.

Constructor's Championship: Reynard 346, Penske 156, Swift 143.

1998

U.S. scientists break the genetic code of the tuberculosis bacterium, the germ that has killed more people than any other infectious agent. ... 15-year-old Tara Lipinski of the U.S. wins the women's figure skating championship at the Winter Olympics.

The CART season schedule grew to 19 events, now including one at the Motegi Speedway in Japan and one on a street course in Houston, and Alex Zanardi grew even more.

Chip Ganassi's Italian import won seven times, was second five times, and ran away with the championship, well ahead of teammate Jimmy Vasser, as Ganassi drivers finished 1-2 and Honda-powered cars finished 1-2-3. Gil de Ferran, driving for Team Kool Green, was third. Vasser and De Ferran won three races apiece, giving Honda 13 for the year. Ford's XD was making a comeback, winning four events, two by Adrian Fernandez.

Ford made arrangements to buy Cosworth Racing midway through the year, so what should have happened decades earlier finally came to pass, and there would be no more discussions as to what the proper name of the engine should be. It hadn't made any difference in the past, since the two had always been so closely related. Now they would be one legally as well.

The tire war saw Firestone dominant, with Michael Andretti the only Goodyear-shod driver able to win a race. It would only be a matter of time before Goodyear retreated to NASCAR, where it was the only supplier, and left CART to Firestone. This would, among other things, enable Penske to use Firestones. As a Goodyear distributor, when they were available he didn't have much choice.

Mexico's hero: Adrian Fernandez.—Ford Motor Company

Attempts to bring CART and IRL back together, or to at least find a common engine formula, went on, but to no avail. Any reunification of the two organizations—aside from their finding a common engine formula—was made more difficult early in the year, when CART became a publicly traded corporation. This move managed to make some of CART's lesser team owners more solvent, but a merger between a public company and a proprietorship could be complicated—and George was the sole owner of the IRL. It also saddled CART with an ongoing need to be aware of the stock price—something not necessarily conducive to a long-range outlook.

In the meantime 1998 marked NASCAR's 50th anniversary, and the media and advertising blitz that accompanied this made the average onlooker doubtful if any other racing series even existed.

This was also Rahal's last year as an active driver. Although he was never in the category of a Foyt or a Mario Andretti he was certainly one of the better ones, winning the CART championship three times and taking the Indianapolis 500 with a thrilling last-lap finish in 1986. He was 45, and had driven 450 races in 29 years, with 264 of them in CART. He was also the owner of a successful CART team, of several auto dealerships and had other business interests. He was, above all, a businessman. When he retired his goals in life were to make his team a winner and to continue the growth of his other holdings.

But in less than two years he would be the interim president of CART, and a few months after that would become the chief executive officer of Jaguar Racing, with the job of bailing out Ford's investment in grand prix racing.

The final point standings: Alex Zanardi (Reynard-Honda) 285, Jimmy Vasser (Reynard-Honda) 169, Dario Franchitti (Reynard-Honda) 160.

Manufacturer's Championship: Honda 365, Ford 293, Mercedes-Benz 225.

Constructor's Championship: Reynard 408, Swift 167, Penske 72.

1999

Only 24 days after the Dow passes 10,000, it tops 11,000.... Viacom takes over CBS.... Denver beats Atlanta in the Super Bowl and quarterback John Elway retires.

Ganassi, with Colombian star Juan Montoya as his new lead driver, made it four championships in a row, and then would announce a switch from Honda to Toyota engines for the following year. And Ganassi was not the only one: Penske, a Daimler-Benz partner in various business deals and a 25 percent owner of Mercedes racing engine manufacturer Ilmor, announced in June year that he would be switching to Honda for 2000.

Montoya, on loan from the Williams Formula One team for two years to gain experience, needed a few races to acclimate himself but then was dominant and ended up winning seven times, a remarkable achievement for a 24-year-old in his first CART season. Franchitti won three times, but his reliability record enabled him to amass enough points for a tie. Montoya was given the title by virtue of the additional victories.

Honda-engined cars won 14 of the 20 races on the schedule, twelve of which were run on road circuits. Zanardi, who left Ganassi and returned to Europe for a Formula One ride, never recovered his 1998 form, and was not a factor in grand prix racing.

Unification talks went on through much of the year, but just when they appeared to be successful, at the end of September George turned down all the proposals. "We're happy with what we have. We don't have to change," he said.

The final point standings: Juan Montoya (Reynard-Honda) 212, Dario Franchitti (Reynard-Honda) 212, Paul Tracy (Reynard-Honda) 161.

Manufacturer's Championship: Honda 383, Ford 301, Mercedes-Benz 193.

Constructor's Championship: Reynard 402, Swift 241, Lola 69.

2000

Tiger Woods wins nine golf tournaments, including the U.S. and British Opens and the PGA championship.... The Los Angeles Lakers, with Shaquille O'Neal and Kobe Bryant, win the NBA championship, defeating Indiana in the finals.

It was a year of comebacks, for Ford, and for Penske. Ford's new XF engine took the manufacturer's championship. Penske's team, now with Honda engines, gave him his eighth championship in CART's 21 years, and the first since 1994.

It was also a year in which the driver's title was not decided until the last event, at Fontana on October 30. Five men had a mathematical chance to win before the race but the championship wound up with Penske driver Gil de Ferran, who finished third at Fontana in an event delayed one day by rain.

Ganassi, who switched over to Toyota, was bothered by various problems during the year and Montoya was therefore not as dominant as in 1999. He won three races, plus the Indianapolis 500 as Ganassi made a side trip on Memorial Day weekend. Equipped with the GM engine that has been standard IRL fare, Montoya dominated the event and added to the IRL-CART controversy. Montoya left with the trophy, Ganassi with several million dollars and great exposure for his sponsors.

The CART schedule grew to 20 races, eleven on road courses and nine on ovals; Honda power won eight, Ford seven and Toyota five. Mercedes-Benz, after a bad season, announced in the fall that it was withdrawing from CART. The company's success in Formula One (with McLaren), it was reported, made involvement in two open-wheel series unnecessary. There was also the question of expenditure for two different racing engines, but this was not mentioned. The television ratings, key to CART's long-term success, were far below those of NASCAR, with no improvement in sight. As a consequence—although there were other factors involved as well— the CART board of directors jettisoned CEO Andrew Craig in mid-June and Rahal took over the job on an interim basis, while keeping to himself the knowledge that he would be chief of Jaguar Racing's Formula One effort beginning December 1. Rahal was succeeded in December by Joseph Heitzler, a TV production veteran with limited racing experience.

Heitzler inherited a multitude of problems, not the least of which were the television ratings. CART races were telecast worldwide, but as far as the bottom line was concerned that number was so much window dressing. What counted with sponsors were the American ratings.

Another problem, never mentioned openly but one that weighed on people's minds, was the makeup of the fields. At the season-opening race in Florida, for example, only two of the top 25 finishers were American born. At most races there were no more than three or four Americans. In the meantime, NASCAR had names like Rusty Wallace, Dale Earnhardt, and Dale Jarrett—and Jeff Gordon, who couldn't get a test drive near his home town in Indiana, and had to go south to find a ride.

The final point standings: Gil de Ferran (Reynard-Honda) 168, Adrian Fernandez (Reynard-Ford) 158, Roberto Moreno (Reynard-Ford) 147.

Manufacturer's Championship: Ford 335, Honda 313, Toyota 275.

Constructor's Championship: Reynard 394, Lola 312, Swift 11.

2001

"The Producers" wins twelve Tony awards.... Julia Roberts wins an Academy Award for her performance in "Erin Brockovich."... Dot com

companies see their market values undergo a drastic downturn.... The Nepalese crown prince assassinates his family, then kills himself.

The struggle between CART and IRL continued, to no good purpose, and now involved engine specifications, as the rival organizations sought ways to make participation in both easier for manufacturers and sponsors. The IRL kept to its V8, 3.5-liter displacement, complete with rpm limit. However, it made a minor technical change, but one important politically, to become effective in 2003. This would enable engines to become more easily adaptable for road racing (the IRL competes only on ovals, where engines can operate in a much narrower rev range). This was seen as throwing an olive branch to CART, still indecisive about its new rules, but needing an engine that would be suitable for road circuits.

CART was down to three major engine suppliers—Ford, Toyota and Honda, and then Toyota announced, on April 3, that it would build an IRL engine in addition to the one it was doing for CART. This was seen as a way of forcing CART's hand regarding the new regulations, and all that was needed was for Ford to go along with Toyota to make the new CART specs virtually the same as those of the IRL—a step toward a possible reunification down the road.

But a management vacuum existed in Dearborn. Bob Rewey and Neil Ressler had retired over the winter and James Schroer, the top marketing man, moved to DaimlerChrysler. There was no one left with a macro view and the understanding that factory involvement in motorsports was a marketing exercise, not an engineering one. So Ford sat on the fence, not realizing that soon there might not be a fence on which to sit.

The situation got worse: CART was embroiled in a major lawsuit because of canceling a race in Texas on the morning of the event, it was losing sponsors, and going through management changes. On the other side, the IRL received another blow when CART (and CART-affiliated) drivers occupied the first six places in the Indianapolis 500, taking with them the bulk of the prize money, funds sorely needed by many of the IRL teams.

The betting in some circles was that CART wouldn't need 2004 engine specifications, as the organization would be out of business by then.

Chapter 22

———●———

COS AND WORTH

The DFV is The One Great Thing for which Cosworth will be remembered as long as racing engines are a topic of conversation.

DFV is Cosworthspeak for Double Four Valve, The Engine That Could, the engine that won more World Driver's Championship Formula One races than any other, that in modified form won the 24 Hours of Le Mans, and modified in another manner was the king of American open-cockpit racing for a decade.

It was basically the work of two men, Keith Duckworth and Mike Costin, who built Britain's preeminent engine design organization starting in a garage in the late 1950s.

In the 15 years from the time it was introduced on June 4, 1967—it won its first race that day, with help from Jimmy Clark—until it propelled Keke Rosberg to its 12th and last title in 1982, the DFV won 152 of the 219 World Driver's Championship events in that period, or roughly 70 percent. This V8 began life producing a little more than 400 horsepower from its three liters, and by 1982 produced approximately 520.

The "worth" was Keith the designer; the "Cos" was Mike, who had the remarkable facility of complementing Keith so that synergistic was an ideal definition of their relationship. Graham Robson, the British author and historian who has known them for more than three decades, says, "Duckworth always swore that without Costin the business would never have survived. The two were completely different in that Keith did all the design and none of the development, while Costin did all the testing, development and rectification and never designed anything. Duckworth told me that Costin could look at a drawing and more than nine times out of ten would be able to say whether something would be a) easy to make, b) would work, and c) was worth pursuing."

If there was a problem with the DFV it was one of image: The One Great Thing tended to hide the fact that Cosworth grew into a flourishing engineering business, one that consulted for manufacturers other than Ford—including Daimler-Benz and General Motors—designed and built many other successful engines, and propelled Costin and Duckworth into the ranks of racing legends.

They are gone from Cosworth, having retired more than a decade ago when the company was being passed from one conglomerate to another, well before Ford finally purchased Cosworth Racing (as opposed to Cosworth Technology, the "road

Keith Duckworth: The father of the DFV.
—Ford Motor Company

Mike Costin: He made things
work.—Ford Motor Company

car" development arm) in 1998. What they left behind, in certain respects, is the basis around which much of the British racing car industry was developed. Constructors needed an engine, and Cossies were available—big ones, small ones, you name it. Cosworth engines, practically all based on Ford production models or designed from scratch for Ford, were dominant (at one time or another) in British sedan racing, Formula Junior, Formula Two, in sports cars, and most certainly in Formula One and CART.

Duckworth was an engineering student in the mid-1950s when he worked for Lotus during his vacations, and came under the spell of Colin Chapman, the Lotus founder, designer, chief engineer, and most everything else. At that time Lotus was located in a small London facility, and had Costin as the team chief for the Lotus racing effort, which was then confined to small-displacement sports cars. Earlier, when they started, Chapman was a project engineer for British Aluminium and Costin was a test rig designer at aircraft manufacturer De Havilland.

"We used to start work at a quarter past seven at night," Costin says, "and work until two in the morning.... We used to build kit cars—by the time we'd made eight we would have the ninth one, and we would share the driving.... Then he got established and we both left our jobs, that was in 1955.... I was responsible for all the development, the building of the prototypes, the cars.... It was the old story of diving in far too deep and you couldn't swim anyway.... The [postwar British] motor industry was in its infancy and had hardly got above the prewar level of ability in terms of design."

And Chapman was the leader of Britain's racing car design movement, a trend that would give Britain preeminence in this field while the rest of the British automotive industry was headed either into oblivion or foreign lands. There were a few proper racing teams—Aston Martin, BRM, Vanwall a bit later, and aside from that there were what the French called *garagistes*—no industry, just a small group of Colin Chapmans, John Coopers, Eric Broadleys and some others. They had dreams, but they didn't have engines to match those of the Continent, the Ferraris, the Maseratis, the Porsches.

And Duckworth came to this, after working there summers in 1955 and 56, "... as a gearbox development engineer, working on the five-speed box, and that only lasted about eleven months, I think it was, and then I decided the box wasn't ever going to be successful. He wanted to carry on with the box and so I decided I would go, and as I'd got friendly with Mike ... We decided we would go in business together and the name of Cosworth was produced, but then Mike was given the job of being technical director of Lotus, forbidding extramural activity, and therefore once he'd given his name to the company he didn't join it for a further three and a bit years."

Costin: "The basis of it was that we wanted to work together—we didn't know what we wanted to do, we hadn't got any notions of building engines, we just decided that we got on well together, we were totally different people, but we thought the same way and we had a good idea that we were pretty able people, and therefore working together we must be able to make a living.

"But then came the crunch. I either had to give up my job and go with Keith.... Now he wasn't married, he could live very cheaply and survive. I had a wife and three children and required an income, and so coincident with that my three-year rolling contract came up for renewal, so I signed ... but of course we were in very close touch."

The early days of Lotus, when Costin and Chapman even shared the wheel in a few sports-car races, saw all manner of people cross their paths.

Costin: "We were racing one day at Brands Hatch and there's this bloke talking to us, talking to Colin when I'm doing something, talking to me when Colin's doing something, with us all day.... Then he wanted to go to London so he scrounged a lift with us, in the transporter.... We drove him back, bought some fish and chips for him and took him to a tube station, we got back in the transporter and I said to Colin, 'Who was that bloke?' 'I don't know,' he said, 'I thought he was a friend of yours!'"

"I've never seen him before in my life—I thought he was a friend of yours!"

On Monday morning the stranger was at the door, and he talked Chapman into hiring him as a mechanic. It was Graham Hill, who used his job as a post from which he could cadge drives with any customer who came through the door. A decade later he would win his second world championship while driving a Lotus-Ford.

In December of 1959 Chapman decided to build cars for the new Formula Junior class, using the 1000cc Ford engine that was also new at the time, "So when we decided in December that we'd make 25 cars, by February we'd sold only three. By September we had built and sold 125."

Duckworth was the engine contractor. "He made 125 engines," Costin says, "so that became his sole activity, and the cost for that engine was 145 pounds (about $400 at 1960 rates of exchange). We used to buy, at a special price from Ford, batches of 105E engines. We'd ship them to Keith and he stripped them, took out all the parts, modified the parts, modified the cylinder head, the ports, ground the camshaft, lightened the flywheel, modified the sump, rebuilt the engine, ran it in, tested it, and then we picked it up—and sent him a check for 145 pounds for each engine. He was allowed to keep the bits—any bits he changed from standard, he could keep."

Duckworth in a garage, with a few helpers, doing 125 engines in about ten months. It was a sort of rite of passage, the same as a Robert Yates, working days for Holman-Moody and nights for Junior Johnson.

By the time Chapman was looking for a three-liter Formula One engine, in the spring of 1966, Cosworth was a going concern in Northampton, and had a string of successful racing engines to its credit.

"Chapman wanted an engine," Duckworth says, "and he thought that I was worthwhile to give it a go.... So he came to me and said, 'How much do you want to design and make a three-liter Formula One engine?'

"So in our usual fashion of no-costing, Mike and I, and Bill Brown and a few others, said, 'Ah, we should be able to make a V8 Formula One engine, make four or five engines, perhaps maintain them for a year or so for 100,000 [pounds—about $280,000],' so we said, 'Colin, 100,000 is the job.'

"So Colin went round to try and get the 100,000.... He first of all went to David Brown of Aston Martin.... For my 100,000 I wanted to preserve the right to manufacture my own, and all design rights and everything else were to remain mine, so I could sell it at my sole discretion. Brown wanted all, so I walked away from that one.... Then Colin had a good go with Walter [Hayes] and Walter decided to take it up."

From start to its first dynamometer run took between nine and ten months, and Duckworth did most of the drawings himself. ("I did work fairly diligently. I didn't start before nine, but worked close to midnight.") Two months later two engines appeared at the Dutch Grand Prix, won by Clark after Hill dropped out. Both engines had the same problem, but Clark's lasted.

Duckworth: "Two teeth had fallen off a cam gear, and therefore a cam had stopped rotating and therefore it went very sick.... Therefore I spent the second half of the race trying to sort out what happened rather than watching the race.... On the way back to the garage Clark's engine was rattling badly and we found there were two teeth off one of his cam gears.... Fortunately there were two with one standing in between, so while it went clickety-bang a bit, it actually managed to keep driving, where the two in line on Graham's allowed the thing to no longer drive."

There is no doubt in Duckworth's mind as to the name of the DFV. It is Ford. Duckworth: "Ford employ all kinds of people to design things, but they are designed for Ford and are Ford property and are Ford engines. It was designed for Ford, and the agreement was ... The important terms of the contract I gave Ford were, that so long as the engine stays in its essential form it will be called a Ford."

The engine, when turbocharged, became a Cosworth in American oval-track racing because Ford was out of motorsports in the mid-'70s when first Parnelli Jones and later Cosworth itself adapted the engine. There was even an internal memo signed by then-president Lee Iacocca making sure Ford kept its distance, which did little except cost the company millions in what could be termed "free" image building. "That's how our name became much better known in America than it was in Europe," Duckworth says.

Although using the engine as a structural member of a racing car had been attempted before (by Lancia in the mid-'50s, BRM in the '60s), the Lotus 49, which the DFV powered, was the first "pure" version of this, where there were no tubes running past the engine. The chassis was simply bolted onto the engine and the rear suspension hung onto the engine. "It was Keith who told Colin," Costin says, "'You don't have any engine mountings, the chassis stops there, and our engine bolts straight on the back of it, and that's all there is to it,' and Colin went along with it.

"When we got down to the stressing of it, we were staggered how low the loads were."

Why didn't someone do this earlier?

"Well, nobody else looked."

That was almost 40 years ago.

One of Duckworth's talents is his ability to cut to the heart of the matter, and do it succinctly.

On the subject of what is most important in a racing car: "Rubber—your tires, totally dominant, way in excess of the importance of drivers.... Rubber is what it's all about, which is why in general you need to have only one manufacturer making rubber, because as soon as you get more than one manufacturer, the manufacturer who produces the best rubber is the one that wins and it wrecks motor racing."

On mandatory pit stops: "As soon as anybody introduces a pit stop it's a change of formula, because your justification for running an eight, when other people are running 12's, is on the grounds of not pit stopping."

Duckworth remained as chairman and chief engineer until 1988, and Ford purchase discussions were going on at that time, but they didn't pan out. When Ford finally took over, "I was pleased for that, because now we've arrived where I thought we should have been all along."

He is clear about the difference between the past and the present: "Trying everything in sight is now the way you get on in Formula One, so you've got to have large teams of people doing lots of development, lots of experimenting, because you need your knowledge base.... We only made money out of motor racing by making our mistakes on paper and scrapping it before we made the hardware, and that's how, whilst everybody else lost their shirts making racing engines, we actually made a reasonable fortune.... It's because we thought of the problems and didn't make too many nonsenses, didn't waste money on development that was unlikely to be successful. I would think about it and decide, 'It's not worth trying that.'

"Unfortunately, in the climate today, that isn't the right attitude, because as you can do your quid's worth, which I think should have been done for a bob, you can get a tenner and do it for a fiver!"

(And even if one doesn't know that a bob is a shilling, a quid is a pound, a tenner is ten pounds and a fiver is five pounds, the point is well made.)

Duckworth and Costin both live on the outskirts of Northampton, comfortable in retirement and still collaborating, doing a consulting job for a motorcycle manufacturer. Keith lost his pilot's license after a bypass but his wife flies their helicopter and "will take me places if I'm good." Mike flies his light plane himself. After he lands he folds the wings up, puts it all on a trailer and takes it home.

Chapter 23

---◆---

TAURUSES AND MONTE CARLOS

1994

Nelson Mandela is elected president of South Africa. ... Richard Nixon, Jacqueline Kennedy Onassis, Linus Pauling, Burt Lancaster die. ... Player strike causes cancellation of World Series. ... Channel Tunnel between England and France opens.

After Michael Kranefuss retired somewhat unexpectedly at the end of the 1993 season Dan Rivard, a veteran engineer and trusted by many at Ford headquarters, was called out of retirement to take over Special Vehicles on what was termed a "temporary" basis. Rivard was supposed to be there for six months while management found a new director. The six-month job would last three years.

Rusty Wallace, still in the Penske stable but now driving a Ford, dominated most of the season and won eight races—double anyone else—and Fords took 20 of the 31 events. But Dale Earnhardt won his seventh championship and even managed to clinch it with two races remaining. It was the second year in a row that Wallace was the big winner and still finished behind Earnhardt in the points race. Ford won the manufacturer's championship for the second time in three years, but it was a season of success and a season of frustration at the same time, and also a year in which still another Robert Yates driver was sidelined by an accident.

Any manufacturer with a team owned by Roger Penske had to be pleased. Penske is the most successful team owner in the history of auto racing, owner, at this writing, of ten Indianapolis 500 championships. His team dominated the SCCA's Can Am series to the point where he ran it out of existence, and was the leader in Trans-Am racing when it attracted major efforts from Ford (and Penske had a Camaro). Reports were that some General Motors racing people were pressuring for Penske Racing South to abandon Pontiac in favor of Chevrolet. At the same time, in the late summer of 1993 GM was giving up its 25 percent interest in Penske-created Ilmor engineering, the Indianapolis engine builder.

The net result was that Penske spoke with persons in Ford management, arrangements were made to sell Detroit Diesel engines for Ford trucks—and Wallace was Winston Cup's leading winner of 1994 with eight victories in a Thunderbird.

Penske Racing South: Rusty Wallace in the Miller Taurus.—Ford Motor Company

There were some cynics who felt that the Penske-Ford commercial alliance was more or less designed to pacify the other front-line Ford teams, but that was never substantiated.

A related result was the walkover victory at the 1994 Indianapolis 500 for the Penske CART team and Mercedes-Benz—with the pushrod Ilmor engine that was first developed while GM had a piece of the action. Roger gave, and Roger took away.

Ernie Irvan, who had taken over Davey Allison's seat on the Robert Yates team after Allison died in a helicopter crash in the summer of 1993, was the fastest driver in the 21 super speedway races and led more laps than anyone else during those events. Then, in late August, he crashed when a tire deflated during practice at Michigan International Speedway and was lucky to escape with his life. His return to racing was, at the time, doubtful.

The old: The Thunderbird stock car, 1994 version.—Ford Motor Company

Despite missing a third of the season Irvan would wind up leading races more times than anyone else, and leading more laps than anyone except Wallace—1781 to 2141 for Wallace and only 1013 for Earnhardt. But Earnhardt was consistent, and consistency (plus four wins) gave him a tie with Richard Petty for the top rung on NASCAR's championship ladder.

Irvan won three of the first ten races. Wallace won five of the first 14, including three in a row in June, but much of the mid-season attention was focused on the inaugural Brickyard 400, the first-ever NASCAR race at the Indianapolis Motor Speedway. For decades the stronghold of America's racing Establishment, IMS was the citadel from which NASCAR founder Bill France was ejected in the early '50s, but his son was now a welcome guest. The fact that NASCAR was coming to the Speedway was no secret, as track modifications had been going on for some time, cars had made test runs, and a formal announcement had been made a year earlier.

The Speedway was sold out in short order, and had to turn down thousands of ticket requests as the Brickyard 400 became the latest jewel in NASCAR's crown. The first race was won, fittingly enough, by a resident of nearby Pittsboro, 23-year-old Jeff Gordon, who regained the lead with five laps to go when Irvan had a freak mishap: The strut holding a fender in place broke and cut a tire, and as a consequence Irvan was forced to pit. Gordon's car took home $613,000, the largest purse in NASCAR history.

Wallace had a bad streak at the season's end, finishing no better than 17th in any of the year's final four races, and being passed for second place in the point standings by Mark Martin, who won the closer at Atlanta and thus moved up. Fords led slightly better than 73 percent of the total of 10,106 laps run during the 31 races, and dominance was fine, but there was a new opponent on the horizon: 1994 was the last year for the Chevrolet Lumina, which would be replaced by the Monte Carlo for 1995.

The final point standings: Dale Earnhardt (Chevrolet) 4694, Mark Martin (Ford) 4250, Rusty Wallace (Ford) 4207.

Wins: Ford 20, Chevrolet 11.

Manufacturer's Trophy: Ford 246, Chevrolet 217.

1995

The Dow-Jones Industrial Average tops 4000 for the first time.... Chase Manhattan and Chemical banks merge, creating the largest bank in U.S. history.

The problems created by aerodynamics, in the form of a Chevrolet Monte Carlo, came to NASCAR in time for the 1995 season. The fact that a new car was imminent was no surprise: GM-supported teams had been testing the model for most of the previous season—and had been busy telling NASCAR it was nothing special. What GM did was to bring the science of aerodynamics into stock-car racing—and do it in a way that escaped the NASCAR technical people. The inspectors were expert at finding hidden fuel tanks and the like, but up to this point they had little experience with wind tunnels.

So when the Monte Carlo's rear end was only 51 inches wide and a 57-inch spoiler was allowed, NASCAR's Gary Nelson allowed GM to extend the body to match the spoiler. It made all the difference. NASCAR did this without benefit of any of its own wind-tunnel data, and so the stock-car wars went through another escalation. The fact that the rear end bore little resemblance to what one could buy in a dealership was shrugged off, and so were Ford's protests.

All of this was probably to the credit of Herb Fishel, GM's veteran racing director. Fishel was not the most popular man in the racing firmament, but he knew his way around, he knew where the bodies were buried, and he had been part of the scene for many years; continuity was a GM plus. What was a GM minus was the fact that by giving the Monte Carlo its additional downforce, sister brand Pontiac was relegated to the back of the pack.

And although few realized it at the time, the entry of the "NASCAR Special" Monte Carlo would pave the way for Ford's creation of the two-door NASCAR Taurus in time for 1998. Cars on the race track were looking less and less like cars in the showroom, but for whatever reason, the fans didn't seem to care.

The new: The first public prototype of the 1998 NASCAR Taurus.
—Ford Motor Company

The net result was that Chevrolets won the first nine races of the 1995 season and Rivard was climbing the walls. He initiated the construction of a NASCAR Monte Carlo, perhaps the only Chevrolet ever built by Ford, ran it through a wind tunnel, then went to France and his inspectors and was able to bring about an increased awareness of aerodynamics. After this, no new model would be admitted to Winston Cup racing without being measured in a wind tunnel first.

In the meantime Dearborn was trying to stem the Chevrolet tide and keep the streak of the past three years alive. The problem was that Chevrolet not only had the Monte Carlo, it had Jeff Gordon as well, and this was the beginning of the Gordon-Hendrick era.

The annals of child psychology are filled with case histories of youngsters pressured by their parents to be something they are not capable of. Little League fields resound with the frustrated cries of parents watching Junior strike out for the third time, the immediate frustration being only the obvious reason for venting. The deeper, potentially more damaging one is the subconscious realization that Junior isn't going to be any better than his father was, two decades earlier. Some fathers demand their sons become great athletes, and sometimes they make it to the edge of greatness before falling victim to the pressures that come from parental ambition.

Jeff Gordon was the exception, the one who showed thousands, even millions, of parents that the child could fulfill all of the parent's dreams, and more. Raised in California by his mother and stepfather, Gordon was driving go-karts and quarter midgets by the time he was five, and wherever he went, he won. He won 46 quarter-midget races at the age of seven, and 52 the next year. When he was 10, he won 25 Kart races. There were no more worlds left to conquer in his age group, so at 13 he moved up to sprint car racing in the Midwest.

Sprint cars are the maker—or breaker—of almost every American oval-track hopeful. These cars, complete with antique suspensions and engine in front, usually have an 86-inch wheelbase, roughly 800-horsepower V8's (alcohol-based fuels) and weigh in the neighborhood of 1500 pounds. They are nervous beasts that run on half-mile dirt and paved tracks, they are unforgiving, and they separate the men from the boys in short order. Now the Midwest, spiritual home of American racing, saw a small boy wanting to run with the men. Stepfather John Bickford talked the promoters into accepting the kid—and by the time he was 17 he was a consistent winner in sprint cars as well. He became U.S. Auto Club midget champion in 1990, one year out of high school, and then made his move away from single-seat cars and into stock-car racing. At first he split his time between the two, but by 1992 he was a Busch Grand National regular, driving a Ford for Bill Davis.

By the end of the year he had been kidnapped, in a manner of speaking, by Rick Hendrick, and the pair, plus crew chief Ray Evernham, started a new era in Winston Cup racing. The reasons for Gordon's leaving were several, depending on whose version one believed: One was that relations between Davis and some members of the Ford organization were strained, and Gordon didn't want to be in the middle of this. The second was that Hendrick was a successful operator who had proven resources, and the third, rarely discussed, was the subtle influence of Fishel, a veteran of the internecine wars common to the sport.

Gordon won seven of the 31 races, his car earned more than $4 million for team owner Hendrick—who also owned three-race winner Terry Labonte's car—and Chevrolets as a marque won 21 of the 31 events. Gordon also led the most laps, took the most poles and led the most miles. About the only thing he didn't lead was in the popularity standings. Despite the fact that stock-car racing was becoming a national sport, its roots were still in the south—and here was this small, almost petite young man looking more like an adolescent than a 24-year-old. He said "yes sir" and "no sir" and his accent was more the California of his birth than the North Carolina of his new residence—and he was beating the pants off everyone's home-grown heroes. It was an interesting study in the psychology of sports fans.

He would go on to win three season championships in the next four years, finish second to teammate Labonte in the other, and would win 40 Winston Cup races from 1995 through 1998. He would be on the crest of the NASCAR publicity wave that was sweeping through media as stock-car racing became a national attraction. The little boy who was raised to be a racing driver became the leader of the pack in more ways than one.

What Ford had going for it in 1995 consisted, basically, of Mark Martin and Rusty Wallace. Martin won four races, Wallace two, Ricky Rudd one—and Dale Jarrett one. Jarrett, whose career had led him to a number of teams with some success but without any great headlines, was spending his first year with Yates as Irvan's replacement. In the years to come this would prove to be a good fit.

The final point standings: Jeff Gordon (Chevrolet) 4614, Dale Earnhardt (Chevrolet) 4580, Sterling Marlin (Chevrolet) 4361, Mark Martin (Ford) 4320.

Wins: Chevrolet 21, Ford 8, Pontiac 2.

Manufacturer's Trophy: Chevrolet 245, Ford 204.

The Yates team: Ricky Rudd in the Texaco Taurus.—Ford Motor Company

1996

The Hubble space telescope returns pictures to earth showing the existence of more than 50 billion galaxies, or more than five times the number previously thought to exist.... The worst drought since the Dust Bowl era of the '30s hits the Southwest and bankrupts tens of thousands of farmers.

Yates' investment in Jarrett proved to be a good one as the son of two-time NASCAR champion Ned won four races in 1996, and three of them were events that drew national attention: He won the Daytona 500 to open the season; won the season's longest event, the 600-mile race at Charlotte; and won the Brickyard 400 at the Indianapolis Motor Speedway. He also won a 400-miler at the Michigan Speedway and finished third in the point standings, but much of Yates' success was overshadowed by the Hendrick Express:

The nation's largest auto dealer was on his way to winning his second championship, this time with Terry Labonte. Gordon won the most races—ten of the 31—and attracted most of the attention. Labonte—the peculiarities of the NASCAR point system working in his favor—won only two races while Rusty Wallace, buried in seventh place, won five. Gordon led 2314 of the 9648 laps in 1996, in other words approximately one quarter of all the racing laps during the year. Labonte led only 973, but consistency in finishing, and a good performance over the final seven races, gave him the title in the final event of the year. Gordon had five races in which he failed to finish and was outside the top ten in two of the final four events. It must have been all the same to Hendrick. His drivers were first and second.

Ford, after the ongoing series of negotiations between Rivard and France, received approval of some small aerodynamic modification in May, but it didn't make much difference. Gordon won three straight in September and Labonte made it four in a row for Hendrick in the next event.

There was also a non-racing related bombshell, one that hit at the time of the NASCAR banquet in New York in December: Hendrick, with 28 Honda franchises in his empire, was involved in a messy affair concerning how dealerships were awarded—one in which several Honda executives were sentenced to jail terms. Hendrick was indicted on 13 counts of money laundering, one of conspiracy and one of mail fraud—and then it was announced that he was suffering from leukemia.

Rivard was retired—again—after three productive years and replaced by Bruce Cambern, who took over in October.

The final point standings: Terry Labonte (Chevrolet) 4657, Jeff Gordon (Chevrolet) 4620, Dale Jarrett (Ford) 4568, Dale Earnhardt (Chevrolet) 4327, Mark Martin (Ford) 4278.

Wins: Chevrolet 17, Ford 13, Pontiac 1.

Manufacturer's Trophy: Chevrolet 233, Ford 223, Pontiac 133.

1997

The tobacco industry agrees to pay $368.5 billion over 25 years to compensate states for the cost of treating smoking-related illnesses.... An Iowa woman gives birth to septuplets.

This would be the last year of the Thunderbird, which was being phased out of production after more than four decades. Ford's first attempt at a sports car, which was born in the mid-'50s, had long since become a two-door coupe—and two-door coupes were not doing well in the marketplace. At the beginning of the season Thunderbirds were also not doing well on the track.

Gordon, on his way to his second championship in three years, led a 1-2-3 sweep of the Daytona 500 for Hendrick-owned cars, the first time for such domination of America's biggest stock-car event. Gordon's start, plus the story of Hendrick's legal problems and his leukemia, served to obscure the fact that Fords won 19 of the 31 races, drove away with the manufacturer's title, and had Jarrett and Martin still in contention for the individual crown at the last race of the year.

Hendrick eventually pled guilty to one count of mail fraud and was sentenced to a year of house arrest as the judge took his illness into consideration. He would return, with the cancer in remission, two years later. He received a Presidential pardon, along with approximately 60 other persons, at Christmastime, 2000.

In house, the problem of replacing the Thunderbird with something suitable for Winston Cup racing was taking precedence over much of the other activity in the Special Vehicles Office. The only full-size model in the Ford Motor Company inventory that could be eligible was the Lincoln Mark VIII, and for obvious marketing reasons, adapting a Lincoln for stock-car racing was ruled out. Bob Rewey, the group vice-president in charge of worldwide sales, service and marketing said, "The car we run needs to be the car we sell the most of," and this meant the Taurus.

Ford, while Rivard was still in his three-year role as director, had kept NASCAR apprised of its new vehicle plans and France, plus others from his organization, had been in Dearborn more than a year earlier to see pre-production models of the new Taurus. And they learned it would be sold with four doors, not two.

When the subject of converting a four-door into a two-door for the track came up, France shrugged. "You're making a NASCAR car," he said, "and it's been a lot of years since we ran stock cars." So the green light, in principle, had been given. And now, with the Thunderbird dropped a year earlier than anticipated, that meant designing, testing and getting approval for a vehicle that would carry a blue oval for the 1998 season, and doing it in a hurry.

The development contract, sought after by all the Ford teams, was awarded to Penske Racing South, with the reason being that PRS was familiar with 40 percent modeling procedures. This would be the fastest way to perfect a body that would look something like the production car, be as aerodynamic as the Chevrolets and Pontiacs, and meet with NASCAR approval. The original schedule called for the succession to take place for the 1999 season, and work was proceeding with all deliberate speed, with this deadline in mind. Then, in late January of the year, the marketing decision to scratch the Thunderbird was changed and the car would be withdrawn from production a year earlier.

Cambern called Penske Racing General Manager Don Miller and gave him the bad news. Development time had to be shortened by a year.

The models were built in Mooresville, North Carolina, home of Penske Racing South and many other teams, wind-tunnel tested in Southampton, England, and in Southern California. It took less than 20 days to build the first model; molds were made, testing took place in Britain at the beginning of April, and on May 14 a super-slick car carrying the name "Taurus" was shown to NASCAR.

The answer was no.

It took only six days to build a second version, and by the end of the month wind-tunnel tests were carried out in San Clemente, California. By the end of June full-size prototypes were tested in the Lockheed tunnel in Marietta, Georgia, and on July 30 a complete car, painted, polished, ready to race, was introduced to the public in Indianapolis.

The only trouble was it had not yet been track tested. That didn't happen until the beginning of September, when further changes were made. Testing went on, day and night work went on, and the Winston Cup season went on as well.

Gordon won ten races, Jarrett seven, Martin four, Jeff Burton three (including the inaugural at Texas Motor Speedway in Fort Worth) and Ricky Rudd two—with the exception of Gordon, all in Fords. NASCAR, always looking for as many winners as possible, had a good year, with eleven drivers splitting the 32 races, and no less than 18 posting fastest qualifying times. Ford drivers led more than 58 percent of all the laps run during 1997 and the manufacturer's title was a shoo-in. But attention, for the most part, was directed elsewhere—the fans toward Gordon, and in-house personnel toward getting the new Taurus ready.

They would do it without Cambern, who despite his engineering talents lacked what were euphemistically known as "people skills." He was replaced in the fall of the year by Dan Davis, who had previous in-house experience working with the Benetton Formula One team earlier in the decade. Rivard was—again—brought back from retirement to help with the Taurus project.

The final point standings: Jeff Gordon (Chevrolet) 4710, Dale Jarrett (Ford) 4696, Mark Martin (Ford) 4681, Jeff Burton (Ford) 4285, Dale Earnhardt (Chevrolet) 4216.

Wins: Ford 19, Chevrolet 11, Pontiac 2.

Manufacturer's Trophy: Ford 245, Chevrolet 209, Pontiac 154.

1998

> *NATO is expanded to include Poland, Hungary and the Czech Republic.... President Clinton testifies that he had an "inappropriate" relationship with White House intern Monica Lewinsky.... The first Federal budget surplus since 1969 is declared.*

The Taurus made it to the starting line at Daytona, and Taurus drivers, with a new car that was still undergoing fine tuning, won 15 races to 16 for the Chevrolet opposition and only two for Pontiac.

But hardly anyone, in a figurative sense, knew about it at the beginning.

The reason was that the season began with Dale Earnhardt finally winning the Daytona 500 after 20 years—and numerous close calls. It was a sort of high-speed morality play to kick-start NASCAR's 50th year, and the organization was understandably promoting the anniversary in every way possible. If this wasn't enough, Jeff Gordon was winning 13 of the 33 races in his Chevrolet for his third championship. The photogenic young driver, complete with counterpoint provided by his sick (and under house arrest) car owner, gave the general-interest and business media a veritable feast.

In the meantime the Tauruses were beginning to make their mark. Hampered by too much downforce at the outset, they improved this and two weeks after Daytona Martin, driving a Roush car, won the inaugural Winston Cup race at Las Vegas' 1½-mile track. Bruton Smith and Humpy Wheeler's Speedway Motorsports had purchased it from Las Vegas interests, and also bought half of tradition-laden North Wilkesboro Speedway in order to get a Winston Cup date for the Vegas acquisition. The old order was changing.

Martin led a Ford sweep of all but one of the first 14 places at Las Vegas, the only intruder being Earnhardt in eighth spot. As an unwished-for consequence, NASCAR clipped pieces off the Taurus spoiler to give the opposition a little help. Penske Racing South, it would seem, had done the job too well. Martin would finish the season as runner-up to Gordon in the point standings—the third time he occupied this position—and also in wins, with seven. Jarrett won three events, but it was Gordon's year. He was not only the darling of the media, but the bankers loved him as well: His cars earned $9.3 million in prize and bonus and point-fund money, more than a million better than the sum won by Martin and Jarrett combined.

The bad news was Jeff Gordon. The good news was that the Taurus was competitive, and that bode well for the future.

The final point standings: Jeff Gordon (Chevrolet) 5328, Mark Martin (Ford) 4964, Dale Jarrett (Ford) 4619, Rusty Wallace (Ford) 4501, Jeff Burton (Ford) 4415.

Wins: Chevrolet 16, Ford 15, Pontiac 2.

Manufacturer's Trophy: Chevrolet 240, Ford 235, Pontiac 152.

The veteran: Roush Racing's Mark Martin.—Ford Motor Company

1999

The Senate votes to acquit President Clinton on both articles of impeachment.... An Oregon jury orders Philip Morris to pay $81.5 million to the family of a 40-year smoker.... The top two organizers of the 2002 Winter Olympics in Salt Lake City resign after investigators discover they bribed persons who voted on the city's bid for the Games.

Gordon, thanks to a daring pass with eleven laps remaining, won the Daytona 500 while Jarrett crashed on the 134th lap and most observers assumed the year would be another one of Gordon-Hendrick-Evernham running away with the title.

It didn't work out that way.

The championships wound up with Jarrett and Yates, and it was a popular victory. For Yates, the only "major" team owner in late-'90s NASCAR who started on one of the lower rungs of the sport and whose livelihood depended on success in racing, this was the culmination of a four-decade involvement, one that saw him begin his career with Holman-Moody in the mid-1960s.

For Jarrett, whose star had been getting brighter ever since he joined Yates in 1995, it was the ultimate validation as a stock-car driver, and incidentally made him the second second-generation NASCAR champion, his father having won in 1961 and 1965 (the Pettys, Lee and Richard, were the first).

For Ford this was the fourth manufacturer's championship in eight years and 13th since the Winston Cup phase of NASCAR competition started in 1972.

Gordon won seven races, Roush driver Jeff Burton six, championship runner-up Bobby Labonte five in his Pontiac and Jarrett had four, but Jarrett's consistency was

The winner: 1999 Winston Cup champion Dale Jarrett.
—Ford Motor Company

outstanding. He failed to finish only one of the 34 events—Daytona—and placed in the top five 24 times. He had the title clinched with one race still to go. Martin finished third, Burton fifth, with rookie of the year Tony Stewart, driving a Pontiac, fourth and having won three races.

Stewart's being classified as a rookie was comparable to Jimmy Clark's carrying the same appellation in front of his name when he first arrived at Indianapolis in 1963. Stewart had been a winner in every form of single-seater competition and was the

Another Roush car: Jeff Burton in the pits, 1999.
—Ford Motor Company

best driver on the IRL circuit before moving to stock cars. Stewart, combined with Bobby Labonte, had given Joe Gibbs' Pontiac operation a first-class team, and one that nearly edged Chevrolet for the runner-up spot in the 1999 manufacturer's points race.

For Yates, after years of working his way up the NASCAR food chain and after originally not wanting to run a second car, Jarrett's victory propelled him into the ranks of championship team owners. This is a rarified atmosphere in the modern era, when most winning owners are multi-millionaires through sources of income separate from their stock-car activities. It was a popular victory in the NASCAR community, and one that came after the 1993 tragedy of Davey Allison, and the major accident involving Irvan in 1995.

The final point standings: Dale Jarrett (Ford) 5262, Bobby Labonte (Pontiac) 5061, Mark Martin (Ford) 4943, Tony Stewart (Pontiac) 4774, Jeff Burton (Ford) 4733.

Wins: Ford 13, Chevrolet 12, Pontiac 9.

Manufacturer's Trophy: Ford 231, Chevrolet 210, Pontiac 205.

2000

George Walker Bush, son of George Herbert Walker Bush, is elected President despite having lost the popular vote, in a acrimonious affair that was not decided until five weeks after election day.... Alex Rodriguez, the 25-year-old shortstop, is signed to a ten-year, $252 million contract by the Texas Rangers, a team formerly owned by the new President.

Dale Jarrett led Fords to a 1-2-3-4-5 finish in the Daytona 500 as the season opened, but it would close in a different manner, as Pontiac driver Labonte, along with Stewart one of two stars on Gibbs' team, won the Winston Cup championship. Ford drivers won 14 of the 34 races, with Pontiacs picking up eleven (Stewart six, Labonte four) and Chevrolet nine, but NASCAR's long-sought goal of parity was achieved.

And it led to a more or less uneventful year, as parity proved less exciting than having a dominant driver in the series, which included 34 events for the last time, two races being added for the 2001 season. The fact that Fords were fastest somehow became submerged in the ceaseless rules-tinkering that was part of NASCAR's management style, and by the fact that the culture was clearly one of drivers, not makes. By the second half of the year it was clear that Rusty Wallace, driving for Penske Racing South, was the fastest, helped by his own talents and by some engine work done by Ilmor, the CART engine designers and builders owned 25 percent by Roger Penske. Wallace was fastest qualifier nine times and Jeremy Mayfield, driving for Penske-Kranefuss Racing, picked up four poles, which meant that Penske engines were quickest almost 40 percent of the time.

Ricky Rudd.
—*Ford Motor Company*

Jeff Burton.
—*Ford Motor Company*

Jeremy Mayfield.
—*Ford Motor Company*

If Wallace wasn't the fastest then it was Stewart, who was becoming one of the true stars of stock-car racing after being known as a great prospect in single-seaters. Everyone seemed to have a fair year, nobody had a great one. Dale Earnhardt, by judicious and steady driving, placed second in the standings even though he won only two races. Wallace and Jeff Burton won four each, Jeff Gordon won three. Ford drivers led more laps (5335 out of 10,167) than Pontiac and Chevrolet drivers combined, and Wallace was the season lap leader with 1731, more than 500 ahead of runner-up Stewart. But Labonte was the champion, thanks to a point system designed to delay the clinching of the championship until the very end, if possible. The current point system, in use since 1975, has been responsible for the winner not being decided until the last race no fewer than 17 times. Labonte clinched it in the next to last event.

There was as much news off the track as on: In December Mike Helton was named to succeed Bill France as president of NASCAR, and earlier in the year it was announced that Dodge would return to NASCAR competition in 2001. The Dodge effort, financed to a great extent by the Dodge dealer organization, would be led by Ray Evernham, who had been lured away from Hendrick and Gordon and who began work on the Dodge effort in the second half of 1999. His lead driver would turn out to be Bill Elliott, who would leave Ford after more than two decades with the blue oval. Elliott, along with Bobby Allison, was one of the first drivers to bring Ford back to respectability in the early '80s. Now it remained to be seen if he could do the same for another make.

Thus NASCAR completed its 53rd year since its founding, its 52nd year since its incorporation, and its 51st year since Big Bill France's creation ran its first "strictly stock" event on a half-mile oval at the Charlotte fairgrounds in 1949. The cars have evolved from those early days to creations nearly as far removed from the term

Table 2 Ford Stock-Car Engine Development

Year	Model	Displ., inches	Engine Family	Type Head	Restrictor Plate	Comp. Ratio	Est. HP (open)	Est. HP (restr.)
1964	Galaxie	427	FE	C/I High Riser	No	12.5	515–520	—
1965	Galaxie	427	FE	C/I Med. Riser	No	12.5	500–505	—
1966	Galaxie	427	FE	C/I Tunnel Port	No	12.5	500–506	—
1967	Galaxie	427*	FE	C/I Tunnel Port	No	12.5	545–555	—
1968	Torino	427	FE	C/I Tunnel Port 8V	No	12.5	570	—
1969	Talladega	429	Boss	C/I Hemi	No	12.5	550–575	—
1970	Torino (short track) Talladega (super speedway)	429	Boss	C/I Hemi	No	12.5	550–575	—
1971	Torino (short track) Talladega (super speedway)	429	Boss	C/I Hemi	No	12.5	575–590	—
1972	Torino	429	Boss	C/I Hemi	No	12.5	590	—
1973	72-3 Torino, 72 Cyclone	429	Boss	C/I Hemi	No	12.5	595	—
1974	72-3 Torino, 72 Cyclone	429	Cleveland	C/I Hemi	No	12.5	600	—
1975	73 Torino, 73-4 Montego	358	Cleveland	4V (iron)	No	12.5	600	—
1976	74 Torino, 74 Montego	358	Cleveland	4V (iron)	No	12.5	600–610	—
1977	75 Torino, 74 Montego	358	Cleveland	4V (iron)	No	12.5	610	—
1978	78 Tbird, 77 Montego	358	Cleveland	4V (iron)	No	12.5	615–620	—
1979	79 Tbird, 77 Montego	358	Cleveland	4V (iron)	No	12.5	620	—
1980	79 Tbird, 77 Montego	358	Cleveland	4V (iron)	No	12.5	625	—
1981	Tbird	358	Cleveland	4V (iron)	No	12.5	635	—
1982	Tbird	358	Cleveland	SVO (alum.)	No	12.5	635	—
1983	Tbird Cougar	358	Cleveland	SVO (alum.)	No	13.0	645	—
1984	Tbird	358	Cleveland	SVO (alum.)	No	13.0	645	—
1985	Tbird	358	Cleveland	SVO (alum.)	No	13.0	650	—
1986	Tbird	358	Cleveland	SVO (alum.)	No	13.0	650	—
1987	Tbird	358	Cleveland	SVO (alum.)	390 carb used as restrictor	13.0	650–675	N/A

Table 2 Ford Stock-Car Engine Development (continued)

Year	Model	Displ., inches	Engine Family	Type Head	Restrictor Plate	Comp. Ratio	Est. HP (open)	Est. HP (restr.)
1988	Tbird	358	Cleveland	SVO (alum.)	1-in. diam. Daytona/Talladega	13.0	675–685	503
1989	Tbird	358	Cleveland	SVO (alum.)	15/16 diam. Daytona/Talladega	13.0	675–685	462
1990	Tbird	358	Cleveland	SVO (alum.)	15/16 diam. Daytona/Talladega	13.5	685–700	469
1991	Tbird	358	Cleveland	SVO (alum.)	7/8 diam. Daytona/Talladega	13.5	700	427
1992	Tbird	358	Windsor	SVO (alum.)	7/8 diam. Daytona/Talladega	14.0	710	433
1993	Tbird	358	Windsor	SVO (alum.)	7/8 diam. Daytona/Talladega	14.0	715–720	438
1994	Tbird	358	Windsor	SVO (alum.)	7/8 diam. Daytona/Talladega	14.5	715–720	438
1995	Tbird	358	Windsor	SVO (alum.)	7/8 diam. Daytona/Talladega	14.5	715–720	442
1996	Tbird	358	Windsor (Siamese)	SVO (alum.)	29/32 diam. Daytona/Talladega	15.0	720–725	416
1997	Tbird	358	Windsor (Siamese)	SVO (alum.)	29/32 diam. Daytona/Talladega	15.0	720–725	418
1998	Taurus	358	Windsor (Siamese)	SVO/Yates	29/32 diam. Daytona/Talladega	14.0	740	421
1999	Taurus	358	Windsor (Siamese)	SVO/Yates	29/32 diam. Daytona/ Talladega	12.0	750	427
2000	Taurus	358	Windsor (Siamese)	SVO/Yates	29/32 diam. Daytona, 7/8 Talladega	12.0	760	433

NASCAR rules in 1967 allowed for a vehicle weight break based on engine displacement: The use of 374-inch engines gave competitors a 300-pound advantage; 396-inch engines were given a 200-pound advantage.
Source: Ford Racing Technology

"stock" as are Formula One machines, but they are—compared to what are otherwise considered "purpose-built" race cars—overweight, undertired, and not very responsive. That being said, in this first year of the Third Millennium they managed, once again, to provide the closest, most competitive racing in the history of the sport.

The following numbers, compiled by longtime stock-car statistician Bob Latford, are of interest: The difference between the pole sitter and the second fastest in the 33 races that had formal qualifying *totaled* 2.5 seconds, or an average of .076 seconds per event. Race leads were held by 48 different drivers and there were 666 lead changes, or an average of 19.6 per event, despite the criticism directed toward the restrictor-plate events. The second race at Talladega saw 40 different lead changes shared by 21 drivers. The average margin of victory in the 28 races that did not finish under a caution flag was 1.658 seconds.

Messrs. Ecclestone and Mosley please note.

The final point standings: Bobby Labonte (Pontiac) 5130, Dale Earnhardt (Chevrolet) 4865, Jeff Burton (Ford) 4836, Dale Jarrett (Ford) 4684, Ricky Rudd (Ford) 4575, Tony Stewart (Pontiac) 4570, Rusty Wallace (Ford) 4544.

Wins: Ford 14, Pontiac 11, Chevrolet 9.

Manufacturer's Trophy: Ford 234, Pontiac 213, Chevrolet 199.

Chapter 24

———◆———

THE DRIVERS

In the 1980s and '90s Ford's banner was carried by Bill Elliott; by Mark Martin, Rusty Wallace and Dale Jarrett, who were still there in 2000; and by Davey Allison and Alan Kulwicki, who weren't, both having been killed in aircraft accidents.

There were others who are (or were) coming up, most notably Jeff Burton (and Ernie Irvan for a time), but the heavy lifting was done by Elliott, Martin, Wallace and Jarrett. Among them, at the close of the 2000 season, they had 116 of Ford's 512 victories in NASCAR championship racing. Adding Allison's 19, Kulwicki's five and Burton's 15 gives this group 155, or slightly better than 30 percent of all the Ford wins since NASCAR held its first championship race in 1949. This total rises to 608 when the 96 Mercury wins are added.

The foursome is different from the current crop of drivers in many other forms of the sport. For one they are older, all between 42 and 46, because working one's way to the top in Winston Cup can be a long, laborious process for all but a few. And the exceptions, for the most part, either move over from single-seat racing, like Jeff Gordon or Tony Stewart, or have family in Winston Cup, like Kyle and the late Adam Petty and Dale Earnhardt, Jr.

Although differing greatly in physical size and personality, they had—aside from driving talent—several things in common:

- When starting out they had considerable support from their families.

- Three of them started early—Martin at the age of 15, Wallace at 16, Elliott at 16.

- By the time they reached the Winston Cup level, most had driven hundreds of races—possibly more than a thousand.

- All worked their way up from the lowest levels of oval-track racing, and had done everything around the car that needed doing.

- They now drive for some of the wealthier, more successful, more technically sophisticated organizations in racing, having made the jump from do-it-yourself operations to where they are only one of the eight factors necessary for winning. The others include a talented crew chief; good in-race communication between the two; an excellent pit stop team; sophisticated engine, chassis and aerodynamics programs; and money to support the other seven.

- The ability to function as part of this relatively large organization.

Although with the exception of Kulwicki none are (or were) in possession of an engineering degree, all have a great deal of empirical knowledge. In modern stock-car racing, where computer modeling and sophisticated engineering is as important as in any other form of the sport, the practical knowledge might not be as necessary before the green flag drops, but is vital once the race starts and chassis setups have to be adjusted on the fly. There is little substitute for experience.

Compare this to Formula One racing, where in the fall of 2000 the International Automobile Federation granted a super license to Kimi Raikkonen, a 21-year-old Finn who had driven a total of 23 races in something called Formula Renault, roughly equivalent to Formula Ford. He was thus approved to graduate from a vehicle with about 140 horsepower to a grand prix car with approximately 800.

In the young Finn's defense (if he needs one) is the fact that like most European and South American drivers of today, he is a graduate of the karting ranks, and top-line "shifter" Karts are excellent training tools. Experience can be found there as well. Two of NASCAR's youngest stars, Gordon and Stewart, both spent time in Karts before moving up, and it certainly was a help. But the old school was the training ground of the Ford drivers of the '80s and '90s.

Elliott was the first, and the one who brought Ford in from the cold. When the company came back from its self-imposed exile in time for the 1981 season Elliott was still scrambling, looking for a sponsor aside from his father's small Ford dealership. He won his first Winston Cup race in 1983, and by 1985 was Million Dollar Bill, the winner of the first Winston Million at a time when the very thought of a million dollars as a prize for a single achievement was staggering.

Mark Martin

Martin and Wallace came from the southern edge of the Midwest, Martin from Arkansas and Wallace from the St. Louis area, and it was a hard road, one Martin started on when he was 15, Wallace at 16. The two knew each other long before arriving in NASCAR, having bumped fenders on the quarter- and half-mile dirt tracks of Missouri and Arkansas when they were on their way up. Martin kept a diary of his early activities and it shows he drove the staggering total of 101 races at the age of 15, winning 22 and finishing in the top three in 86. These may have been in a six-cylinder Chevrolet on the clay of Bentonville, Locust Grove and Heber Springs, but they were races, there was competition, and in addition to winning he was learning. Heber Springs might not be Indianapolis or Daytona, but there is a flag at the start, one at the finish, other drivers against whom you can compete, and you learn something about yourself every time.

Mark Martin: A hard road from Arkansas.
—Ford Motor Company

The road up, in Martin's case, led to a V8-engined Camaro in 1976, and he spent the 1977 season running against Wallace almost every week. In 1978 he moved to the American Speed Association series, a sort of AA minor league for Winston Cup, and won the championship his first year, when he was 19. He won it again the following two years, despite an accident that saw him break both feet and one ankle in 1980.

He tried to run his own team and moved to Winston Cup racing in 1981 and '82, but by the end of that season was bankrupt and back in the minors. It took five years before he hooked up with Jack Roush for the 1988 season. Fourteen years after his first race, a half-dozen years after his first unsuccessful foray into Winston Cup, Martin was with a winning team.

It took Roush, fresh from dominance of the SCCA Trans-Am series, a year to get his team organized, but by the 1989 season they were ready. Martin, with Roush's resources at his disposal, has been a front-line Winston Cup contender ever since.

It was a long way from the Benton Speedbowl to one's own jet.

Bill Elliott

Elliott is from Dawsonville, now on the outer edge of the vast urban sprawl known as Atlanta, but not so many years ago just a small town in the foothills, on the southern ramp of the Great Smokies. Just north of Dawsonville is the hill country, with all sorts of crevices and hollows where a man could hide a still or do almost anything else if he were of a mind to, as long as he didn't make any noise.

Bill Elliott: It started with his father.
—Ford Motor Company

Dahlonega, just up past Dawsonville, now has a new Jack Nicklaus golf course and a Holiday Inn Express.

Elliott's father was a race car owner before he ever became the Ford dealer in Dahlonega: "My father was involved in racing when I was a small child, he had cars that went to Daytona in the '60s, modified or some other class ... he got the Ford dealership in '69 ... he was always a Ford fanatic. He would show up at a race track, everybody else would have Chevrolets ... he'd be the only Ford there and it wouldn't matter how it ran or whatever it did, he was 100 percent Ford and that was that.

"Along in the late '60s, because my oldest brother Ernie was interested in the racing side we started a speed shop business selling parts to local racers and that evolved into building engines and we started doing other things that were associated with the racing side of the business.... I was helping build cars and build engines, helping keep a race car up for Jody Ridley from Chatsworth.... When I got to be around 16 or a little better maybe I wanted to try driving a little bit.... I was out there working on this old car one afternoon and my dad saw that I was kind of serious about doing this and he said, 'Well here, let me get you a car that's safe enough to go race.... Ernie drove it a bit and didn't like it, my middle brother, Dan, he was going to college, starting a family and stuff and he really couldn't commit the time that he needed to do it.... Then I came along and I was young and happy and didn't know any better and here I was. I got in a race car and enjoyed it, and that led me to where I'm at today."

"But I look back, and I really didn't start young enough.... You look at these kids today, four and five years old, and they're running these quarter midgets and stuff like that, it's pretty amazing what these kids come through.... In today's world they have so many avenues to get information from. When I started, back then, for example, when we built a race car, we'd take a '56 Ford, we'd cut the body off of it, we'd take a '65 Ford Falcon body off that chassis and put it on the '56 Ford chassis ... Put a roll cage on it, an engine, you know, do whatever we had to do, change the rear end, change the suspension parts, and that's what we went and ran.... I mean back then you talked about building a race car, you know, it was three, four thousand dollars, where today it's astronomical, you couldn't put a real dollar number on it.... Sponsorship in the late '70s, you could sponsor a Winston Cup team for $100,000.... We can spend that on a single road race just in transmissions in this day and time...."

In the spring of 1976, with a four-year-old car they bought from Bobby Allison and rebuilt over the winter, Bill and Ernie went to Rockingham, and qualified. "We didn't have a clue what we were doing," says Elliott. "We were so excited when we left the track that afternoon after qualifying that we didn't do anything to prepare the car for the race.... You know back then you'd cover up the duct for the oil cooler so the car would run faster [for qualifying].... We forgot to uncover the oil cooler, so during the race we had to come in and knock the cover off so the air would get in.... We were like, you talk about the hillbillies going to Beverly Hills, I mean that was pretty much the way we looked back then.... To look back on those days and the way NASCAR was, how laid back NASCAR was, back then there was probably a second and a half, two seconds from the fastest qualifier to the slowest."

In the fall of 1977 the Elliotts bought a Ford skinned as a Mercury from Roger Penske, who was getting out of stock-car racing, and "We took it home, and that's what really started my career.... I ran it in numerous races, ran well at Daytona, and that led into—at the end of 1980 we met up with Harry Melling."

Melling was a machine-tool manufacturer from Jackson, Michigan, near the Michigan International Speedway, and he became a partial sponsor that year. (Elliott: "A lot of times we didn't have the money to come up.... A group of business people in Brooklyn [where the track is located] and Jackson put up $500, whatever, some people were giving us $100, and we'd put their names on the side of the car.")

By 1982 Melling was the principal sponsor for the entire season, in 1983 Elliott won his first Winston Cup event at Riverside, and another major league racing driver arrived on the scene, not quite a decade after he first stepped into something Bill and his brother put together in Dawsonville. In 1985 Elliott won eleven races, all on super-speedways, a mark that has yet to be touched. In 1987 he qualified at Talladega with a mark of 212.8 mph, which also stands to this day.

They had a decade's worth of success with Melling, including a Winston Cup championship in 1988. Bill then spent three years with Junior Johnson before setting up his own team in 1995.

It didn't work. Elliott was seemingly as fast as ever, but he went six years without winning, discovering, somewhat painfully, that driving and owning a team at the same time doesn't work well.

Then, in the late summer of 1999, Elliott was approached by Ray Evernham, the king of the crew chiefs, who was leaving Rick Hendrick and Jeff Gordon to set up his own operation for Dodge, which was planning a return to NASCAR for the 2001 season. "Ray came to me at the New Hampshire race and said, 'I want you to drive my car in 2001,' and I'm picking myself up off the floor, because he said, 'I came to you, you're the only guy I want to go to, and I hope you'll say yes.'"

For Elliott, despite a quarter century with Ford and 40 major-league victories, it was impossible to say no. He left camp with all good wishes, because after so many years, it is not often that a person gets a new lease on life.

Dale Jarrett

The other members of this quartet began their racing lives in the hinterlands of the sport, while Jarrett's early introduction came in the form of NASCAR champion father Ned, and a look at what the top of the stock-car racing pyramid was like in the 1960s.

But it took him a quarter of a century to return there, which must set some sort of record for determination and faith in one's own ability.

Jarrett the Younger didn't get into any sort of a racing car until he was 20, it took another eight years before his first Winston Cup start, he was 31 before he ran a full Cup season and 35 before he won his first championship event. Yet at 44 he has been in the front ranks of the stock-car community for nearly a decade.

Dale Jarrett: The second-generation champion.—CIA stock photos

Whereas the others had fathers filled with enthusiasm, Jarrett had one who knew exactly what life at the top was like, and explained it to his son. Dale: "We had that discussion—I think I was probably 17 or 18 when I really got interested and tried to get involved.... He tried to make me understand what he'd been through, how difficult a business it was, and that there were only a very small number of drivers who got to race every weekend in the Winston Cup series, and an even smaller percentage that were really known to be successful and could make a good living at it. He didn't try to persuade me to stay away from it, but he wanted me to understand that if this was the choice I was going to make it was going to be very difficult to get to that top level."

Jarrett's Odyssey began in the spring of 1977 at the half-mile track once owned and operated by his father in Hickory, his hometown about an hour northwest of Charlotte. That was in a so-called limited sportsman car, a nine-year-old Chevrolet Nova. From there it was a long succession of "Daytona Dash" cars, late-model sportsmen, and finally in 1982, when the Busch Grand National series began the two Jarretts owned a team. With some outside backing he ran that for five years before getting a second-rate Winston Cup ride in 1987, and he spent three years in the back of the Winston Cup pack.

Jarrett: "It was difficult, but it was better than the alternative of not being there at all, even running at the back I was still learning, we had enough relatively good days when I could be around good drivers in good cars.... Everyone has different ways that they get there, I felt that I had to pay my dues, and there was a lot I had to learn, maybe, than a lot of other people.... But I tried to pay attention, still working on the cars myself and again, running toward the back, was better than the 18–20 hour days I had to put in running my own Busch team."

Jarrett got his first break in the spring of 1990 when Neil Bonnett was injured and the Wood Brothers' Ford needed a driver—right now. He drove the season for the Woods and outran Davey Allison by a few feet at Michigan for his first Cup win. It was, in one sense, a validation of his years of trying: "I raced Davey side by side for the last couple of laps.... I was able to beat Davey with a Wood Brothers car, and with Robert Yates having built Davey's car and the engine, that gave me a lot more confidence."

The next step was in the winter of 1993, Jarrett's second year with Joe Gibbs, when he won the Daytona 500 and passed Dale Earnhardt at the end: "That to me was very special, you know, here's a guy considered the best on this type of track and I was able to pass him, be patient at the end of the race ... Make my move at the right time, and I think that told me, right then and there, that I had exactly what it took, with the right equipment and the right people, that I could compete."

Jarrett had moved up to the Wood Brothers because of Bonnett's accident, and when Irvan was seriously injured at Michigan in the late summer of 1994 and Yates went looking for another driver he looked at Dale. ("Actually the first call came from a mutual friend, and there seemed to be some interest on both sides, and as we went on we were able to work out a release from Joe Gibbs Racing.")

There was a comfort feeling from the start. Jarrett: "Even before the 1994 season was over they were inviting me to the race shop and I knew that not a lot of people get to tour his engine facility, but I was invited in there to see what was going on and to see what their plans were for the future, and this knowing that more than likely this was going to be a one-year deal for me."

"When we got to Daytona to test," Jarrett says, "it wasn't, 'This is what we always do, you just get in and drive,' it was, 'How can we make this work together,' and they liked my input."

The year was not that successful, Irvan was—figuratively at least—looking over Jarrett's shoulder, and the problem of the future was upon them. Yates did not want to run a two-car team, even though he wanted Jarrett, but Irvan was due back by the end of the 1995 season. The problem was fixed by Rivard. He knew that Quality Care, known by its proper name as the Ford Customer Service Division, was pulling its sponsorship away from the Bud Moore team, and was also canceling its sponsorship of drag racing star Bob Glidden.

He also knew that Ford Credit was the sponsor of Elton Sawyer's Busch series car. Rivard went to Edsel Ford, at the time president of Ford Credit, tapped the Busch sponsorship money, was able to convince Customer Service to invest in Jarrett, talked Yates into a second car, and Jarrett's new number 88 was born for the 1996 season. Three years later the Yates-Jarrett combination, with Todd Parrott as crew chief, was the Winston Cup titleholder.

The top of the pyramid, described to Dale by father Ned decades earlier, had been reached.

Rusty Wallace

Russell Wallace's father was the track champion at Lake Hill Speedway, a third-mile paved oval in the St. Louis area which was the focal point of life for Rusty and his two brothers when they were in their teens. Rusty's father was also a man with an entrepreneurial bent, involved in several businesses, including running a suburban paper route in Creve Coeur, with Rusty driving one of the delivery vans.

The aspiring driver, whose parents had gotten a judge's permission to let him compete when he reached the age of 16—he drove and won that night—would go past a house that had "Penske Racing" trucks usually parked outside, and this intrigued young Wallace. "I thought, man, he's a racer, what's going on with this guy? Who is this guy? So finally one day I met him and he's one of Roger's right-hand guys, he ran the whole show-car program...."

The man with the trucks was Don Miller. He was in charge of Motorsports International, one of Penske's numerous racing-related companies, this one supplying exhibition versions of his racing cars for displays throughout the nation. Don Miller had a close personal relationship with his boss. The relationship, which has now lasted more than three decades, resulted in the 1991 creation of Penske Racing

*Rusty Wallace: From the Midwest to
NASCAR.—Ford Motor Company*

South, one of the sport's premier organizations, one which has Miller and Wallace as substantial minority shareholders, and Wallace as its star driver.

There were a lot of miles between Lake Hill Speedway in the early '70s and three aircraft and shares in four auto dealerships in 2000.

At first it was the bullrings of the Midwest, where he would meet up with Martin, another of the ambitious youngsters, and where they both had to go through a rite of passage—beating Springfield, Missouri, star Larry Phillips, who was almost untouchable on the tracks that he frequented, but who seldom, if ever, left his neighborhood. Wallace became a full-time driver when he was "about 19," getting fired by his uncle for spending too much time on the race car and not enough working in the family vacuum cleaner business. But as Wallace says, "That was the happiest day of my life, because that made me go out and stand on my own two feet racing."

The path led to places where the various Midwest acronyms held sway— CARRA, ARTGO, ASA, USAC, and whatever else he could find. Wallace drove, Miller gave him whatever advice he could. By 1979 he was voted USAC stock-car rookie of the year. In 1980 Penske gave him a ride at the season-ending Winston Cup race in Atlanta and Rusty finished second, but the next year it was back to the bush leagues; "not enough experience" was the call. He won the American Speed Association championship in 1983 and then got a full-time Winston Cup ride with Cliff Stewart the next year. By that time he had 201 short-track victories.

Stewart's team was underfunded and the competition was better than Wallace was used to, and at the beginning "I felt like I couldn't even drive, everything I was so good at, everything went wrong.... I crashed in every race. Then Neil Bonnett grabbed hold of me—I never will forget—during the Firecracker 400 at Daytona, drug me on top of a truck, and said, 'Look, I've watched you race, your whole career, I've watched you on those high banks at Winchester, I've watched you at Michigan.... Do not lose confidence in yourself, you know how to drive.' That stuck in my mind, that's when I started thinking you know, this isn't all my fault, it's not my fault these engines are blowing up, that the car won't handle.... But I really didn't understand Winston Cup cars and 1985 was worse."

What it took was a new owner, and Wallace had been watched by Raymond Beadle, the bigtime drag racer who was also a stock-car owner. He signed with Beadle for 1986, driving a Pontiac. He placed sixth in the season standings, and never looked back. He won six races in 1988 and '89, won the Winston Cup championship the latter year, then Beadle ran out of money at the end of 1990. Penske, Wallace and Miller, complete with Miller Brewing Company sponsorship (Penske was on the board of directors of parent company Phillip Morris), founded Penske Racing South that winter, and the team stayed with Pontiacs until moving to Ford for the 1994 season.

By the end of 2000 Wallace had 53 Winston Cup wins, placing him eighth on the all-time list. It was a long way from Lake Hill Speedway.

Allison and Kulwicki—The Ones Who Left Early

Davey Allison was a member of NASCAR's star-crossed family. His father Bobby, one of the biggest winners in the history of the organization, has never completely recovered from a horrendous crash at Pocono in the early summer of 1988 that ended his driving career, and Davey's younger brother Cliff was killed during practice at Michigan Speedway in 1992. Davey, one of the great natural talents of stock-car racing, made it to the age of 32 before dying in the crash of his helicopter in July of 1993.

This was just a few months after Kulwicki, the northerner who ran his own team and was the defending Winston Cup champion, died in a private plane crash in April of that year.

Although there are always new drivers to take the place of the old ones, Allison and Kulwicki were part of the younger generation that was putting Ford back on top, and was giving NASCAR one of the menu items needed for continuing success— drivers who are more than simply new names and new faces. Allison and Kulwicki were winners, and they were unfortunately reminders that life off the track can be as fragile as it is on.

Allison, who grew up practically in the shadow of his father's race car, barely made it through high school because he was more interested in cars than books. Then came the usual short-track, dirt-track experience, but by 1987 he had a ride in Harry Ranier's Ford, with Yates as crew chief. He became the first driver to win a

Winston Cup race in his rookie season—won two, actually—and when Yates bought Ranier out for the 1988 season, he had a budding star as his pilot.

Desire, ambition, or whatever its name, was part of the Allison makeup. In July of 1992 he fractured his right forearm in two places, fractured his right wrist and broke a collarbone in an accident at Pocono. The next week he took the start at Talladega and drove until the first caution flag before giving way to a relief driver. A few weeks later, in August, brother Cliff was killed in a Friday crash at Michigan Speedway, but Davey drove the Sunday race and finished fifth before heading home for the funeral.

The final race of the season was in Atlanta, and Davey, Kulwicki and Elliott all had mathematical chances to win the 1992 title. All Davey needed was to finish in the top five, regardless of where the other two placed. He was running a conservative fifth after 253 of the 328-lap event when Irvan spun in front of him. Allison couldn't avoid Irvan and was out of the race.

He was, in some odd way, the NASCAR version of Icarus: He flew close to real stardom, but didn't fly well enough in his new helicopter.

Kulwicki was the beneficiary of Allison's Atlanta crash, winning the 1992 championship by the narrowest margin in NASCAR history, ten points in front of Elliott. The only engineer-driver in the Winston Cup ranks since Mark Donohue's brief appearance in the early '70s, Kulwicki was a graduate of the University of Wisconsin. He drove his first race at the age of 19, went through the ASA and USAC stock-car circuits, moved up to NASCAR's Busch series in 1984, and by the 1986 season was running a full Winston Cup schedule with his own, woefully underfinanced team.

In 1990 he turned down a lucrative offer from Junior Johnson to give up his team and function strictly as a driver to keep going on his own. In the spring of 1991 he finally found a major sponsor and enough financing to improve his operation, and 1992 was his year—by ten points.

Kulwicki finished second in that famous season-ender in which Allison crashed and Elliott won, but Elliott led 102 laps and Kulwicki 103, and the bonus points difference gave Kulwicki the championship. He came along at a time when engineering knowledge was becoming increasingly important in stock-car racing, and the fact that he could combine his driving talents with a formal education put him ahead of many others. He called his Thunderbird his "Underbird," because of the size and financial situation of his team. But his engineering skills worked to put most of the others in the underdog role.

Ironically, when he was killed in that April plane crash he was only a passenger. The preparation and the piloting were done by others.

Chapter 25

---•---

THE OWNERS

By the last decade of the century major-league stock-car racing had reached a level of sophistication undreamed of even ten years earlier. Increased sponsorship, television and ancillary revenues flowing into the sport made the leading teams able to afford the latest computer expertise in design, development and race management; squads of graduate engineers; and personnel rosters numbering in the hundreds.

As a consequence Winston Cup racing took on a look similar to major league baseball, with only the big-budget teams having a realistic shot at the championship. There were six of these, three with a Ford relationship and four with General Motors: Robert Yates, Roger Penske and Jack Roush for Ford and Joe Gibbs (Pontiac), Rick Hendrick, Richard Childress and Dale Earnhardt (all Chevrolet) for GM.

Evidence of their dominance is best seen by the results of the 2000 Winston Cup season: All but one of the 34 races were won by a car owned, engineered, or otherwise controlled by one of the Big Seven. The members of this group all had more than one entry, although some cars were run as the property of "other" owners. The owner-driver was fast becoming a thing of the past, with Bill Elliott giving up his team to join Ray Evernham's Dodge-sponsored organization for 2001, and Ricky Rudd having joined Yates the year before. The ones who were left, on either side of the aisle, Ford or GM, were in the make-weight category, although with the increased sponsorship dollars they could show a profit even without being contenders.

The major owners are of several types: Penske, Hendrick, Roush and Gibbs are in categories by themselves, while Yates, Childress and Earnhardt are prime examples of men who worked themselves up through the racing ranks. Penske is one of America's more visible industrialists and the most successful non-factory car owner in racing history. Hendrick is the country's largest single automobile dealer. Roush is a former Ford employee who built a successful group of engineering businesses in addition to the largest stock-car team the sport has ever seen. Gibbs is a former National Football League coach whose teams won the Super Bowl three times, then decided to use his management skills to set up a racing activity.

They have two things in common: Great self-motivation, and the ability to adapt to changing circumstances.

Many of the earlier-era owners have dropped out, either because of age, failure to keep up with advancing technology, or failure to concentrate on the business aspects. On the Ford side of the equation, those remaining include the Wood Brothers and Junie Donlavey. The Wood organization is now run by the children of patriarch Glen, while Donlavey, who has been entering Fords for a half century, continues to run his own small operation. There are always new ones, but it has become increasingly difficult for the smaller teams to keep up with the big-budget, marketing-oriented Big Seven.

The major Ford team owners:

Robert Yates Racing

When Dale Jarrett won the 1999 Winston Cup title it was a particularly popular victory in stock-car circles, because Jarrett was the number one driver for Robert Yates Racing, and Robert Yates was One of Them, and one of the Childress-Earnhardt-Yates trio that came up through the ranks.

"Them," in this case, means the vast majority of the men who make up the stock-car industry, people raised, for the most part, in the Southeast. They are skilled manually, highly motivated, and very good at what they do. They are men who have done it themselves, and then learned how to let someone else do the work and concentrate on being managers. Yates is a product of this environment, a graduate of the College of Holman-Moody, Ford's remarkable Charlotte-based racing arm of the 1950s and '60s.

Childress was an unsuccessful owner-driver in the mid '70s when John Cooper, then NASCAR's vice-president of marketing, arranged for a sponsor and thus helped make him profitable. A few years later Childress decided owning had a better future than driving, picked up Ricky Rudd for the 1982 and '83 seasons, and signed Dale Earnhardt for 1984. Childress and Earnhardt were a great team—until Earnhardt was killed at Daytona in February 2001.

If there is a cult figure in modern-day stock-car racing it is Earnhardt, one of NASCAR's two seven-time champions (Richard Petty is the other). At the age of 49 he was not only a threat to win, but he had built himself into a business empire with a worth estimated at $50 million. Earnhardt drove for Childress, but his eponymous operation owns cars run by his son, by Steve Park, by Kevin Harvick, and also had the 1999 Craftsman Truck champion in Ron Hornaday.

Winston Cup racing is long past the day when a great driver, a Curtis Turner or a Fireball Roberts, could get sideways on a half-mile dirt track and make up for the shortcomings of the car or crew. It now takes managerial skills, both technical and business skills, to compete in an arena where a half-second is often the difference between being the pole sitter or the 25th car in the starting lineup. The number of employees needed depends on the number of cars the owner is running, but Hendrick has more than 300, and Roush averages 40 per car, not to mention the backup in his 2000-person engineering organization.

Even in his late 50s Yates has little gray creeping into his blond hair or mustache. He is heavy through the shoulders and despite more hard work than many men could achieve in three lifetimes, looks no older than his years, possibly younger.

He first learned his managerial skills from John Holman when he was in his early 20s. A Charlotte native, a minister's son and along with his fraternal twin the young-est of nine children, Yates went to work for H-M in the summer of 1967, when the team was coming back from Ford's second straight victory at Le Mans. He was working as a heavy-equipment mechanic when a friend told him there were jobs available and so Yates wanted to come by after work but was worried H-M might be closed.

No, we work until ten o'clock every night, he was told, "So I went over there and I walked into this place, from out of a bulldozer shop to a white-collar—almost—job, they knew I'd been to college for several years and could do the math.... Jack Sullivan sent me over to Howard DeHart and Howard said, 'When do you want to start?' The money ... I was making two dollars an hour and they were paying four, and the overtime, time and a half after eight [hours], and they said we expect you to work until ten.... So I went back, and the [bulldozer] shop foreman said, 'I'll kill you if you don't take this job!' I pretty much got them to promise me if it didn't work out I could have my job back."

"It was the booming-est place, 325 employees, people making four times what they could make on the outside.... I worked on a lot of engines, 1968, '69, going through the different engine changes, and got a lot of race experience, actually working on the pit crews.... Work ethics were good, you really worked hard, but nobody ever missed a day of work.... I ended up working on a lot of the development stuff.... I put together an engine for Junior Johnson [LeeRoy Yarbrough was the driver], an overnight deal, that won the Daytona 500 in '69.... All the engines for the factory-backed teams came out of H-M."

Ford's withdrawal in the fall of 1970 was traumatic: "The money pump was cut off.... There were a lot of tears but nobody volunteered to leave.... A lot of people had gotten into financing houses.... That deal taught me a lesson: Don't buy anything unless you can pay for it, and I've done that pretty much, because I saw 300 people really devastated...."

"When the pump cut off," Yates says, "I probably had a better education to go out and do something by myself, so I went and did Chevrolets at night ... Built the first Chevrolets for Junior while I was working for Holman.... I'm standing in the middle of the race track watching the three-car of Junior's qualifying on the pole, when I'm supposed to be working on the Wood Brothers engines and I'm trying not to show it on my face...."

Yates' early racing education came from both ends of Holman-Moody: "I learned a lot from John Holman and from Ralph Moody, too. I used to stay with Ralph when we'd go to races, room with him, and we'd talk until midnight every night."

"Holman would really chew people out and everybody was afraid of him.... One night at three in the morning he comes by, and I was operating three or four machines and he saw some oil, and he came down the aisle raising hell and then he saw who it was and he stopped, and I got the oil cleaned up, he helped me clean it up, and I'll always remember, I was just shaking, here he was, actually talking to me, and he was so calm, and with a different tone of voice, and I remember him telling me, standing right there, with the rod grinder running, he was apologizing for screaming, and he said, 'You know, I wasn't born a sonofabitch, people made me a sonofabitch,' and from then on I understood why he had to be firm.... He and Moody were totally different people; John took care of the business and Ralph, he raced. If it had been left to one or the other they never would have made it, but together they made it work. I think I learned a lesson there."

Yates built his own Chevrolet dirt-track car in 1971 while working for Holman, a car that won 18 out of 23 races in area events ("We beat Ralph Earnhardt every night"), and wound up as engine builder with Johnson's team for four years after that, then went to the DiGard team in 1975 and stayed ten years.

Robert Yates' management school was a hard one. From April of 1971, when he started working for Johnson after spending the day at Holman-Moody, he made the 160-mile round trip (no interstates then) to Wilkes County every night and spent weekends at the track with Johnson. He kept the dirt car for a while until demands on his time forced a sale ("I knew if I wasn't around it wasn't going to be very successful"), and was also the operator of a service station, working, in a real sense, around the clock.

"But I never set out and said I just want to own something," Yates says, "until the day we were sitting on the pit wall at Charlotte and Davey [Allison] comes over and says, 'You got that much money? You don't need any partners, just go ahead and do it." It was the summer of 1988, Yates was the crew chief for Harry Ranier's team, and Ranier was in financial difficulty and having to sell out.

"Went round and round with different deals, thought I might have to end up taking a partner [but didn't].... I knew I could be very responsible for my money, never late, always paid my bills first, so I was a good steward of the funds, but I went and sold my house, hocked everything—but it just worked out."

It did work, with Davey as one of the young stars of NASCAR, and they were successful, finishing third in points in 1991 when a win in the last race would have meant the championship, and third again the following year, when one of the realities of auto racing parked itself next door.

In August of 1992, Davey's brother Cliff was killed during practice at Michigan International Speedway. Yates: "I was still in the house, must have been about one in the afternoon, I mean, I just couldn't believe it.... Davey was at the track, we met him at the track, and it was knee-weakening, it really hurt ... Even if it wasn't part of our business, but it was very close. When I talked to Davey he said, 'Clifford loved to race, he was doing what he wanted to do,' and if anything he picked us up off the floor.... He was good, loved his brother ... But he said, 'This is what we're going to do,' and he made the decision. I wouldn't have expected him to race.... I don't remember much about the race but I know it was awful tough on me."

The next year, in mid-July, Yates was in his headquarters when Bill France called "... and told me that Davey's been in a bad helicopter accident.... of course I knew he had his helicopter (a recent purchase).... The last words I ever spoke to him were, 'Make sure you keep a good instructor with you, you've got plenty of money.'"

There was the personal tragedy, and there was the need to hire another driver, and quickly. "Ernie wasn't even on the list, then the phone rang and it was Lee Morse (number two man in SVO at the time), and he said, 'I think you need to look at Ernie.' I said, 'He's not available,' and Lee said, 'I think you need to look at him,' and I said, 'I know he's under contract, he's got to come to me, I can't go to him,' and he

Robert Yates with son Douglas (top) and with crew chief Todd Parrott (bottom).
—Don Hunter (top), CIA stock photos (bottom)

said, 'Well, do you like the idea?' I sat there with Larry (McReynolds, his crew chief) and Doug Yates and we wadded up our list of drivers and stuffed it in the trash can."

Irvan became a charger for Yates, winning twice in the remainder of 1993 season and the next season winning twice, finishing second six times and third three times before the August race at Michigan. Then Irvan crashed, badly, after qualifying, and for a day it wasn't sure if he would live, much less drive again. Yates was affected deeply, since he takes pride in his work, and his reflections on this accident, and mishaps in general, are a key to his work ethic: "The very first engine I put together, when I started putting the rods in, an engineer told me, 'This is like a loaded gun, you got to make sure it doesn't go off.' I forget exactly how he worded it, but it was like, in other words, 'You don't screw this up,' you mess with it, you can hurt somebody, and always try to do it skillfully.... When you're working on a car it's a skill, not a dare.... You just don't throw something out and expect it not—well, maybe it won't wreck. You do it skillfully."

Skillful is an important word in his vocabulary. In Yatespeak it means considerably more than it did to Noah Webster.

After losing Allison and Irvan, Yates came up with the driver who would take him to the Winston Cup championship in a few years, but at the time he was an unlikely one. Jarrett was driving for Gibbs, and looking to make a change. So was Bobby Labonte, driving for Bill Davis. Yates had to choose between the two, had to arrange for Gibbs to release Jarrett, and "I was talking to Bobby, and he wanted to drive, and well, Ford says no, we won't support you on that."

At the same time, Yates had a note from Jarrett, and he called him, and "Dale says, 'I tried to call you, I'll drive it six months, I'll drive it two races. If I can't win races in that car I'd rather play golf,' he says, 'I need to find out.'"

Yates was trying to sign a driver and still not knowing if Irvan would—or could—come back, Labonte wanted the ride, and Jarrett wanted to know if, after years of trying, he was good enough to run up front with the poster boys of racing. He was having an indifferent season, after a number of them, and it was time.

Ford wanted Labonte to drive for Bud Moore, but in the end Yates paid Gibbs to get Jarrett out of his contract, and Gibbs paid Davis to get Labonte. Irvan came back but only briefly, and Yates finally got his Winston Cup champion, although it took a few more years, Jarrett not winning until 1999. Gibbs got one too, Labonte doing the same in 2000.

It also took a lot of days and nights of doing things skillfully, and it took getting over the emotional shocks of losing drivers to deaths and injuries, and it took keeping one's eye on the prize—regardless of what else happened.

Penske Racing South

Perhaps the best way to describe the influence of Roger Penske on motorsports in general and Winston Cup in particular is to say that Penske Racing South, a major player in NASCAR, is a minor part of Penske's performance activities and a miniscule part of the Penske Corporation.

Penske Racing South can be found in Mooresville, North Carolina, the home base for several stock-car teams, and can also be found on one of the lower rungs of one of the four divisions of the Penske Corporation, a $10 billion closely held company more than 50 percent owned by Penske himself. Even after selling his controlling stake in Detroit Diesel Corporation—which he bought from GM in 1988 and rehabilitated—to Daimler Chrysler in 2000, Penske Corporation employed roughly 30,000 persons at 3000 locations worldwide.

Penske's nine components are all oriented to things automotive, and include such undertakings as Penske Truck Leasing (more than 200,000 vehicles), United Automotive Group (approximately 125 dealerships nationwide), and Penske Auto Centers (more than 650 service centers at Kmarts across the country). In addition to the United holding, there is another dealership operation, Penske Automotive, which sells approximately 39,000 vehicles annually from five locations in Southern California.

The performance group is the one of interest here, not only because of Penske Racing South, of which its namesake owns approximately 52 percent, but because of its influence on the sport in general. Penske teams have been dominant in Trans-Am racing, sports-car racing, and have paced American single-seater racing from 1972, when Penske driver Mark Donohue won the Indianapolis 500, to 1994, when Al Unser Jr. gave Penske his tenth win at Indianapolis.

Penske helped create Ilmor, the engineering organization that designed and built the Mercedes Indy-car engines and still builds the Mercedes-McLaren Formula One engines, and owns 25 percent of that company. Yet when Ilmor's performance fell off in 1999, he did not hesitate to switch to Honda for 2000—and won the CART season championship as a result. It was fairly obvious—and others could have gotten a clue merely by opening their eyes—Penske knew a year in advance that Mercedes might pull out of its CART involvement.

Penske's stock-car involvement, which has been an off-again, on-again relationship, goes back as far as 1963 when he drove a Ray Nichels Pontiac and won a NASCAR 250-miler at the Riverside road course. This was two years before he decided that being a racing car owner would be more profitable and would allow him to pursue other interests as well.

Penske's racing interests lay, for the most part, in non-stock-car areas, but he was never one to miss an opportunity, and he was good at reading rulebooks. In 1973, when he was trying to give American Motors a performance image, he found that NASCAR did not prohibit disc brakes. Ford, GM and Chrysler didn't have them on production cars, so the subject had fallen between the cracks. But AMC did, and a Penske-prepared Matador, known internally as the Kenosha Canoe and driven by Mark Donohue, won the Riverside 500.

Penske Racing South had its genesis in the relationship between Penske and Don Miller, who had been with Roger since 1971 and who was also Rusty Wallace's longtime friend and advisor. When Wallace and Miller split from Raymond Beadle at the end of the 1990 season, MR Racing became PRS in October. Still with Pontiac at the time, they moved to Ford in time for the 1994 season—at the same time that Penske was preparing to beat the Fords at Indianapolis.

Penske took a major interest in what then became Penske-Kranefuss in the fall of 1997 so that he was then involved in two teams, with engines for both coming out of his separate stock-car engine building facility. John Erickson, a bright young ex-Pontiac employee, came in as general manager of PRS in late 1998 as Miller moved into semi-retirement, and Penske began a consolidation move in 2000 when he bought out Kranefuss.

By the start of 2001 he then had Wallace in one car, Jeremy Mayfield in the other, and a promising prospect in Ryan Newman, who was about to get his mechanical engineering degree from Purdue and was already a minor star in Midwest midget and sprint-car circles. Newman, who many were already comparing to a young Donohue because of the latter's engineering background, was scheduled for a season of ARCA and Busch races, with just enough Winston Cup thrown in to give him a taste of the major leagues.

Penske Racing South, it would seem, was looking good. The man in Detroit had made the arrangements.

Roush Racing

This is the largest multiple-car team in stock-car racing, and it revolves around Jack Roush, its 59-year-old creator, who can perhaps best be described by an incident that retired Ford racing engineer Don Hayward remembers from the '80s. Hayward was the Trans-Am and IMSA program manager then, and at that time Roush cars were busy winning their class in the Daytona 24-hour race for ten consecutive years. Hayward and Roush were leaning against the Daytona pit wall at 3 or 4 a.m., a time when crews are normally more concerned with staying awake than anything else.

Conversation is usually at a minimum, but Roush made a remark and Hayward asked him what he meant, and Roush said, "I'm thinking about what we can do better next year."

Jack Roush is an intense man of less than medium height, distinguished at race tracks by his straw hat, in other arenas by his entrepreneurial talents or even by the World War II P-51 he flies as a hobby. Although he doesn't smile much, when he chooses to it is a good one, and when he stands on his accomplishments he is about nine feet tall.

Born and raised in southern Ohio, his parents couldn't afford to send him to college so he worked his way through at Berea in Kentucky. This was a cooperative institution that didn't offer a mechanical engineering degree, so he composed his own curriculum to go with the empirical engineering knowledge he was already amassing.

*Jack Roush: From drag racing to
an industry.—Roush Museum*

He was graduated in 1964, and went right to Ford when the Air Force said he was wanted as a navigator and ordnance officer, not as a pilot. He got involved with a group of Ford employees who were drag racing, and also got involved with what can be called the underground high-performance market in the Detroit area. It was the time when Ford and Chrysler were into all types of racing and GM was busy with under-the-table funding.

Performance was king, there was a demand for hot street machines, and Roush knew where to get the parts and how to put them together. He was working for Ford, building engines at night at his home in Taylor, and was part of the Fastbacks, the Ford employee drag-racing club. ("We had two cars.... one was a '64 Galaxie, the other was a high-performance Mustang 2+2, and we raced those cars in the NHRA stock class, in regional and national events.... This was '65, '66, '67.... We went as far as California, New Jersey, Florida....")

The group was shrinking in size, so Roush picked up one of the cars and joined forces with Wayne Gapp, another Ford engineer, and Gapp and Roush, complete with a Pro Stock car, became national champions, Gapp driving most of the time, but Roush winning the AHRA title in 1972.

In the meantime he left Ford in 1969, came back in 1970, taught junior college for two years (physics, trigonometry, basic engine and electrical), got his master's degree in mathematics at Eastern Michigan University—and was in the performance business, somehow managing to squeeze it all into the 24 hours available each day.

Gapp also left Ford in 1972 to devote more time to racing and to the engineering business he and Roush were building, a business that got off the ground, at its start, by the emission-control crisis that hit the industry in the early '70s. Roush and Gapp were under contract to Ford, as were other outside agencies. Roush and Gapp divided their assets in 1976: "We had differing views of how the business should be run.... He took the race cars and ran them one more year, and I took the prototype business and the work for Ford.... We would make oil pans, we would make little parts for the engine-build activities, an intake manifold or a dual-exhaust system for an American Motors car...."

Roush had six people by the close of 1977, but this had grown to "25 or so" by 1979, and then "The parts and service people started to feel the grip on the motorsports side release a little and they started looking around to see what kind of tooling we had for valve springs and rods.... We were getting all these phone calls from people who wanted to buy engine parts...."

Ford came to Roush to prepare the pace cars for the 1979 Indianapolis 500; he'd work on the Ford family's privately owned GT40, so when the performance program started up again in 1981 he was in town, he had a facility, and he had a relationship with the company. And it went from there.

As big as Roush Racing has become, it is only approximately 20 percent of Roush's activities. The company has grown from its owner's garage in 1970 to where it employed more than 2000 people at the start of 2001. These people were located in 58 facilities in three countries and were involved in doing engineering and prototype work for Ford, General Motors, DaimlerChrysler, John Deere, and even for a golf shaft manufacturer, as Roush holds the patent on True Temper's Sensicor vibration-dampening device.

The breakdown is Roush Racing, Roush Performance Products (about 10 percent of the company) and Roush Industries (the remaining 70 percent). Among other things Roush builds engines for the IRL series, and for the Sports Car Club of America's Pro-Spec series.

By the time Roush entered major-league stock-car competition in 1988, his cars had won national championships in drag racing and had been the scourge of the Sports Car Club of America's Trans-Am series. Through his engineering business and his relationship with Ford he was well connected with many teams involved in Winston Cup, and was aware of the effort it would take to be successful in this arena.

A NASCAR entry had been his goal for five years. But, in the '80s, he tired of supporting other people's efforts in SCCA and IMSA and decided to run his own cars on both circuits.

"I figured that I had," says Roush, "a half million dollars [in 1983] that I could spend on my racing and not eat the seed corn that I needed for my engineering businesses, so that I was able to do the salaries right, that I was able to buy the equipment that I needed, to staff and facilitate, to meet the opportunities.... I'd been pretty good at figuring out where I needed to go and spending my limited resources ... and I really wanted to go stock-car racing—for Jack.... I was friends with the Wood Brothers, and I was friends with Bud Moore, from helping them and also being helped by them ... Buying old NASCAR parts from them and they would give me information sometimes that would be useful for my drag racing when I was drag racing.... I would give them some information that would be helpful for their stock-car racing.... But I figured, based on where I was, and watching the Trans-Am series and being involved with Zakspeed, and IMSA, I figured I could go make a name for myself with road racing and then would be able to garner more sponsorship and have a chance to practice and develop my racing skills, my judgements and my people...."

Roush's information-gathering process began back then, and when he showed up with a Winston Cup car he had Mark Martin, fresh from the Busch series and with a long history in Midwest short-track racing, as his driver. Martin was not the first person to be interviewed. Roush: "The drivers that were in Winston Cup, which Mark was not, they were all, I'm sure, looking at me with some risk, so given the risk of a new team owner and somebody who was suspect, somebody who'd been drag racing and sports cars, you couldn't believe that they were going to have the right stuff for a while so it was, 'Yeah, we might do this, but for a lot of money.'

"When I had my conversation with Mark he was the opposite, he was more interested in who was going to work on the car, how much could we test.... We discussed salary as an afterthought and it was a low salary for a Winston Cup driver, certainly for a driver who was able to get poles and was able to race with the kind of dispatch and enthusiasm that he could."

It took Martin-Roush two years to win its first race, but by the second season Mark was considered a contender. Since then, through the 2000 Winston Cup campaign, Martin never finished lower than eighth in the point standings, was runner-up three times and third four times.

Roush had run multiple-car teams in drag racing and sports-car racing, and started his NASCAR expansion in 1992 with Wally Dallenbach. He tried Ted Musgrave for a number of years and finally settled on Jeff Burton, whom he signed for the 1996 season after Burton had two unsuccessful years with his first team. Burton has become one of Winston Cup's biggest winners, and together with Martin, and 2000 rookie of the year Matt Kenseth, has given Roush three drivers capable of winning in racing's most competitive arena. They are part of an organization that dwarfs anything seen previously in NASCAR. No one else has ever run so many cars in so many different stock-car divisions. In the 2000 season Roush Racing included five Winston Cup teams, two Busch teams and two Craftsman Truck teams. This would be cut back to four Cup teams for 2001.

The 2000 effort required ten new Winston Cup cars per team, six Busch cars per team, and eight Craftsman trucks per team—a total of 78 new cars. Although some would be built during the season, approximately 80 percent of the tube-frame chassis would be finished by January. There would be a total of between 215 and 220 entries in races, which meant the following for the engine builders:

A new engine for each race, plus a high-horsepower qualifying engine that will run an average of three times before a rebuild, plus another 70 engines that will get built or rebuilt, plus engines that will fail in practice or the race (perhaps ten), and approximately 30 test engines. The total number can be rounded off to 340 engines for the season, of which 75 percent were built at Roush headquarters in Michigan and the rest at Roush Racing just north of Charlotte.

Even with the economies of scale that come with nine cars, each team needs its own personnel, which averages out to 40 per car, not including engine builders, but including administrative, marketing, fabrication and pit crews. In addition, there are engineers available for consultation.

The logistics involved in moving an operation of this size from headquarters to races and back again finally resulted in Roush's chartering a Boeing 727 for the 2001 season.

And it started with a garage at home and a drag racer's dream.

Chapter 26

———◆———

ROUSH'S HUNTING GROUND

The Sports Car Club of America's Trans-Am series was created in time for the 1966 season and has survived, despite various crises, ups and downs, politics and what have you until today, making it the oldest road racing championship in America. With the exception of its first few years it was not as good as its IMSA opposition, but the SCCA survived whereas IMSA didn't. The Trans-Am series is testimony to the fact that if you are the only game in town catering to a particular type of car, there will be people—and sometimes even manufacturers—willing to compete.

In its early years the Trans-Am was the performance arena in which the new Mustang and even newer Camaro fought for attention, the stage on which Mark Donohue became a driver of national stature, and where Roger Penske attracted notice as a team owner who was not only as good as the rest, but might even be better.

Much of that went away after the 1970 season, when Ford and Chevrolet withdrew support, although American Motors stayed around for another year. The series survived, but just barely, became a Porsche picnic for a few years in the '70s, and then a basic change in the regulations changed its nature in 1980. After that it was practically the personal hunting ground of Roush Racing until Ford (again) withdrew support after the 1997 season.

Once they got into it, Roush cars and drivers were dominant, although oddly enough one of Roush's principal competitors was another Ford team, this one run by driver Tom Gloy, who also took a year off from the Trans-Am to drive Ford's ill-fated GTP Probe in IMSA. Some of Roush's titles were won when the cars were called Capris, some when they were Mustangs, and some when they were Merkur XR4Ti's.

Underneath they were all basically the same, since Trans-Am rules, beginning in 1980, specified tube frames, with only the skins—and sometimes the engines—representing the brand listed in the program. Roush cars and drivers won six championships in the 14 years they competed in the Trans-Am series, and although statistics do not necessarily tell the whole story, both Roush and Gloy have impressive numbers.

Roush's cars made 519 starts in 181 races, won 69 of them, and had 216 top five finishes. All of these marks are far and away the best of any team that ever entered the Trans-Am. Gloy, whose efforts were not on the same big-budget scale as Roush, had

Roger Penske (left) and Mark Donohue: The beginning.
—Penske Archives

Tom Gloy.—Ford Motor Company

the following record when Ford pulled its support of Trans-Am at the end of 1997: 27 wins (fourth all time) in 347 starts (second) and 142 top five finishes (second).

But all that was later. The Trans-Am opener in 1966, run at Sebring the day before the twelve-hour race, was a four-hour event called the Governor's Cup and drew 44 cars, including A.J. Foyt in a Mustang and Monte Carlo Rally winner Paddy Hopkirk in a Mini Cooper. The winner came out of the under two-liter class and was an Alfa Romeo coupe handled by grand prix driver Jochen Rindt, who had rolled his mount in practice the day before. The result was not greeted with pleasure in Detroit.

There were seven races that first year and participation from both Dodge and Plymouth, but Ford won the over two-liter title, thanks to Jerry Titus' performance in the closing race at Riverside. The editor of *Sports Car Graphic* magazine, Titus was a late pick to drive for Carroll Shelby's factory-backed Mustang team. He had to carve his way through the field twice, once after a bad start and once after a long pit stop, and thus made himself into a role model for every auto writer who ever fantasized about being a racing driver.

The Mustang made its debut in the spring of 1964 and was an instant sales success, and racing it was simply another step in the company's total performance campaign of the 1960s. It was a way of building an image that would, hopefully, depend not only on the car's looks, but also on its performance. It took GM two years to catch up, the Camaro was introduced in 1966 as a 1967 model, and it was the ideal car to pit against Shelby. And Penske was the ideal team owner. He had an excellent reputation as a driver, but retired at the end of the 1964 season in favor of his budding automobile business, and then spent weekends in 1965 acting as racing manager for Texan John Mecom's team. He owned a Chevrolet dealership, he had connections with GM engineering, and he made good use of them, even at a time when most of GM's under-the-table racing support was going to Jim Hall's Chaparral organization. Penske made his debut as an owner in 1966, and in 1967 he had Donohue, whom he had chosen from the ranks of the SCCA's amateur drivers. Their car was factory supported, and was not only a credit to Donohue's ability to drive, but also to Penske's talents in organizing sponsors and in making sure the paperwork was right. Although the car was not listed for sale with a 305-inch engine (the five-liter maximum for the series), Chevrolet soon came up with one and put the Mustangs and Cougars at an immediate disadvantage—they had 289-inch motors.

Had there been a driver's championship (at the start there was only a manufacturer's award) Titus would have won it, just ahead of Donohue. But most of the noise was made by Lincoln-Mercury's Cougar team. That division, which now had its own version of the Mustang, had a performance program operated by veteran NASCAR team owner Bud Moore, and the drivers were Dan Gurney, Parnelli Jones, Peter Revson, Ed Leslie, and even David Pearson for two events and Cale Yarborough and LeeRoy Yarbrough for one. It wasn't their dominance on the track, it was more a case of their presence in the series attracting attention to it. Titus was the only man to drive all twelve races, while Donohue missed two (at the same time Donohue was driving for Ford in major long-distance sports-car races, it should be noted). Ford Division edged Lincoln-Mercury by two points for the manufacturer's title, which led to some acrimony in Dearborn, as the smaller division was getting most of the press even though it finished second. The Cougars were retired after the season, and Moore went back to stock-car racing for a year.

From then on, it looked like this:

1968

Donohue dominated the series, winning ten of the 13 events, including eight in a row, and in the fall Jacque Passino, then the head of Ford's performance effort, called Spartanburg, South Carolina, and spoke with Moore, who had gone back to running his NASCAR team.

"Passino called me and he says, 'How about comin' up here,'" Moore says, "So I go to Detroit, I get up there, and he says, 'I need you to work on this Trans-Am series, we can't get beat like we did this year,' and he said, 'Parnelli and they all are out at Riverside testing right now....' so I got on a plane and went to Riverside."

The long and short of it, after shedding the operation of close to two dozen Ford and Holley carburetor engineers, was that Moore asked for, and got, three engineers: Denny Wu for the chassis, Lee Morse for the engines, and Harold Droste from Holley for the carburetors, and they managed to make the Mustangs competitive.

1969

The result of Moore's work, although it brought about improvements, was not enough. Donohue won six of the ten races he entered, Ronnie Bucknum added another two for the Camaros, Jones won two and George Follmer one driving Mustangs. The manufacturer's title again went to Chevrolet.

Pit stop: Bud Moore takes care of George Follmer's Mustang.
—Ford/Dave Friedman

1970

This was Jones' year, by a single point ahead of Donohue, who was driving a Penske Javelin, the latter having embarked on one of the few unsuccessful efforts of his career—trying to boost American Motors' sagging fortunes with a performance campaign. Penske's cars did better than AMC. Parnelli drove in all ten events on the schedule and won five of them while Donohue won three. Follmer, who was rapidly becoming one of America's better drivers, won one and placed third in the standings, thus giving Ford a comfortable lead for the manufacturer's title.

This would be the last year of strong American factory participation for a decade. Penske had Revson and Vic Elford in addition to Donohue, while Chrysler supported Sam Posey in a Dodge Challenger and Swede Savage in a Plymouth Barracuda. They finished fourth and fifth, respectively.

1971

With Ford out of the picture for the next decade, Moore tried to keep the Trans-Am effort alive on his own, but Penske still had American Motors' backing and Donohue came close to sweeping the field again, winning seven of nine events. Follmer, spending half the season with Moore and then moving over to Penske, placed second. Peter Gregg, who would make his reputation in Porsches, drove for Moore and finished third, ahead of Revson, again in a Javelin.

Donohue finished his Trans-Am career with a record that has yet to be matched. He won 29 races and did this in only 55 starts, or 52.7 percent of those in which he took part. Ford took one positive away from the season, and that was Moore's experience with the small-block V8, which would come in handy in the years ahead, when the company dropped its 429-inch engine and moved to the 351 for NASCAR competition. In fact it was Moore who did it, while Ford was on the sidelines.

Ford's withdrawal wasn't the only bad news for the SCCA. The other one was the inauguration of IMSA's GT series, which would run in direct competition in an area the older club had thought of as its private preserve.

1972

Follmer became the only man ever to win both the Trans-Am and Can Am championships in the same year, taking the Trans-Am title in an ex-Penske Javelin, now operated by Roy Woods Racing, as he won four of the six races he started. He won the Can Am series in Penske's Porsche 917, taking over Donohue's seat after the latter was injured in a June crash while practicing at Road Atlanta, a month after he won the Indianapolis 500.

Warren Tope, the son of Ford vice president Don Tope (who would be instrumental in helping stock-car teams procure good blocks in the mid-'70s thanks to his connections in Australia) was the only bright light for Ford, winning the last two of the six races.

1973–79

The Trans-Am series was faced with two major problems in 1973, and both of them were named IMSA. One was the fact that the IMSA GT series was more attractive to prospective contestants, and the other was that IMSA had signed Camel cigarettes as its principal sponsor, a far more affluent sponsor than any the SCCA could round up for the Trans-Am. The SCCA's reaction was to change the Trans-Am rules to replicate IMSA regulations for 1973 and '74, the latter year being one in which only four events were scheduled, including two on the same weekend at Watkins Glen. Gregg won the title both years with Porsches, which were seemingly everywhere.

By 1975 the Trans-Am was little more than a professional version of the SCCA's amateur-only national championship series, and John Greenwood was the winner with a Corvette. Turbocharged Porsches were allowed starting in 1976, and Follmer returned and won again, this time with a Porsche 934, and Canadian Ludwig Heimrath won with the same model in 1977. What this was, in effect, was IMSA cars plus amateurs. The next two seasons saw the SCCA make it even more confusing in an effort to keep the series alive, with a split into Categories I and II. Veteran Jaguar driver and team manager Bob Tullius took Category I both years in an XJS, while Category II went to Greg Pickett in a Corvette in 1978 and John Paul in a Porsche 935 in 1979.

The series was in danger of folding, and steps had to be taken in order to keep it alive. Veterans of the SCCA maintain the only reason it remained solvent was because of the club's ownership of the name Trans-Am. General Motors was paying the club a royalty of $5 for every Pontiac that carried the Trans-Am name, and the popularity—at the time—of the Burt Reynolds movie "Smokey and the Bandit" caused a minor boom in Trans-Am sales.

Help, it would seem, can come from the strangest places.

1980

The start of the first tube-frame year saw few tube frames, as there hadn't been enough time to design and build them since the new rules were passed. The basic configuration said five liters and 2600 pounds minimum, but that was academic in 1980, as John Bauer won the championship in a Porsche 911SC. The season covered nine races, and Bauer won four of the eight he started. The basic vehicle configuration, under the new rules, amounted to a sophisticated version of NASCAR.

This was also the year in which driver point standings were created for the first six years of Trans-Am competition, as the club indulged in some harmless revisionist history. The championship, from 1966 through 1971, had been for manufacturers only. Then, in the winter of 1980, public relations man Mac Demere went back through the records and figured out what the driver point standings would have been—and simply assigned the points.

1981

Walter Hayes may have been the man who brought Ford back to racing in the United States, but Hayes was a newcomer to the country and there were some things he didn't know, and others he didn't want to admit. As a consequence, Ford's first Trans-Am appearance was a peculiar one.

Somewhere along the line Hayes had met a young man from Arizona by the name of Dennis Meacham, and Meacham had a new Trans-Am Mustang, said car being built, supposedly, to meet the tube-frame regulations. Somehow Hayes got the idea that Dennis Meacham was John Mecom, who at the time was one of the leading car owners in both sports-car and single-seater circles (Jackie Stewart and Graham Hill drove for him at Indianapolis, A.J. Foyt drove his sports cars at times). Hayes knew Mecom was successful, thought Meacham was Mecom, and the word went out to new SVO Director Michael Kranefuss to support him.

And Hayes put his foot down when people tried to explain.

The road course at Charlotte Speedway, which combined with the banking, was the scene of the season's first race and Meacham showed up, but it was obvious that the car was a long way from complying with the regulations. Some horse trading finally got the technical inspectors to where they said if the doors would open and close, they would let the car in. Roush was there and he took the car to a garage, along with a Mustang rental, and worked most of the night cutting the welded doors out and installing the ones from the rental vehicle.

Then came bad news. Meacham didn't drive very well. He was running far back in the pack when the hood flew off and landed in the middle of the track, and one of the other drivers ran over it to make sure it wouldn't be used again. Kranefuss stayed upstairs in the VIP box, too embarrassed to come down to the pits.

No one recalls what happened to the rental car.

There was a bright side to the story, and that was what happened to the race car. Meacham's crew was a good one and they knew Gloy, who had been Formula Atlantic champion the year before, and by midway through the season Gloy was the driver. They were rebuilding and changing the car for every race, Gloy says, trying to get it into some sort of competitive shape, and by Trois Rivieres in Canada, in late summer, Gloy managed to finish third. He put the car on the pole at Mosport but dropped out early, then closed the season with a win at Sears Point, the first post-comeback victory for a Ford.

Gloy was one of the very first drivers to win a championship for the company. He would run his own Ford team in Trans-Am, practically always in competition with Roush. In addition he sometimes drove for Roush or Zakspeed, and finally wound up, after retiring from active driving in 1989, as a team owner—in the NASCAR Craftsman Truck series for a while, and in Trans-Am.

1982

While Roush was busy trying to make Zakspeed into a competitive force in IMSA, Gloy carried on in the Trans-Am series with a Capri and managed to win the last race of a ten-event season, but finished fourth. Elliott Forbes-Robinson, driving a GM-backed Pontiac Trans-Am, won four races and finished second twice and the championship was all his.

1983

Racing success is in many respects a function of budget size, and in 1983 General Motors backed the DeAtley team, which a few years previously had been unsuccessful with a Mercedes-Benz 450SL, a car thoroughly unsuited for Trans-Am racing. This time DeAtley had a pair of Camaros, Englishman David Hobbs and the mercurial Willy T. Ribbs. Ironically, the engineer on DeAtley's cars was John Dick, who had been one of those who talked Gloy into the Meacham car in 1981. Dick's theory, Gloy says, was to more or less build a NASCAR stock car underneath a Camaro skin. He was right.

They finished first and second, in that order, with Gloy third in the twelve-race season. Lyn St. James, now moved over from IMSA's Kelly American series, was Gloy's teammate and finished tenth.

1984

Designer Bob Riley, still with Ford at the time, came up with his new chassis for 1984, one that was used by both Gloy and Roush as the Capris swept the top three spots in what had grown to a 16-event series, with Gloy on top at the finish.

The Capris won eleven races with Gloy taking three, runner-up Greg Pickett and third-place finisher Ribbs four apiece. Gloy was a model of consistency during the year, with six second-place finishes, two thirds and two fourths. Included in Gloy's wins was one in Detroit, in the preliminary race before the U.S. Grand Prix. That prelim was sponsored by GM. The manufacturer's title went to Lincoln-Mercury for the first time.

1985

The Capris swept nearly everything for the second year, finishing 1-2-3-5-6, this time with Wally Dallenbach Jr. as champion, Ribbs second, Gloy third, Chris Kneifel fourth and Jim Miller fifth. Dallenbach won five of the 15 events and Ribbs seven, and Lincoln-Mercury's manufacturer's title was a foregone conclusion.

1986

Dallenbach won the title again, and he was once again driving a Riley-designed chassis, but this time it carried a Camaro body and a Chevrolet engine, as Riley had moved to GM-funded Protofab at the end of the previous season.

Lincoln-Mercury had the satisfaction of taking the manufacturer's title for the third straight year, and did it in spectacular fashion. The Roush and Gloy cars had to sweep the top four spots in the final race of the season, at St. Petersburg, Florida, to clinch it—and they did.

Pete Halsmer and Kneifel, both driving for Roush, finished second and third. Gloy had left the Trans-Am series, at Ford's request, to drive the Probe in the IMSA GTP series. He would have been better off staying where he was.

1987

Scott Pruett was the new leader of Roush's Trans-Am team, which switched to the turbocharged Merkur XR4Ti for this season, and he won seven of the twelve races and placed second twice, so the competition for the driver's title wasn't even close. Halsmer finished third, also in an XR4Ti.

The Roush team recorded its 32nd victory during the season, moving it ahead of Penske's 31, a mark that stood for 16 years. Lincoln-Mercury picked up its fourth consecutive manufacturer's championship.

The leader: Scott Pruett in the Detroit Trans-Am.—Ford Motor Company

1988

Pruett's success of the previous season prompted the SCCA to impose what veteran Ford engineer Don Hayward called "the Pruett rule," which was intended to handicap his car more than any other. As a consequence Roush ran his two Merkurs—one for Pruett, the other for Halsmer—with V8's, and they were admitted even though they were not standard production.

Regardless of whether the Roush cars used turbo fours or V8's, the series was taking on a different complexion: Audi came in and was making major effort with its Quattro, and wound up with Hurley Haywood as the season's titleholder. Haywood, perhaps America's most successful long-distance driver, combined with German teammates Hans Stuck and Walter Roehrl to win seven of the 13 races. Haywood drove all of the events and won two, Stuck drove eight and won four, Roehrl drove six and won two. Audi wasn't the only new contender: GM was backing a campaign for Oldsmobile, and Cutlasses began appearing. One, driven by Irv Hoerr, finished second in the standings.

1989

With drivers moving onward—and in some cases upward to bigger series—Ford held what was called, inside SVO, a "gong show" to find new driving talent, and one who looked promising, at the end of the 1988 season, was Dorsey Schroeder, who would drive for Gloy. A veteran of SCCA racing for nearly two decades, he turned professional in 1984 and had been the IMSA Firehawk champion in 1986 and '87. Now he was back, and Ford went back to Mustangs for the 1989 Trans-Am campaign since this was the 25th anniversary of the model, and Schroeder was in the lead car. He ran away with the season, winning six of the 14 events and giving the Ford Division its first manufacturer's title since 1970—all the others the company won in the interim having gone to Lincoln-Mercury.

But the GM presence became stronger, now with Chevrolet Berettas in addition to the Cutlasses. Hoerr was again second in his Cutlass and won four times, while a youngster from Southern California, Tommy Kendall, finished third in a Beretta. He would be heard from again, and soon.

1990

The season grew to 15 races again for the first time in six years, and Kendall won six of them, finishing well ahead of Beretta teammate Kneifel. The Mustangs were far back, as Roush was devoting much of his time to his NASCAR team and Gloy out of the picture for the moment. Finn Robert Lappalainen in fourth, Max Jones seventh and Ron Fellows in tenth were the leading Mustangs.

1991

The only Mustang in the top ten at the end of the season was driven by Fellows, who finished fifth as GM-backed cars dominated. The 23-year-old Scott Sharp won the title, well ahead of fellow Camaro driver Jack Baldwin. Sharp won six times in 14 starts, Baldwin once. Ford had dropped the program for the time being.

1992

Baldwin and Sharp traded places at the end of the 1992 season, with Baldwin winning the title by a four-point margin, and Fellows moved up to fourth while winning two events, the same as Baldwin and Sharp. Fellows was driving for Gloy, who was making a comeback as a Ford team owner.

1993

Gloy's group won the first three races of the season, with Fellows taking two and Schroeder one. Sharp won his second championship in three years before moving on to single seaters. Sharp, still in a Camaro, won six of the 13 races, Fellows won three and was second in the standings, Baldwin won the last two of the year and finished third.

1994

Ford had enough of GM's Trans-Am dominance of the past five years and upped the budget for 1994. The one thing that was missing, however, was Pruett, now driving a Camaro. Pruett took the series by winning three times and placing second six times in the 13-race season, but the manufacturer's trophy went to Ford.

Fellows, Kendall and Schroeder won the other ten events and placed second, third and fourth in that order. Fellows and Kendall each won four times, and had Kendall not dropped out of the last two races of the season he might have won his second championship.

1995

Fellows switched to General Motors starting with this season and won five of the eleven races, but still finished second to Kendall, who won only once but who had enough good finishing positions. Schroeder placed third, and a private-entry Mustang, driven by Brian Simo, was fourth.

1996

Kendall, driving for Roush, and Schroeder, who was the leader of Gloy's team, placed one-two in the last year in which there was factory support for the Camaro effort. Ford would continue for another year. Kendall won his second consecutive driver's championship, and the manufacturer's title went to Ford as well.

1997

Tommy Kendall was the fastest driver in the field, he had the fastest car, and GM had pulled out. The result was that Kendall won the first eleven races on the 13-event schedule, something never accomplished before or since. The driver's title was his third in a row, and the manufacturer's honors were all Ford's.

Tom Kendall: Eleven wins in one season.—Ford Motor Company

Simo, driving for Gloy, and rookie Mike Borkowski, also on Gloy's team, finished second and third and Mustangs occupied the first five places in the season standings. Borkowski, in his rookie Trans-Am season, was the one who snapped Kendall's streak, coming out ahead in a last-lap fender-banging contest.

It was also a year in which the SCCA came close to losing the entire series. Upset by the high-handed manner in which the club was running the series, 17 of the drivers signed a petition that the SCCA practically ignored until Professional Sports Car Racing—the successor to IMSA—made an offer to start a rival series. Things were patched up, but this kind of disagreement did little to encourage manufacturers to stay involved.

1998

Ford also withdrew after the 1997 season and the series was left to teams that had to look elsewhere for their funding. Paul Gentilozzi, a veteran Trans-Am competitor, won the championship with a Corvette, ahead of Simo in his Mustang, after eleven years of trying. Gentilozzi won seven of the 13 races, Simo won two.

1999

Gentilozzi switched to Mustang for this season and won again, and Simo was runner-up for the third straight year. Mustangs occupied the first four places in the standings, and Gentilozzi won six times, as did Simo. The margin at the end was only 13 points. Ford, however, took its sixth manufacturer's championship, plus the four taken by Lincoln-Mercury.

2000

Gentilozzi switched his body shell to Jaguar for the 2000 season, keeping everything underneath more or less as before, and was on his way to his third straight title until the last race, when a broken oil pump shaft sidelined him. Simo, who drove a Ford-powered Qvale Mangusta, finished third and gained points for the championship. This was only the third time in the Trans-Am's 35 years that the points lead moved from one driver to another in the last race of the season. The manufacturer's championship went to Chevrolet.

The marketing rights to the series, now obviously for private entries, were taken over, on a ten-year lease, by the Panoz-Sanchez Group, beginning with the 2000 season. Whether Panoz-Sanchez can elevate the Trans-Am from its current status remains to be seen.

Chapter 27

————◆————

FORCE AND THE FOCUS

There have been a few instances in the history of the automobile when a car or an engine—sometimes the combination of car and engine—has provoked a major change in the market, or in motorsports, or both.

The first of these was the Model T. This creation not only put America on wheels, but also provided performance-oriented people, mostly young people, with a real opportunity to add horsepower over and above that offered by the manufacturer. The Model T, as it turned out, also functioned as the base for everyman's racing car from before World War I through the 1920s.

The next was Ford's flathead V8, born in 1932 and the object of affection of the youth market that Ford, in the '30s and '40s, didn't know it owned. As in the case of the Model T's four cylinder it was basically a strong engine, understressed in stock form, and performance parts were available. They were not available from Ford, but rather from speed equipment manufacturers located primarily in Southern California, a part of the country that was (and still is) the automotive trendsetter.

Ford lost its youth-market preeminence in the fall of 1954, when the Chevrolet V8 was introduced. It took over this market in short order, not only because it was the best engine, but because performance parts were readily available and were priced right. Ford has been trying to catch up ever since.

Then along came the Focus, introduced in the U.S. in various forms, including a hatchback coupe, in the fall of 1999. It was small, appealingly ugly, and with a 130-horsepower, two-liter engine. This was the replacement for the 32-year-old Escort and although no one at Ford would verbalize it, the hoped-for World Car. The first of these, announced with great fanfare in 1993, was the Mondeo-Contour-Mystique, the name depending on the market and the brand. This one was soon sentenced to the fleet lease-rental car category, and so the Focus was billed, simply, as Ford's new small car.

(The fact that people think of Focus-sized cars as potential performance machines is indicative of the progress in engineering in the past four decades: The specific output of the seven-liter "muscle cars" of the '60s is less that that of the standard production Focus, and the Focus, despite the high-performance handicap of being a front-wheel drive machine, is possibly quicker, point to point, than the 1960s Galaxies, Pontiac GTO's and their cousins.)

In Europe the Focus became Ford's World Rally Championship entry, complete with acid-dipped body, a number of carbon fiber parts, four-wheel drive and a turbocharged engine producing better than 300 horsepower. In the U.S. the car became the newest subject of the speed-equipment manufacturers because of the "pocket rocket" phenomena. A typical pocket rocket is a Honda Civic with a turbocharged engine producing, in some cases, more than 400 horsepower in a small street machine—up to 750 hp when set up for drag racing. It is also equipped with racing wheels, fat tires, lowered suspensions, and any number of look-faster pieces.

In the year 2001 the pocket rocket represents the youth market, the potential for the high-performance market, the entry-level car, the chance to build brand loyalty, and possibly a few other things. It has been dominated by Honda for the past several years, and Ford management got a look at this in the winter of 1998 during a "market immersion" trip to Southern California, where CEO Jac Nasser, Bob Rewey and others got a look at the hot Hondas that were leading in sales in this area. They found demand was so great that used Civics were selling for over new-car prices, in some instances.

The decision to push the Focus coupe came from that trip, and as a result Ford engineers began using some of the enthusiast magazines as a sounding board, and also got in touch with the speed-equipment manufacturers. Ford funded tooling, granted the manufacturers permission to put the parts in their catalogs, and made prototypes available to the manufacturers to foster more research and development.

The ZX3 coupe was introduced, it sold well, the performance parts were being made and sold by the equipment houses, but there was more to be done in the field. As former Focus vehicle line director engineer Al Kammerer said, "No manufacturer can call themselves cool—the kids do that." And for the kids to see it there had to be a road show, a caravan that traveled around the country to places where the kids gather.

It is 8 a.m. on Saturday of Labor Day weekend, and Ford's Mike Gearhart is at Fontana Speedway, near the junction of Interstates 10 and 15, east of Los Angeles, busy unloading his trailer at a drag race. This one is off the radar screen as far as the NHRA is concerned, but draws hundreds of cars from all over Southern California, and it is being run in the pit lane of the speedway, where the course measures only an eighth of a mile.

This is missionary work, the most unglamorous kind. Gearhart has towed his trailer from Detroit to Pennsylvania, to the State of Washington, now here, and next he's headed to Atlanta for what is considered a "major" event. The trailer holds a hot Focus, display boards with performance parts on them and literature. It is augmented by other hot Focuses from the area, and the cars are easy to distinguish from the bulk of those on hand—the rest, almost without exception, are of Japanese manufacture.

But this is where it happens, this is where a good performance by Focus in the drags gets the word out, under the radar. The NHRA, after several years of watching this phenomenon and doing nothing about it, finally came up with a separate six-race import series for 2001. The Establishment finally accepted the pocket rockets.

If one paid attention to the basic rules of automotive design, none of this should be happening. The terms front-wheel drive and drag racing should be mutually exclusive. They don't go together for a number of reasons, the principal one being that acceleration shifts the weight to the rear of a vehicle and therefore something with the front wheels doing the driving is unsuited for such an activity. But the kids never bothered about this when they were converting their cars for high performance—somewhat like the bumblebee, who was never told his wings were too short, and that he wouldn't be able to fly.

This was the company's first management-endorsed, conscious attempt to regain a portion of the high-performance market it gave up more than four decades earlier.

While the Focus was finding its niche, what Ford had going for it in drag racing was John Force.

When Force started driving high-performance equipment, he was far removed from the United States and he was even farther removed from being known by anyone. This included Ray Brock, the former Petersen Publishing executive who was the link between Australian promoters and American drag-racing talent.

Brock, beginning in 1969, had been arranging for a few cars and drivers to spend a month Down Under, to run exhibition races at the resort city of Surfer's Paradise, in Melbourne, and in Sydney. One year in the mid-'70s he was set with a fuel dragster

John Force: Ten national championships.
—Ford Motor Company

and a Funny Car, the dragster was already in the container at the Long Beach docks, and suddenly the Funny Car driver decided to stay home.

Brock: "So I called a fellow by the name of Gene Beaver, who had a Funny Car, and I had sent him to Australia the year before, and I said, 'Gene, where's your car?'

"He said, 'It's sitting out in the garage,' and I said, 'Is it together?' and he said, 'Yeah, it's together.'

"I said, 'Well, I need a car to go to Australia real quick, can I use your car to go back to Australia?' and he said, 'Well, yeah, I can do that.' So he brings it down to the dock, we throw it into the container, and away it goes.

"Then I said, 'Who's the driver?' and he said, 'I don't have one right now, I'll find one.'

" Just before Christmas I got back to Gene and said, 'Gene, I've got to have a driver,' and Gene said, 'Well, I've got one—he's my nephew,' and I said, 'What's his name?' and he said, 'John Force.'

"I said, 'I've never heard of him, is he a good driver?' and he said, 'Oh yeah, he's good.' Well, I hope so, because we want to put on a good show. So about a week before Christmas, I go down to the airport and I meet this guy, a young kid, sort of polite in those days, and the dragster driver, he was there, we got them on an airplane and sent them off, and I sat back and thought, 'Well, I've got that taken care of.'"

"After the first race I get a phone call from the guy who was running the track down there and he said, 'We're in trouble,' and I said, 'What's the matter?' and he said, 'Well, John Force blew up his car, we need some pieces,' and I said, 'What do you need? And he said, 'Well, we need a new block, and we need this and we need that,' and I said, 'For chrissakes, what did he do?' and he said, 'Well, he blew it up.'

"So I had to run around and get blocks and crankshafts and pistons and get them on an airplane in time for the next race, which was a week later—we got that done—they had one spare motor so they put the motor in while I was getting parts to build another spare and after the second run I get another phone call. He says, 'We need more pieces!' and I said, 'What the hell happened?' and he said, 'Well, he blew it up again.'

"This went on for five straight races—I'm chasing parts and stuff—in some cases it wasn't as severe as others, maybe just burned a couple of pistons, but what it ended up was that John Force had never driven a race car in his entire life."

"What he'd do—he wasn't short on bravery—when the light turned green he'd put it to the floor and leave it there, and if it got loose he didn't feather, he just held it down until it blew up!"

When Force, who was a truck driver, returned from Australia, Brock says, "Now he thought he was a race driver and was going to go Funny Car racing.... So one day later I was going down the 91 Freeway and I saw this trailer, a sort of modest trailer, with an old pickup pulling the thing, and on the side it said, 'John Force, Funny Car.'

"And from there, he became a race driver."

That was then. Today Force is probably the only American in any form of racing who can carry a brand along with him.

Superlatives are always risky, but there is little doubt that Force, in his early 50s, is the dominant force in the drag racing, regardless of whether Top Fuel, Funny Car or Pro Stock. Surveys have shown that more than a third of the spectators at any NHRA championship event come to see him. Ford got to Force, or Force to Ford, depending on one's outlook, in January 1996, when he showed up at one of Bob Tasca's dealerships in the Providence suburb of Seekonk, Massachusetts. Tasca was, and is, one of Ford's top dealers, dominating the southern New England area for both Ford and Lincoln-Mercury, and is a person of influence with Ford management. Dealers who know how to sell cars always have a friendly ear on the twelfth floor. Tasca had used drag racing to sell cars ever since the early '60s. At one time he had been the owner of a national championship entry, and he still kept his contacts in the sport.

"I was at a restaurant," Tasca says, "when I got a call saying, 'John Force is in the showroom,' and I said, 'Bring him up here.' He and I knew each other from racing, but we were never close, and now here he was in the neighborhood, he was looking to buy a car for someone and he said, 'Tasca? Is that the same guy? I'll buy one from him.'"

Force was unhappy with the relationship he had with GM at the time and Tasca jumped on it. "If you have a problem," Tasca said, " If you get out of the GM contract I'll get you a deal with Ford—that day."

Tasca knew, as he put it, he had the "wherewithal" to get it done, with his line to the executive floor of Ford.

"At 8 am," Tasca says, "I got a call from Force's lawyer in Los Angeles—it was five there, and Force had been on the phone with him all night—telling me that he was resigning from GM, and he wanted my approval to mail the letter. I told him that was John's business, I couldn't approve anything. He mailed the letter, and then we signed him up. Bob Rewey said OK, and they sent him a check for $1.5 million.

"To own John Force for $1.5 million, with two cars, is the steal of the century," he said, "and you don't even have to give him a spark plug. He handles everything himself." GM, in order to save face, made a show of firing Force, who got immediate revenge that April: When running with his new Mustang body, he won the Winston Invitational at Rockingham, North Carolina. Ford got a twofer with Force, as he runs a two-car Mustang team along with Tony Pedregon, a member of one drag racing's best-known families.

Force has been with Ford ever since, he became the NHRA's all-time winner last year when he passed Bob Glidden and then ended the season with a total of 92 victories in championship events. He had been the points champion a total of ten times. He and Pedregon recently signed up for another five years, with a slight increase and with five trucks thrown in.

Tony Pedregon: A member of drag racing's
top family.—Ford Motor Company

Teammates: Tony Pedregon (left) and John Force (right) face off
at the Winternationals.—Ford Motor Company

Chapter 28

———◆———

"You Should Get Out"

1995—The Return Flight

A low point of Ford's Formula One involvement was reached on June 11 at the Grand Prix of Canada in Montreal. It was bad enough that none of the eight cars with Ford engines were competitive. It was worse that only one of them managed to finish: Luca Badoer, an eternal also-ran driving a Minardi, was a lap back in eighth place.

It was bad enough that Ford had lost Benetton and Schumacher, it was bad enough that Ford was now engine supplier to also-ran Sauber. But to members of management, having to sit there and watch all this was too much. The old days of F1 dominance with the DFV engine, to which hardly anyone in Dearborn paid attention, were long gone. The new era was one of pouring money into Cosworth, watching Vickers use Cosworth as a cash cow, and watching the increasing worldwide popularity of Formula One being used by others to win races, improve image, get rich, or all three. Ford was reduced to being a spear carrier on this grand opera-like stage of international auto racing.

What made it worse was being there. It was bad enough to read Monday morning reports from Europe or Japan, but this was something else. Bob Rewey, Neil Ressler, Dan Rivard and Jackie Stewart were on the company plane back to Dearborn afterward and it was a quiet flight until someone asked Stewart what he would do about the situation.

Stewart: "They said how unhappy they were and I said, 'You're right, you want to get out, you're not doing it properly, and if you're not going to do it correctly, get out.' They were very unhappy with Sauber. Nothing against Sauber, but it just wasn't working, and then Rewey said, 'How about making a proposal for how you think it should be done?' I remember he said, 'You put a plan together and tell us if you would be interested in putting together a proposal.' Well, we had been talking about where we were going and what we were going to do, and we thought, 'This will be a big job, a mammoth task, but if a *car* maker is part of your program then it could be worthwhile.... So we sent them a paper and they said now let's move further with it, now give us a full proposal. We gave them a program, and it was accepted."

From this point until he retired in February 2001, Ressler would be more involved in Ford's Formula One effort than anyone else in the company. A man with a doctorate in physics and an MBA in addition to his engineering degree, when he was chief of car product development he was still taking vacation time to attend races ("I was told it would not be a good idea for me to turn up at auto races," he says). This stopped at the Canadian Grand Prix of 1989, when he happened to attend the same reception as then-Chairman Don Petersen. There Ressler was introduced to the press as an example of "Ford's technical involvement in auto racing."

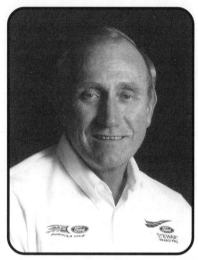

Neil Ressler: Took over when Ford bought out Stewart.—Ford Motor Company

After that he considered it part of the job, and soon had development engineers assigned to the Benetton F1 team in Europe in an official capacity. Ressler (as did the Honda management) felt racing was a good place for young engineers to spend time, he felt there could be technology transfer between racing and production, and coincident with the Stewart announcement formed the Motorsport Technology Group for this purpose.

The official announcement of Stewart Grand Prix, complete with a new tartan known as Racing Stewart, was made January 4, 1996. The deal was a five-year arrangement, with options for renewal. Ford would pay for the engines, to be built by Cosworth, and would guarantee a certain sum toward the operation of the team. Stewart, however, would have to find additional sponsors in order to make the proposition viable from a business standpoint. Cigarette manufacturers, normally a prime source of racing sponsorship money, Ford insisted, could not be on a car in which the company was involved. Now all Jackie had to do was find the money, form a grand-prix level organization, build a car, and do it all in time for the 1997 season.

While Ford and Stewart were working on their Formula One future Schumacher was busy dealing with the present, winning nine of the 17 races that comprised the 1995 season. His total tied Mansell's 1992 performance, and although most observers thought this could not happen again it would, within a few years.

The season, such as it was, was dominated by the Renault-powered Benetton and Williams teams, Benetton winning the Constructor's Cup with 137 points to 112 for Williams and their combined total being far ahead of the total points collected by the other eleven teams that competed during 1995. Schumacher wound up with 102, well ahead of Williams driver Damon Hill's 69. Scotsman David Coulthard, in his second grand prix season (and second with Williams), was third with 49. Englishman Johnny Herbert, Schumacher's backup at Benetton, was fourth with 45. The rest of the field, figuratively and almost literally, was nowhere.

It was the first year of the return to 3.0 liters, a maximum engine size that has remained in effect. The Renault V10's were still thought of as the best engines in F1, despite being reduced in displacement, and this was proven by Benetton and Williams. The Fords used by Sauber were a redesign of the Zetec-R and produced approximately 670 horsepower and could be revved to slightly over 14,500 rpm. This engine would also be the "customer" engine—for teams other than Sauber and in 1997, Stewart. Customers—a euphemism for those who paid—used the ED engine in 1995, one that began life with a maximum output of about 650 horsepower. All electronic "driver assist" devices were now banned, fuel consumption was unlimited, and the weight minimum was now 595 kilograms (approximately 1310 pounds) with oil, water and driver—the driver's weight being added for the first time.

1996—Like Fathers, Like Sons

Damon Hill, after a few years of being in one of the best cars, led the Williams team's continuing domination of the Formula One picture, winning the world driver's championship that his father Graham captured in 1962 and 1968. Damon won eight of the season's 16 events, but by the time he won Hill knew he was out of a job. Frank Williams, the austere, hard-driving creator and owner of his organization, who ruled from a wheelchair ever since breaking his neck in a traffic accident in 1986, told Hill in mid-season that his contract would not be renewed. Since all first-class seats for 1997 were taken, this move effectively ended Hill's grand prix career, and after three more mediocre seasons with Arrows and Jordan he would retire. Williams never gave a reason, but at least two scenarios appeared plausible: The first was a disagreement over money, and the second was that the owner felt Hill would never be able to beat Schumacher in a wheel-to-wheel contest.

A third reason could well have been the arrival of Hill's new teammate, Canadian Jacques Villeneuve, who arrived fresh from winning the 1995 CART championship plus the Indianapolis 500. Villeneuve soon let everyone know that he was as fast, if not faster, than anyone out there. He wound up with four wins and five seconds as Williams reclaimed the FIA Constructor's Cup. Schumacher, who moved to Ferrari in the off-season (the deal was done before the previous September), won three of the remaining four events and also became the world's best-paid athlete, not counting endorsement fees. Villeneuve's father, an idol of racing fans in his own country, was the famous Gilles, the lead Ferrari driver who was killed in a 1982 crash.

Schumacher, it was reported, was being paid $25 million per year, with the bulk of the money coming from Shell and Marlboro. John Barnard, who had been the Ferrari designer (with offices in Britain), was now replaced by two more Benetton engineers, Ross Brawn as technical director and Rory Byrne as chief designer.

While Stewart was getting his team together Peter Sauber struggled on, knowing before the season started he would be losing Ford power when Stewart was ready. Sauber had German Heinz-Harald Frentzen and Englishman Johnny Herbert as drivers and it was a season of being non-competitive. They amassed a total of eleven points to put the team eighth out of eleven that took part.

1997—Hard Times at the Start

There were 17 races in the season, which meant that Stewart Grand Prix, with Brazilian Rubens Barrichello and Dane Jan Magnusson as drivers, would start a total of 34 times. The next result, with a new team and new, still fragile Zetec-R V10 engines, was that the finish line was reached only eight times. Only one car placed in the top six and managed to earn points.

That was Barrichello, who was the runner-up in a rain-soaked Grand Prix of Monte Carlo when many contenders either crashed or were wearing the wrong tires for the conditions. The expectations in both Dearborn and Warley added up to a miserable season and the recognition that there was still a long way to go to even be competitive, much less a winner. Anyone who expected instant success was disabused of that notion. There were several problems, but a big one was lack of budget. Formula One racing had turned in to a high-dollar exercise, and Stewart was not in the financial league of a Ferrari or McLaren.

Jacques Villeneuve, who made his Formula One debut the previous season and proved himself a threat right from the start, won the championship after a season-long battle with Schumacher, Villeneuve winning in the last race of the season, the Grand Prix of Europe at Jerez, Spain. The little Canadian went into the event one point behind Schumacher. When he attempted to pass the Ferrari driver for the lead on the 48th of 69 laps, the German pulled the same maneuver he used in 1994, when he ran Hill off the road in the last race to preserve his title.

This time it didn't work. Schumacher crashed and Villeneuve kept his Williams on the road. Needing only a third place to clinch the title, Villeneuve sportingly let McLaren drivers Mika Hakkinen and David Coulthard pass him on the last lap.

The first Stewart grand prix car, 1997.—Ford Motor Company

Villeneuve ended with 81 points to 78 for Schumacher, but the FIA soon wiped out Schumacher's total, eliminating him from the standings. Ferrari kept those points in its Constructor's Cup total but it was academic, since Williams finished first in that category. It is presumed that Schumacher kept his paycheck.

In addition to being non-competitive in qualifying, Stewart's two cars weren't much better in the races. They dropped out with engine problems eleven times, were involved in ten accidents and were sidelined five times by gearbox or transmission troubles.

Villeneuve won seven races, Schumacher five, and the oncoming McLaren team, complete with Mercedes engines, won three events, two by Coulthard and the Jerez race that was presented to Hakkinen by Villeneuve.

1998—Finally: Ford Buys Cosworth

While Stewart was moving into his second season, in Dearborn the oft-voiced idea of buying Cosworth Racing was becoming a reality. Ressler: "In the beginning it looked like we had the best of both worlds because we had good racing engines and we didn't have to actually own and manage the asset.

"But, as time passed, as we worked our way through the '90s, we became less and less enchanted with the way it was working. They were in the hands of some people who didn't know what business they were in and they didn't share things with us. Here we were, funding the engines, buying the engines, and we didn't know what the power was, we didn't know anything! As time passed I was the one beating the drums to be more involved with Cosworth—at least to be in a management position, to be on the board of directors, on the management steering committee, and as we talked about it they kind of resisted.

"It was the owners—the guys from Vickers, not the actual Cosworth guys—they were taking money out of it, they were clearly not investing to keep the thing alive. I began pressing, let's just buy this; then we'll know, we can manage it ourselves, invest enough to keep them alive, doing well, and even start to think about Cosworth-branded products down the line."

Negotiations were concluded successfully, Ford thought, and on a Friday morning in July Ressler was scheduled to have his photo taken with a Cosworth Formula One engine for a press release announcing the acquisition. He never got to the appointment, as he was awakened early and heard the news that Vickers, as he put it, "Had sold the whole thing, lock, stock and barrel, to Audi."

Ressler was in CEO Jac Nasser's office later that morning when Nasser phoned Volkswagen's Ferdinand Piech, the chairman of Audi's parent company Volkswagen. Nasser explained the situation to Piech, and got Piech's word that Ford could have Cosworth Racing, while Audi would take over Cosworth Technology. It took a few months, and there were some at VW who were not happy with this, but Piech kept his promise.

Meanwhile, the Formula One season kept right on:

Hakkinen, who was involved in a near-fatal accident in 1995, led McLaren in its return to the Constructor's Cup it last won in 1991 as he defeated Schumacher for the championship by winning the last two races of the year. Hakkinen won eight of the 16 races and scored points in 13 events, Schumacher won six and earned points in twelve. It was another bitterly fought season, but one in which the Ford-powered Stewarts had no role except as also-rans. The second year was hardly more successful than the first.

Barrichello was still the lead driver, and Magnusson was replaced by Dutchman Jos Verstappen halfway through the season, but there was little improvement. The 32 starts produced twelve finishes, the best being two fifth places by Barrichello. Ten cars were retired by gearbox or transmission troubles, five due to accidents, two because of engine failure, two with suspension problems and one with bad brakes.

Renault, the most successful engine supplier of the past decade, had left the scene at the close of the previous season and its engines now carried the Mecachrome name on the valve covers, as the engine building equipment had been turned over to a private organization.

But little was spent on development, and the engines were no longer competitive with either the Ilmor-built Mercedes or Ferrari competition.

1999—First Cosworth, then Stewart, then Change the Name

Even before the season started it was clear that Dearborn was not happy with the progress made in the first two years of the Stewart effort, although this had been kept out of the media. Formula One had progressed to the point where business skills were as necessary as racing expertise, and the team, with no one in management having this kind of training, was suffering from this as well as from its technical shortcomings. Consultants were brought in at one point to help.

Another problem, in Ford's view, was that the company was becoming "lost in the shuffle," as one executive put it. Jackie Stewart was overshadowing Ford, it was felt, although if anyone had thought about this in advance it was inevitable. Stewart's name was on the team and on the car. Ford's was on the check, and now on some engines.

Jackie Stewart and son Paul.
—Ford Motor Company

The search for a way out was undertaken.

"We began talking to teams," Ressler says. "It wasn't a foregone conclusion that we would buy out Jackie. I talked with several other teams—Benetton, Arrows— we even thought about starting our own team when there was a twelfth spot available.... Of course we were talking to Jackie also.... Jackie wasn't sure he wanted to sell, but as time passed he began thinking about the financial demands.

"It was clear that he was going to have to do something, that costs were going up faster than he was able to get sponsorship money, and so we kind of came back together."

So John Young Stewart, the three-time world champion and one of the great personalities of auto racing, gave up the Formula One organization he started thinking about when he was managing his son Paul's Formula Three team in the early 1990s.

The price was approximately $100 million.

While negotiations with Stewart and the others were taking place, on February 9 there was a management change taking place at BMW in Germany. The company's investment in the British Rover Group had proven to be disastrous, and as a consequence the chairman was being fired. Wolfgang Reitzle, the heir apparent and the man greatly responsible for the reputation of BMW's products, was the logical successor. But when he didn't get the expected support from the labor unions he quit that same day.

Then, on March 19, Reitzle was announced as the head of Ford's new Premier Automotive Group, which includes Jaguar, Lincoln, Volvo and Aston Martin. Although unrelated at the time, this would eventually have an impact on Ford's Formula One efforts.

Negotiations for the Stewart buyout culminated in June when the announcement was made. Ford was to purchase Stewart Grand Prix, with the name being changed in time for the 2000 season. Although Jackie was to remain as CEO and Paul as chief operating officer and this was acknowledged at the time of the sale, it was clear that there would be a management change. Jackie turned 60 in mid-June, and it was not known for how long he would want to continue in what had become a stressful business. There was, however, the problem of finding a graceful exit.

Stewart had been identified with the company for more than three decades, and had been a valuable consultant to the engineering division. He had a positive role as a Ford spokesman, and was a friend of the Ford family and of many persons in management. In his dealings with Ford, as Dan Rivard once put it, he had "always under-promised and over-delivered." This time was different.

Ressler, it was decided, would take over as chairman of Jaguar Racing, and would also be chairman of Cosworth Racing and the recently acquired Pi, a data-acquisition company located in Cambridge that was known throughout the racing industry. Along with the top-level personnel changes, a search for a new and better site was undertaken. At this juncture Stewart was in Milton Keynes, about 60 miles north of central London, with Northampton roughly 15 miles northeast of Stewart. The trick would be to find a location that could fit both Jaguar and Cosworth, include all the additional facilities—such as a wind tunnel—and be close enough to their homes so that personnel would stay.

For Ressler, who was chief technical officer of the Ford Motor Company, this meant a move to Britain between the two seasons, and a management job that required his presence on both sides of the Atlantic at once. He would become a frequent presence on the British Airways flight from Detroit to London.

A new managing director for Cosworth was found in Trevor Crisp, the chief engineer of the power train group at Jaguar, who moved to Northampton to replace the retiring Dick Scammell. The latter had come back from his first retirement to help out at Cosworth, and was now going back to his native Bath for the second time.

The season itself saw Hakkinen win his second straight championship in a year when both he and his McLaren-Mercedes team took turns trying to lose the title. Hakkinen won five of the 16 races, and when he wasn't winning he was either being bumped off the track by teammate Coulthard or leaving the track himself when in the lead. Hakkinen, who was fastest qualifier eleven times during the season, was thought to have been "given" the title in July when Schumacher broke his leg during a crash at the British Grand Prix and as a consequence missing the next six events while his leg healed. But both the Finn and his team contrived to make their own mistakes, such as Hakkinen's leaving the road while well in the lead of the Italian Grand Prix in September, or when he lost a wheel after a pit stop at the British event.

In the end, Hakkinen had to beat Ferrari's number two driver, Eddie Irvine, in the last race of the season to clinch the championship.

Stewart's team had its most successful season and won the European Grand Prix at the Nürburgring, as Johnny Herbert inherited the rain-spattered event when a number of the front-runners dropped back or dropped out for one reason or another. Nevertheless it was a win, the first after two and a half years of trying. Stewart also finished fourth in the constructor's championship behind Ferrari, which edged McLaren for first, and Jordan, which placed third.

The changes for the next season would include drivers as well as management, with Irvine coming over from Ferrari to be the team leader at a salary in the neighborhood of $10 million per year. Rubens Barrichello, the young Brazilian who had made such a favorable impression despite Stewart's problems of the past two seasons, would move over to Ferrari. Herbert would stay with the new Jaguar team.

The three years of Stewart Grand Prix: 49 races, 98 cars started, 35 finished (36 percent), one win.

Chapter 29

─────────●─────────

BOY'S NAMES, GROWN MEN

Of all the thousands of drivers who have carried the Ford oval, a few have been close to the company in one way or another, and a number of these were profiled earlier. There are two, however, who have relationships with Ford that go beyond, in either number of years or number of dollars involved, any of the others.

Jackie Stewart

He is of less than medium height, with a permanent combination of a squint and smile, most articulate and always well dressed, and he was probably the first racing driver in Europe to make what can be termed real money. He was able to do this because he was not only the best of his day, but because he never lost sight of the fact that driving racing cars was not an end in itself, but rather a step toward something else.

That, aside from a recitation of his obvious driving talents, is a thumbnail description of three-time world champion Sir John Young Stewart. A friend of royalty, friend of the Ford family, he left his racing career at his peak to step up to other things—things that have moved him into the ranks of Britain's wealthiest people. He did it, however, realizing that the victories had to come first. Without them, nothing would happen. Over the past century Ford has developed close relationships with many of its drivers, but none so close or so long-lived as that with Jackie.

Thirty-one years ago, in the fall of 1964, when he was in the midst of his meteoric rise from working in the family garage near Glasgow to becoming a three-time world champion, Stewart, ever with his eye on the prize, journeyed to London for the Earl's Court motor show.

He went by train.

"I had won the British and European championships of Formula Three that year and had won the Monaco Grand Prix [the preliminary race], had a sort of rocket-ship ride, and by October was already getting offers to drive Formula One cars from BRM, from Lotus, and from Cooper. And I had been driving a Lotus Cortina for a garage dealer in Chester. At that time everybody went to the London Motor Show because that's where the Dunlops were, and the Essos were, and the BP's and the Shells and of course the Fords and etcetera, and I'm on the Ford stand not knowing who to look for...."

*Sir John Young Stewart, O.B.E., and three-time
world champion.—Ford Motor Company*

"There was a white Ford Zodiac with whitewall tires and red upholstery and lots of chrome and gold on it.... There had clearly been an American over there ... And I was looking at this car and not knowing what to do with myself, and a fellow came alongside me and said, 'Do you like it?' And I said, 'Yes, it's very nice.' He says, 'Would you like it?' and I thought what a strange thing for somebody to say to a man who didn't have a car at the time.

"I had asked Stuart Turner (then British Motor Corporation motorsports director) if I could borrow a Mini to come down to Earl's Court because I couldn't afford to rent a car in those days, and he said no, after I had won all those races with a BMC engine. I was very upset....

"And this man was saying, 'Would you like it?' And I turned around and the man's name was Walter Hayes.... I didn't really know who he was but I'd seen him around, and he said, 'Well look, I'm with Ford. I know who you are. If you drive— if you sign a contract with me for next year—we'll not ask you to do much, maybe drive some cars, maybe a Lotus Cortina or some things like that. And I'll give you some money with it.'

"And that was my deal with the Ford Motor Company. And the amount was 500 pounds (about $1400 at 1964 exchange rates) with this car off the show stand. And I thought it was the biggest deal in the whole world. And since that day I have been under contract with Ford every single year."

Deals with famous athletes have a way of going sour for many reasons, among them the fact that some athletes think all they have to do is cash the check. Stewart, on the other hand, understood that delivery was the important thing. At first he was there in a public relations capacity, as he was for ABC Sports, for Goodyear, Rolex, and Elf Aquitaine, the French oil company. But then, in the early '80s, after Hayes moved to the U.S., Stewart was brought in to act as a consultant to the engineering staff, and it wasn't easy.

Stewart: "I was having no fun at all. I couldn't get through the barrier, I mean, 'not invented here,' some of them.... You know, he's got nothing to do with us, these race drivers...."

"The corner turned when I went to drive with Dan Rivard, a very good engineer who held the lap record at the Dearborn proving grounds. He was a very aggressive and good driver, a fast driver, not a very sophisticated driver because he had been self-taught and he just drove by the seat of his pants. But he was good.

"Somebody said, 'For God's sake, you better go out there, the management are going on about this Jackie Stewart. Go and drive with him because he doesn't approve of one of our cars....'

"And so I drove Dan, telling him what I didn't like about it, and in so doing he was a great stopwatch man, and he had all the lap times logged, and I of course, put in a lap quicker than his lap record, which wasn't what was supposed to happen. So then he went back out to try and go quicker.... But obviously, I mean, it was my business, I was a professional racing driver, he was a professional engineer, but he was the best driver at the Ford Motor Company.

"And the fact that I was quicker was for him very confusing, because I was clearly doing it with technique, whereas he was doing it with aggression, so it's a 'Hello, there's something to be learned here,' and we built up a fantastic relationship, which I think was the cornerstone of me being able to communicate with the engineering community in North America. And from that point it grew to working, I think the high was something like 123 days a year.... It was always over 100 days.... Romeo, Dearborn, Geelong in Australia, down to South America, to Mazda in Hiroshima."

The engineering consultancy was what maintained his relationship with Ford, because at the beginning he thought the promotional work might be the end of the line. It was the same as when he was young: Hayes got him involved.

"While I've been with Ford I've had five chairmen," he says, "and I've seen a lot of presidents and vice presidents come and go, and lots of them would say, 'Well, that was in my time, you know, that was my decision.' But indeed, it was a little man with a pipe and hands that rubbed themselves together, and he puffed and he walked and sort of sneaked around and got deals done that to my knowledge, nobody in the history of the company has ever been able to get through.

"If there is a trouble in a major manufacturer in the industry it is the bureaucracy they have to deal with. The endless meetings and committees that have to be approving something of this kind. By the time it's approved, it's already obsolete in Formula One, and Walter was able to surpass that. They will have called him maverick, they will have called him a pain in the ass, but the fact is, he got it done."

When Stewart dropped out of the 1966 Indianapolis 500 with a commanding lead and only eight laps to go he was a kid, in his first major race in America, and the disappointment must have been huge—but he was gracious and quotable at the end. When 34 years later he was removed—a harsh word but appropriate—as chairman of the Formula One team he founded he was just as gracious, and continued to be helpful.

Neither had anything to do with driving fast.

On the subject of driving fast: Stewart participated in 99 world championship events, fewer than about 50 other men. He won 27, more than all but four others, and three of them drove in many more races.

He won the title three times. With technique.

Bobby Rahal

When he was named to succeed Neil Ressler as leader of the Jaguar Formula One team, the news surprised the racing community on both sides of the Atlantic. Yes, he had been a good driver and yes, he had a successful CART entry, but ... Formula One?

What hardly anyone outside Ford knew was that Bobby Rahal's relationship with the company was one that went well beyond the normal race team-factory engine provider scenario, and that this relationship had been established five years ago. Although there was certainly no thought of it at the time, the genesis of Rahal's new appointment took place in 1995.

At that time Rahal had already reached several goals: He was a three-time CART champion, he was a winner of the Indianapolis 500, he was the owner of a successful team and he was financially well fixed, with majority positions in four auto dealerships (more came later) and other investments.

And he was getting ready to retire from driving.

Rahal: "I saw a lot of drivers ... who raced for years and really ended up with nothing. Either there wasn't enough money, or they took the attitude that the money was always going to be there, or they got hurt, or they didn't take care of themselves, or God knows what, so I think when I started to achieve success, particularly when I got into CART, and I was starting to make some money.... I was 29 when I entered CART in 1982 and at that time it was young—today it's old—as I started to achieve success the thing that frightened me was that I would turn 40 and that I would achieve all these things and there was nothing there ... that I had squandered whatever I had made, or that I'd been stupid.... I have a very good advisor, he's my CPA, one of my best friends.... I think my nature is conservative.... We set up a pension plan, we incorporated, we did a lot of things at the time, because I knew there would be a life after racing, that I wasn't going to race forever.

"Initially I thought I'll be retired when I'm about 40.... Of course when you're successful and you're 39 you sit there and you say, 'Maybe not quite,' but I will say when I was 40 I said, 'Well, 45's about max, and I'm kind of proud that I held to that."

Rahal retired from driving in 1998, but three years earlier he gave up Ilmor-Mercedes as engine supplier and moved to Ford. Rahal and Ford had been close to an agreement in 1994, when Rahal left Honda, but that hadn't worked out and he went to Mercedes instead. Now, a year later, he had something long range in mind.

"I was looking to create a strategic partnership with a manufacturer," Rahal says, "because I felt that in the years to come if I didn't have that kind of a relationship, opportunities for being successful would be minimized.

"I remember calling Dan Rivard to say that I decided to go back to Ilmor since we had been with Ilmor prior to the Honda program.... I was sorry I had to make the decision I did—for him—but I thought we should stay in touch because I liked him, and he agreed, and so I evolved this concept for the need to create a strategic relationship. I knew I couldn't get it at Honda, because that bridge was gone, I knew I couldn't get it at Mercedes because of Roger [Penske, who was close to Daimler-Benz in many ways], so I went back, we made a proposal.

"It was about a relationship whose nature would be different from what they had with anybody else in American racing. I would make a five-year commitment if they would do certain things for us, and in return, aside from making a commitment to run the engines, we would open our company to Ford participation. Usually people say, 'Give me the money, or give me the engines,' and you know, that's that. The hallmark of our relationship has been that Ford engineering has people within this team that we're helping to teach, and they helping us."

As a consequence, John Valentine's motorsports technology group had a presence at Rahal's operation, and it was good for both sides. When the time came, five years later, Ressler knew exactly what kind of a manager he was. The only question was one of availability, and Rahal was willing to leave his team in the hands of an employee and make the move to Britain.

There was a period of a few months in the summer when Rahal was asked to become the interim president of CART, which he did until a replacement could be found, but throughout that period he already knew where the future lay.

No American since Teddy Mayer in the late '70s had ever run a major Formula One team, and Mayer did so when the dollars involved were considerably fewer and Formula One bore more of a resemblance to a sport than it did to a marketing effort for major manufacturers. The public announcement of his new job was made in late September, at the U.S. Grand Prix, and he took over from Ressler on December 1.

Chapter 30

———◆———

NEW CAR, NEW ERA

The good news for Ford's rally team in 1996, although few realized it at the time, was the appointment of Martin Whitaker as Director of European motorsports, a move that brought with it a major change in the effort. Whitaker had joined Ford the season before as the public relations man for performance in Europe, but when it was found that Peter Gillitzer was not working out as director of the motorsports operation, he was replaced by Whitaker in the late spring.

Whitaker had been a journalist, had worked for the FIA and for McLaren, and knew his way around the European scene. On paper he was also responsible for Ford's new Formula One venture, but Jackie Stewart had his own lines of communication to Dearborn and as a consequence Whitaker's principal job was to revive a flagging rally program.

Dan Rivard, at the time Ford's director of Special Vehicle Operations in Dearborn: "I don't know how he did it, but he did. I told him Americans weren't interested in rallying to begin with, didn't know what it was, and that I could only fund half of what he wanted. But he explained how important it was in the rest of the world, went out and raised the other half, and somehow he made it work."

Whitaker got some from departments inside Ford, made new deals with sponsors, and made the decision to get the aging Escort ready for the "new" World Rally Championship. This would start with the 1997 season—14 rallies per year, and the automakers required to enter all if they wanted manufacturer's championship points.

The FIA was saying that if you want to advertise something worthwhile, we want something for our organizing clubs, and for whatever television package we may sell—namely the guarantee of a full field at the end of the year, when the championship may have been decided. This also ensured that manufacturers who chose to enter would be major ones—automakers who marketed worldwide. In addition, the rotation system of the past few years was abandoned. From now on all the rallies would count.

Engine size was limited to 2.0 liters (about 122 cubic inches) turbocharged, with the turbo inlet restricted to 34 millimeters. This restriction had been in place since 1997, and meant that engines would be producing about 300 horsepower. Minimum weight was set at 1230 kg (about 2700 pounds) with oil and water, but without fuel, and aside from that, most everything else was allowed, including four-wheel drive—

which was a necessity. This came to pass through a rather creative directive from the FIA, an organization not normally associated with creativity, but in this case assisted by the manufacturers, who had some input to the new regulations.

The engine specifications and vehicle weights were hardly different from those of the few years preceding, but there was one significant difference: The WRC rules said you needed to use a production car, but—a big but—you could add to that car from a factory-prepared kit of special parts. The only limitation was that you made at least 20 kits, so that they could be sold to whomever could afford one. What this did, in effect, was to ensure that every WRC car was a rally version of a NASCAR stock car, with the institution of the "20 kit" rule making this more affordable for the manufacturers. It was, in effect, a silhouette formula. As long as the car looked like a production car on the outside, and as long as the minimum weight and engine specs were met, you could do just about anything.

What would make it anything but affordable, however, was the requirement that manufacturers had to enter *all* events in order for points to count, and this meant shipping entire teams, complete with service vehicles, spare parts, etc., around the world on a continuing basis. In 2000, for example, Ford had two complete sets of equipment. One was used in European events. The other, loaded in two 40-foot containers and two 20-foot containers that were filled to the brim, went by sea from one distant rally site to the other, returning to Britain only at the close of the season. The cars themselves—Ford used 14 during 2000—were shipped by air. This was typical of all the manufacturers who ran for the title.

Championship events would be held everywhere from Monte Carlo to China, Australia and New Zealand, and the title was competed for by big-budget teams from Mitsubishi, Toyota, Nissan, Subaru, Peugeot, Volkswagen's SEAT and Skoda marques, plus Ford.

As usual, there were (and are) other, minor FIA rally championships, something called the two-liter World Cup (no turbos, 2.0 liters, front-wheel drive only) and another entitled Group N (very close to production specs) but the WRC was and is the big one—the one worth advertising and marketing, all around the world.

Except, maybe, in the U.S.—the biggest market of all.

1996

South Africa gets a new constitution. ... Virginia Military Institute agrees to admit women. ... Madeline Albright is appointed America's first woman secretary of state. ... Kofi Annan is named UN secretary-general.

Tommi Makinen (no relation to Timo, an earlier Finnish star) won the first of what would eventually be four consecutive world titles while driving for Mitsubishi, this year's model being the Lancer Evolution. The team title, however, went to Subaru, paced again by Colin McRae, who was second in the individual standings.

Ford, as the previous year, was third in the team results, and had Spaniards Carlos Sainz and co-driver Luis Moya as the lead pair. This was Sainz-Moya's second time with Ford, and the combination would stay with the company for still another year, just as in 1987–88. The pair was originally scheduled to move to Toyota, but that team's suspension gave Ford the opportunity to sign them. (It is common practice in rallying for the team to sign the driver. He then makes his own arrangement with the navigator.)

The rally team: Colin McRae (left) and Nicky Grist.—Ford Motor Company

Sainz-Moya were signed in the fall of 1995, soon after the news of Toyota's being banned for 1996, and they were signed by Whitaker—still the public relations man at the time—and John Taylor, the operations manager at Boreham and a Sainz fan. "It really wasn't my job to do any of this," Whitaker said, "and he had a big sponsor, the state-run Spanish national oil company Repsol, and we went and saw him and said, 'We want you to be in our car,' and at the time Ford's reputation was absolutely dreadful. He said 'No.' Anyway, I convinced him to come, I got Repsol to sponsor the program and they wanted to have a press conference to announce and I went back and told them I had signed Sainz, and somebody said, 'I thought we were out of the rally championship,' and I said, 'We're just back in it.'"

Corsican Patrick Bernardini, a private entrant who had won the French rally championship twice, was the surprise winner in Monte Carlo in an Escort RS Cosworth, as the rally was skipped by several factory teams, including Ford. Sainz did well for much of the year, winning in Indonesia and finishing second in Argentina, Italy and Sweden, but reliability problems cost him dearly and besides, Makinen won five events. Sainz was backed, for part of the season, by Belgian veteran Bruno Thiry, and before Thiry by Stig Blomqvist, another experienced pilot.

The rally team: Carlos Sainz (left) and Luis Moya.—Ford Motor Company

Much of the year was devoted to preparations for 1997 and the revised World Rally Championship, and for Whitaker and the Ford team, budget approvals and the like did not come until mid-November—about nine weeks before the opening event of the year. In addition to the late approval, which meant day and night work for the next two months, Ford's rally team also had a new face—that of Malcolm Wilson, the head of M-Sport, an organization roughly comparable to the Yates or Roush NASCAR teams.

Ford had for years been hampered by the fact that the Boreham mechanics were unionized. This meant that not only were their hours restricted, but their overtime, travel compensation, and a host of other things foreign to the all-out effort needed were holding back the program. They were not only more expensive, but some of them were more interested in piling up overtime than they were in making a contribution. This came to an end with the selection of Wilson, a former British rally champion who had been running his own team.

Wilson's M-Sport was located in the town of Cockermouth, in the far northwest of England, beyond the Cumbrian mountains, just below Carlisle and the Scottish border. He had been British champion three times, had been Ford's chief test driver, was good at organization, and he was ambitious. There was some hesitancy at first, this revolving around the remote location of his facility, but that was overcome and he was signed. It was another major step on the return to being competitive.

Manufacturer's points: Subaru 401, Mitsubishi 322, Ford 299.

Driver's points: Makinen (Mitsubishi) 123, McRae (Subaru) 92, Sainz (Ford) 89.

1997

Newt Gingrich is reelected as House speaker, and shortly thereafter found guilty of ethics violations. ... Tiger Woods breaks records in winning his first Masters golf title. ... Hong Kong returns to Chinese rule, but life goes on as usual.

This was the first year of the revised championship, now known by the initials WRC, and Subaru was again on top in what was becoming a Japan versus Ford affair, this time in a 14-event season, with all events counting. But Makinen, in his Mitsubishi, won the individual title again. Point systems, under the new rules, were returned to something similar to Formula One: 10-6-4-3-2-1 for the first six places in the driver's championship, and the same for the manufacturer's. In the latter, however, if a team finished first and second in an event, it would collect 16 points.

There were, as in the past, classes for other cars, but the WRC, complete with its opportunities for publicity, marketing and the like, dominated the media reports. It was a good year for excitement, as five events were won by less than ten seconds.

Makinen won four of the 13 rallies. McRae, still with Subaru, lost the driver's championship by a point and won five, including the last three—San Remo (Italy), Australia, and the Rally of Britain.

Sainz, amazingly, finished second in Monte Carlo in the debut of the revised Escort, then finished second in Sweden as well—a remarkable performance in a rally that has never been won by a non-Scandinavian. He was second to McRae by eight seconds in the Tour de Corse, second to Subaru's Kenneth Eriksson by 13 seconds in New Zealand, and led a 1-2 Sainz-Kankkunen finish in the Indonesian Rally. When one considers that the car was already scheduled for oblivion, his performance was even more sensational. Sainz would return to Toyota for the next two years, and be missed in both Cockermouth and Warley, the home of Ford of Europe.

Manufacturer's points: Subaru 114, Ford 91, Mitsubishi 86.

Driver's points: Makinen (Mitsubishi) 63, McRae (Subaru) 62, Sainz (Ford) 51.

1998

Theodore Kaczynski, the Unabomber, pleads guilty. ... The Food and Drug Administration approves Viagra. ... The Good Friday Accords are reached in Northern Ireland.

Mitsubishi was back on top again, in a season that was the last year for the Escort as Ford's entry, as the Focus would be the entry beginning in 1999.

The Focus, in the meantime, was getting ready for its production debut and was being prepared for competition—simultaneously. The decision to give M-Sport the development contract in addition to the one it had for the rally season was another ground-breaking step, but was a logical one, as those who would compete with the car were obviously better fitted to develop it. Millbrook, considerably closer to Ford headquarters than Wilson's place in Cumbria, was picked as the site. The first "bodies in white" were delivered there in February, contracts were signed with engine builder Mountune and with transmission manufacturer Xtrac for the six-speed sequential gearbox. The prototype was introduced at the Paris auto show in October, the first car was track tested later that month and the car, ready to run, was introduced again at the Autosport show in January—just a few weeks before the 1999 season would start in Monte Carlo.

The 1998 season, however, saw Sainz's Toyota and Makinen's Mitsubishi in a close race until the very end—literally. Sainz was cruising home, in the season-ending RAC Rally, the obvious winner of the year's championship, when his engine blew up a few hundred yards from the finish line. Makinen, who had crashed the day before, was on his way to the airport when he was called back to be awarded his third consecutive title. Richard Burns, also in a Mitsubishi, won the rally, the first of three straight in this event.

M-Sport had the veteran Kankkunen and Thiry as its regular drivers, with Ari Vatanen taking part in several events. Kankkunen finished second in Monte Carlo and the Safari, third in Sweden, the Acropolis and Finland, and placed fourth for the year.

Manufacturer's points: Mitsubishi 91, Toyota 85, Subaru 65, Ford 53.

Driver's points: Makinen (Mitsubishi) 58, Sainz (Toyota) 56, McRae (Subaru) 45.

1999

> *Astronomers announce the detection of three large planets around a solar-type star 44 light-years away, the first confirmation that our solar system is not a singular phenomenon.... John F. Kennedy Jr., his wife and her sister die a plane crash on their way to Cape Cod.*

The car wasn't the only new item for 1999. Colin McRae was the other, as Ford signed the Scotsman away from Subaru for an amount estimated in the $10 million range, this to be spread over two years. Rallying thus took another step in the direction of Formula One. McRae, together with co-driver Nicky Grist, would drive the lead car, while the second vehicle would be handled by various drivers—Sweden's Thomas Raedstrom and Petter Sollberg, and Martinique's Simon Jean-Joseph. Fred Gallagher would be the navigator for whichever one would be driving.

The Focus made its competition debut not on the road, but in the press, when the new car's homologation papers became a subject of discussion. The focus was on the Focus' water pump, which the FIA rejected as being wrong in both size and location. The FIA gave the car provisional approval, based on the water pump problem being corrected, and then the Focus team showed up at the season-opening Monte Carlo Rally with the pump that was ruled illegal.

*In the snow: Colin McRae and Nicky Grist at the 1999 Monte Carlo Rally.
—Ford Motor Company*

The other teams, with an eye on perhaps needing some help from Ford in the future, agreed to let the Focus run in the event, but it still had to pass technical inspection at the end, and this result was a foregone conclusion. McRae finished a brilliant third over-all in a car that was well over the minimum weight limit—and then was disqualified.

Taking the jumps: Petter Solberg in Kenya, 1999.—Ford Motor Company

Raedstrom finished third in the Swedish Rally a month later, with the water pump in the place demanded by the FIA. McRae and Grist then won the East African Safari and the Rally of Portugal in back-to-back performances, and it looked as if the Focus was on its way. That would, however, be all for 1999. McRae dropped out of several events due to accidents, mechanical problems sidelined him at other times, and the second drivers were not able to run with Makinen (Mitsubishi), Burns (Subaru), Didier Auriol (Toyota), Sainz (Toyota) or Kankkunen (Subaru). Four things were needed: Greater reliability, a faster second driver, more durable engines, and a way to keep McRae on the road.

Manufacturer's points: Toyota 109, Subaru 105, Mitsubishi 83, Ford 37.

Driver's points: Makinen (Mitsubishi) 62, Richard Burns (Subaru) 55, Didier Auriol (Toyota) 44, Kankkunen (Ford) 44.

2000

> *The New York Yankees win the World Series, defeating the Mets in five games.... The St. Louis Rams beat Tennessee in the Super Bowl, in a game not decided until the last play.*

Ford had been able to sign Sainz and Moya for the 1996 and 1997 seasons when Toyota was forced to pull out for a year after being caught cheating. Now Toyota withdrew from rallying again, this time in favor of a 2002 entry into Formula One. Technical personnel and budgets were directed toward this effort, and thus Whitaker was able to bring them back into the fold. That meant Ford had the strongest—and most expensive—team it had ever assembled, with both Sainz and McRae in the same salary range.

The Focus had been through a year's worth of competition and thus the bugs—hopefully—had been worked out, and the engines were now coming from Cosworth, Ford's wholly owned subsidiary and the manufacturer of both the Formula One and CART powerplants.

The team would also have, starting halfway through the season, Dovenby Hall, Wilson's magnificent new headquarters a few miles away from his old garage. Dovenby Hall, listed as an estate of historic interest, includes a 60,000-square foot workshop and parts area, with 26 individual bays for cars. The property covers 115 acres, and would put most of the comparable NASCAR facilities to shame. Wilson, ever the entrepreneur, convinced the Cumbria Inward Investment Agency, a government organization, to fund part of the project.

The opposition was as before, except that Peugeot was mounting an all-out campaign similar to what the French company did in the mid-'80s, with the underlying reason for this being Peugeot's dissatisfaction with—and withdrawal from—grand prix racing. Peugeot had Markus Grönholm and Francois Delecour as drivers, Subaru had Richard Burns and four-time titleholder Juha Kankkunen, and Mitsubishi had four-time world champion Tommi Makinen, his four coming in the last four seasons.

McRae failed to finish his ninth consecutive rally when he retired due to engine trouble at season-opening Monte Carlo, then finished third in Sweden before dropping out of the East African Safari and the Portuguese event, giving him a remarkable eleven DNF's in twelve attempts. Meanwhile Sainz had been soldiering on, second in Monte Carlo, fourth in Kenya and third in Portugal.

The turnaround came in Spain, where McRae won and Sainz placed third after some four hours of racing-speed special stages. Argentina saw both drivers run into problems, but they were 1-2 in Greece's Acropolis Rally, again with McRae in front. Sollberg, driving the third M-Sport entry, placed sixth. New Zealand, the eighth event of the year, saw McRae and Sainz finish 2-3 behind eventual season champion Grönholm, and McRae's second place in Finland gave Ford its first lead in the chase for the manufacturer's title, 63-60 over Subaru.

Sainz, who led from the start, paced a 1-2 Ford finish in Cyprus, which gave the team a 79-64 lead over Subaru; the win was Sainz's 23rd in world championship rallying, tying him with all-time leader Kankkunen, and with four events to go, the outlook was good.

But it was not to be.

McRae crashed in Corsica, fracturing his cheekbone and destroying the car—Grist was not injured—and Sainz finished third. Peugeot then ran 1-2 in Italy's San Remo Rally and moved ahead in points, 90-88, which meant the title would be decided in the season's last two events—Australia and Britain.

Australia proved to be the end of it. McRae went out with engine trouble right after the start of the first day, and Sainz was disqualified for stopping in the wrong place while waiting to enter a control. It was over, except for what could have been a "hometown" finish in the Rally of Britain.

That was also not to be.

McRae had a commanding lead more than halfway through the event and ran off the road, Sainz finished fourth, and that was the end of it. Grönholm, leading for the individual title, drove carefully, placed second behind three-time British Rally winner Burns to clinch his championship, and Peugeot finished well ahead of Ford for the manufacturer's award.

Consistency, as well as speed, won for Grönholm. He finished in the top six in the ten of the 14 rallies he finished, and was the fastest on 42 of the special stages conducted during the season. The fastest, unquestionably, was Burns, who was first in 69 special stages but failed to finish five events. Grönholm and Burns each won four events. McRae was fastest over 36 special stages, but dropped out of half the events, troubled by engine problems or by roads that turned left when he was turning right. Either Grönholm, Burns, McRae, Sainz (28) or Makinen (27) were fastest on 202 of the 266 special stages run during the season.

The Focuses were competitive, in fact more than competitive, but if this, if that, if the other thing had happened....

Kipling had something to say about that.

In the meantime, practice for the 2001 season started the next week.

Manufacturer's points: Peugeot 111, Ford 91, Subaru 88, Mitsubishi 43, SEAT 11.

Driver's points: Markus Grönholm (Peugeot) 65, Richard Burns (Subaru) 60, Carlos Sainz (Ford) 46, Colin McRae (Ford) 43, Tommi Makinen (Mitsubishi) 36.

Chapter 31

ALL THE KING'S HORSES

Jaguar, which for years benefited from America's predilection for things British, and which had dined out for decades on a few Le Mans victories, came under the Ford umbrella in the winter of 1989. The two had reached an agreement the previous November, the sum of $2.5 billion changed hands at the end of February, then Ford discovered it had purchased a company with a great image, but with serious short-comings.

It took nearly a decade and multiples of the purchase price to make the problems go away from the production models and to build a proper infrastructure, and in the meantime Jaguar survived—just barely—on its image and on good exterior design.

It was what Jaguar represented, rather than the car itself, that made up its initial appeal. When Americans were becoming aware of "road" racing, a young man from Santa Monica, Phil Hill, won the first feature event ever held in the Del Monte Forest at Pebble Beach in 1950, driving an XK120 roadster. Jaguars won the 24 Hours of Le Mans in 1951, 1953, 1955, 1956 and 1957, and since that was about the only European race anyone in the U.S. had heard of, the reputation was made.

The C-Types that won in 1951 and 1953, and the D-Types that did so the next three times were not competitive except where the road surfaces were smooth. They had live rear axles that were not happy on circuits such as the Nürburgring or the roads of the Mille Miglia or Targa Florio. They were not, for example, a match for the Aston Martins, which dominated even the Ferraris at the 1000 Kilometers of the Nürburgring.

But Jaguar became a household name, even for those who would never buy one. And they stood for something upscale, even if that something was not clear in the eye of the beholder.

In the late '80s and 1990 the racing successes returned, this time with the team being run by Tom Walkinshaw as a factory-supported effort, and with Walkinshaw being the British equivalent of a Holman-Moody or Roush Racing. In 1987, sponsored by Silk Cut cigarettes, the team won the world sports car prototype championship, they repeated in 1988 and won at Le Mans to boot, and the U.S. Jaguar team was a factor in IMSA GTP racing in the early '90s.

All of this, however, attracted little or no notice in Dearborn. Jaguar was Over There, Jaguar had problems that winning some races wouldn't fix, and Jaguar faded from the motorsports scene.

The C-Type, winner at Le Mans 1951, 1953.—Jaguar Cars

The D-Type, winner at Le Mans 1955-56-57.—Jaguar Cars

Then, in 1999, Jaguar became an entry in the rarified world of Formula One, thanks to marketing considerations. This came to pass, in simple terms, because Ford decided to buy out Jackie Stewart and take over the team it had financed and decided that Jaguar, with its upscale image, was a better fit for Formula One than was the Blue Oval.

Jaguar was hoping to compete for market share with Mercedes-Benz (more than one million cars per year, worldwide) and BMW (about 800,000 annually). Jaguar's total sales in 2000 would be roughly 90,000, and less than that when the decision was

The XJR 12, winner at Le Mans 1990.—Jaguar Cars

The Jaguar R1 Formula One car.—Jaguar Racing

made. So it figured, the thinking went, that any Jaguar success in grand prix racing would be a direct benefit to the production car image.

There was also the job of finding someone to run the racing team. Ressler never thought of himself as the race director, but rather as the over-all manager, the person who would get the three companies (data acquisition firm Pi was the third) in good shape and then turn it over to someone else. At the time of the Stewart takeover Ressler was 60 and had spent more than 35 successful years with the company. He had responsibilities in Dearborn and he was also considering retirement due to family obligations.

In the meantime, the racing effort went down the drain from the start. All the king's horses and all the king's men managed only four points during the 17-race season, one that saw Ferrari and McLaren fight for the title and reduce the rest of the field to the also-ran category.

The points for the FIA Constructor's Cup are awarded on a 10-6-4-3-2-1 basis, and points are awarded to both team cars if both finish in the top six. There were a total of 432 points available during the season, 391 points for the first four places. Ferrari and McLaren combined for 322 of these, or 82 percent. It was a year in which Schumacher won nine races and his third championship and thus gave Ferrari its first driver's title since 1979. Hakkinen won four, Coulthard three and Barrichello one, so no one other than a Ferrari or a McLaren driver had so much as a hope for a win, much less a finish in the top three or four.

Irvine managed to finish ten of the 16 events he drove (he missed one due to illness), and managed a fourth at Monte Carlo plus a sixth in Malaysia. He never qualified better than sixth. Herbert finished eight of 17 and was never close to anything. Jaguar Racing collected four points in the Constructor's Cup standings—ninth of eleven teams.

Someone had to take the blame, or at least explain. Ressler: "There were a variety of reasons. Our car was a better car last year, designed by the prior design team, Alan Jenkins and Egbal Hamidy. This was their [the new team, led by Gary Anderson] first car ... and they didn't get the car right to start with, and really never did get on top of the whole development, and that's the harsh truth.

"And we made a mistake on the engine as well. The engine in 1999 was a very good engine, but we went to higher revving, bigger bore, smaller stroke for 2000. It started out OK, and then as time passed and the weather got hotter we think combustion instability sort of doomed it to failure, so we did a basically new engine starting in July."

Ressler knew he had to live with it, and met with Nasser, who was supportive. Ressler: "I told him I can blow it up in the middle of the season and go to the F1 unemployment office, or you've got to give me some time to get the right guys." Dearborn said OK, and as the year struggled on, Ressler was also looking for a new chief executive officer. Almost from the start, he had his eye on Bobby Rahal.

*Bobby Rahal: From the cockpit to
CART to Jaguar.—Jaguar Racing*

It seemed an odd choice. No one questioned Rahal's driving experience or his business reputation—he was running a successful CART operation and was the owner of several dealerships and had other investments—but he was an Outsider, not a member of the Formula One club. But Ressler was convinced. "May was when I talked to him first. I hadn't been here a month, full time, when I was on the phone with him and he was interested from the first [this was before Rahal accepted the temporary post of CEO of CART].... I had some misgivings about whether he'd be accepted because he's an American and this is a sport that views itself as a British sport, but I began asking around and got a very good and very positive read."

Ressler informed Nasser, Bob Rewey, Richard Parry-Jones and Wolfgang Reitzle of what he was doing, and found no objections. The deal was kept quiet for some weeks, but in the few days before the U.S. Grand Prix at the Indianapolis Motor Speedway, the news was out and an announcement was made. Indianapolis was an appropriate place for Rahal's new job to be formalized, as so much of his driving career had centered around the Speedway, where he won the 500 in 1986. There was some symbolism, too, in the fact that the U.S. would have a world driver's championship event for the first time since 1991, when a makeshift street circuit in Phoenix attracted a small crowd.

Now, despite his differences with CART and his efforts to keep his own Indy Racing League alive, Speedway President Tony George had transformed the giant facility into something unique: the only place where a major American oval track race, a major NASCAR event and a world driver's championship race would use the same venue. It had cost millions—some estimated as much as $40 million—but the result was impressive.

The so-called road circuit was as good as could be expected, considering the fact that the several golf course holes inside the Speedway had been left inviolate, but there was no criticism from the visitors, who were happy to be there, and who were impressed with the facilities.

When the Formula One circus descended upon Indiana, in certain respects it was like arriving on another planet. The "home" audience, for want of a better word, was split between locals used to counterclockwise oval racing and fan-friendly drivers, and Formula One adherents who weren't quite sure what to expect but were willing to put up with most anything to be near their heroes.

Indianapolis hotel rooms went up to $400 per night at some of the better hostelries; there were even reports that one team bought a house in the suburb of Carmel, just so they would have a residence one week a year. No one could verify this, but it all made for good theater. The Paddock Club, Bernie Ecclestone's $3000 per person lunchroom for Those Who Needed To Be Seen, even managed to keep the Indiana State Police out. Among the more interesting episodes of the weekend was the scene at the Detroit airport, where immigration officials turned back a group of 52 waiters and busboys who were flown in from Europe to work at the Paddock Club, and who didn't have the proper papers.

When a Formula One insider was queried as to why local personnel weren't hired for what were basically simple jobs, he explained that "Our clientele like to have the same waiters in America that they have in Japan and the rest of the world."

In town, George was seen as a hero. Criticized by many after reducing the Indianapolis 500 to almost also-ran status with the IRL-CART split, Tony Hulman's grandson had now become the man who was providing his city with no less than three positive economic impacts. The race itself was almost secondary to the sights and sounds of the newcomers.

And after about ten laps, when Schumacher passed Coulthard, it was all over. Schumacher's lead was big enough so that when he spun a few laps from the end he had plenty of time to get going again.

Rahal took over on December 1, by which time Anderson and some others had been fired; the new technical team would be led by Steve Nichols, John Russell and Mark Handford. Test driver Luciano Burti had replaced Herbert, and Ressler was ready to retire, which he did at the beginning of February after having brought some order to the situation.

Then another penny dropped. Coincident with Ressler's retirement Jaguar, Cosworth and Pi, were renamed the Premier Performance Division and put under Reitzle's control, the rationale being that since the division's purpose was to build a marketable image for Jaguar, Reitzle should be in charge. He agreed to take over the budgets, which was key.

Niki Lauda: Rahal's new boss.—Jaguar Racing

And Reitzle brought in his friend Niki Lauda to be chairman of the new PPD, something Rahal had not dreamed of when he consented to take the job. Just what qualifications Lauda had were not explained. He was a three-time world champion, but no one expected him to drive one of the cars. He was in his early 50s, and had just been forced out of Lauda Air, the airline he had founded some years earlier which was in financial difficulties.

It was, as Alice once said in her own wonderland, curiouser and curiouser. A brand-new chapter was unfolding.

At the same time Ecclestone was selling off another piece of his holding company, this time to a German television conglomerate that already owned 50 percent. The price for the newest 25 percent was reported at $987 million.

So the former motorcycle dealer, at the age of 70 and with no business heir on the horizon, now owned only a quarter of the Formula One business, but the manner in which the contracts were written allowed him to keep control. In 30 years he had not only brought a different lifestyle to this particular type of racing, he had also built it into the most profitable.

And there was more to come—maybe even another century's worth.

Chapter 32

———◆———

MORE DUST ...

One form of racing almost always evolves from another, going back to the days when someone took the fenders off a touring vehicle and converted it into what we now call a race car. In a somewhat more complicated manner, off-road racing became the parent of the NASCAR Craftsman Truck series, and it began at the Ford motorsports banquet in January of 1993, when Dave Ashley heard Ford Division General Manager Ross Roberts talk about the changing automotive scene.

"He was saying that as long as Ford made trucks they would be in NASCAR, because 71 percent of NASCAR fans were truck buyers," Ashley says, "and that's when I started to think about it." He then went to Dick Landfield, the owner of his team, and from there the idea took form.

At about the same time, Landfield says, "NASCAR had come to a bunch of us off-road racers and said they wanted to get us into the Winston West series.... We had three or four meetings and so I got hold of Frank Vessels, Jimmy Smith and Jim Venable. These were guys who were heavily involved in off-road racing, spending their own money on it, spending a couple hundred thousand, three hundred, five hundred, I don't know, of their own money, just to have some fun. And so I told them, 'This NASCAR thing is crazy, you're not gonna get anywhere. One out of a hundred is gonna make it to the big show and the rest of us are gonna be running around the bullrings for the rest of our lives. Listen to this. Truck sales are rapidly approaching car sales. The truck market is booming. People relate to trucks.

"Why don't we race trucks?"

"Dave had come up with the idea of just taking a regular NASCAR chassis and reskinning it with truck sheet metal. We thought it was a good idea and flew back to Florida to see Bill France, and he said, 'I understand you boys want to race pick-me-ups. What gives you that idea?'

"If you look at the demographics of the people who are driving pickup trucks," Landfield said to France, "it has grown from the farmer and the construction worker to where it's an everyday passenger car. The market is expanding—people relate to trucks."

The foursome gave France their business plan and he said, "You get this thing started and we'll take a look at it and see what we can do to support you."

They went to Marion Collins, a stock-car builder and driver in Bakersfield, for the prototype, Mose Nowland of Ford Racing supplied the engine, they invited NASCAR's Ken Clapp and Dennis Huth to the debut, and took the truck to Mesa Marin Speedway, the local half-mile oval. Collins "rolled out of his garage, down the track, fired it, took a couple of warm-up laps, then went out there and started turning ... no setup, no tire person, he just went out there," Landfield says. "They were timing him, and his time would have put him third on the grid for the fourth of July race, which was their big one."

They took the truck back to Daytona Speed Weeks in February and everyone got a look at it, but soon, Landfield says, "It was obvious we couldn't handle something like this. We came back, the four of us, and realized we weren't willing to put a million bucks apiece of our own money into a dream. So we made the phone call to Dennis and NASCAR took it over."

That was the genesis of the truck series, which was announced in May of 1994, and which has given NASCAR and the France-controlled International Speedway Corporation a useful attraction to support Winston Cup and Busch Grand National. Fittingly, the first truck race was held at Collins' Bakersfield track and was won by Parnelli Jones' son P.J. in a truck owned by Vessels.

And the off-road racers went back to doing their thing, even though Ashley managed to drive five Craftsman races before he returned to the desert.

Off-road racing can consist of weeks, even months, of work to get ready for several hundred miles, sometimes close to a thousand miles, of frantic activity, in which luck can play as big a part as driving skill or good preparation. And in the case of the Baja, off-road racing includes the mystique, says Ashley: "What has always appealed to me is the stories—every times I've ever gone down there I've had an experience I'll never forget.... It's unexplainable to the average person. If you haven't been there, you'll never know...."

And as far as mystique and stories were concerned, there would never be a better opportunity for Ashley and co-driver Dan Smith than there was in the Baja 2000, SCORE's longest-ever event which ran in November 2000. It was preceded by considerable hype and should have been, as the distance—approximately 1680 miles—was the greatest for an event of this type in the western hemisphere. It attracted the big names—Ivan Stewart and Larry Roeseler sharing a Toyota, and a two-car Chevrolet entry, with Larry Ragland and Brian Stewart in one trophy truck, and Mark Miller and Ryan Arciero in the other.

Chevrolet would have more than 100 support personnel on the ground for this one, with what was estimated at 20 chase trucks and a half-dozen SUV's as personnel carrier, plus two helicopters and a fixed-wing aircraft. Landfield's Enduro Racing, or in other words Ashley-Smith, had a volunteer support crew of 23, plus chase trucks, the rolling workshop 18-wheeler, and two planes so that one was in the air at all times to maintain the necessary radio contact to the race truck.

Roaring through Mexico: Ashley and Smith in the Baja 2000.
—Trackside Photo

Ashley and Smith knew each other from their motorcycle days, both having been champions on two wheels, the 37-year-old Smith having been the American Motorcycle Association's Hare and Hounds titleholder five straight years with 500cc bikes. ("They're strong. You point it at a mountain and it'll go up it.") They met in the late '80s when they were both pre-running desert motorcycle races, and then, Smith says, "One day in 1990 the phone rang at home and Dave was on the other end, and asked if I'd like to drive a truck. It's the dream of all motorcycle riders to drive a race truck."

By the time the Baja 2000 rolled around Ashley and Smith had been a team for a decade, sharing the wheel in longer events and each handling his own vehicle in shorter ones. They were members of the Rough Riders from 1991 through 1997, and were busy running six to ten races a year, in both SCORE and Best in the Desert, when the Baja 2000 was announced.

Trophy trucks, barring serious accident, can last for a few years before needing replacement if one is to be a serious contender for over-all honors, and they can go on for several years after that, if necessary. One of Ashley's older trucks, in which he won more than 40 events, was sold to another competitor in 1999 and at last report was still running. (If the tube frame cracks, and they do, one brings out the torch and welds it back together again.) Work on a new truck for Baja 2000 began in January of the year, when Ashley, Smith, Mike Backholdin and Danny Gonzales began welding a new frame.

They use a surface plate, thus ensuring a level platform, but the design is as much empirical as anything else, depending on years of experience and knowing what works rather than on an engineering study. The build took nine months ("Like a baby," Ashley says with a smile), and in the meantime, the pair headed for Mexico to practice, using their older race vehicle, plus a tow truck and a trailer.

The reconnaissance, or pre-run, involved two trips, as "something broke" during the first attempt and they had to return for a second. Earlier in the year, when Ashley was on a Ford motorsports panel along with CART driver Kenny Brack and NASCAR's Benny Parsons, the latter asked Ashley how he practiced for something like the Baja 2000 and was nonplussed when he found what it would take: At least one trip around the entire course, and several passes through what are deemed the critical sections. "You've got to run over that dime for 1700 miles," Ashley says. "We both drive better in different areas," Smith says. "I like to drive the tighter, more technical sections and Dave is better at night, and in the faster sections."

When they went back for the second pre-run Ashley was hit by what is sometimes known as Montezuma's Revenge, and lost a week and twelve pounds as the result. But on Sunday morning of November 12 they were at the line, together with 261 other entries, running in 30 classes—everything from motorcycles and trucks to a few cars and even some all-terrain vehicles. Ashley and Smith had a 5.4-liter overhead camshaft Ford, modified to produce about 600 horsepower, and located in the middle of the tube frame.

Since no one had ever run a race of this distance, part of the guessing game was to pick a predetermined pace and stick to it, either figuring to outrun everyone or to drive relatively conservatively and expect the others to break or crash.

Ashley and Smith took the conservative route—conservative being a relative term in this case. They got their first break when one of the factory Chevrolets left the road just ten miles from the start, and lost three hours. This truck, driven by

Miller and Arciero, would throw caution to the wind the rest of the way and eventually finish fourth, about an hour behind the winner, but it was effectively out of contention almost as soon as its engine reached operating temperature.

Smith drove the first and third legs, Ashley the second and fourth, each leg being about 400 miles—and after 260 miles, Smith saw the water temperature gauge heading up. They had a head gasket leak, and in order to keep going Smith started pouring sealant in with the water. Before the race was over Smith and Ashley would pour a lot of water—and a lot of sealant—but the engine held.

Transmission trouble hit the pair at about the 700-mile mark, when fifth and sixth gears became inoperable, which meant they would have to over-rev the engine the rest of the way if they hoped to stay on the pace. This meant turning above 8000 rpm, and doing it on a steady basis.

Then, at about the 900-mile mark, there was good news for a change. The race-leading Toyota of Stewart and Roeseler had coughed up its engine.

By the time they got to the last driver change, at approximately 11 a.m., with 450 miles to go, Ashley knew what he had to do and how he had to do it, running at 8200 rpm in fourth, then backing down to 7500 for a while to let the water temperature drop from 230 degrees so that he could hit it hard again on the paved sections, at speeds over 100 with the engine above 8000.

The next to last act in the drama took place, with between 65 and 70 miles to go, at the end of the final paved stage. Ashley: "The last place I really had to run hard was through a town called Todo Santo.... he [Ragland] had two corners to go, and he spun and hit a building"

Ashley knew that Ragland, in the only other truck remaining in contention, was just a few minutes behind. He also knew that since Ragland had started in front of him, the Chevy would have to pass him to win, and then pull out a lead of more than a minute. "I knew if I could hold him off until we got back to the dirt he'd have to drive through my dust...."

Then they were back into the dirt and the desert, and Ragland was getting close again, coming within 16 seconds (Ashley: "I knew where he was because I was aware of his helicopter"). Then Ragland was in Ashley's dust cloud, he pulled out to make a pass, and rolled it.

It was all over, even though the Chevrolet managed to finish third, 44 minutes astern.

On the way to the finish, Ashley says, "You have something you've planned for so long, when it was happening you almost had to laugh.... It was just unfolding ... I knew what he [Ragland] was thinking, and I knew what I was thinking.... I was in more of a relaxed state than anyone else."

Thirty-two hours and 15 minutes after they started, at about 5:30 on a warm, clear evening, they were winners, 35 minutes ahead of the Class 1 Ford-powered "Truggy"—an oversized Baja Bug, in simple terms—of Troy Herbst and Jim Smith, and another nine minutes ahead of Ragland and Stewart.

Their truck was covered with dust—as well as a little glory.

INDEX

Note: Page numbers followed by *t* or *ph* refer to tables and photographs, respectively. Page numbers directly following a main heading refer to brief mentions of the topic. Subheadings refer to more substantial discussion of a topic.

Off-road racing *(continued)*
  Best in the Desert Racing Association,
    255, 259–260
  dealer participation, 253–255
  early history, 175–180
  Rough Riders, 257–259
  truck series, 383–384
  venues, 255
  see also SCORE
Offenhauser engines
  1968–1980 USAC seasons, 108–120
  "DGS-Offy," 116
  Drake-Offenhauser success, 109–115
Oil embargo (1973), 66
Ojjeh, Mansour, 240, 241
Oldsmobile division (GM)
  CART racing, 275
  NASCAR racing, 71–74
  Trans-Am racing, 338
Oliver, Jackie, 167
Olympia Brewing Company, 179
Ongais, Danny, 127
Opel AG, 44, 45, 47, 48
Open-cockpit racing. *See* Championship
  Auto Racing Teams; Formula One racing;
  United States Auto Club
Open-road racing. *See* Road racing
Open-wheel racing. *See* Championship
  Auto Racing Teams; Formula One racing;
  United States Auto Club
Owen, Sir Alfred, 148
Owens, Cotton, 13, 15, 77, 80

Paddock Club, 380
Palm, Gunnar, 38, 42
Panch, Marvin, 78, 85
Panoz, Don, 98, 165, 341
Pardue, Jimmy, 83
Park, Steve, 318
Parks, Wally, 181, 183*ph*
Parnelli. *See* Jones, Rufus Parnell; Vel's-
  Parnelli Jones team
Parrott, Todd, 312, 321*ph*
Parry-Jones, Richard, 379
Parsons, Benny
  1973–1980 seasons, 63–74

1981 season, 209–210
Dave Ashley and, 386
retires, 219
Passino, Jacque, 11, 22, 79, 88, 332
Patrese, Riccardo, 142, 239, 248
Patrick, U.E. (Pat), 106, 121
Patton, George, 80–81
Paul, John, 334
PDA (Professional Drivers Association),
  18, 65
Pearlman, Ed, 176*ph*
  early off-road racing, 175–177
  Mickey Thompson and, 180
  mini-truck classes, 255
Pearson, David, 75*ph*, 78, 331
  1968–1969 seasons, 13–20
  1971–1979 seasons, 60–72
  biographical notes, 75–77
  retires, 219
  Wood brothers and, 85, 86
Pedregon, Tony, 347, 348*ph*
Penske-Kranefuss Racing, 299, 324
Penske, Roger, 64*ph*, 74, 193, 269*ph*, 309,
  313, 314, 329, 330*ph*, 363
  1970–1972 USAC/CART seasons, 111–
    112
  1974–1975 Formula One seasons, 229–
    230
  1974 NASCAR season, 65
  1977 NASCAR season, 71
  1978–1989 USAC/CART seasons, 117–
    129
  1990–2000 USAC/CART seasons, 264–
    278
  1994 NASCAR season, 287
  biographical notes, 317, 322–324
  CART formation, 106
  disc brakes use, 64
  NASCAR Taurus and, 294–295
  Trans-Am series racing, 331–333
  see also Ilmor Engineering Ltd.
Petersen, Don, 73, 242, 350
Petersen Publishing, 181
Peterson, Ronnie, 159, 228, 234
Petrol. *See* Fuel regulations
Petty, Adam, 305
Petty, Kyle, 216, 305

ABOUT THE AUTHOR

---●---

When Volume 1 of *Ford: The Dust and the Glory* was first published in 1968, Leo Levine was fresh from a career as a newspaperman (highlighted by stints with the European edition of *The Stars and Stripes* and with *The New York Herald Tribune*) and as a racing driver in Europe and South America. Soon after publication he joined Mercedes-Benz of North America and spent two decades with the company, retiring as one of the company's general managers in 1989. In late 1998, the Ford Motor Company asked him if he would write Volume 2 of the firm's racing history, which has been published at the time of Ford's 100th anniversary of involvement in motorsports. Volume 1 was republished earlier this year.